The First Civil Right

Studies in Postwar American Political Development
Steven Teles, Series Editor

Series Board Members:
Jennifer Hochschild
Desmond King
Sanford Levinson
Taeku Lee
Shep Melnick
Paul Pierson
John Skrentny
Adam Sheingate
Reva Siegel
Thomas Sugrue

The Delegated Welfare State: Medicare, Markets, and
the Governance of Social Policy
Kimberly J. Morgan and Andrea Louise Campbell

Rule and Ruin: The Downfall of Moderation and the Destruction
of the Republican Party, From Eisenhower to the Tea Party
Geoffrey Kabaservice

Engines of Change: Party Factions in American Politics, 1868–2010
Daniel DiSalvo

Follow the Money: How Foundation Dollars Change Public School Politics
Sarah Reckhow

The Allure of Order: High Hopes, Dashed Expectations, and the Troubled
Quest to Remake American Schooling
Jal Mehta

Rich People's Movements: Grassroots Campaigns to Untax the One Percent
Isaac William Martin

The First Civil Right

How Liberals Built Prison America

NAOMI MURAKAWA

OXFORD
UNIVERSITY PRESS

OXFORD
UNIVERSITY PRESS

Oxford University Press is a department of the University of
Oxford. It furthers the University's objective of excellence in research,
scholarship, and education by publishing worldwide.

Oxford   New York
Auckland   Cape Town   Dar es Salaam   Hong Kong   Karachi
Kuala Lumpur   Madrid   Melbourne   Mexico City   Nairobi
New Delhi   Shanghai   Taipei   Toronto

With offices in
Argentina   Austria   Brazil   Chile   Czech Republic   France   Greece
Guatemala   Hungary   Italy   Japan   Poland   Portugal   Singapore
South Korea   Switzerland   Thailand   Turkey   Ukraine   Vietnam

Oxford is a registered trademark of Oxford University Press
in the UK and certain other countries.

Published in the United States of America by
Oxford University Press
198 Madison Avenue, New York, NY 10016

© Oxford University Press 2014

Library of Congress Cataloging-in-Publication Data

CIP record is available from the Library of Congress

ISBN 978-0-19-989278-5 (hbk)
ISBN 978-0-19-989280-8 (pbk)

CONTENTS

List of Illustrations vii
List of Tables ix
List of Abbreviations xi

1. The First Civil Right: Protection from Lawless Racial Violence 1

2. Freedom from Fear: White Violence, Black Criminality, and the
   Ideological Fight for Law-and-Order 27

3. Policing the Great Society: Modernizing Law Enforcement and
   Rehabilitating Criminal Sentencing 69

4. The Era of Big Punishment: Mandatory Minimums, Community
   Policing, and Death Penalty Bidding Wars 113

5. The Last Civil Right: Freedom from State-Sanctioned Racial
   Violence 148

Appendix Tables 157
Author's Notes and Acknowledgments 205
Abbreviations in Notes 209
Notes 211
Index 253

LIST OF ILLUSTRATIONS

1.1   Number and Rate of Persons Incarcerated in State and Federal
      Prisons, 1925–2010   5

1.2   Admission Rates to State and Federal Prisons by Race, 1926–1997   6

2.1   "A Colored Man Is Held by Unconcerned Detroit Cops While a
      White Man Slaps His Face," 1943   33

2.2   "Race Riots Emerge from Inequities, Discriminations & Segregation,"
      American Council on Race Relations, 1945   37

2.3   "Four Essential Rights," 1947   42

3.1   Join the Oakland Police Department, 1967   84

4.1   Cumulative Net Number of Mandatory Minimum Expansions,
      1790–2010   116

4.2   Racial Distribution of Narcotics Arrests and the Cumulative Net
      Number of Expansions to Narcotics Mandatory Minimums,
      1933–2000   120

4.3   President Clinton with Police Officers, 1993   128

4.4   Number of Capital Crimes in Selected House Proposals,
      1988–1994   138

4.5   Number of Capital Crimes in Selected Senate Proposals,
      1988–1994   138

LIST OF TABLES

2.1   Incarceration Rates by Race in Selected States, 1950   62

3.1   Disparate Penalties for Identical Cases, *The Second Circuit Sentencing Study*, 1974   88

3.2   Selected Senate Proposals for Sentencing Guidelines, 1977–1984   101

A.1   Overview of Major Federal Crime Legislation, 1790–2010   157

A.2   Selected Votes on the Omnibus Crime Control and Safe Streets Act of 1968   164

A.3   U.S. Sentencing Guidelines, 1987   166

A.4   Current Federal Mandatory Minimums Statutes, 2010   168

A.5   Capital Crimes, by the 1993 Democratic Count and by Year of Enactment, 1974–2010   190

A.6   Selected House Votes on Capital Punishment Proposals, 1988–1994   198

A.7   Selected Senate Votes on Capital Punishment Proposals, 1988–1994   202

LIST OF ABBREVIATIONS

ABA	American Bar Association
ABF	American Bar Foundation
ACLU	American Civil Liberties Union
ALI	American Law Institute
BOP	Bureau of Prisons
CBC	Congressional Black Caucus
COPS	Office of Community Oriented Policing Services
CRC	Civil Rights Congress
CORE	Congress of Racial Equality
DEA	Drug Enforcement Administration
DOJ	U.S. Department of Justice
FBI	Federal Bureau of Investigation
FDPA	Federal Death Penalty Act of 1994
ICE	Immigration and Customs Enforcement
IIRIRA	Illegal Immigration Reform and Immigrant Responsibility Act of 1996
LEAA	Law Enforcement Assistance Administration
NCCD	National Council on Crime and Delinquency
NIJ	National Institute of Justice
OLEA	Office of Law Enforcement Assistance
NAACP	National Association for the Advancement of Colored People
PCCR	President's Committee on Civil Rights
PRWORA	Personal Responsibility and Work Opportunity Reconciliation Act of 1996
RJA	Racial Justice Act
SNCC	Student Non-Violent Coordinating Committee

SRA	Sentencing Reform Act of 1984
TANF	Temporary Assistance to Needy Families
USCRC	U.S. Civil Rights Commission
USSC	U.S. Sentencing Commission
U.S.C.	*United States Code*

The First Civil Right

The First Civil Right

Protection From Lawless Racial Violence

The first civil right of every American is to be free from domestic violence....We shall re-establish freedom from fear in America so that
America can take the lead of re-establishing freedom from fear in the
world. And to those who say that law-and-order is the code word for
racism, here is a reply: Our goal is justice—justice for every American.[1]
—*Richard Nixon's Acceptance of the Republican Party Nomination
for President, August 8, 1968*

The [first] Condition of Our Rights [is] the Right to Safety and
Security of the Person.... Too many of our people still live under the
harrowing fear of violence or death at the hands of a mob or of brutal treatment by police officers. Many fear entanglement with the law
because of the knowledge that the justice rendered in some courts is
not equal for all persons.[2]
—*President Harry S. Truman's Committee on
Civil Rights, To Secure These Rights, 1947*

One black man in the White House, one million black men in the Big House.
This juxtaposition, used by many, captures the seemingly impossible reality of
post–civil rights America. On the night of his election as forty-fourth president
of the United States, Barack Obama took the stage in Chicago's Grant Park as
self-declared proof that "America is a place where all things are possible," and
more than one commentator marked the first African American president as
Exhibit A for the case that "we have overcome."[3] From that November 2008 cel-
ebration in Grant Park, home to Frank Gehry's stainless steel footbridge and
Jaume Plensa's interactive video sculpture, any election-night reveler might
have journeyed just six miles to witness another of Chicago's distinctive edi-
fices—the nation's largest single-site jail. A 96-acre compound on Chicago's
west side, the Cook County Jail of 2008 held nearly 10,000 people. African
Americans comprised 70 percent of the jail's population, twice their share in
Cook County. As former home to Al Capone and backdrop to MSNBC's reality

show *The Squeeze*, the Cook County Jail has long attracted a certain lurid fascination, but a Department of Justice report from July 2008 documented the jail's unconstitutional practices in sober and technical terms. As an example of "unjust restriction[s] on pretrial detainees," the Department of Justice noted that general-population inmates spent every other day in "a continuous 26-hour period locked inside the cells." Due to a "lack of uniformity of policies and procedures" regarding "adequate sanitation and environmental conditions," many cells had overflowing toilets and exposed electrical wires. In one instance, jail medics fitted a cast to a man's broken leg but subsequently failed "to provide adequate and timely" medical care, letting three weeks pass before answering his complaints of pain, numbness, and a "malodorous discharge" dripping from the cast. When finally treated, he had lost so much soft tissue that doctors amputated his leg.[4]

This is the strange racial present, when talk of futuristic post-racialism coexists with a punishment system deemed a bridge to the racial past, even "the new Jim Crow." This post–civil rights condition is so perfectly insidious that it seems the outcome of a grand plan. Indeed, the rise of mass incarceration appears to fulfill Richard Nixon's 1968 campaign pledge to restore "the first civil right of every American," which Nixon alternatively characterized as freedom from domestic violence, the right to be safe, and freedom from fear. Of course, Nixon's "first civil right" was striking precisely because it was not the first civil right of its time, following as it did the Civil Rights Act of 1964, the Voting Rights Act of 1965, and the Warren Court's expansion of rights of the accused. As a co-optation of civil rights discourse, Nixon's messages established a rank order: the implicitly white right to safety was paramount, not to be threatened by special "minority" and "criminal" rights. As if following Nixon's 1968 call to fight "narcotics peddlers" and "merchants of crime," lawmakers have over time enacted mandatory penalties and funded prison construction, facilitating the septupling of the incarcerated population from 1968 to 2010. When witnessed through a Nixonian lens of law-and-order as racism-free "justice for every American," occupants of the White House and the Big House simply confirm each other's legitimacy. Taken together, the president's successes and the prisoners' failures authenticate meritocracy, untainted by venomous white hatred and sentimental white lenience. As African American prisoners catapult the U.S. incarceration rate to the highest in the world, it seems that Nixon's "first civil right" was promise and prophecy of what was to come.[5]

This book's title, *The First Civil Right*, announces that I begin with a simple observation: two decades before Nixon's anti-black law-and-order campaign, *liberal* law-and-order campaigns pursued "the right to safety" as the first step toward racial equality. At the close of World War II, President Harry S. Truman's Committee on Civil Rights designated the "right to safety and security of the person" the first condition of all rights, and in so doing, fired the Democratic Party's opening salvo against white mob violence and racial prejudice in the criminal justice system. At this juncture, race liberals of the national Democratic Party tentatively committed to an integrationist platform for voting rights and fair employment, with a central plank of reforming criminal justice to secure racial justice.[6] As the black freedom struggle gained momentum, as lynchings of black veterans caused international embarrassment, and as all feared impending "race wars," liberals established a law-and-order mandate: build a better carceral state, one strong enough to control racial violence in the streets and regimented enough to control racial bias in criminal justice administration. As such, the 1947 right to safety was an explicit sanction against white-on-black violence, and not, as it was for Nixon two decades later, an implicit summoning of black-on-white crime.

More than a shared rhetorical flourish, the liberal-cum-conservative "right to safety" invites us to reexamine the scaffolding beneath our explanations for the rise of mass incarceration. The assumed competition of Democratic civil rights versus Republican law-and-order makes it commonplace to interpret history in lurching terms, as if two steps toward racial equality provoked one step backward through carceral expansion. When sorted into binary terms, the rise of mass incarceration becomes the triumph of retribution over rehabilitation, of personal responsibility over "root causes," and, in the parlance of election campaigns, of "tough-on-crime" Republicans over "soft" Democrats.[7] *The First Civil Right* approaches civil rights versus law-and-order categories as the subjects of, not the tools for, investigating the politics of punishment. As such, this book attempts to defamiliarize keywords by foregrounding what is typically seen as the background of carceral expansion: the actors deemed history's virtuous losers, and the times designated prehistory or respite from the war on crime. Examining federal crime policy since World War II, I shine a bright spotlight on race liberals, that is, those who aspired to incorporate African Americans and other "minorities" into the meritocratic pursuit of the good life, and, under the brightest spotlight, race liberals of the national Democratic Party.[8]

With agnosticism toward the ideological valence of law-and-order and recast in expanded historical context, my history of federal crime politics inverts the conventional wisdom: the United States did not face a crime problem that was racialized; it faced a race problem that was criminalized. Rising crime of the 1960s was not uniquely racialized as a conservative strategy to conflate civil rights with black criminality; rather, the race "problem" of the civil rights movement from the 1940s onward was answered with pledges of carceral state development— from racially liberal and conservative lawmakers alike. My overarching claim is therefore that lawmakers constructed the civil rights carceral state, in which liberal notions of racial violence and agendas for race-neutral machinery actually propelled development of a punitive carceral state. Crime politics were at once symptomatic and uniquely structuring of postwar racial liberalism, as efforts to govern a racially explosive society ultimately affirmed the sensibility that only the proceduralist, rights-based state could diffuse what racially threatened the nation. In this sense, crime policy and carceral expansion were not reactions against civil rights; they were the very progeny of civil rights as lawmakers defined them.

Searching for Racism in the Colorblind Carceral State

The rise of mass incarceration is often introduced as a puzzle. Through the late twentieth century, crime policymaking was largely divorced from crime rates, from calls for small government, and from the conventional wisdom of racial progress.[9] Disjunctions between crime rates and tough policy are striking: crime rates and public punitiveness escalated most rapidly through the late 1960s and early 1970s, yet federal lawmakers enacted notoriously punitive drug penalties and three-strikes provisions two decades later, during the stable and declining crime rates of the late 1980s and 1990s. Referencing crime "waves" and drug "epidemics" renders lawbreaking a natural disaster to which good lawmakers simply respond, but a vast literature challenges any straightforward or "natural" relationship between crime rates and punitive policy.[10] Similarly, the most expensive and expansive crime policies emerged along with calls for lean and devolved government. Even as President Bill Clinton vowed to remake big government, prisons expanded as the institutional catchall for drug addiction, mental illness, and homelessness, and federal criminal justice holds the front in ever-aggressive wars on crime, drugs, immigration, and terror.[11]

Post-racial triumphalism seemingly compounds the carceral puzzle. It is well known that the post–civil rights era maintains acute black-to-white disparities, such as two-to-one unemployment, two-to-one infant mortality, and four-to-one poverty, all frequently characterized as legacies of racism past. Not dismissible as Jim Crow "residue," the black-to-white ratio for incarceration rates jumped from three-to-one at Nixon's inauguration to eight-to-one by the turn of the millennium.[12] The White House versus Big House image that opened this chapter called attention to African American men, but African American women faced the fastest growing incarceration rates through the 1990s, and their 2010 incarceration rate was three times that of white women. In the early twenty-first century, nearly one in 10 African American adults could not vote due to felon disenfranchisement laws and, in 2007 alone, one in 15 African American children had a parent held in state or federal prison.[13]

Given its devastating consequences for African Americans, carceral expansion is usually seen as the offspring of conservative interests and ideologies, with anti-black animus close if not central to the causal core. The timing and racial concentration of carceral expansion align cleanly with accounts of conservative backlash against the perceived excesses of African American advancement. From 1925 through 1973, state and federal incarceration rates remained remarkably steady. As shown in Figure 1.1, incarceration rates held at roughly 110 persons incarcerated per 100,000 population, with the slight Depression-era increase and modest World War II decrease followed by a period of such notable constancy that in 1973 two prominent criminologists declared the "stability of punishment" and predicted more of the same. Against prediction, the number of people incarcerated in state and federal prisons jumped from 196,000 persons in 1970 to more than 1.4 million persons in 2010. These numbers reflect state and federal prisons, only part of the carceral state. Counting jails with prisons gives the United States an incarceration rate that outstrips those of other Western democracies by a factor of roughly seven to one.[14] Counting probation and parole with jails and prisons is more astonishing still: this population grew from 780,000 in 1965 to seven million in 2010.[15]

Racial disparity is no detail of carceral expansion. Instead, the last third of the twentieth century saw an equilibrium break in the racial concentration of

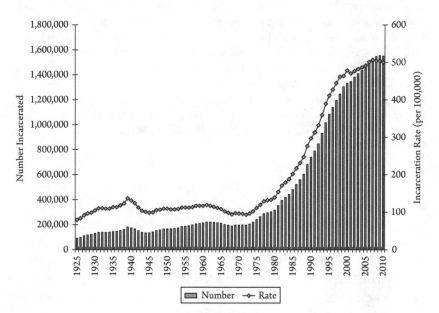

Figure 1.1 Number and Rate of Persons Incarcerated in State and Federal Prisons, 1925–2010. *Source*: Bureau of Justice Statistics, *Sourcebook of Criminal Justice Statistics* (Washington, DC: Department of Justice), various years.

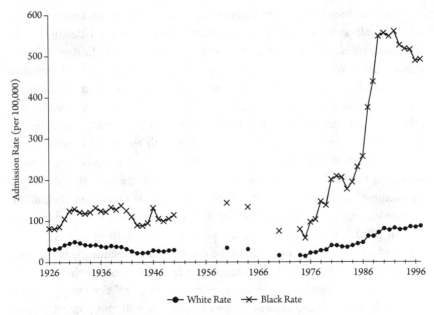

Figure 1.2 Admission Rates to State and Federal Prisons by Race, 1926–1997. *Note*: The Bureau of Justice Statistics compiled federal and state admissions data through 1997, though it did not distinguish between Latino and non-Latino racial categories. This figure therefore represents a significant overcount of white admissions. Admissions data since 1998 are problematic in several ways. The Federal Justice Statistics Program, which collects and makes publicly available federal data, altered its measurement system and began distinguishing between Latino and non-Latino racial categories in 1998. The National Corrections Reporting Program, which collects and restricts access to state data, works with variegated state systems. Many states did not distinguish between Latino and non-Latino racial categories prior to 2000; several states still do not. *Sources*: Bureau of Justice Statistics, *Race of Prisoners Admitted to State and Federal Institutions, 1926–1986* (Washington, DC: Department of Justice, 1991); Bureau of Justice Statistics, *Correctional Populations in the United States, 1994* (Washington, DC: Department of Justice, 1996), table 1.15; Bureau of Justice Statistics, *Correctional Populations in the United States, 1997* (Washington, DC: Department of Justice, 2000), table 1.20; U.S. Census Bureau, *Statistical Abstract of the United States* (Washington, DC: Government Printing Office, various years).

punishment. Between 1926 and 1976, black admission rates to state and federal prisons varied between 81 and 137 admitted per 100,000, and white admission rates varied between 22 and 50 admitted per 100,000 (Figure 1.2). Overall, black-to-white prison admission rates held steady at a three-to-one ratio from 1926 through 1976; this ratio is striking for its severe and steady overrepresentation of African Americans. After 1976, however, the black admission rate broke from its historic norm, and by 1997 the black-to-white admission rate hit a six-to-one ratio.[16] The combination of scale expansion and racial shift produced seismic demographic ruptures for African Americans. Even a relatively

short prison sentence triggers what sociologist Bruce Western calls "a cumulative spiral of disadvantage," reducing wages, slowing wage growth over the life
course, and impairing health over the long term.[17] Intersectionally disadvan-
taged African Americans are especially vulnerable to carceral enmeshment and
the injuries of abusive, excessive, and negligent law enforcement.[18] Transgender
and gender-nonconforming African Americans confront ongoing police harassment, high incarceration rates, and heightened risks of violence in sex-segregated
detention facilities. Low income and educational attainment compound racial
marginalization. An African American man born in the late 1960s who gradu-
ated high school faced a 30 percent chance of going to prison in his lifetime; one
who did not complete high school had a 60 percent chance of going to prison in
his lifetime.[19]

If the problem of the twentieth century was, in W. E. B. Du Bois's famous
words, "the problem of the color line," then the problem of the twenty-first
century is the problem of colorblindness, the refusal to acknowledge the
causes and consequences of enduring racial stratification.[20] In the context of
this stubborn refusal, many scholarly and journalistic accounts explain racialized carceral expansion as the outcome of a conservative backlash or Nixon's
"Southern Strategy," the narrative pivoting on readily identifiable actors with
known motives: anxious or resentful white voters, and Republican sentiments
through coded anti-black appeals. Referenced since at least the 1964 presidential election and canonized in Thomas and Mary Edsall's 1991 Pulitzer Prize
finalist *Chain Reaction*, the backlash thesis holds that Republicans used racially
coded appeals to win white voters who had became disillusioned with the late
1960s "excesses" of civil rights, Black Power, and the disorder of mass protests
and violent uprisings.[21] For more than four decades, the backlash thesis has
traveled through journalistic and academic works; such traveling confirms the
theory's dominance but simultaneously "stretches" its terminology. That the
backlash thesis holds conventional-wisdom status is evidenced by the fact that
so many scholars offer it en route to presenting their original research. [22] As a
theory that pivots on anxious whites and opportunistic conservatives, backlash
encourages certain analytical practices of "finding" racial power in a post–civil
rights context.[23]

Evidence of conservative racialization flows in a stream of familiar
moments: Barry Goldwater's 1964 equation of civil disobedience with black
criminality, Richard Nixon's 1971 commencement of the drug war, and George
H. W. Bush's infamous 1988 Willie Horton campaign ad.[24] The strongest evidence of "coding," therefore, is "smoking gun" proof of racist scheming or a "got-
cha" moment when the real motive slips out from the cover of colorblindness.
Perhaps this is why dozens of backlash tomes cite Kevin Phillips's *The Emerging*

Republican Majority as nothing less than the official playbook for anti-black campaigns, and nearly as many recount Richard Nixon's 1968 campaign advertisement followed by his candid racial slip. In an advertisement addressing a recent teachers' strike, Nixon explained, "The heart of the problem is law-and-order in our schools." His voiceover continued, "Discipline in the classroom is essential if our children are to learn." Having read his script, Nixon accidentally recorded this statement to his staff: "Yep, this hits it right on the nose, the thing about this whole teacher—it's all about law-and-order and the damn Negro–Puerto Rican groups out there."[25] To code is to disguise racism for political gain; the moniker itself retains meaning as deliberate subterfuge. Undeniably repulsive, Nixon's slip exposes the intent beneath the disavowal.

With eyes fixed on the incendiary sins of conservative law-and-order, liberal agendas become contrast background, glossed quickly and presumed virtuous. Accounts of conservative backlash are not wrong; rather, I believe that they are so overwhelmingly persuasive that they eclipse the specificity of racial liberalism against which they respond. Our explanations too quickly dichotomize the late-1960s crime debate into "two schools of thought": conservatives blamed crime on black culture, and "liberals, by contrast, insisted that social reforms" like "the War on Poverty and civil rights legislation would get at the 'root causes' of criminal behavior and stressed the social conditions that predictably generate crime."[26] Polarizing conservative law-and-order versus liberal civil rights risks depoliticizing racial power by reducing racism to white animus, and it risks naturalizing some non-racial backdrop against which conservative "racialization" was dramatized.

Searching for racism as emotional white "resentment" or strategic, subtextual "coding" means missing liberal racial criminalization that thrived in the full light of day.[27] Recognizing racial power requires eschewing the search for animus or calculation that Republicans "*cynically* manipulated the *anxieties* of southern and working-class whites by focusing on issues like crime and welfare fraud that served as code words for race." White animus too often propels backlash accounts, as if some primordial racism among southern and working-class whites simply presented a political opportunity for conservatives.[28] Racial power is not something that "an individual or a group exercises directly or intentionally over another individual or group," as political scientist Claire Kim tells us; it is "rather a system property, permeating, circulating throughout and continuously constituting society."[29] Indeed, the mandate to discount intentions must extend to what might appear to be goodwill. On the dangers of liberal reforms mobilized through white pity or paternalism, it is worth quoting historian Daryl Michael Scott's *Contempt & Pity* at length: "Oppression was wrong, liberals suggested, because it damaged personalities, and changes had to be made to protect and promote the well-being of African Americans. Rather than standing on the ideals of the American creed and making reparations for the nation's failure to live up to the separate-but-equal doctrine set forth in *Plessy v. Ferguson*, liberals capitulated to the historic tendency of posing blacks as objects of pity."[30]

Consider, for example, the banner case of civil rights victories: *Brown v. Board of Education* (1954). In making the case for school desegregation, legal strategists centralized the idea that segregation damaged black personality development. The potency of black damage imagery is evident in the fact that the Supreme Court cited several psychological studies, most famously Kenneth and Mamie Clark's "doll experiment" in which black children selected white dolls as nicer, prettier, and smarter than brown dolls. Evidence that segregation injured black self-esteem, however, was quite mixed. Indeed, other psychological studies of the early 1950s concluded that school segregation psychologically protected black youth, and even the "doll experiment" data allowed for a similar interpretation. Despite contradictory and thin evidence, the Supreme Court's *Brown* decision granted authoritative status to the idea that segregation damaged black self-esteem and personality development. By foregrounding black psychology rather than white economic advantage, *Brown* posited interracial contact in desegregated schools as the palliative cure. Moreover, since psychological studies "tested" segregation's impact on black children without examining segregation's damage to white personality development, *Brown* and its social scientific evidence reinforced paternal notions that blacks benefit from proximity to white superiors.[31]

It is only by turning away from animus that a racial promise of liberal law-and-order becomes clear: liberals "criminalized" the race problem, often toward the end of compelling reform. Across the postwar period, liberals explained a range of disparate phenomenon—organized civil disobedience, mass uprisings, individual acts of petty crime—as indicators that white supremacy was unsustainable. Characterized as "volcanic threat" or "socio-racial dynamite," black lawlessness was, for liberals, an expression of rage, frustration, or aggression. Not biologically preordained, black lawlessness was a product of white social engineering. President John Kennedy urged passage of civil rights legislation in June 1963 because the "fires of frustration and discord are burning in every city," where "redress is sought in the streets, in demonstrations, parades, and protests which create tensions and threaten violence and threaten lives."[32] By 1967, Johnson Democrats explained black lawlessness as a social, psychological, and familial adaptation to white racism. President Johnson's 1967 Commission on Law Enforcement and Administration of Justice articulated this quintessential philosophy with the statement: "A civil rights law is a law against crime."[33]

By bracketing the search for coded, ill-willed racialization, the double edge of liberal advocacy becomes clear: perhaps the explosive volatility of black rage necessitated civil rights legislation, but the imagery militated against recognition of black humanity. That uncontrollable fire of black rage conjured "the black criminal," the figure used to justify lynching, chain gangs, exploitative labor, segregation, and the overall maintenance of white supremacy. We might surmise the complicated mix of righteousness, fear, and empathy in Vice President Hubert Humphrey's statement in July 1966: "If I had to live in the slums I think you'd have more trouble than you have already, because I've got enough spark left in me to lead a mighty good revolt." Like a furious President Johnson, many criticized Humphrey's statement as easy fodder in the 1968 campaign, as Nixon and his vice presidential candidate Spiro Agnew denounced Humphrey for "condon[ing] violence and advocate[ing] overthrow of the government."[34] But we might note the dangers of his "facile intimacy," as if he can slide into some predictable, easily knowable black anger. Observing his pride of "spunk" and his pleasure of indignation, we might situate Humphrey's comments in political constructions of the black male figure—physically strong, socially irreverent, presumptively criminal—that is at once enviable, enticing, and menacing to white men, such that it "so seduces America just as often as the bogeyman that keeps America awake at night."[35] By forgetting animus, it becomes clear that there was no post–civil rights exit from racial criminalization. There were "competing" constructions of black criminality, one callous, another with a tenor of sympathy and cowering paternalism.[36]

With racialization understood as the extension of racial meaning, it is clear that, in the words of legal scholar Michelle Alexander, "the racialized nature of this [crime] imagery became a crucial resource for conservatives" in the late 1960s. With racialized imagery, conservatives "succeeded in using law-and-order rhetoric in their effort to mobilize the resentment of white working-class voters, many of whom felt threatened by the sudden progress of African Americans."[37] If racialization is, as defined in Michael Omi and Howard Winant's germinal *Racial Formation in the United States,* a historically specific ideological process that "extends racial meaning to a previously racially unclassified relationship, social practice or group," then it is the "backdrop" to conservative racialization that warrants study.

Turning away from the callously "racialized" to mundane agendas for neutrality reveals the promise of liberal law-and-order: to modernize and deracialize carceral machinery. For liberal reformers, racial "bias" infiltrated the unmodernized machine: byzantine systems of administration, contradictory laws, and ill-defined procedures allowed the whims of individual discretion to supplant rule of law. "Different standards of justice" across the country and "unfettered police lawlessness" allowed criminal-justice administrators to act out their irrationalities against "unpopular minorities" like union organizers, "Negroes, Mexicans, or Jehovah's Witnesses," explained by Truman's Committee on Civil Rights in

The First Civil Right

1947.[38] Bemoaning the same incoherence two decades later, President Johnson's Commission on Law Enforcement and the Administration of Justice flat out denied the existence of a criminal justice "system" worthy of the name. The "system" was merely a "philosophical core" that valued the "impartial and deliberate process." In language familiar to scholars of American Political Development, the Commission chastised lawmakers for adding "layer upon layer of institutions and procedures" around that core, "some carefully constructed and some improvised, some inspired by principle and some by expediency."[39] By "layering" new policies and institutions in piecemeal fashion, lawmakers built a contradictory, and, in the eyes of liberal reformers, easy expression of animus toward "unpopular minorities."[40]

In this sense, liberal law-and-order agendas flowed from an underlying assumption of racism: racism was an individual whim, an irrationality, and therefore racism could be corrected with "state-building" in the Weberian sense—that is, the replacement of the personalized power of government officials with codified, standardized, and formalized authority.[41] Following scholars like Lani Guinier, Daniel HoSang, Jodi Melamed, Chandan Reddy, and Nikhil Singh, I use the term "postwar racial liberalism" to capture the historically grounded understanding of the American race "problem" as psychological in nature, with "solutions" of teaching tolerance and creating colorblind institutions. The close of World War II opened a "therapeutic war against prejudice": civil, professional, and religious organizations devised educational programs about the wrongs of scapegoating, and, by one count, the number of organizations attempting to correct ethnic "misconceptions" jumped from 300 in 1945 to more than 1,350 by 1950.[42] As a political formation, postwar racial liberalism should be understood vis-à-vis the frameworks it eclipsed. On one side, postwar racial liberalism came to overshadow biological racism, which naturalized racial hierarchy (and became the referent of conservative "coded" racism). On another side, postwar racial liberalism eclipsed conceptions of structural racism, which situated domestic racism and colonialism abroad in an integrated critique of global capitalism (and became the discredited thinking of a communist fringe). Postwar racial liberalism conceived of racism as "an anachronistic prejudice and a personal and psychological problem, rather than as a systemic problem rooted in specific social practices and pervading relations of political economy and culture."[43]

In the construction of liberal law-and-order, then, *racist* violence became *arbitrary* violence. Racism was an irrational belief, erratic and baseless, and therefore, correcting racial violence meant criminalizing "private" acts, and, more significantly, modernizing carceral machinery to increase procedural protections, decrease discretionary decisions, and insulate the system from arbitrary bias.

The Perils of Liberal Law-and-Order

Over the second half of the twentieth century, liberal law-and-order became an ethos that safety from "racial violence" was a right, a logos that rights and rules could insulate racial bias from carceral machinery, and a pathos that black criminality expressed black deprivation, frustration, and rage, perhaps dysfunctional but "pitiable" as a byproduct of white prejudice. To grasp the perils of liberal law-and-order, consider first the grand promises of liberal law-and-order. Federal lawmakers since Reconstruction regularly neglected calls to redress white supremacist violence in the North and South, including the routine violence of white riots, lynch mobs, police brutality, and "third-degree" methods to extort (false) confessions. Given the lawlessness of state and local carceral machinery, it is unsurprising that calls for federal law-and-order came from Ida B. Wells in her campaign against lynching, from the National Negro Congress in calling for all murder to be a federal offense, and from the National Association for the Advancement of Colored People in demanding punishment for inhibiting voting rights by use of threat, assault, arson, and murder. When confronted with racial violence, federal lawmakers sometimes invoked legal fictions that African Americans enjoyed equal protection under the law, or they hid behind the cover of federalism. Silence on racial violence, like silence on most civil rights matters, preserved the fragile alliance of the national Democratic Party.[44] Based on this history of non-intervention, postwar liberal Democrats launched their law-and-order agenda, not with a punitive bang, but with a proceduralist whimper. As it congealed after World War II, the agenda for liberal law-and-order included more protective rules of criminal procedure, federally sponsored police professionalization, enforceable civil rights crimes, an organized criminal code, and predictable criminal sentencing.

Liberal law-and-order agendas might sound less violent than the "new Jim Crow," less scheming than the Republican "Southern Strategy." But we should not indulge what Gillian Harkins has called a "nostalgic remembrance of liberalisms past," as if there were ever a full-throated, unambiguous commitment to ameliorating structural violence or eliminating "root causes."[45] If the conservative racialization directs us to research how political actors maintain constraint by "coding" racism into law-and-order policies, then understanding carceral racial liberalism encourages an examination of how political actors come to obscure racial power through vocabularies of bland administrative reform and soft racial paternalism.

This study of federal crime politics and policies highlights central moments in the postwar development of liberal law-and-order—from Truman Democrats and the problem of racial violence, to Johnson Democrats and the problem of black crime, and to Clinton Democrats and the problem of (colorblind) crime. Following crime policy development in four domains—federal funding for law enforcement, sentencing guidelines, mandatory minimums, and the death penalty—I identify the ways in which liberal problem framings and policy solutions shaped, complicated, and ultimately accelerated carceral state development. Construction of the civil rights carceral state has many moving parts, no clean periodization, and pivots on the minutiae of legislative history and institutional development, the legacies of partisan commitments. To introduce the argument in broad strokes, however, I explain the three interrelated perils of liberal law-and-order: its potential to entrench notions of black criminality, to fuel carceral state-building, and to fortify the legitimacy of the carceral state. As a sensibility of racial pity and administrative quality, liberal law-and-order could not contain or even critique the distinctive features of the late-twentieth-century carceral state—its scale and its intense racial concentration.

Peril One: Entrenches Notions of Black Criminality

The first peril of liberal law-and-order was its potential to entrench notions of black criminality. Liberal racial pity mirrored conservative racial contempt, and, as mirror images, "competing" partisan frames locked linkages of blackness to criminality. By repeating terms of warped, deprived, and even justifiably rageful blackness, liberal law-and-order entrenched notions of black criminality.

Ultimately, liberal Democrats defined "the crime problem" as a subset of "the Negro problem." Race liberals framed a whole host of black transgressions—civil disobedience, Black Power, street crime—as indicators that civil rights had not gone far enough. Unfulfilled civil rights agendas breed crime, they claimed, because racial inequality sustained relative deprivation and perceptions of law's illegitimacy. By the mid-1960s, Johnson Democrats worried about street crime and urban riots, addressing "black criminality" as a social, psychological, and familial adaptation to white racism. In the logic of postwar racial liberalism, therefore, racism was a psychological defect, but its symptoms manifested differently on the white-black binary. For white people, racism was an irrationality, a pollutant to the real self. For black people, racism was an injury, a disfigurement of psychological development and therefore constitutive of the real self. Liberals relied on a political strategy of compelling reform by making black people seem damaged and potentially violent. Like many political constructions, the liberals' profile of black criminality derived neither from evidence nor intellectual coherence. A mélange of psychological terms diagnosed black disruptions, whether seen as rudeness, social protest, or criminal act, as "concealed aggression," a byproduct of low self-esteem, black subculture, or the pathological black family. By making political protest an explosive emotion that extended to violence, crime, and riots, liberals were guilty of a strategy most associated with conservatives: they blurred together organized civil disobedience, street crime, and riots into one mess of psychological disorder.[46]

Postwar liberal law-and-order converged with emergent Republican positions on a basic premise: civil rights liberalization would require carceral modernization. Civil rights opponents, mostly Republicans and southern Democrats, argued that crime was a manifestation of black civil rights gone too far. Civil rights generated crime, they claimed, by disrupting the harmonious segregation of the races and by validating black civil disobedience. Federal civil rights liberalization implicated the federal government in crime control; simply put, federal lawmakers were principally responsible for civil rights, and therefore federal lawmakers should clean up the ensuing criminological mess. While seemingly opposite interpretations, both race-liberal and race-conservative explanations attributed crime to black civil rights, and both interpretations identified blacks as default suspects in the crime problem.

To "differentiate" conservative anti-black animus from liberal goodwill, consider two archetypal profiles: the conservative Republicans' Willie Horton and the liberal Democrats' Bigger Thomas. As part of George H. W. Bush's 1988 presidential campaign against Democratic candidate Michael Dukakis, the William ("Willie") Horton television ad described the young black man's life sentence for a first-degree murder in Massachusetts, where, through Governor Michael Dukakis's furlough system, Horton left prison on a weekend pass. While on the weekend furlough, Horton assaulted a white married couple in their home, raping the woman and stabbing her husband.[47] In a sense, the advertisement retold the conservative's appraisal of civil rights history in simple narrative structure: orientation begins with a married, home-owning white couple; the story's confrontation is Willie Horton entering their home, his prison furlough a manifestation of Great Society liberalism in all its permissive "lenience" toward criminals and African Americans; the story's resolution was left to voters.

More than two decades after the campaign, the Willie Horton ad still attracts attention as a textbook example of conservative racial coding, a model of disavowing racist intent while displaying racist positions. We recognize Willie Horton in the historical pantheon of the "black male rapist," that particular political construction of the violent, hypersexual black man with alleged desire for white women. Attending to this construction draws a straight line from the 1988 Republican campaign ad through conservatives' 1950s opposition to civil rights on grounds that desegregation would make white women vulnerable to assaults by black men, to 1930s and 1940s opposition to anti-lynching legislation for the same reasons, and the infamous 1915 film *Birth of the Nation* that allegorized as rape the dangers of black freedom for the white nation. In his 1906 State of the Union Address, President Theodore Roosevelt asserted that "the greatest existing cause of lynching is the perpetration, especially by black men, of the hideous crime of rape," building on long-standing nineteenth-century uses of the myth of the black rapist to justify brutality and policing of African Americans.[48]

If conservative racialization is exemplified in Willie Horton, liberal racialization is exemplified in Bigger Thomas. As the protagonist of Richard Wright's 1940 novel *Native Son*, Bigger Thomas was a black man who killed a white woman, but Richard Wright crafted the character as a product of the racist social environment, not biologically driven beastly impulses. Wright's novel was popular in its own right, while Bigger Thomas was referenced in the touchstone book of racial politics, Gunnar Myrdal's *An American Dilemma*. The Swedish researcher worried about the ongoing creation of Bigger Thomases in urban "Negro slums." Bigger Thomas recurred in liberal politics as a symbol of the dangers caused by race prejudice: he was a black man engineered for frustration and violence. This frame was used as a call for political change to improve the lives of black people, lest a generation of Biggers come to express their frustration through criminal acts that destroyed white lives and social order.[49]

We may or may not think of those who advocated reform through Bigger Thomas as holding racist attitudes; discerning the real intentions matters less than the larger institutional dynamic: the two major political parties, staking claims that effectively set the spectrum of reasonable debate and motivated reforms with reference to the threat of black criminality. Here we should attend to Paul Frymer's trenchant-if-controversial analysis: racism does not become problematic "simply because some or even many individuals hold racist attitudes; it becomes so because institutional dynamics legitimate and promote racist behavior in a concentrated and systematic manner."[50] Partisan racial criminalization is precisely the kind of practice that legitimates racist realities in systemic fashion. Liberal racial pity mirrored conservative racial contempt, and, as mirror images, "competing" partisan frames locked blackness to criminality.

Peril Two: Fuels "Neutral" State-Building

Proposals for carceral modernization were so powerful precisely because of their seeming "neutrality." Calls to improve criminal justice administration, whether for more police training or for reorganization of the byzantine criminal code, garnered support from lawmakers and interest groups with distinct and even oppositional goals.[51] Like shared fear of the "Negro problem," opposing partisan, regional coalitions agreed on policies to "modernize" criminal justice.

While liberals fought for professionalized police and modernized sentencing to bring fairness and reason to discretionary machinery, race conservatives also demanded federal modernization to guard against the specter of black criminality in a desegregated racial regime. Consider, for example, that civil rights proponents and opponents supported federal funding to local police, but for different racial reasons. Many liberal Democrats like Senator Joseph Tydings of Maryland supported police professionalization to improve police-community "relations" and to correct the "deep-seated belief amongst our Negro citizens that equal law enforcement in police practices does not exist anywhere in our land." At the same time, racially conservative Republicans like Senator John Tower of Texas supported police professionalization because, during a time when people "accept as normal the use of riots, civil disorder, disobedience, and even individual violence," funding police would allegedly reinforce "common decency" and "self-control" behind the notion that "Americans need not rob and assault" to achieve "progress."[52]

Liberal agendas to modernize were vulnerable to co-optation, in part because liberal lawmakers obscured outcome-based measures of racial justice as a parenthetical matter. Skilled policy entrepreneurs generally maintain ambiguity to build winning coalitions, but the particular vernacular of liberal law-and-order aimed to protect due process and control discretionary power in criminal justice administration. Reducing "discretion" is an example par excellence of process-oriented metrics of racial fairness: discretion was not a problem because it produced over-punishment or under-punishment; its problem was unpredictability, variation so extreme that it impugned the rule of law without transgressing any specific rule.

Many scholars have demonstrated the power of crime "policy feedbacks"; that is, the ways in which policies "produce social effects that reinforce their own stability."[53] Even referencing the "prison industrial complex" implicitly affirms political scientist E. E. Schattschneider's claim that "new policies create new politics." In this case, new punitive policies fortified police unions and private detention corporations, thereby strengthening interest groups with incentives to "reinforce the stability" of punitive policies. The California Correctional Peace Officers Association, for example, gradually accrued the economic and political capital to lobby for and fund advertising for the 1994 Three Strikes and You're Out ballot initiatives.[54] Others emphasized the ways in which expanded criminalization ratchets up electoral incentives for even more criminalization, because, in the long run, reliance on short-term punitive fixes raises the costs of jumping tracks to invest in better systems of education, health care, and employment.[55] Carceral expansion also weakened oppositional interests—that is, it impeded the development of potential "negative" feedbacks that might have undercut carceral expansion. Felon

disenfranchisement laws have eliminated votes for individuals likely to support Democratic candidates, and unsolicited contact with police officers sup-
presses proclivity for civic engagement.[56]

In this same vein, postwar reforms to improve criminal justice administration directed future reforms down the same path. The combination of a meager welfare state but a capacious carceral state had led interest groups to rely on
criminal justice for social change. Acting within existing institutional arrange-
ments, mainstream anti-violence movements, for example, pursued restraining
orders, specialized domestic violence courts, and mandatory arrest policies that
fortified existing institutions.[57] Not necessarily a reflection of pro-punitive sentiments, reformers tend to build on or adapt existing institutional structures;
destroying and building anew is costly, requires challenged entrenched interests,
and poses coordination problems.[58]

Undoubtedly, the outcomes of Democratic proposals might be called defeats.
The conservative coalition of Republicans and southern Democrats won crucial
policy details. In many ways, the rise of the "New Democrats" after 1984 demonstrated just how much ground liberals had lost or conceded. Democrats lost
many wars of parliamentary maneuver, but they built something more fundamental, harder to see. By promoting the ideology of liberal law-and-order, they
established a way of asking and answering the question of how we see racism in
criminal justice.

Peril Three: Secures Legitimacy, or, Seeing Racial Violence as an Administrative Deficiency

The carceral state exerts extreme coercive power in forcing a person to wear an
ankle bracelet, to live in a cell, or to die by lethal injection, but this naked violence is licensed by adherence to rights, secured through race-free administrative
protocol, and enabled by a sympathetic preoccupation with black criminality.[59]
Liberal law-and-order set a lens for seeing racial violence as correctable with
reformed carceral machinery.[60] In this sense, liberal law-and-order anchored the
pro-rights "left" in a conversation that assumed the fundamental institutional
structure of criminalizing, policing, and incarcerating. On that invisible shared
ground, the "heated" conflict between the parties became simply a matter of
"how *best* to run prisons, organize probation, or enforce fines, rather than question why these measures are used in the first place," as sociologist David Garland
put it.[61]

Liberal law-and-order constrained the ideological terrain for addressing racial
violence. This ideological contraction is an historical process, visible only by calling attention to neglected and quashed visions of law-and-order, before conservatives successfully captured the term and petrified its meaning. In the postwar

years, organizations like the National Negro Congress, the Civil Rights Congress, the Anti-Defamation League of B'nai B'rith, and the National Association for the Advancement of Colored People forced a reluctant Democratic Party to address lynching, but lynching was more than a single criminal incident with a handful of culpable individuals. Lynching was paradigmatic of the indivisibility of white violence: it was violence achieved at once through "private" white actors, through complicit local police, and through the unearned accumulation of white economic and political power and the oppositional definitions of rational, law-abiding whites over irrational, criminal blacks. In this understanding, which I think of as the fight for structural law-and-order, carceral harm was not measured by adherence to due process. It is an ideology against all state-sanctioned racism that demanded the elimination of carceral practices and institutions that maintained or exacerbated race-differentiated vulnerability to premature death.[62]

Liberal lawmakers, however, confronted racial violence as an administrative deficiency. In the ideology of liberal law-and-order, police brutality was the unsanctioned use of force, but more procedures and professionalization could define *acceptable use* of force. Lynching was lawless mob violence, but capital punishment could be fair with adequate legal defense for the poor, proper jury instructions, and clear lists of mitigating and aggravating circumstances. Seen as an administrative deficiency, racial violence could be corrected through the establishment of well-defined, rule-bound, and rights-laden uniform state processes. Liberal lawmakers would come to evaluate fairness through finely honed, step-by-step questions: Did legislators enact a sufficiently clear criminal statute? Did police properly *Mirandize*? Did prosecutors follow protocol in offering a plea bargain or filing charges? Did parole officers follow administrative rules of revocation? And, in any single step, did a specific actor deviate from the protocol or intentionally discriminate? As a methodology for "finding racism" in the criminal justice system, liberal law-and order reinforced the common sense that racism is a ghost in the machine, some immaterial force detached from the institutional terrain of racialized wealth inequality and the possessive investment in whiteness.[63] At the core of liberal law-and-order was the promise to move each individual qua individual through a system of clear rules that allow little room for individual bias.[64] In effect, a lasting legacy of liberal law-and-order is this: we evaluate the rightness of criminal justice through the administrative quality by which each individual is searched, arrested, warehoused, or put to death.

Taken together, the liberal's brand of racial criminalization and administrative deracialization legitimized extreme penal harm to African Americans: the more carceral machinery was rights-based and rule-bound, the more racial disparity was isolatable to "real" black criminality. This mutually reinforcing dynamic is evident, for example, in the changing assumptions of criminological research. Beginning with positivist faith that crime rates measured misconduct rather than social control, researchers have long attempted to isolate the real crime rate. The excess of black punishment, as interpreted by many liberal "race relations" theorists, demonstrated the consequences of black disadvantage. As sociologist Darnell Hawkins has explained, liberal "race relations" researchers presented black crime as reactive, a product of black subculture, social disorganization, family structure, and normlessness. By the 1970s, prominent criminological research attributed racially disparate carceral outcomes to black criminality, not administrative bias.[65] With gestures of pity for black deprivation and with agendas for system deracialization, liberal law-and-order covered the basic quandary of twentieth-century punishment: given that the outcomes are as they are, why does the criminal justice system maintain legitimacy as a non-racist institution?[66]

Approach

My perspective on racial and carceral power compels a particular methodological course. Race, crime, and punishment are all politically constructed, enmeshed in institutions and ideologies that develop over time, continually remaking the common sense of who is dangerous, where the bad neighborhoods are, what constitutes excessive police force, and why some narcotics heal and others hurt. Implicitly this perspective discounts intentions, recognizing that racial power is not necessarily exerted by will. Likewise, complexities in crime policymaking and coalition building, especially with a large omnibus bill, belie the notion of legislative intent. Empirically, individual or legislative "intentions" may be unknown, unknowable, or of questionable relevance in explaining outcomes. Normatively, I discount intentions because penal harm—that is, the actual pain of punishment as experienced by individuals and groups—varies least by what the partisans value most: the "message" of punishment. Stated interests in minimizing bias or increasing rehabilitation do not necessarily mitigate penal harm. The harm of a 16-month prison sentence holds, I suspect, whether imposed by unfettered judicial discretion or a sentencing guideline. Legal rituals and administrative technicalities do not dull the fact that, as legal scholar Robert Cover so famously stated, law acts on the "field of pain and death."[67]

Anti-functionalism is the sine qua non of American Political Development, beginning as it does with the recognition that policies and institutions are more than congealed tastes, elite interests, and the "the natural and adaptive reaction of governments to changing conditions." Methodologically, therefore, by emphasizing policy development, I hope to avoid functionalist deductions that bypass history through a shortcut that takes the logical form, "X exists because

it serves the function Y."[68] Proposals for indigent defense and community policing may have been touched by the better angels of our nature, but, as scholars
of American Political Development insist, crime policymaking and carceral
state-building worked within existing institutional and ideological arrange-
ments, often resulting in suboptimal policies with unintended outcomes.[69]

I anchor my study in four crime policy domains: federal funding to state and
local law enforcement, sentencing guidelines, mandatory minimum statutes,
and the death penalty. Federal funding for law enforcement, my first domain, has
a relatively small impact on mammoth state and local budgets, but this policy
domain nonetheless attracts national commentary on ideal police-community
relations, the role of "minority" police, and the import of Supreme Court decisions like *Miranda*. My second and third domains—sentencing guidelines and
mandatory minimums—matter as engines of mass incarceration, and, taken
together, the emergence of guidelines and the explosive growth of mandatory minimums constitute the most important developments in the history of
U.S. sentencing policies. Prior to 1970, the federal government and states operated by a system known as indeterminate sentencing, in which judicial decisions
were constrained by statutory maximums and a handful of statutory minimums.
If incarcerated, a person usually became eligible for release after serving one-third
of their sentence, with final release date decided by a parole board. This changed
in the last third of the twentieth century, when Congress and state legislatures
enacted sentencing guidelines and mandatory minimums that curtailed judicial
discretion. With the creation of sentencing guidelines, an extra-judicial body
devised uniform sentencing "grids" for judges to follow. Seventeen states and the
federal government have created sentencing guidelines since 1979. Mandatory
minimums are legislatively predetermined sentences, triggered upon conviction
regardless of case-specific mitigating factors such as playing a peripheral role in
the crime or having no prior offenses. Between 1970 and 1996, most state legislatures enacted mandatory minimum penalties for repeat offenses (40 states),
crimes committed using a deadly weapon (38 states), drug possession or trafficking (36 states), and drunk driving (31 states).[70] My fourth domain, the death
penalty, warrants study as the outer extreme of carceral violence, anomalous
among Western democracies.

These four policy domains are worthy of study, but I neglect equally worthy
areas. To evaluate my domain selection, I compiled a list of federal crime enactments that are significant by at least one of two measures: the enactment qualified as important on political scientist David Mayhew's much-referenced roster
of postwar enactments, or the enactment contained a mandatory minimum.[71]
(Important enactments are given special denotation in Table A.1, which lists
major federal crime legislation enacted from 1790 to 2010 and is intended as a
quick reference for readers.) I do not address three major domains: gun control;

organized and corporate crime; and hate crimes and violence against women. These omitted domains, however, are likely the "usual suspects" of claims that liberals fortified carceral machinery, often with aspirations of mitigating economic inequality and social hierarchy.[72]

To see politics and policy development most closely from the inside, I examine how proposals originate and change over time, how federal lawmakers articulate preferences and justifications in particular crime policy issues, and how partisan stances developed over the course of the postwar period. I therefore make use of floor statements in the *Congressional Record* and judiciary committee hearings and reports, reports from presidential commissions, and party platforms. To see how policymakers discuss and strategize, I examine documents gathered from the Harry S. Truman, Lyndon B. Johnson, and William J. Clinton presidential libraries.

This book toggles between different scales of investigation: the granular (sometimes tedious) history of selected federal enactments, and the grand (sometimes lavish) interpretation of commonsense standards for fair punishment. Given the difficulties of jumping between these registers, I offer some qualifications and clarifications. First, I examine the politics of carceral expansion in one relatively small, unusual site: the federal government. Having increased its population from 17,000 persons in 1947 to more than 200,000 in 2010, the federal government has surpassed Texas to become the largest prison system in the union. Nonetheless, states and localities hold roughly 85 percent of all incarcerated people. The federal government is no typical case study; in fact, federal lawmakers tend to exhibit greater punitiveness than local lawmakers.[73] Despite these major limitations, federal crime policy is uniquely important in terms of specifying criminal procedure, funding to local police and state prison construction, and for some specifications of "felon exclusions" from federal benefits.[74] More significant, however, federal lawmakers have generated a national conversation on law-and-order in everything from Johnson's sweeping demand for "jobs, education and hope" as crime control to Nancy Reagan's schmaltzy "just say no" campaign by making crime a reference point on matters of race, rights, and morality. In the end, I selected federal crime policy recognizing its major tradeoff: federal crime policy carries light institutional but hefty symbolic weight.

In this study, liberal law-and-order is an ideology, and as such not synonymous with northern Democrats, the Warren Court, or any other single actor. Ideologies circulate through different actors and congeal over time. That said, I occasionally reference law-and-order themes by Democratic presidencies, from Truman to Johnson to Clinton. This shorthand is problematic because it wrongly signals sharp ideological breaks between presidencies, and it highlights presidents instead of the House and Senate judiciary chairs who forged coalitions across Congresses and presidencies.[75] Despite serious limitations,

Democratic presidencies are convenient shorthand references, and, in the end, presidencies reference thematic if messy change in characterizations of the crime problem, from white-on-black racial violence for Truman's presidency, to black-on-white crime during Johnson's presidency, to allegedly colorblind (but frequently black-on-black) crime during Clinton's presidency.

Looking Ahead: The Path of Liberal Law-and-Order

The promises and perils of liberal law-and-order are presented above in analytically discrete and static form, but these are merely conceptual markers to hold on to while I undertake the true work of my argument: to show how struggles over law-and-order unfold over time. I highlight and weave together two historical narratives: a story of carceral state-building, and a story of commitments to racial equality. The history of carceral state-building is, in many ways, a straightforward story of the continual layering of carceral machinery and rules. The history of racial equality focuses mostly on the Democratic Party, and it is a story of turning away. As black voters were securely "captured" in the Democratic Party, Democrats of the 1980s feared that defending "lenient" punishment was politically synonymous with defending black criminality. It is the nexus of these two historical narratives that matters. Aspirations and good intentions could not contain carceral machinery. Perhaps the 1980s and 1990s secured a punitive cultural hegemony, but the carceral state developed over the decades, "unaware" that it would serve conservative ends.[76]

Chapter 2, "Freedom from Fear," explores the formation of liberal law-and-order with the crisis of white supremacy at World War II. With white riots in the North and lynching in the South, liberal Democrats advocated anti-lynching legislation, civil rights crimes, enhanced criminal procedure, and police training. Lawmakers made civil rights the venue to discuss a national conversation: what, if anything, constituted unacceptable carceral violence against black people? The answers were developed through regional comparisons with southern criminal justice seen as backward and unprofessional, and local police viewed as having no special discipline to elevate themselves as professionals. Evidencing their claims that integration brings chaos, southern lawmakers advertised that black incarceration rates in the North were roughly twice those in the South, and in cities like Detroit and Cleveland, African Americans comprised 90 percent of all narcotics arrestees. These discrepancies were no challenge to Myrdal's conclusion that northern criminal justice was professional and race-neutral.

True to Kimberlé Crenshaw's insight that winning and losing are part of the same experience in the fight for racial justice, the victories of national lawmakers addressing the racial terrorism of lynching and explosives entailed the discrediting of more ambitious agendas for structural law-and-order. Visions of structural law-and-order from the Civil Rights Congress, for example, critiqued white violence as systemic in world economic terms. Private lynching and state executions mutually reinforced and protected white supremacy. Liberals, by contrast, would correct racial violence by criminalizing private racial violence and rationalizing state bias. Truman Democratic policies for anti-lynching laws, civil rights crimes, reform of criminal procedure, and training against police brutality gained little traction in the short-run, but they transmogrified into a more fundamental policy platform among Johnson Democrats: federal civil rights liberalization would necessitate federally spearheaded criminal justice modernization.

The power of liberal law-and-order and its homologies with race conservatism is evident in Chapter 3, "Policing the Great Society." This chapter traces the development of two banner policies of police professionalization and sentencing reform with shared liberal logics: the Law Enforcement Assistance Act of 1968 (Title I of the Omnibus Crime Control and Safe Streets Act of 1968), which established the Law Enforcement Assistance Administration and charged it with supporting state and local police forces, and the Sentencing Reform Act of 1984 (Title II of the Comprehensive Crime Control Act), which created the U.S. Sentencing Commission and charged its development of the U.S. Sentencing Guidelines. If witnessed at the moment of enactment, each law appears to be a conservative victory. By tracing longer policy development, however, I argue that these policies share liberal origins. In the tradition of Truman-era identification of prejudice in criminal justice, Johnson Democrats supported police funding to recruit and train the racism out of local police departments, through varied policy actions such as the Law Enforcement Assistance Act of 1968, a string of antecedent recommendations from the U.S. Civil Rights Commission, the Juvenile Justice Act of 1961, and the Law Enforcement Assistance Act of 1965. I then follow the key policy entrepreneur for sentencing guidelines, Democratic Senator Edward "Ted" Kennedy, as I track changes in Kennedy's six antecedent proposals from 1977 to 1984. Across his proposals, I give special attention to four crucial subsections: maintaining parole, increasing early release through "good time," capping prison capacity, and providing alternatives to incarceration.

Police professionalization and sentencing reform shared a particular logic: bringing rules, rights, and procedure to carceral machinery would quell racial violence through trust. As reforms to the administration of justice, these policies did not fall on a single dimension of "root causes" versus "individual responsibility," and the political catchphrases were not only "soft" versus "tough" and "rehabilitative" versus "retributive." In this logic, many liberal reformers advocated carceral modernization because it would quell racial violence. By this logic, enhanced criminal justice administration would control urban uprisings and prison rebellions, not by repressive crackdown but by minimizing provocations that come in the form of police misconduct, judicial bias, and ill-defined standards for granting parole. Combining imagery of defective machinery and eruptive "ghetto residents," President Johnson's infamously liberal attorney general Ramsey Clark openly criticized "police lawlessness" because it provoked "savage outbursts" in cities. He supported, therefore, higher salaries and better training to build a truly "professional and disciplined" police force, one capable of sustaining calm "police community relations."[77] Liberal advocates of police professionalization may not have known of polling data confirming the depth of the racial divide, the fact that 49 percent of Newark's African Americans viewed police as "too brutal" but only 5 percent of whites held this view in 1968. Polling data from 1969 documented the magnitude of the credibility gap, with 72 percent of African Americans in Watts agreeing that police frisked or searched blacks without good reason, and 81 percent of African Americans in Detroit believing that police treated some groups better than others.[78]

Following three sweeping policy domains—mandatory minimums, federal funding for community policing, and capital punishment—Chapter 4, "The Era of Big Punishment," examines the explosion of punitive crime policy from the opening of the Reagan administration through the close of the Clinton administration. In the last two decades of the twentieth century, "centrist" New Democrats accelerated punitive escalation through a new strategy: they attempted to neutralize their soft-on-crime moniker by outbidding Republicans on the number of crimes and severity of penalties. Democratic punitive outbidding was no generic tough-on-crime strategy; instead, centrist Democrats supported mandatory minimums most likely to affect African Americans, and centrist Democrats distanced themselves from the Congressional Black Caucus.

Descriptive statistics of punitive bidding wars are stunning. Cataloguing mandatory minimum enactments from 1790 to 2010, I identify Congress' transition from incremental passage of mandatory minimums to sudden, dramatic passage beginning in 1984. The *tripling* of mandatory minimum expansions from 1985 to 2000 is all the more noteworthy because Clinton's two terms (1993 to 2000) saw the enactment of more mandatory penalties than the tough-on-crime terms of Reagan and Bush (1985 to 1992). Capital crime escalation was uniquely demonstrative of Democratic punitive outbidding. While federal legislation authorized only one death-eligible crime in 1976 and only three in 1988, the Federal Death Penalty Act of 1994 (Title VI of the Violent Crime Control and Law Enforcement Act of 1994) authorized a new total of 66 death-eligible crimes. Focusing on the crucial years of escalation, from 1988 through 1994, I demonstrate that the total number of capital crimes increased via alternate high bids between the political parties. Democratic Party capacity to compete in death penalty bidding wars ultimately hinged on its willingness to forfeit the Congressional Black Caucus's Racial Justice Act, which would have allowed statistically based challenges to the racial fairness of individual death sentences. This chapter documents the Democratic rightward turn, its rejection of racial egalitarianism, and its embrace of neoliberal "small government" for the economic top but big punishment for others.[79]

Situating these enactments in the arc of postwar liberal law-and-order, a certain dynamic becomes clear: early Democratic efforts to *limit* racialized carceral expansion actually *amplified* consequences of the Democratic punitive turn. Consider mandatory minimums. In mandatory minimum escalations from 1984 onward, many Democrats confessed that electoral self-preservation compelled their support for mandatory minimums. However reluctant their support, Democrats unwittingly raised penalties *beyond* isolated mandatory minimums via a liberal institutional brainchild: the U.S. Sentencing Commission. In Chapter 3, we note that liberals like Senator Edward Kennedy initially proposed creation of the U.S. Sentencing Commission with aspirations for less incarceration and more racial equity, but Kennedy relinquished anti-carceral provisions. Instructed to devise rational, proportional punishment grids, the U.S. Sentencing Commission incorporated mandatory penalties into the grid and concomitantly raised other penalties for proportionality. Similarly, Clinton's initiative for Community-Oriented Policing, which ultimately contributed to aggressive order-maintenance policing, might have faced resistance on federalist grounds, but Great Society Democrats cleared this federalist hurdle through the 1960s, with aspirations that federal funding would build better police-community relations. Finally, ambiguous Democratic opposition to the death penalty in the 1970s could not constrain death penalty escalation of the 1980s and 1990s. With opposition framed in administrative rather than absolute terms, liberal death penalty opponents invited, however inadvertently, administrative perfection of the death penalty.

The final chapter, "The Last Civil Right," situates the history of liberal law-and-order in two contexts: the twentieth-century arc of civil rights and twenty-first-century discontents with carceral practices. When seen in light of crime rates, demands for small government, or expectations of linear racial progress, the rise of mass incarceration seems puzzling. It becomes tragically recognizable, however, when examined as a trajectory of liberal civil rights reforms. When liberal lawmakers selectively answered activist calls to combat racial violence, they did so in ways that transformed, decontextualized, and even inverted animating visions of justice. In this construction of the civil rights carceral state, lawful racial violence was routinized, performed by trained professionals, and licensed by the proceduralist alignment of *Miranda*'s "right to remain silent" with Martin Luther King Jr.'s call to judge individuals "by the content of their character." With each administrative layer to protect African Americans from *lawless* racial violence, liberals propelled carceral development that, through perverse turns, expanded *lawful* racial violence. This history matters because many twenty-first-century proposals—calls for less prosecutorial discretion and more judicial discretion, for clearer written standards to initiate stop-and-frisks, and for more police training to stop racial profiling—remain locked in the same perilous if well-intentioned pursuit of administrative perfection.

Freedom from Fear

White Violence, Black Criminality, and the Ideological Fight for Law-and-Order

"Since the police and the courts stand behind any practices which preserve white dominance, the white population, acting individually or in groups, has not hesitated to make extensive use of violence and intimidation.... The administration of justice, violence and intimidation, and lynching are all cut from the same cloth."[1]

—*Robert Carr, Executive Secretary of President Harry S. Truman's Committee on Civil Rights, 1947*

"If the multitude of bills proposing Federal legislation on so-called civil rights constitutes a legitimate exercise of power on the part of the Federal Government under the Constitution, certainly security of person should also be classified as one of the paramount Federal rights.... If the Negro is entitled to equal social status, why does not he earn equality? Why is he responsible for most of the crimes in this country?"[2]

—*Democratic Senator James Eastland of Mississippi, Chair of the Senate Judiciary Committee, 1960*

They had been warned. In August 1943, the Office of War Information advised the Franklin D. Roosevelt administration to stay silent on "the problem of law-and-order." The problem was not measured in crime rates. Instead, "the problem of law-and-order" was a racial "tension" so thick that, according to the Office of War Information, it was "burst[ing] into active conflict." By one count, 47 cities experienced 242 violent "racial battles" in 1943.[3] Consider one "racial battle." In the Los Angeles "zoot suit riots," over 1,000 white people, many of whom were soldiers and sailors, marched through East Los Angeles and assaulted "zoot-suit hoodlums," mostly Mexican Americans as well as some African Americans and Filipino Americans. Zoot suits were a distinctive style of broad-shouldered jackets matched with peg-legged trousers; analogous to baggy pants or hoodies of the early twenty-first century, this clothing marked young people of color as delinquent and defiant. White mobs ruled the streets for 10 days. Some attackers stripped victims of their suits and stole their money, but this violence could not in any practical sense be called "lawless." Los Angeles police officers followed the white rioters, observed their assaults, and participated in beatings. Police officers arrested Mexican Americans on "vagrancy" charges. The Los Angeles City Council made it a misdemeanor to wear a zoot suit.[4] Labels of the day— "the problem of law-and-order," "race riots," "racial battles"—covered a kind of violence that was more accurately called state-sponsored white violence, and, even more specific to my purpose, white violence enabled and administered by the criminal justice system.

So when the Office of War Information advised silence, it counseled Roosevelt to do what the national Democratic Party had done for years: ignore white brutality. Philleo Nash, the Office of War Information advisor who penned this particular advisory memo, was well aware that "the problem of law-and-order is certainly fundamental to the minorities question." Nash condemned the law's racial double standard, defined, in his words as "the failure to provide negroes [sic] with the full protection of the law" while still "hold[ing] them fully responsible before the law." Despite his recognition of the problem, Nash advised the Roosevelt administration to avoid all "pronouncements or public statements" against "the law-and-order problem." On one hand, Nash feared that pronouncements linking race to law-and-order might be turned against "racial minorities." Reforms to provide "minorities" the "full protection of the law," he speculated, were "open to manipulation by people who want law enforcement as a cloak for repressive activities." If federal lawmakers built a stronger criminal justice system, it might prove difficult to control as a means for racially just ends. The potential for carceral development to increase "minority" repression was too great. On the other hand, Nash feared that the risk for politicians was too high. He continued, "If any public relations program in race relations is developed around a pronouncement from a high official on the importance of law-and-order, then every breach of law-and-order is a slap in the face at the program and the speaker."[5] The warning was clear. If Democrats stood for law-and-order to improve race relations, both would fail. Law-and-order agendas would be subverted toward repressive ends, and aspirations for better "race relations" would suffer with every breach of law-and-order.

Against the warning of this obscure and prescient memo, President Harry S. Truman nudged the Democratic Party toward law-and-order pronouncements and, ipso facto, its nascent civil rights agenda. This chapter traces the development of liberal law-and-order chronologically from World War II through the end of the Kennedy administration. By historicizing law-and-order, I challenge notions that Barry Goldwater and Richard Nixon "set the scene for debate about crime." Deeper racial antecedents emerge when law-and-order itself is studied in a long-term political sequence rather than in a cross-sectional moment of all factors contemporaneous with the 1964 presidential campaign. This chapter retraces how concerns for racial order were articulated as law-and-order over the longer trajectory of postwar civil rights struggles, even before the perfect-storm conditions of increasing crime and more riots emerged. This prehistory to the 1960s war on crime does not aim for completeness. Instead, I write this history with the goal of understanding the formation of liberal law-and-order: when it congealed, what it excluded, and how it converged with racially conservative ideas.

First, lasting partisan positions on crime policy developed slowly and in the shadow of the rising black freedom struggle through the 1940s, with race liberals playing offense. Old forms of racist violence took on new meaning during World War II and the Cold War, as national proclamations against fascism, genocide, and communism heightened the shame and hypocrisy of lynching, police brutality, and prison abuses. In this context, the Truman administration gave "official" party voice to a major tenet of liberal law-and-order: white lawlessness, like the lawlessness of all racial groups, stemmed from the injuries of prejudice and collective disrespect for arbitrary biases in criminal justice administration. Democratic Party policy solutions entailed more enforcement of civil rights crimes, more regulation of police brutality, more funding to professionalize police, and more federal influence in criminal procedure. Most fundamentally, they included far-reaching civil rights liberalization in everything from voting to education to employment. As a response to the lynching of black veterans, Harry S. Truman created the President's Committee on Civil Rights. Its final report declared that the first right of every American is security of person and freedom from violent aggression, which included not only white-on-black violence, but also white assaults on Mexican Americans in the zoot-suit riots and beyond, along with state aggression as in the Japanese American internment. Unlike Nixon's famous "first civil right" that emerged two decades later, Truman's first essential right—the *first* "first civil right"—identified the *paucity* of civil rights, not an *overabundance*, as the root of violence.

Second, the construction of liberal law-and-order occluded the larger system of racial violence. At midcentury, organizations like the National Negro Congress and the Civil Rights Congress challenged carceral machinery as the very core of state-sanctioned racial violence. From the perspective of structural law-and-order, white violence spanned "private" crimes such as lynching and state punishments such as execution; inextricably linked, individual and state violence preserved racial hierarchy. In contrast, liberal law-and-order depoliticized white violence by dividing "private" white lawlessness from prejudiced administration, correcting the former through criminalization and the latter through rationalization. During this period, race liberals experienced

international embarrassment, personal fear, and genuine disgust over white violence. They problematized the most visible and geopolitically distinct forms of
southern white lawlessness, but did not see illegitimate white violence in, for
example, the drug war in the urban North. Studying this period allows us to see
how liberal lawmakers defined "the right to safety" in constrained terms: it was
not freedom from state-sanctioned racial violence; it was protection from lawless private violence vis-à-vis an enhanced, neutral carceral state.

Third, northern Democrats converged with southern Democrats and, later,
Republicans in critical ways: they framed "the crime problem" as a subset of "the
Negro problem," with the solution of building stronger federal carceral machinery. As the black freedom struggle accelerated from *Brown v. Board of Education*
to Little Rock to the Freedom Rides, Republicans and southern Democrats
attributed criminological effect to racial cause: too much racial liberalization
caused crime, as forced race-mixing disrupted harmonious "race relations" and
exposed white innocents to black criminality. Moreover, as the black freedom
struggle turned to nonviolent civil disobedience, race conservatives held that
civil rights legislation rewarded and encouraged black disobedience. Senator
Eastland's statement at the opening of this chapter captures a typical equation
cast by race conservatives: if black civil rights are the legitimate domain of federal power, then so, too, is black crime; if blacks assume full citizenship, then
they must face full punishment for their crimes; and if the federal government
promotes black civil rights, then it must control the black criminological mess.

At first glance, northern Democrats appeared to have a dramatically different
stance on civil rights than did Republicans and southern Democrats. They converged, however, in the alignment of civil rights with the causes of black crime.
While northern Democrats identified state-recognized civil rights as the solution to black crime, southern Democrats positioned them as the cause. Race
liberals shared conservatives' prognostications of racial catastrophe, although
they inverted the cause-and-effect logic attributed to civil rights. This resulted
in a political struggle over how to define racial violence as criminal violence.
Southern Democrats spearheaded severe mandatory minimum sentences for
drug crimes in the Boggs Act of 1951 and 1956 by focusing on the allegedly special racial problems of the urban North: black drug users using heroin from "Red
China," who disseminated dope and communist propaganda in jazz clubs and
sparked white juvenile crime. At the same time, northern Democrats focused
on the allegedly special racial problems of the South: police complicity in white
mob violence and explosives, regulated through the Civil Rights Acts of 1957
and 1960. In this sense, the internally conflicted national Democratic Party
developed crime policy in a game of regional displacement over who won the
prize for the worst racial violence. Ultimately, when liberals set black criminality
as the barometer of racial progress, they joined conservatives in obscuring all the

ways in which "blackness" and "criminality" were created by law, policed with threat, and enforced through private and state violence.

Old Racial Violence and New Racial Liberalism

Even as national crime rates remained low and stable in the years during and immediately following World War II, challenges to Jim Crow's racial order cast the criminological system in a new light. Through the 1940s, rising black activism, changing racial consciousness, and early instances of civil rights liberalization produced new ways of seeing "crime": white riots in the urban North seemed to suggest an impending race war; black women who bumped into white men on the bus were accused of organized racial aggression; and lynching came to be seen as a crime of southern atavism and international embarrassment. This section attempts to answer a strange question: why did state-sanctioned white violence become, just for a moment in the 1940s, the national law-and-order problem? The question is strange because the horrors of white violence were neither new nor exceptionally cruel. The white rioters who looted and burned black, Mexican, and Filipino American neighborhoods did so with impunity—even with police assistance—in many cities in the Red Summer of 1919, in Tulsa in 1921, and in Watsonville in 1930. Sheriffs or deputies participated in roughly half of all lynchings between 1930 and 1933.[6] White violence enabled and administered by the criminal justice system was normal.

State-sanctioned white violence became visible through a certain political triangulation: international threats to U.S. credibility through World War II and the Cold War; domestic threats to U.S. credibility through "race wars" at home; and the growing strength of the black freedom struggle and its power to "use" these threats to force concessions. Indeed, in the great "racial break" of World War II, as sociologist Howard Winant called it, international battles against fascism and concerns for domestic peace compelled rejection of "official white supremacy." World War II opened what historian Harvard Sitkoff called "a quarter century of increasing hope and frustration" for African Americans. The president of the Brotherhood of Sleeping Car Porters, A. Philip Randolph, spearheaded the March on Washington Movement to "demand the right to work and fight for our country." Together with Walter White, executive secretary of the National Association for the Advancement of Colored People, and Lester Granger, executive director of the Urban League, Randolph organized the first national mass demonstration for immediate federal intervention. The March on Washington Movement gathered steam quickly, as 36 March on Washington Movement chapters formed across the nation, including 10 in the South. Randolph pledged that 100,000 blacks would March on Washington on July 1, 1941. The Congress of Racial Equality (CORE), founded in 1942, began high-profile experimentation with nonviolent direct action, such as working with Howard University students to begin sit-ins to end segregation in the North. During World War II, black newspapers with growing circulations headlined stories about black exclusion from defense jobs, the segregation of blood plasma by the Red Cross, and white brutality against black soldiers and civilians alike.[7]

During World War II, white riots in the urban North and lynching in the South forced a national conversation on crime and violence. In this context, the growing black freedom struggle brought something to light: state violence, when seen through a racial lens, was indistinguishable from the violence delivered by private citizens. As white police officers joined white mobs in murdering black veterans and international newspapers ridiculed the hypocrisy of incarcerating Japanese Americans while battling Emperor Hirohito in the name of democracy, there was no longer enough, in Charles Tilly's words, "to make the division between 'legitimate' and 'illegitimate' force credible."[8] National attention pivoted on two seemingly new crises in the division between legitimate and illegitimate force: "race wars" in the North and lynching in the South.

"Race Riots Coming"

By August 1943, the Office of War Information listed "law-and-order" as a top problem of the time. *Newsweek* gave the typical diagnosis that the 1943 riots were "a symptom of racial tension festering all over the country." In 1943 emerging conflicts over racial hierarchy and the rule of law moved through these absorptive code phrases: "racial tension" described challenges to the existing racial hierarchy of white supremacy and "law-and-order" described possible solutions to such "racial tensions," in which the rule of law might be updated to secure new racial orders. Struggle over language reflected struggles on the streets, where the ability to name the relationship between racial hierarchy and law was immediately at stake. While some named this relationship "black hoodlumism" and called for law-and-order to reinforce existing racial hierarchies, others called it the "American Gestapo" and insisted that the 1943 riots revealed the inextricability of white "private" violence and state violence. Throughout the riots of 1943, law enforcement officers openly allied with white rioters. In New York City, for example, riots erupted after a white police officer shot a black military police officer. As part of the state response, the New York City police arrested 500 people, almost all of whom were black. In Beaumont, Texas, white mobs set fire to the city's black neighborhood. The proximate cause was rumor of a black man having raped a white woman, but the more smoldering cause was white-shipyard-workers-turned-rioters who feared that President Roosevelt's fair employment commission would hand "their" jobs to black workers.[9]

In August 1943, Detroit erupted with the spread of rumors, one that a group of white people had thrown a black woman and her baby into the river, another that a black man had shot a white woman on the Belle Isle Bridge. White mobs assaulted black people caught in white neighborhoods. Black people looted white-owned stores in black neighborhoods and threw rocks at police. As Sitkoff explains, black Detroiters were "tired of finding the North too much like the South, tired of being Jim-Crowed," and they "struck out against 'whitey' and his property and symbols of authority." In response, Detroit Mayor Edward Jeffries mobilized all local police and called in the Michigan State Troops, but they were slow to arrive and "their training and equipment were insufficient." In the three-day uprising, Detroit police killed 17 people, all of whom were black, and arrested 1,800 people, 85 percent of whom were black.[10]

Given these numbers, it is unsurprising that the American Council on Race Relations suggested that the U.S. Army attend to such racial battles because local police "too often make common cause with the white rioters."[11] There was no shortage of images that confirmed police making "common cause with white rioters." In September 1943, *Collier's* weekly magazine, with a 2.5-million-strong readership through World War II, announced with certainty: "Race Riots Coming." With that ominous prediction, *Collier's* presented a photograph that sharply demonstrates, I believe, a discrete moment of state-sanctioned white

Figure 2.1 "A Colored Man Is Held by Unconcerned Detroit Cops While a White Man Slaps His Face," 1943. *Note: Collier's* national weekly magazine published this photograph with an editorial note that "this picture did much to further the Negro cause." *Source*: Photo courtesy of Associated Press; Walter Davenport, "Race Riots Coming," *Collier's*, September 18, 1943, 11.

violence. The photograph, taken by the *Detroit Free Press* on June 21, 1943, shows a white man striking a black man in the face, while "unconcerned Detroit cops" restrain the victim (see Figure 2.1). According to *Collier's*, the photograph captured the actuality of white-on-black violence, and its greatest power was its explosive potential to bring reform.

> Perhaps nothing that has been written or that will be written has done more for the Negro's cause than the photograph of the Negro with his arms being held by two policemen while he was being struck in the face by a white hoodlum, and a mounted cop watched. This photograph has taken its place in hundreds of Negro headquarters and meeting places. It has been preprinted and rephotographed and broadcast amongst Negroes. It has brought shoals of letters of sympathy to Negro leaders. It has caused many whites to donate money to Negro organizations.[12]

Such images of police brutality, long ignored by lawmakers, had become a conspicuous blight on U.S. international reputation.

In the context of World War II, the criminal justice system performed precisely the "kind of racism" that threatened state legitimacy: its racism was directly, photogenically violent and undeniably that of "the state." When leaders of the NAACP and the National Urban League demanded federal investigation of the Detroit mayor, Detroit police, and Michigan police, they challenged criminal justice legitimacy by likening it to fascist violence. William Hastie, dean of Howard University Law School, along with NAACP legal counsel Thurgood Marshall, called Detroit police "the Gestapo" of America. Police brutality was ammunition for the Axis powers, according to the president of the National Urban League. In Detroit's "twenty-four torrid hours of rioting and blood-lust," the city known as the "Arsenal of Democracy" became "ammunition for the propaganda of the Axis in Europe, Africa, the Near East, and particularly the Far East; and that ammunition was handed to our enemies not by slow convoys but by short wave."[13]

As the spotlight on the American Gestapo grew brighter, a common political response redirected light and heat onto "black hoodlums." Through the summer of 1943, Roosevelt said nothing of the brutality, and his aides quashed Congress' plan to investigate. The head of the Civil Rights Section, Victor Rotnem, discouraged the attorney general from pursuing an investigation, because Detroit police "did a very fair job." In Detroit, Harlem, and Baltimore, "rioting and looting are outstanding examples of Negro hoodlumism and wanton murder," wrote the head of the Civil Rights Section. In fact, it was "Negroes themselves" who "would be in a sorry national plight if the truth of the Detroit riots were made clear to America." Like others in the Roosevelt administration, Rotnem concluded that "we should very carefully keep our hands off the Detroit riot." With a political sensibility similar to the August 1943 Office of War Information memo, he added, "Certainly I should not want us to give him [William Hastie, dean of Howard University Law School] such an answer in writing."[14]

Roosevelt's strategic silence allowed southern Democrats to fill the airwaves with charges of black criminality. In this sense, the "racial battles" of 1943 occasioned the kind of race conservative rhetoric so powerful through the 1960s: black violence was the predictable outcome of black activism pushing too far too fast. In January 1943, well before the summer riots, the editor of the *Richmond Times Dispatch* warned that "Negro agitators" like A. Philip Randolph and the NAACP, along with "white rabble rousers," were "pushing this country closer and closer to an interracial explosion" in which hundreds if not thousands would be killed. In more muted tones, the Michigan Governor's Committee on the Causes of the Detroit Race Riot blamed A. Philip Randolph and the black press. Even though Randolph was not in Detroit, he deserved "vigorous criticism" for inspiring "a disregard for law, order and judicial process, in seeking the racial equality to which they are entitled." The Michigan Committee interpreted Randolph's statement that "justice is never granted, it is extracted" as "an appeal to extract 'justice' by violence." The Michigan Committee also noted that blacks constituted less than 10 percent of Detroit's population but committed more than 70 percent of major crimes. Detroit's police department reported that blacks constituted well over half of those arrested for narcotics violations (88 percent), gambling (65 percent), and liquor law violations (62 percent). The precise relationship of riots to narcotics, gambling, and drinking—all victimless crimes for which police held the highest discretionary power for making arrests—was taken for granted in the report. The Committee concluded that "Negroes" and "youths" were at fault, while local law enforcement behaved admirably.[15] In short, black lawbreaking in every form, from gambling to cocaine use to civil disobedience, was the initial violence to which criminal justice was merely necessary counter-violence.

For southern Democrats, northern riots proved that racial equality yielded disappointment, violence, and crime. After the Detroit riots, the governors of Tennessee, Virginia, Georgia, Alabama, North Carolina, and South Carolina boasted that southern race relations were stable and healthy compared to those in the North. Governor J. Melville Broughton of North Carolina was apparently assured that a "satisfactory relationship" between races would hold as long as "outside agitators do not stir up strife." Governor Chauncey Sparks of Alabama advised that "when the Negro quits chasing rainbows and butterflies, such as social equality and the abolishment of segregation," then there will be no "future race rioting" and "he will be better off." One governor (who wanted his name withheld) said that "misguided people," especially "the inflammatory Negro press," did "the Negro" a "great injustice by urging him to take advantage of the war period to demand social equality."[16]

In sum, the actuality of state-sponsored white violence provoked ever-loud accusations of black criminality. This political dynamic imbued quotidian interracial interactions with danger. Immediately following the Detroit riot, Walter White of the NAACP sent letters to black ministers and social clubs in Harlem and Brooklyn warning young black people to avoid "rudeness" that might provoke violence. African Americans were "justifiably resentful of the terrible discrimination" but must, White urged, "check lawlessness and bad manners by a minority of irresponsible Negroes," especially "vulgarity, rudeness and other unseemly conduct on subway trains and beaches."[17] Walter White also requested reports from NAACP branches on the status of "racial tension." Reports suggested looming threat; Baltimore NAACP leaders reported, "Race riots might break out at any time." The Philadelphia branch reported "a rising tension," including white Marines assaulting black people riding street cars; four black people assaulting a white man driving through "a thickly populated Negro area"; and white boys clearing a housing project's swimming pool by threatening to "drown all Negroes who were not out of the pool in 10 minutes." In response, the Philadelphia NAACP pressured the mayor and heads of the police department to stop discrimination, particularly "in the arresting of Negroes and permitting whites to remain at liberty."[18]

While some claimed that black activism and "hoodlumism" caused riots, others articulated a version of psychological "root causes": prejudice was the basis for racial violence. In the liberal parlance of the time, white violence was a "symptom" of misguided beliefs. In the final years of the war, the American Council on Race Relations, an academic organization established with the help of University of Chicago sociologist Louis Wirth, led the way in creating hundreds of interracial committees across the country, all with the objective of working with police to prevent any incident that might provoke racial confrontation. The organization created pamphlets to train people out of their violence, using the war to teach people that "scapegoatism" fueled racism, which was "the core of the diseases called Nazism in Germany and Fascism in Italy." The mentality of scapegoatism similarly drove "the Ku Klux Klan after the Civil War and after World War I, and in 1943 it produced the Detroit race riot." The American Council on Race Relations depicted the "race riot" as but the tip of the iceberg of "inequities, discriminations & segregation" (see Figure 2.2). Proper solutions should address the entire iceberg, including promoting nondiscrimination in housing and strengthening federal and state Fair Employment Practices Committees. Similarly, the Anti-Defamation League of B'nai B'rith published the "ABCs of Scapegoating" as part of their "Freedom Pamphlets" series. Their 1948 pamphlet, written by Harvard psychologist Gordon Allport, gave a similar formula

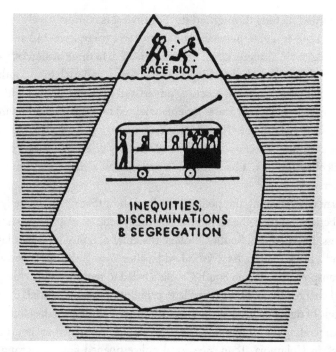

Figure 2.2 "Race Riots Emerge from Inequities, Discriminations & Segregation," American Council on Race Relations, 1945. *Note:* The race riot was but "the small part of an iceberg that juts above the water line." *Source:* Alfred McClung Lee in cooperation with the American Council on Race Relations, *Race Riots Aren't Necessary* (Chicago: American Council on Race Relations, 1945), 2, Box 47, Nash Papers, HSTL.

for racial violence. The "strains and irritations of the cold war" plus a "mixed population" produce "fertile soil for prejudice and scapegoating." Vigilant awareness of irrationalities and strains stop the spread of scapegoatism, illustrated in the horrors of Nazi Germany.[19]

"The Four Freedoms: Dixie Style"

If race riots were represented as a problem of the urban North, then lynching was presented as the problem of the South. Even as lynchings declined through the 1920s, they remained a problem explicitly associated with the U.S. South. Of the 171 recorded lynchings between 1927 and 1946, 160 were in the 11 states of the former confederacy; of this total, 157 of the victims were black. During those two decades, the leading lynch states were Mississippi (47), Georgia (29), Florida (22), Louisiana (17), Tennessee (12), Texas (13), Alabama (9), South Carolina (7), Missouri (5), and North Carolina (4).[20] Lynch mobs murdered at least 150 African American women in the South between 1880 and 1965, and anti-Mexican lynching throughout the Southwest is conservatively estimated at 597 from 1848 to 1928. Between 1882 and 1951 there were 248 anti-lynching bills introduced in Congress. Not one was enacted. In three instances, the House passed legislation to make lynching a federal crime, and each time southern senators killed it. The politics of lynching advertised to the world that white brutality was legal in the United States, openly wielded by local law enforcement, and unchecked by federal law. The *Chicago Defender* spoofed Roosevelt's freedoms with the cartoon, "The Four Freedoms: Dixie Style," showing a lynch noose, a poll tax collection box, a ball labeled "peonage" on a chain, and Jim Crow as a tattered man.[21]

By way of explicating the political configuration that finally made lynching a national crisis, consider the ways in which the lynchings of 1946 exposed federal feebleness. In Batesburg, South Carolina, the chief of police used his club to beat and blind a black veteran, Isaac Woodard Jr., after Woodard complained about Jim Crow transportation. When South Carolina failed to reprimand the chief of police, the DOJ charged him with violating laws prohibiting "public officials from depriving anyone of rights 'secured by the Constitution and the laws of the United States.'" After deliberating for 30 minutes, the all-white jury of the federal court acquitted the chief. In Columbia, Tennessee, local police opened fire on a group of black citizens trying to stop the planned lynching of a black veteran. Police arrested 28 black people for attempted murder, and killed two black protesters who were, at the time, being held in jail. Walter White warned the White House that the "Columbia [Tennessee] disorder" was "but a symptom" of "widespread violence" and "a possible beginning of country-wide disorders." U.S. Attorney General Tom Clark impaneled a grand jury investigation of the massacre; no indictments followed.

In Monroe, Georgia, a group of white men gunned down two black women, one of whom was seven months pregnant, and two black men, one of whom was a veteran. One of the lynching victims, George Dorsey, had completed his five-year service in the U.S. Army without serious injury, but in Georgia he and his companions were massacred, their bodies found riddled with at least 60 bullets. The NAACP gave the DOJ materials to prosecute, including affidavits confirming that Monroe Police had participated in the violence, in violation of federal law. It was a national embarrassment, wrote Thurgood Marshall to the attorney general, that the NAACP's own "inexperienced investigators" found murder witnesses but the FBI could not, even though the FBI had an "incomparable record for ferreting out" gangsters. Representative Adam Clayton Powell (D-New York) called for the president to "send troops into Georgia or such incidents would increase." Even Attorney General Tom Clark worried that "such violence leaps like wildfire from one community to another." Members of the National Association of Colored Women marched in front of the White House to demand justice.[22]

In August 1946, after a year of internationally scandalous lynchings, the National Association for the Advancement of Colored People, the Civil Rights Congress, and the National Negro Congress joined forces and demanded that the federal government "check the rising tide of mob violence." By December 1946, Truman issued Executive Order 9808 to create the President's Committee on Civil Rights and authorized its 15 members to recommend "effective means and procedures" to protect civil rights. At the close of World War II, the black freedom struggle forced recognition that lynching was not "racial tension"; it was white supremacist violence. But the political responses from Truman and the Democratic Party also constrained the scope of understanding white violence in relation to state violence. As reframed by race liberals, southern lynching was a regional exception to federal law-and-order, which was fully competent in differentiating lawful from lawless white violence.[23]

Postwar lawmakers thereby confronted lynching in ways that constrained remediation of racial injustice and enabled carceral growth. I elaborate on this dynamic in the next section and preview two points here. First, political focus on lynching forced eyes on violence in the South, while other criminal justice violence was protected from scrutiny. This exacerbated a regional dynamic of competing racial hierarchies rather than a federal strategy to address structural racism within and across regions. Southern lawmakers deflected blame by claiming that riots in the urban North were far more chaotic than the occasional murder in the South. In response to the Monroe lynching, for example, governor-nominate Eugene Talmadge said that the current Georgia governor felt "chagrin and embarrassment" about the lynching but added that there was "a great deal of mob violence in Detroit, Chicago and other sections of the country during the past few years." Second, Truman and his attorney general called lynchings "crimes" and, in so doing, individualized them as isolated acts of white criminality. After the Monroe massacre, Attorney General Tom Clark answered calls for justice in legal, nationalistic terms. "These crimes," Clark stated, "are an affront to decent Americanism. Only due process of law sustains our claim to orderly self-government." Clark urged the white citizens of Monroe to "assist the authorities to bring these criminals to justice."[24] To call lynching a "crime" acknowledged lawbreaking worthy of moral opprobrium and challenged notions of lynching as "punishment" for alleged crimes against white women. But to call lynching a crime is also to acknowledge constraints on its redress.

Emergent Democratic Commitments to Liberal Law-and-Order

"Today, Freedom from Fear, and the democratic institutions which sustain it, are again under attack," wrote President Harry S. Truman in December 1946. With this, Truman signed Executive Order 9808 to create the President's Committee on Civil Rights. Only five years before, President Franklin D. Roosevelt defined "Freedom from Fear" in "world terms," as security from the violent aggression of other nations. At the end of World War II, Truman redefined his predecessor's "Freedom from Fear" in domestic terms, as security from the violent aggression of individuals and mobs fueled by "hatred and intolerance." Truman did not reference "lynching" by name. He described it with qualifications: "In some places, from time to time, *the local enforcement of law-and-order has broken down*, and individuals—sometimes ex-servicemen, even women—have been killed, maimed, intimidated." With this, Truman tasked his 15-member Committee on Civil Rights to determine if "current law-enforcement measures" may be "strengthened and improved to safeguard the civil rights of the people."[25] The President's Committee on Civil Rights produced an agenda far beyond the scope of law enforcement, with profound consequences for the Democratic Party and its positions on crime and violence.[26] Specifically, the PCCR Report *To Secure These Rights* articulated two themes that the national Democratic Party would come to embrace: first, prejudice engendered lawlessness, and, second, the criminal justice system can be purged of discrimination with greater federal leadership.

The Right to Safety

To Secure These Rights might be easily dismissed as merely a report, a way of replacing real political action with a commission. But *To Secure These Rights* was a uniquely telling cultural document. In addition to soliciting written statements from 184 organizations, the PCCR relied on the keystone "race relations" text of the day, Gunnar Myrdal's *An American Dilemma*. *To Secure These Rights* also deepened fractures in the Democratic Party. In the words of the director of the Southern Regional Council, *To Secure These Rights* was nothing less than "the Democratic Party's rejection of the Compromise of 1877."[27] The stand for racial fairness was a radical break from recent Democratic Party history. Theodore Roosevelt's Progressive Party refused to seat black delegates from the South at its 1912 convention, and Woodrow Wilson condoned increased segregation in government offices. The New Deal had not challenged Dixie's sovereignty in white dominance: Old Age Insurance excluded domestic and agricultural workers, and Roosevelt refused to support anti-lynching legislation. The national Democratic Party's deference to Dixie, concluded John Temple Graves II, made Franklin D. Roosevelt "the Democratic party, the rebel yell, Woodrow Wilson and Robert E. Lee rolled into one."[28]

Rising black activism during World War II strained the New Deal coalition between northern and southern Democrats on issues of race. In June

1941, Roosevelt issued Executive Order 8802 to create the Fair Employment Practices Committee, the first national commitment to a policy of racial equality in employment. For the first time since Reconstruction, a president—this time a Democrat—made open cause with black civil rights. Myrdal designated Roosevelt's FEPC order "the most definite break in the tradition of federal unconcernedness about racial discrimination."[29] In 1942, the House of Representatives passed a federal anti-poll tax bill, which would affect eight southern states. Democrats were finding it harder to ignore black voters, and Roosevelt himself calculated that black voters in the North were essential to Democratic victories in 1940. The Democratic Party had begun to win over black voters in northern cities during the New Deal of the 1930s, and civil rights was becoming a winning issue—or, at the very least, a significant losing issue, as Democrats feared party defections.

To Secure These Rights opened by listing four rights as essential to individual well-being and social progress. Of the Four Essential Rights, the "right to safety and security" had its own spotlight, shining alongside the rights to citizenship, freedom of conscience, and equality of opportunity (see Figure 2.3). These last-mentioned rights, I believe, are more familiar and more easily recognized in the canon of civil rights. The right to citizenship and its privileges meant full access to the cornerstones of national voice and belonging—the vote and military service. To secure this right, lawmakers should have ended the poll tax, protected voters, and ended segregation in the armed services. The right to freedom of conscience and expression entailed non-interference in religion, speech, press, and assembly. To secure this right, lawmakers should have deterred civil servants from anti-communist "Red hunting." The right to equality of opportunity meant providing the individual an equal chance "to utilize fully his skills and knowledge." As the most capacious right, equality of opportunity included policies to correct discriminatory hiring practices, on-the-job discrimination, discriminatory public and private schools, and equal access to housing. The PCCR supported an end to discrimination in government employment, an end to restrictive housing covenants, and an end to segregation in interstate transportation.[30]

The right to safety stood in this pantheon of civil rights, along with rights to citizenship, expression, and opportunity. The PCCR defined the "right to safety and security of the person" (which I will shorthand as Truman's "right to safety") as a prerequisite to freedom:

> Freedom can exist only where the citizen is assured that his person is secure against bondage, lawless violence, and arbitrary arrest and punishment. Freedom from slavery in all its forms is clearly necessary if all men are to have equal opportunity to use their talents and to lead

FOUR ESSENTIAL RIGHTS

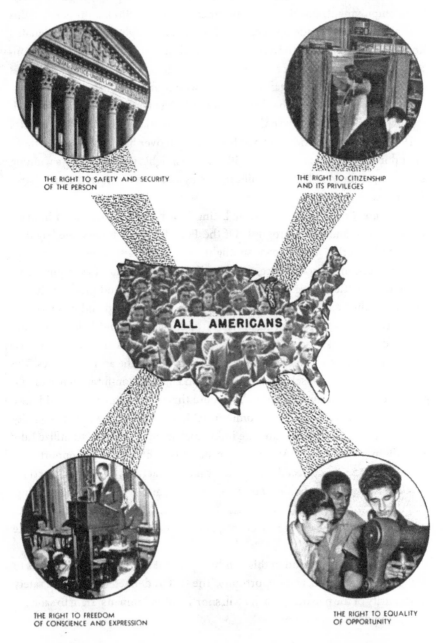

THE RIGHT TO SAFETY AND SECURITY
OF THE PERSON

THE RIGHT TO CITIZENSHIP
AND ITS PRIVILEGES

ALL AMERICANS

THE RIGHT TO FREEDOM
OF CONSCIENCE AND EXPRESSION

THE RIGHT TO EQUALITY
OF OPPORTUNITY

Figure 2.3 "Four Essential Rights," 1947. *Note*: This bubble diagram presented the four rights "essential to the well-being of the individual and to the progress of society." *Source*: President's Committee on Civil Rights, *To Secure These Rights: The Report of the President's Committee on Civil Rights* (Washington, DC: GPO, 1947), 7.

worthwhile lives. Moreover, to be free, men must be subject to discipline by society only for commission of offenses clearly defined by law and only after trial by due process of law. Where the administration of justice is discriminatory, no man can be sure of his security. Where the threat of violence by private persons or mobs exists, a cruel inhibition of the sense of freedom of activity and security of the person inevitably results. Where a society permits private and arbitrary violence to be done to its members, its own integrity is inevitably corrupted. It cannot permit human beings to be imprisoned or killed in the absence of due process of law without degrading its entire fabric.[31]

What, precisely, would be protected under this right to safety? What is most notable is the threat of arbitrariness—the dangers of "arbitrary" arrest, of "discriminatory" administration, and of "private and arbitrary violence." The problem they identified was not violence. The problem was "lawless violence"— violence absent state officials and legal formality. To be killed by private persons or a mob was cruel; to be imprisoned or killed through due process of law preserved the nation's moral fabric.

To theorize more broadly, the right to safety established the predictability of violence; that is, it protected against private and arbitrary violence. In this sense, liberal law-and-order established a division between legitimate and illegitimate force: legitimate force was exercised when the state followed predictable rules; illegitimate force was exercised when private citizens did not follow the state's rules. The category of "violence" was thereby reserved for the exercise of illegitimate force—private, arbitrary violence. In contrast, the carceral state merely protected the person's right to safety and security. In other words, the carceral state was permitted limitless violence so long as it conformed to clearly defined laws, administrative protocol, and due process. The final sentence of the paragraph cited above showcases the legitimating logic of proceduralism: "It [society] cannot permit human beings to be imprisoned or killed in the absence of due process of law without degrading its entire fabric." The right to safety evaluated imprisonment and execution by "due process of law," or the procedural and administrative quality through which the state cages and kills.

To be clear, the right to safety in *To Secure These Rights* was not a stand-alone abstraction. In context, the right to safety attached to specific policies that, if enacted, would have tempered the racial lethality of the criminal justice system. *To Secure These Rights* recommended punishment for white murderers, and it tasked lawmakers to discipline police who harassed "Negroes, Mexicans, or Jehovah's Witnesses." It called for an inclusionary jury system. It proposed elimination of the "fee system," in which court officials received their pay by levying fines. *To Secure These Rights* had a flash of radicalism, I believe, in that it acknowledged a basic fact: in matters of crime and punishment, the state was a perpetrator of racist violence. The report listed five violations of the right to safety, indicting the state as perpetrator of three violations: police brutality, the administration of justice, and the wartime internment of Japanese Americans.[32]

To Secure These Rights also acknowledged the everyday brutality, corruption, and unbridled power of local criminal justice as a consequence of the failed First Reconstruction. Designating the right to safety a federal civil right was bold because, at midcentury, the federal criminal justice system remained a scraggly collection of small agencies. The federal government established the Department of Justice in 1870, and the Federal Bureau of Investigation in 1909, and it took an additional two decades for FBI agents to gain the authority to carry guns, serve warrants and subpoenas, and make arrests and seizures. The Federal Bureau of Prisons was established only in 1930.[33] Activists turned to the federal government to provide real law-and-order, protection from the abuse of "vagrancy" laws, kangaroo courts, and sheriffs participating in lynchings. It is from this federalist history that Ida B. Wells, in her campaign against lynching, insisted that "lawbreakers must be made to know that human life is sacred and that every citizen of this country is first a citizen of the United States and secondly a citizen of the state in which he belongs."[34] Wells issued this demand in 1909. Four decades later, the national Democratic Party gave tentative assent.

Still, recognition of structural violence was nested in a more constrained vision of civil rights. The liberal right to safety translated race-based vulnerability to *excessive* arrest and punishment into a problem of "*arbitrary* arrest and punishment." Lost in translation was the fact that carceral violence was so lethal precisely because it was *not* arbitrary. Consistent with the logic of postwar racial liberalism, prejudice was baseless and irrational, as arbitrary as the designation of race itself. So long as state-sponsored racial violence, or white violence enabled and administered by the criminal justice system, was predictable, it might be construed as legitimate. Racial equality might therefore be achieved by ensuring predictability.

The Liberal Agenda: Tighten the Hardware and Heal the Heart

Within the framework of liberal law-and-order, securing the right to safety necessitated tightening carceral hardware and healing the heart of (white) prejudice. Tightening machinery meant leaving no slack for the "arbitrary" biases of parochial administrators; more procedures and higher professional standards could insulate criminal justice from personal prejudices. Robert Carr, executive secretary to the PCCR, articulated this philosophy with the quote that opened this chapter: "Out of the discriminatory administration of justice has grown a disregard of the law." The solution, therefore, was federal intervention to stop "the police and the courts" from following "practices which preserve white dominance." Truman's Committee on Civil Rights recommended "increased professionalization of state and local police forces," particularly to "indoctrinate officers with an awareness of civil rights problems." Higher salaries to "attract and hold competent personnel" would do much "to make police forces genuinely professional."[35]

Given that lynching scandals compelled Truman to impanel the PCCR, it is little surprise that southern criminal justice dominated the agenda. Witnesses before the PCCR testified to the horrors of southern criminal justice. The executive director of the Southern Regional Council, for example, recounted the common practice of justice. Police officers jailed potential witnesses just to keep them on hand. Police beat people held in custody before trial. Some southern counties operated on the fee system, and the "Saturday-night round-up of crap-shooters and 'vagrants' is the time-worn way to bringing in the fees." Even J. Edgar Hoover testified to the brutality, arrogance, and paranoia of southern criminal justice. The head of the FBI told the President's Committee on Civil Rights that he knew of one southern jail where "it was seldom that a Negro man or woman was incarcerated who was not given a severe beating, which started off with a pistol whipping and ended with a rubber hose." Hoover blamed white southerners for blocking federal lynching investigations, erecting what Hoover called "an iron curtain" of steely silence. According to Hoover, "the arrogance" of the white population "was unbelievable, and the fear of the Negroes was almost as unbelievable."[36]

We can see aspirations for criminal justice modernization in Gunnar Myrdal's praise for police and judges in the North and his disdain for lagging professional standards in the South. The sheer size of northern cities insulated legal machinery from parochial prejudice and "objectif[ied] its operations." To the extent that northern systems arrested and jailed African Americans in high numbers, it was for reasons of class and education level, not racism. "Since, on the whole, Negroes do not meet much more discrimination from officers of the law than do white persons of the same economic and cultural level, there is in the North no special problem of getting justice for Negroes, outside the general one of improving the working of the machinery of the law for the equal protection of the rights of poor and uneducated people." Myrdal's conclusion was sanguine: "In the North, for the most part, Negroes enjoy equitable justice."[37]

While size insulated northern criminal justice from "local prejudice," southern criminal justice was maximally vulnerable to prejudice through the "extreme democracy" of electing rather than appointing sheriffs, court clerks, and judges. For Myrdal, the "extreme democracy" of southern criminal justice destroyed rule of law, full stop. Elected officers hewed to the whims and bloodlust of the

white voting public. Whites-only primaries, grandfather clauses, poll taxes, literacy tests, and brute force from the very law enforcement agents supposedly
held accountable to voters enforced the electorate's racial purity. "A white man
can steal from or maltreat a Negro in almost any way without fear of reprisal,
because the Negro cannot claim the protection of the police or courts, and personal vengeance on the part of the offended Negro usually results in organized
retaliation in the form of bodily injury (including lynching), home burning or
banishment." Prejudice in white hearts could not seep into tight northern legal
machinery of the urban North. The sanguine functionality of northern criminal
justice made southern criminal justice look all the worse, but its solution all the
easier. Myrdal italicized his solution: "*Lingering inequality in justice in the South is
probably due more to low and lagging professional standards—certainly among the
police, and in many regions even among the lawyers who are willing to enter into court
service—than it is to opinion in favor of legal inequality.*"[38]

Central recommendations to address the security of people were filtered
through the narrow remnants of post-Reconstruction federal criminal jurisdiction—the civil rights crimes of Sections 51 and 52 of Title 18 of the U.S. Code.
The weakness of Sections 51 and 52, "plus the failure of the Department of
Justice fully to exercise" its powers, was, according to the Civil Rights Congress,
"making lynching America's No. 1 crime which grants complete immunity to
killers." The report recommended strengthening Section 51 of the criminal code,
an anti-conspiracy statute criminalizing *two or more persons* who conspire to
"injure, oppress, threaten or intimidate any citizen in the free exercise or enjoy-
ment of any right or privilege secured to him by the Constitution," by imposing
the same liability on *one* person acting alone.[39]

Recommended expansions to Section 52 were more ambitious, opening the
possibility of broad federal regulation of police brutality in local law enforcement. Specifically, *To Secure These Rights* recommended redefining Section 52
as protection from police brutality, including the right to be "free from personal
injury inflicted by a public officer; the right to engage in a lawful activity without
interference by a public officer; and the right to be free from discriminatory law
enforcement resulting from either *active* or *passive* conduct by a public officer."
This recommendation posed a radical rewriting of Section 52, which had been
defined only as criminalizing the "*willful*" deprivation "under color of any law" of
the "rights, privileges, or immunities" secured by the Constitution. Under these
narrow terms, the Supreme Court in *Screws v. United States* (1945) restrictively
interpreted the term "willful" in Section 52. After a Georgia sheriff and two other
officers beat to death a black man accused of stealing a tire, the DOJ charged
the three officers as acting "under color of law" to deprive the accused of his
Fourteenth Amendment right to be tried by due process of law. The three officers had been convicted in federal trial court, but the Supreme Court set aside

the conviction on grounds that the trial judge failed to charge the jury properly. Under Section 52, the Supreme Court held that "willful" implied both knowledge of the existence of a specific federal right and willful intention to deprive one of that right. The failure of the judge to analyze the law in this fashion in his charge to the jury entitled the defendant to a new trial. When the federal government brought Screws and his associates to trial a second time, they were acquitted.[40]

Along with broadening federal regulation of police brutality, the PCCR also recommended "increased professionalization of state and local police forces." Northern Democrats would come to propose police professionalization through the 1950s and 1960s, and massive funding for police modernization was ultimately enacted in the Law Enforcement Assistance Act of 1965 and the Safe Streets Act of 1968. Recommendations for federal assistance to professionalize police were not new; it was different, however, to encourage police professionalization in the name of racial progress. President Hoover's famous Wickersham Commission of 1929, for example, called for improved police training, more racial minorities on police forces, centralized prosecution systems in the states, better communication within and between law enforcement agencies, and improved monitoring and aggregation of criminal statistics. Aside from the FBI's effort to improve criminal statistics with creation of the *Uniform Crime Reports,* most modernization recommendations went unheeded.[41] But while the Wickersham Commission encouraged modernization with all the keywords of the late Progressive Era—ending corruption and deploying scientific logics for governance—the President's Commission on Civil Rights proposed modernization with the keywords of the early federal civil rights—ending discriminatory practices, formalizing racially fair procedures, and protecting the "unpopular, weak, [and] defenseless." As if anticipating federal finger-pointing, southern lawmakers sputtered over police professionalization through the 1930s. Between 1929 and 1939, they scrambled to establish state-level police departments in hopes that state police and highway patrol might rise above the rogue racial violence of local, rural police officers.[42]

Following from the President's Committee on Civil Rights, northern Democrats introduced a flurry of bills to build a stronger and more racially fair criminal justice system. A typical bill was the Civil Rights Bill of 1949, which introduced enhanced criminal justice procedural reform alongside core civil rights proposals for protection of voting rights and prohibition of segregation in interstate commerce. Specifically, the bill (S. 1725, S. 1734) proposed adding to the criminal code (Title 18, section 242) the right to immunity from abuses of fines and punishment without due process of law, immunity from physical violence to coerce confession of crime, the right to be free of illegal restraint, and the right to police protection of person and property without discrimination. It is clear that the focus on criminal justice abuses had moved beyond lynching; here, the focus was on the very nature of appropriate expectations from criminal justice, cast in both negative rights (no excess punishment, no coerced confessions, no illegal restraints) and positive rights (protection from the criminal justice system).[43] As Thurgood Marshall explained in his support for the bills, only deep criminal justice reform could quell "that everlasting threat, that feeling of violence and threatened violence." The civil rights bills of 1949 did not pass, though they were supported by many civil rights organizations, including the National Citizens' Council on Civil Rights, the NAACP, the Anti-Defamation League of B'nai B'rith, the American Jewish Congress, and the American Civil Liberties Union.[44] In 1949, procedural reform seemed to promise relief from "that everlasting threat" of racial violence; two decades later, the Supreme Court enhanced criminal procedure amid the same anticipation of alleviating racial animus.

Liberal Racial Profiling

The question of what constituted racial animus, however, was widely debated. Northern and southern Democrats diverged on the relationship of racial animus to racial progress, each insisting that inequitable race relations were endemic to the opposing region. While northern Democrats argued that racial animus was reduced by racial progress, southern Democrats argued instead that racial progress produced racial animus. In responding to bills for strengthened civil rights crimes, southern Democrats argued that "the social structure of the South is best for all concerned," and it yields "less inter-racial crime and less racial friction than any section of the country." Southern Democrats in Congress claimed to "understand the Negro," and southern officers knew to be "more lenient on the Negro who violates the law." Assuming that the lynching of a black man was a response to his actual raping of a white woman, southern Democrats suggested that the anti-lynching bill "ought to be called a bill to encourage rape." Southern Democrats suggested that Truman should show less concern for black men and more concern for "bringing about the conditions whereby the women of the Nation can walk without fear of attack and assault."[45]

While southern Democrats insisted on black racial animus against whites, and white women in particular, they also asserted that overall, the South had more benign race relations than the North. Of course, the political idea of the "black male rapist" had deep historical antecedents: opponents of Emancipation and Reconstruction frequently spoke of the hypersexual black male and his uncontrollable lust for white women.[46] Following World War II, the political idea of the "black male rapist" held renewed currency because of challenges to Jim Crow and gender conventions, as many questioned whether white women would return home happily after their war-time jobs. Once again, traditional conceptions of white femininity both undermined black women's claims to normative womanhood and white women's agency in ways that bolstered constructions of black male criminality. This construction of 1940s black criminality was, however, not isolated to the U.S. South. Northern understandings of racial animus and racial progress also produced a particular profile of black criminality: the Biggers and Bumpers of liberal sociology. This liberal criminal profile of black men, black women, and black youth ossified with the hardening of post–World War II sensibilities of the psychological costs of discrimination. In contrast to the Southern Democratic position, race liberals came to embrace the idea that curing racial animus was a struggle over the heart and soul. What is crucial about the liberal paradigm of racial animus is that its core logic cycled white violence "back" to black criminality. This set the stage for "healing the heart" of racism as a kind of crime control within liberal law-and-order, one that would shut down more structural approaches to race, equity, and justice.

"Biggers," "Bumpers," and Concealed Aggression

Several factors contributed to this psychological common sense: a therapeutic ethos about how social environment shapes personality, trends in social science research, and anti-communism so strong that it crushed alternative visions of colonial- and economic-based racism. Healing the heart of American racism echoed Gunnar Myrdal's oft-cited statement: "*The American Negro problem is a problem in the heart of the American.*" The problem in the heart of the (white) American was racial prejudice, an external evil that marred the true American Creed of democratic egalitarianism. In this scenario, prejudice was a matter of irrational and false beliefs, and the scene of the crime was the heart. White "people will twist and mutilate their beliefs of how social reality actually is," explained Myrdal, to defend their behavior to others and to themselves. In Myrdalian terms, the gap between our aims and our actions "is creating a kind of moral dry rot which eats away at the emotional and rational bases of democratic beliefs." Prejudice was an individual problem, but one that swept everyone into its destructive cycle. Prejudicial beliefs self-reinforce through Myrdal's famous "vicious circle." In this circle, white prejudice and discrimination "keep the Negro low in standards of living, health, education, manners and morals," which in turn supported white prejudice. In sum, "White prejudice and Negro standards thus "mutually 'cause' each other." According to Myrdal, white people might commit acts of violence, misguided by twisted prejudice and "scapegoating," but white violence was a deviation from the American Creed.[47]

To Secure These Rights echoed Myrdal's insistent pluralism: discrimination damaged everyone. Prejudice eroded *our* national morality, slowed *our* national economy, and sullied *our* international reputation. Prejudices hurt everyone economically, too. In the vicious circle, discrimination depressed the employment and wages of "minority groups," which in turn reduced their purchasing power, which in turn reduced production, which in turn reduced employment and wages. In the end, prejudice and insecurity "aggravate the very discrimination in employment which sets the vicious circle in motion." And international attention to discrimination impaired the collective goal of making "the United States an enormous positive influence for peace and progress throughout the world."[48] Based on this pluralism, it is logical that *To Secure These Rights* opened with murdered black men and black women, but closed with national injury. If white lynch mobs forced a national reckoning, then reckoning cycled the problem of white violence back into a problem of black criminality.

Crime and violence were the "cost[s] of prejudice," asserted Truman's Committee on Civil Rights, because minority "frustrations [with] their restricted existence are translated into aggression against the dominant group." The government report then inserts this block quote from Gunnar Myrdal:

> Not only occasional acts of violence, but most laziness, carelessness, unreliability, petty stealing and lying are undoubtedly to be explained as concealed aggression.... The truth is that Negroes generally do not feel they have unqualified moral obligations to white people.... The voluntary withdrawal which has intensified the isolation between the two castes is also an expression of Negro protest under cover.[49]

Before considering the "concealed aggression" diagnosis, we should reflect on the list of symptoms it is meant to explain. Black "laziness," "carelessness," and "lying" apparently just exist in the world, awaiting illumination. Myrdal was certainly race liberal in his disavowal of biological distinction, and his *American Dilemma* found "no reasons to assume that Negroes are endowed with a greater innate propensity to violence than other people." But his analysis, like that of so many liberal Democrats to come, matched the race conservative formulation of the question: what explains black criminality? Liberal focus on black criminality relied on quasi-scientific phrases of "concealed aggression," "Negro protest under cover," and the truism "people relegated to second-class citizenship should behave as second-class citizens," which is at once paternal and cowering.[50]

To better understand the diagnosis, consider the scholarship in the citation chain that brought "concealed aggression" to the Democratic Party's civil rights report. Moving backward in the chain, Truman's 1947 *To Secure These Rights* presented "concealed aggression" in a block quote attributed to Myrdal's 1944 *An American Dilemma,* in which that precise line is supported by citations to Richard Wright's 1940 *Native Son* and John Dollard's 1937 *Caste and Class in a Southern Town.* I believe that this is the liberal's alchemy of racial violence: white violence was the input, absorbed and interwoven into black psyches, producing the output of black criminality. Many who reproduced such imagery of black damage and rage were, as historian Daryl Michael Scott has documented, "race liberals, who often generated the images specifically to aid the cause of obtaining black rights and opportunities." Myrdal saw black-on-white crime as "concealed aggression" and intra-black crime as the "*misplaced aggression* of a severely frustrated subordinate caste."[51] Myrdal supported such claims with fiction and scholarship that sketched portraits of black rage in gendered, classed, and regionally distinct forms.

In the "Negro slums of American cities," Myrdal saw a "growing generation" of "individuals like Bigger Thomas." In his 1940 novel *Native Son,* Richard Wright created Bigger Thomas as a black man who murdered two women, one white and one black. Wright created Bigger Thomas as the product of racist structure; Wright was a "fiction writer posing as a social psychiatrist," in the words of historian Daryl Michael Scott. Within the novel, Bigger Thomas's defense lawyer delivered the now-familiar thesis of socially engineered black rage: "The hate and fear which we have inspired in him, woven by our civilization into the very structure of his consciousness and into his blood and bones, into the hourly functioning of his personality, have become the justification of his existence." If our "civilization" mass-produced Bigger Thomases, punishing one Bigger Thomas with a death sentence would only aggravate the others: "Kill him and swell the tide of pent-up lava that will some day break loose, not in a single, blundering crime, but in a wild cataract of emotion that will brook no control." Myrdal used the novel to show what social science could not: a causal sequence in the development of "the Negro male," from a "civilization" of racist structure, to black "consciousness" of hate and fear, to acts of violence.

From this fictional profile, Myrdal identified a sociological generation of Bigger Thomases in urban "Negro slums." Myrdal claimed that he could see them "walking the streets unemployed" and "standing around on the corners." With the Bigger Thomas profile in mind, Myrdal observed physical gestures that, to a psychologically attuned observer like himself, revealed a broiling inner life: "They have a bearing of their whole body, a way of carrying their hats, a way of looking cheeky and talking coolly, and a general recklessness about their own and others' personal security and property, which gives one a feeling that carelessness, asociality, and fear have reached their zenith."[52]

Myrdal's portrait of southern black aggression also drew on John Dollard's sociological study of *Caste and Class in a Southern Town.* In Dollard's analysis, black people reacted to racial caste with a hostility that could only turn inward, against self and community. "Since the hostility of Negroes against whites is violently and effectively suppressed," wrote Dollard, "we have a boiling of aggressive affect within the Negro group." Black criminality was not biologically determined; it was a *psychological adaption,* borne of a justifiable anger toward white domination. For Dollard, black aggression moved most freely among poor black southerners, not because of poverty per se, but because of "weak" family structure. Lower-class black families could not contain black aggression because, in Dollard's Freudian-heavy training, their "unstable, non-monogamous" family structure "was much less tightly organized to control impulse expression." Dollard could not "help wondering if it does not serve the ends of the white caste to have a high level of violence in the Negro group, since disunity in the Negro caste tends to make it less resistant to the white domination."[53]

In this citation chain, *To Secure These Rights* connected its civil rights recommendations to a racial psychology emerging in the era. Broader trends in social science research reveal this more general belief in the interdependence of social environment and criminality. If race liberals feared a "Bigger" inside every northern black man, then they feared a "Bumper" inside every northern black woman. The "bumpers," as black sociologist Charles Johnson explained in a 1944 article, were "Negro women with grievances, said to be organized for the purpose of harassing whites by bumping into them in crowded cars and on the streets." Johnson hastened to add that social scientific theories of concealed aggression "are not attempts to condone or excuse this behavior, but to help explain it." Some bumping, Johnson acknowledged, was "simple awkwardness," unavoidable in crowded city streets and buses. But Johnson suspected a deeper psychological trigger: for northern black women, especially recent migrants from the South, contact with white urban dwellers set off "long, bitter accumulations of racial resentment." Johnson elaborated: "These delayed and often *concealed or deflected aggressions* may appear in a wide range of behavior from inter-race or intra-race fights to petty and otherwise meaningless offenses against property. It is this type of delayed guerrilla warfare of a few individuals that becomes magnified in the imagination to cover the entire Negro population."[54]

Like the construction of "bumpers," in the North and South there were rumors of "pushy" black women. In the South, and throughout New York, Los Angeles, and Chicago, whites invented rumors of "Eleanor Clubs," named after black "sympathizer" First Lady Eleanor Roosevelt. As Howard Odum documented in his study of race rumors from July 1942 through July 1945, "Eleanor Clubs" were said to be collectives of black women, particularly black women employed as domestic workers plotting to achieve their mission statement: "A white woman in every kitchen by 1943." Vice President Harry Truman apparently believed rumors of organized bumpers and Eleanor Clubs, and the African American newspaper the *Pittsburgh Courier* reported that Truman forbade his daughter Margaret from riding Washington, D.C., streetcars on Thursdays. On Thursdays, rumor had it, black women pushed white women and men off streetcars with particular gusto.[55]

True to political scientist James Scott's observation that rumor is "the second cousin of gossip and magical aggression," rumors of racial aggression had the lurid specificity of town gossip. Tales of black aggression revealed that white fears exceeded the PCCR and Myrdal's predictions of black laziness and lying. Racial progress would be nothing less than subversion of the economic, gendered, and sexuality-based order of Jim Crow. Rumor of Eleanor Clubs reflected a particular fear: if black women as workers commanded proper wages, then white households would lose cheap domestic service and, assuming fixed gender-based division of labor, wealthier white women would have to cook and clean. This was devalued work, demeaned more still during the 1920s and 1930s as labor reserved for African American women, Mexican American women in the Southwest, Japanese American women in the West, and immigrant white women in the Northeast. Another rumor documented by Howard Odum was that white men submitted to the draft more than black men, leaving white women vulnerable to assault and seduction by draft-dodging black men. To prepare for sexual violence, black men were rumored to be stockpiling ice picks, knives, and guns, waiting for the first blackout to begin the attack.[56]

Liberal Obfuscation of Structural Law-and-Order

This section is purportedly about the *liberal* profile of the black criminal, but certainly the rumors listed above circulated through gossiping white racial conservatives. Race conservatives—again, those who wished to conserve status quo privileges and powers for white people—bear primary responsibility for spreading rumors of conspiring bumpers, of Eleanor Clubs, and of draft-dodging black men wielding ice picks. Yet race liberals—again, those who applied liberalism to race and racism with wishes of incorporation based on individually assessed merit—accepted black aggression as the center of debate. Why did so many presumably well-intentioned people accept and recirculate the liberal profile of the black criminal? Given entrenched notions of black criminality, perhaps recoding this image seemed the only strategically viable move. Or perhaps the liberal profile of black criminality accommodated mixed, even dissonant, ideas, including self-interested hopes to forestall "race wars." After all, white fears of black violence shaped the history of how Gunnar Myrdal came to write *An American*

Dilemma. As historian Walter Jackson discovered, the massive study of race relations was the pet project of a particular trustee of the Carnegie Corporation who
predicted racial wars in the urban North, mostly due to the influx of "untidy"
southern African Americans. In the end, it was "fear, not philanthropy" that
drove the Carnegie Corporation to underwrite Myrdal's study.[57]

By making black violence (against whites) the barometer of progress, liberals
doubly abnegated structural law-and-order—once in the circumscribed definition of violence, and once again in the mismeasure of racial justice. Thus, even
as liberal law-and-order represented a fledgling Democratic commitment to civil
rights, civil rights activists themselves proffered a very different vision of violence and justice. For liberal Democrats, individual crimes from lawless whites
and "lazy" blacks were the byproduct of racial prejudice. For many black activists, violence was neither individualized nor was a byproduct; it was the strong
arm of white supremacy that permeated the state itself. For black progressives,
racial violence was a centerpiece of demands for civil rights; demands for federal
intervention were sometimes procedural, sometimes substantive, but always
focused on structures of white supremacy.

Groups like the National Negro Congress, the Southern Regional Congress,
the NAACP, and the ACLU pushed for even more aggressive federal intervention. It should be underscored that black civil rights activists turned to federal
lawmakers as potential refuge from the abuses of local criminal justice, and they
demanded even more regulation than was proposed by the PCCR. Notably, the
Southern Regional Council, as well as the National Negro Congress, wanted
to make all murder a federal offense. Guy Johnson, executive director of the
Southern Regional Council in Atlanta, Georgia, testified, "Since the federal
government seems to pursue offenders with more skill and persistence than the
state governments, as a general rule, it seems to me to be highly desirable to
strengthen the hand of the federal government against lynching to the fullest
possible extend under the Constitution."[58]

Moreover, questions of the appropriate scope of federal criminal justice
were seemingly resolved through capacious interpretations of the Fourteenth
Amendment. Internal memos of the National Lawyers Guild, the National
Bar Association, and the NAACP claimed that the congressional intent of the
Fourteenth Amendment was "overwhelmingly" in support of "national govern-
ment power to punish unlawful acts of individuals as well as states." These advo-
cates recalled that Congressman Bingham of Ohio, who drafted the first section
of the Fourteenth Amendment, suggested that the Thirteenth, Fourteenth, and
Fifteenth Amendments vest Congress with the power to protect "citizens against
States" *and* "citizens in States." The National Lawyers Guild, the National Bar
Association, and the NAACP concluded that the federal government had an
"affirmative obligation to protect its citizens and to preserve its free institutions

from violent overthrow by avowed terrorists and fascists." Moreover, no "new concept" or "new law" was required for Congress and the attorney general to prosecute the misconduct of individuals and states—through the Fourteenth Amendment "states as well as the Federal government may prosecute." In contrast, in 1946, the chief of the Civil Rights Section, Turner Smith, worried about risking the extension of federal power over "mob violence cases," because the Supreme Court in *U.S. v. Harris* (1882) "flatly held that there was no Federal jurisdiction... unless there were affirmative acts on the part of the state denying due process or equal protection of the law." The chief of the Civil Rights Section further puzzled: "Where is any language in the Constitution of the Amendments thereto that even by implication confer any right upon Congress to pass laws governing private assaults?"[59]

The limited liberal vision of violence is best illuminated when juxtaposed with its contemporaneous appeals for international justice. Between 1946 and 1951, the National Negro Congress, the NAACP, and the Civil Rights Congress all petitioned the United Nations to indict the U.S. government as propagating genocidal criminal violence. At the end of World War II, the Nuremberg Trials offered an international stage to hold soldiers and police accountable for "crimes against peace" and "crimes against humanity," even when acting under government orders. International Cold War pressures compelled greater domestic attention to civil rights, as many have argued. The international arena also offered, for a brief moment, a spotlight on violence and a different way to conceive of criminality. In this context, the National Negro Congress submitted its 1946 "Petition to the United Nations on Behalf of 13 Million Oppressed Negro Citizens of the United States of America," which called upon the UN to honor its stated purpose of promoting fundamental freedoms for all. The National Negro Congress indicted the Truman administration for "its failure to implement Constitutional guarantees."[60] The following year, after the UN issued the Universal Declaration of Human Rights, the NAACP petitioned the United Nations with *An Appeal to the World,* edited by W. E. B. Du Bois. The *Appeal* claimed that the Soviet Union was perhaps less a threat to American democracy than was Mississippi—"not Stalin and Molotov but Bilbo and Rankin."[61]

Perhaps the broadest challenge against violence appeared in 1951 with the Civil Rights Congress petition, *We Charge Genocide: The Historic Petition to the United Nations for Relief from a Crime of the United States Government Against the Negro People.* The definition of genocide, adopted by the UN General Assembly in 1948, included actions "with the intent to destroy, in whole or in part, a national, ethnic, racial or religious group." By this definition, violence was criminal even if it was part of legal, normal state action. In this framework, lynching was not merely a form of murder, but it generated "a constant fear" conveyed through the "thousands of glances from white supremacists all over the land every day." Police brutality was neither exceptional nor contained in the South; it pervaded every part of the country, as evidenced by the nearly 200 racially motivated murders and executions, as well as hundreds of nonfatal assaults from the period 1945 to early 1951 alone. The petition did not distinguish between illegal white violence and legal violence; between murder and execution; between "private" white violence and white violence administered "under color of law." In its campaigns in New York and Oakland, the CRC challenged criminal justice brutality as "legal lynching," different from southern violence only for donning the police uniform or the judge's robe. The Civil Rights Congress indicted the totality of violence and "the willful creation of conditions making for premature death, poverty, and disease."[62]

The Civil Rights Congress harnessed an international perspective that, in the United States, "lynching" by lawless white mobs differed little from "capital punishment" by state officials. Consider the CRC's defense of Willie McGee. In November 1945, Willie McGee, a Mississippi black man accused of raping a married white woman, was sentenced to death after an all-white jury, having deliberated for a full two-and-a-half minutes, found him guilty as charged. McGee appealed his conviction with the help of the Civil Rights Congress and one of its attorneys, a young Bella Abzug. The Mississippi Supreme Court overturned McGee's conviction twice, once to grant a change of venue and once again because prosecutors excluded blacks from the grand jury list. The U.S. Supreme Court allowed him two reprieves, but denied his last petition. In May 1951, after nearly six years of legal battles, the state of Mississippi killed Willie McGee. Radio stations broadcast live from the courthouse where McGee was strapped into Mississippi's portable electric chair. The "event" closed after one radio announcer stated, "Well, ladies and gentlemen, we just assume that that last surge was the final 2,000 volts of electricity that meant the end of Willie McGee."[63]

Wrongful execution of a black man is unremarkable. What is remarkable is the intensity of international protest it inspired. The Civil Rights Congress facilitated "Save Willie McGee" marches and petition campaigns through England and France, and people protested in Africa, Asia, and Communist-bloc countries. A 1951 political cartoon in the *Daily Worker* depicted "Dixiecrats," the Supreme Court, and the Truman White House all together with their hands of "white supremacy" flipping the switch to execute Willie McGee. The CRC petition to the United Nations described Willie McGee as "ignored by the American white press but known nevertheless the world over." McGee was the "tragic cause celèbre" among "the virtually unknown killed almost casually, as an almost incidental aspect of institutionalized murder."[64]

Yet liberal critics dismissed the petitions as communist propaganda and national betrayal. John Temple Graves ridiculed Walter White for "tattling on his country to the United Nations," as if international charges were at once subversive and childish. Reception within black organizations was also mixed; many in the NAACP dismissed the genocidal charge as communist subversion, and the *Pittsburgh Courier* rejected the charge of genocide as turning black Americans into the "cat's paws for the Soviet Fifth Column."[65] Even as international petitions gained little political traction, they demonstrated the limits of the liberal construction of violence: by attempting to correct prejudice in the administration of justice, liberal law-and-order was a project to secure the legitimacy of state violence. The rise of white massive resistance and black civil disobedience further entrenched liberal and conservative constructions of the crisis of "law-and-order."

The Regional Isolation of Illegitimate Racial Violence

At its most fundamental level, the black freedom struggle from 1954 through 1963 ignited explicit challenges to federal rule of law itself. Benchmarks of the black freedom struggle prior to the Civil Rights Act of 1964—*Brown*, Montgomery Bus Boycotts, the Civil Rights Acts of 1957 and 1960—created lasting characterizations of law-and-order. Even as battles against civil rights *generated* violence against black people and their allies—with beatings, arson, and explosives directed at civil rights advocates—race conservatives *displaced* the root of violence onto civil rights liberalization itself. This displacement highlighted sectional and partisan divisions, with southern Democrats and southern massive resisters claiming that crime in the allegedly integrated North was far worse than crime in the South. The underlying reason, they implied, was that forced race-mixing exposed white innocents to black criminality. Moreover, with the rise of boycotts and civil disobedience, civil rights legislation was cast as a reward for black lawlessness. In short, for race conservatives and southern Democrats, civil rights liberalization was criminogenic.

Race liberals saw a different law-and-order crisis. The civil rights movement exposed the magnitude of unregulated white violence, of police brutality, and of excessive punishments for civil rights protesters. Sins of southern criminal justice, once unremarkable as "normal" manifestations of Jim Crow, achieved prominence as the seemingly atavistic violence of an outdated form of racism. Each episode of racial violence, from Emmett Till to the use of explosives against black activists, became modernizing moments that propelled demands for federal civil rights protection via enhanced criminal justice. In an oft-quoted speech at the Holt Street Baptist Church during the Montgomery bus boycotts, Martin Luther King Jr. indicted the sanctity of federal law: "If we are wrong, the Supreme Court of this nation is wrong. If we are wrong, the Constitution of the United States is wrong. If we are wrong, God Almighty is wrong." The movement would be guided, in King's words, "by *the highest principles* of law-and-order."[66] This was, of course, a commitment to nonviolent protest "with dignity and Christian love," but it also underscored that state and local authorities operated by the *lowest principles* of "law-and-order."

Illegitimate Racial Violence: Rogues in the South

A year after the bus boycotts, the Democratic Congress passed, and President Dwight Eisenhower signed, the Civil Rights Act of 1957—the first law to address racial inequality since the Civil Rights Act of 1875. The enacted legislation established a national Commission on Civil Rights and a civil rights division at the Justice Department. When Attorney General Herbert Brownell Jr. defended the proposed civil rights bill, he insisted that the Eisenhower administration did not seek to change the system that placed primary responsibility for "maintaining law-and-order" on local communities and states. After passage of the 1957 Civil Rights Act, black leaders attempted to use threat of criminal law for protection of voting rights. Clarence Mitchell, director of the NAACP's Washington branch, urged black leaders to "make it plain throughout the Southland that a cell in jail is waiting for those who capriciously interfere with the right to vote because of a person's color."[67]

Southern Democrats in Congress mobilized familiar arguments against the Civil Rights Act of 1957: federal civil rights legislation violated states' rights, duplicated protections already imparted to blacks, and threatened to destroy the salutary and natural social system of segregation. Southern Democrats also issued another, less commonly recognized set of arguments against civil rights legislation: segregation maintains law-and-order, while integration breeds crime. Such arguments were heard in individual floor statements, but it was no mere handful of southern legislators claiming civil rights would engender violence and fuel race "agitators." As a kind of second Southern Manifesto, southern members of Congress produced a "Warning of Grave Dangers" in July 1956, in opposition to the Civil Rights Bill of 1956. The "Warning" was a House document, written by Representatives William Muck (D-Virginia), William Colmer (D-Mississippi), and Edwin Willis (D-Louisiana) and signed by 83 southern members. What were these dangers? The civil rights bill would "fuel and flame" the "discord" of race "agitators," and if adopted "could only result in deterioration" of race relations.[68]

In vocalizing opposition to the Civil Rights Act of 1957 and its failed previous version in 1956, southern Democrats argued that integration made whites vulnerable to black criminality. Representative Elijah Forrester (D-Georgia) put forth this line of argument: "where segregation has been abolished, such as public parks, restaurants, theaters, schools, and transportation, the Negro has virtually had the full use thereof." This problem was especially pronounced in Washington,

D.C., "the guinea pig for social experiments," where "the white race" enters public parks only "at the risk of assaults upon their person or the robbery of their personal effects." In this account, integration gave way to black domination of public places, which then gave way to black assault and robbery of whites, which finally gave way to an inability to safely walk the streets. White fear of social equality between the races was decidedly spatial, and reminiscent of post-bellum claims that blacks were pushy on sidewalks.[69]

Like White Citizens' Councils, many southern Democrats who protested the Civil Rights Act of 1957 offered "proof" of segregation's benefits by favorably comparing southern crime rates to northern crime rates. Representative Thomas Abernathy (D-Mississippi) reasoned that "race relations are much better in the South than in the North," and civil rights legislation will only "stir strife and discord among us." Representative Abernathy highlighted crime control as a specific benefit of segregation, stating that "there is less crime among the Negroes of the South than among those in the North." In the same vein, Representative James Davis (D-Georgia) asserted that "racial violence between southern white people and southern Negroes is rare indeed," while "racial animosity and racial violence is greater in your section than it is in mine."[70]

In addition to perpetuating the argument that integration engendered crime, southern Democrats also contended that the Civil Rights Act of 1957 would empower black organizations to defend black criminals under the guise of civil rights. Representative Basil Whitener (D-North Carolina) opposed the establishment of a Civil Rights Division on the grounds that it was simply an avenue for the exoneration of black criminals. Representative Whitener stated "there are many good law-abiding Negroes in this country," but "nevertheless the bulk of the crimes of violence are committed by Negroes." "Radical" organizations like the NAACP, "under the guise of protecting civil rights," run to "the assistance of Negro criminals and seeks to protect them from the punishment for the crimes they commit." In this line of thinking, the establishment of a Civil Rights Division would therefore "tie the hands of law-enforcement officers throughout the country, and would place law-abiding men, women, and children at the mercy of brutal, merciless, hardened criminals." In this argument, the Civil Rights Division was a special privilege, a vehicle for black organizations to defend the worst of their race. This logic was not new to Congress: opponents of Reconstruction argued that efforts to redress racial inequality, such as the Fourteenth and Fifteenth Amendments and the Freedman's Bureau, were giving blacks undeserved and unfair privileges.[71] In this framework, efforts to redress racial inequality were nothing more than special privileges for blacks, and, in the case of a Civil Rights Division, such special privileges could lead to the dangerous exoneration of black criminals.

In contrast, civil rights advocates defined the Civil Rights Act of 1957 as a step toward law-and-order. It was high time for federal law to punish "shootings and bombings of homes and churches" and "threats of bodily harm" generated by extra-legal and legal forces in the South, declared Roy Wilkins, executive director of the NAACP, testifying before Congress in favor of the bill. Opponents of the civil rights bill, according to Wilkins, were "anti-law-and-order forces." Wilkins added that blacks had maintained "nonviolence in the face of extreme provocation," but added that he could not predict "what mood might be engendered" if the 1957 bill stalled. Few challenged the focus on black criminality, even though it was white violence that prompted the legislation. Senator Jacob Javits (R-New York), a supporter of the Civil Rights Act of 1957, characterized crime in the North and the South as the "penalty for a long number of years in which we have failed to bring up to parity the education, housing, and employment opportunities of the Negro members of all our communities."[72]

The Civil Rights Act of 1960 was a modest federal effort to regulate violence and a rehearsal ground for partisan positions on the racial roots of crime. In 1959, there were 38 bills to create federal criminal penalties for explosives, which had been used regularly against civil rights activists in the South. Typical liberal proposals, such as H.R. 15 introduced by Emanuel Celler (D-New York) in the 86th Congress (1959), allowed for a fine of up to $10,000 or imprisonment up to five years for the possession of explosives with "the knowledge or intent that it will be used to damage or destroy any building" used for "educational, religious, charitable, or civil objectives," or to intimidate any person pursuing such objectives. A modest version of the criminalization of the use of explosives emerged in the Civil Rights Act of 1960. Title I of the Civil Rights Act of 1960 made it a *misdemeanor* to use threat or force to interfere with the exercise of rights or of performance of duties under a federal court order punishable by a fine of up to $1,000 and/or imprisonment for up to one year. Title II created three new federal offenses: (1) fleeing across a state line to avoid prosecution or punishment under state law for destroying by fire or explosives a building used for religious, educational, or other purposes; (2) transporting explosives in interstate or foreign commerce with the intent to damage such a structure; and (3) using the mail, telephone, telegraph, or any "other instrument of commerce" to make a bomb threat.[73]

The enacted legislation was a meek effort to secure black voting rights and regulate violence, and did little to "promote integration" per se, but southern Democrats still warned that the new civil rights legislation would bring crime waves because of increased race-mixing. In opposing the bill in 1959, Senator Strom Thurmond predicted that "political demands for integration of the races" would bring a "wave of terror, crime, and juvenile delinquency." As proof for this claim, Senator Thurmond pointed to "crime after crime in integrated New York" and other "integrated sections of the country." Senator James Eastland presented the incarceration rates listed in Table 2.1 as proof that racial segregation made the South "the most peaceful section of the United States." Eastland advised north-ern politicians to address "the rape, the murder, the muggings, the crime on the streets of northern cities" rather than shame the South, even though incarcera-tion rates do not speak for themselves as proof of criminality or "friction."[74]

Senator William Fulbright (D-Arkansas) stated that southern cities have seen an upsurge in strife "that grew out of the Supreme Court decision," and in inte-grated northern cities like Washington, D.C., "one does not feel safe to walk on any street." Southern Democrats were quick to cite mainstream news sources that validated their claims, including a *U.S. News & World Report* article that announced: "terror on the streets is a growing problem in big American cities." The reason: "police say racial frictions are closely related to the upsurge in crime. Trouble brews, for example, when Negroes or Puerto Ricans move into neighbor-hoods once regarded as predominantly Irish or Italian." Echoing their opposition to anti-lynching bills, southern Democrats again suggested that the Civil Rights Act of 1960 would encourage race-mixing and all it entailed for black men's access to white women. Senator Eastland stated that the culture and conditions of the integrated North meant "a white woman is not safe on the streets of their cities or in their schools or within the walls of an apartment house." Senator Johnston (D-South Carolina) listed multiple rape cases in the North, adding that "a colored man instigated and is tied in with each of these cases."

Southern Democrats were so insistent that civil rights generated crime that they proposed making the new U.S. Civil Rights Commission responsible for collecting crime data. Following a recommendation from former President Herbert Hoover, in 1960 Senator Eastland proposed a bill (H.R. 8315) requir-ing the recently established Civil Rights Commission to conduct a census of all criminal victimizations in the country. Specifically, this census would show "what races the offenders come from," with the intended effect of "stir[ring] the leaders of various racial groups to action" in disciplining their own. This task was rightly entrusted to the Civil Rights Commission, argued Senator Eastland, because the Commission served no "useful purpose," and because there was no civil right more important than "the God-given right of all people to be secure in both their persons and property from the trespass of others."[75]

Legitimate Racial Violence: Drug Wars in the North

Democratic Representative Hale Boggs of Louisiana secured enactment of some of the most aggressive narcotics mandatory minimums in history, and his 1951 legislation mandated a two-year sentence for first-offense narcotics *pos-session*. With its opening bid of two years for simple possession, the Boggs Act

Table 2.1 Incarceration Rates by Race in Selected States, 1950

State	Negro population, 1950 census	Negroes admitted to prison on felony charges, 1950	Rate of Negro felony prisoners per 100,000, 1950	White population, 1950 census	Whites admitted to prison on felony charges, 1950	Rate of white felony prisoners per 100,000, 1950	Percent of population Negro, 1950	Percent of felony prisoners Negro, 1950	Negro rate over white rate
California	462,172	596	129	9,915,173	2,472	25	4.0	19.0	516
District of Columbia	280,803	444	158	517,865	136	26	35.0	50.0	608
Illinois	645,980	639	99	8,040,058	1,225	15	7.0	32.0	660
Indiana	174,168	189	108	3,758,512	944	23	4.0	17.0	432
Kentucky	201,921	277	132	2,742,090	1,083	39	7.0	21.0	338
Maryland	385,972	1,484	386	1,945,975	993	51	16.0	60.0	757
Michigan (1952)	442,296	1,058	236	5,917,825	1,834	31	7.0	37.0	761
Missouri	297,088	413	139	3,655,593	1,133	31	8.0	47.0	448
New Jersey	318,565	478	150	4,511,585	883	19	7.0	33.0	789
New York	918,191	1,051	114	13,872,095	1,218	13	6.0	37.0	877
Ohio	513,072	922	179	7,428,222	1,729	23	6.0	35.0	773
Oklahoma	145,503	208	143	2,032,526	892	44	7.0	19.0	325
Pennsylvania	638,485	493	77	9,853,848	935	9	6.0	35.0	855
West Virginia	115,867	93	81	1,890,282	609	32	6.0	13.0	253
Total	5,539,083	8,345	145	76,096,649	16,694	22	6.3	33.3	659

Alabama	979,617	790	80	2,079,591	719	35	32.0	52.0	229
Arkansas	426,639	282	66	1,481,507	405	27	22.0	41.0	244
Florida	603,101	620	102	2,166,051	895	41	22.0	41.0	249
Georgia (1952)	1,062,762	979	92	2,386,577	799	33	30.0	55.0	297
Louisiana	882,428	642	72	1,796,683	515	29	33.0	55.0	248
Mississippi	986,494	530	53	1,188,632	222	19	45.0	70.0	279
North Carolina	1,047,353	622	59	2,983,121	633	21	26.0	50.0	281
South Carolina	822,077	183	22	1,293,405	420	32	39.0	30.0	[1] 145
Tennessee	530,603	334	63	2,760,257	691	25	16.0	32.0	252
Texas	977,458	867	38	6,726,534	2,125	32	13.0	30.0	275
Virginia	734,211	941	128	2,581,555	800	35	22.0	54.0	366
Total	9,052,743	6,790	75	27,437,879	8,222	30	25.0	45.0	250

[1] White over Negro.

Note: In a voting rights debate, Democratic Senator James Eastland of Mississippi submitted this table as proof that the "segregated society of the South" maintains peace through social segregation, not incarceration.

Source: *Congressional Record*, March 1, 1960, 4021.

ratcheted up penalties in the two-five-ten-twenty-year increments characteristic of federal mandatory minimums. Second-offense and third-offense narcotics possession triggered, respectively, five- and ten-year mandatory penalties, and first-offense and second-offense narcotics sales triggered five- and ten-year mandatory penalties. Passed by uncontroversial voice votes in the House and Senate, the Boggs Act of 1951 became law with President Truman's unadorned signing statement: "the tragic effects of drug addiction are only too self-evident." This apparently self-evident tragedy compelled Congress to enact the Narcotic Control Act of 1956, which increased Boggs's mandatory penalties and added new ones for narcotics importation, selling heroin to minors, and using the telephone for drug transactions.[76] President Nixon repealed these mandatory penalties in 1970; the next mandatory penalty for drug possession was enacted in the Anti-Drug Abuse Act of 1988. As I detail in Chapter 5, Congress set a five-year sentence for first-offense crack possession as an emergency measure against the scare of cocaine use by the "black underclass." The 1950s prequel developed in a similar racial scare.

Federal lawmakers launched the 1950s war on drugs to combat "red" and "black" threats: red heroin-pushing communists and black heroin addicts. Turkey, Iran, Lebanon, and Mexico allegedly exported heroin to the United States, but "Red China" was the "biggest offender," pushing heroin "to try to demoralize us" according to Democratic Senator Price Daniel of Texas. Daniel's Senate committee report concluded that "subversion through drug addiction is an established aim of Communist China." The United States was a "target," and drug addicts had been exposed to "contagion" and must be placed in "quarantine."[77] Harry Anslinger regularly accused the "Red Chinese" of maintaining an official trade bureau "to promote the distribution of heroin." Lois Higgins of the crime prevention bureau in Chicago warned that "our Communist enemies are waging a deadly and tragically successful war against us here at home" with "narcotic drugs" as "weapons." As a Cold War weapon, heroin was "as deadly and as dangerous as an atomic bomb," in the words of an Illinois Democratic representative.[78]

But while the 1950s narcotics mandatory minimums increased federal prison populations, the numerical change was puny compared to the supersized impact wrought by the contemporary drug war. Between 1950 and 1965, the number of narcotics offenders held in federal institutions almost doubled, from 2,017 in 1950 to 3,998 in 1965; proportionately, these numbers represent a jump from 11.2 percent of all federal offenders in 1950 to 17.9 percent of all offenders in 1965. Average sentence length for drug offenders in 1965 was 87.6 months, nearly double that of 1945. Perhaps the greater impact was in the spread of "Little Boggs" narcotics laws across states, named in recognition of Hale Boggs and his influence in encouraging state-level narcotics mandatory minimums. For example, in 1953, Illinois required "drug addicts" to get a state "registration card" to be carried at all times, and the law specified that "multiple punctures on body surfaces or scars or abrasions resulting from hypodermic needle punctures, shall be prima facie evidence of the repeated use of narcotic drugs."[79]

In debating drug policy, southern lawmakers found what they interpreted as indisputable proof of the North's "Negro problem." For 47 days in 1955, Texas Senator Price Daniel chaired hearings on illicit narcotics traffic in northern cities like New York City, Washington, D.C., Philadelphia, Los Angeles, San Francisco, Chicago, Detroit, and Cleveland, as well as the one southern city, Houston. With 345 witnesses and 8,000 pages of testimony, Senator Daniel's hearings documented the astoundingly high arrest rates of black, Mexican, and Puerto Rican people. Officers from city-level narcotic squads and bureaus delivered the "cold facts" of racial dysfunction in the North. Detroit's Narcotics Bureau reported that, although blacks constituted 20 percent of the city, they constituted 89 percent of drug arrestees. Cleveland's Narcotics Squad reported that the "colored, Negro class" constituted 95 percent of the narcotics arrestees. The Cleveland lieutenant did not fault policing practices; instead, he explained that Cleveland African Americans enjoy high disposable incomes too often used for social drug use in their "associations and in their meeting places." Chicago's Narcotics Bureau reported that 1 in 71 black Chicagoans had been arrested on drug charges, compared to 1 in 1,100 white Chicagoans. Of the 7,639 persons "processed" through the Chicago Narcotics Bureau in 1954, 5,335 were "colored male," 1,266 were "colored female," 605 were "white male," 147 were "white female," and 286 were categorized as "other" and said to include "Chinamen, Mexicans, and Puerto Ricans." The Bureau of Narcotics commissioner Harry Anslinger called addiction the special problem of the "Negroes in a few northern cities," where social problems became more acute with the "migration of large numbers of Negroes from the South during World War II."[80]

As high as these numbers were, narcotics squad lieutenants insinuated that they might be higher still if white administrators could insulate themselves against unwarranted, humiliating charges of racism. Too many judges excused black lawbreakers because, according to Cleveland's narcotics lieutenant, "they feel that these Negro citizens haven't had the advantages that others have and they should be excused because they don't know." The Cleveland Chief of Police had faced accusations of harboring "some feeling against their race," but he felt no self-consciousness because narcotics arrests were "a matter of cold statistical fact." Like Senator Daniel, white lawmakers and law enforcement agents categorized narcotics arrests as cold hard facts.

Senator Daniel concluded, "The narcotics problem [was] centered among the Negro people," but then he qualified, "Except in the Southern States." Senator Daniel was well aware of sectional divisions that would make him look opportunistic. "The first time I ever got any figures like this, I was afraid to even bring them out, because someone would say, 'Oh, well, that man from the South is trying to point up something here.'" In the spirit of patriotism and fact-finding, however, he had decided that there are "facts that are essential for Congress and other legislative bodies and law enforcement officers to have in order to know how to whip the problem." Senator Daniel then asked, "Is there any reason why the figures are reversed down in our part of the country?"[81]

Senator Daniel implied that northern lawmakers were, as historian Heather Ann Thompson might explain it, "blinded by a 'barbaric' South." Forms of southern criminal justice hold the racial-economic architecture of slavery—from slavery, to plantation-style prison farms, to convict leasing, to chain gangs. Based on this history, Thompson explains, we can barely interrogate "the popular premise that the southern justice system was uniquely brutal because of the region's ugly past."[82] Dominant accounts of race, crime, and punishment are too often "told through southern criminal justice practices and framed as pre-modern," as argued by historian Khalil Gibran Muhammad. In contrast, histories of northern criminal justice maintained a "modernizing narrative," in which innovations in policing, probation, prison, and parole turned on native and foreign-born whites only. Many have challenged southern exceptionalism for reinforcing a selective historical consciousness about the civil rights era, which is typically portrayed as an epic showdown between "the retrograde South and a progressive nation."[83] This southern exceptionalism took particular form in national crime policy: as southern white violence became the scene of the nation's racial crimes, the routinized racial drug war of the North was rendered normal.

The Agenda for Lawful Racial Violence

This chapter might have been titled "The *First* 'First Civil Right'": before Richard Nixon's 1968 invocation of the right to protection from (black) crime, Truman Democrats advocated protection from (white) lawlessness as the first essential right. Race conservatives did not uniquely link "the Negro problem" to the law-and-order problem. By the end of the Truman administration, liberal Democrats had taken a position that would shape the development of federal crime policy over the next 50 years: a strong civil rights carceral state would reduce crime through racially fair machinery.

Even as it was a step forward on the march of racial progress, the liberal construction of law-and-order obscured as much as it illuminated. Most centrally, liberal and conservative constructions converged on a seemingly uncontroversial point—crime reflected the status of "the Negro problem." Like their northern Democratic counterparts, southern Democrats and race conservatives articulated their position on crime in the shadow of civil rights. In arguing that integration led to crime, southern Democrats blended criminological street crime—robbery, assault, stranger rape, with black people simply being in the streets unregulated by Jim Crow—using parks, schools, buses, and other public spaces as if they had equal right to them. In arguing that civil rights rewarded black lawlessness, southern Democrats conflated predatory street crime with politically motivated, group-organized law breaking in the form of civil disobedience. This early conflation of black freedom with black crime makes it difficult to conclude that Barry Goldwater "constructed what would become the standard conservative formulation of law-and-order." Instead, Goldwater simply inhabited a dialogue framed by southern Democrats nearly two decades ago.[84]

This chapter opened with a warning to the national Democratic Party: if Democrats stood for law-and-order in the name of racial equality, both would fail. As the next chapters illustrate, this warning held true on both counts. As the Democratic Party fought for modernized carceral machinery in the name of racial progress, their plans were easily subverted toward repressive ends. Moreover, the Democratic dream of reducing crime through racial fairness ultimately strained their civil rights agenda, as crime rates rose through the late 1960s. But beyond errors of strategy, the liberal construction of law-and-order limited the ideological terrain of seeing racial violence and understanding its remediation. Liberal Democrats attempted to correct narrow illegalities while offering modest reforms to carceral machinery; moreover, they highlighted sensational southern violence while neglecting the routine violence of standard policing and legal incarceration throughout the nation. Liberal law-and-order translated international battles against colonialism and genocidal racial violence into an agenda of procedural fairness, race-neutral machinery, and formal equality. Race liberals, anchoring the "left" of the national stage, set out to correct the lawlessness, not the lethality, of racial violence. In this sense, the fight for racially just law-and-order was already lost.

This chapter demonstrated the formation of liberal law-and-order as a set of procedural, psychological standards for evaluating racial fairness in crime and punishment. The next two chapters investigate how the standards of liberal law-and-order guided policymaking for the next four decades. I will follow the aspirational thread in three policy areas. First, the first civil right was freedom from discriminatory policing and "arbitrary arrest." A fair police force would protect against—and be easily distinguishable from—chaotic "private and arbitrary" white violence. Liberal reformers pursued and replicated this standard in the Warren Court's criminal procedure "revolution" and in policy development that culminated in the Safe Streets Act of 1968. Second, the first civil right demanded clean presentation of criminal law: "To be free, men [sic] must be subject to discipline by society only for commission of offenses clearly defined in the laws." Democratic and liberal pursuit of this standard manifested in President Lyndon Johnson's effort to reorganize federal criminal codes for consistency, a fight later pursued by Senator Edward Kennedy that culminated with enactment of the Sentencing Reform Act of 1984. Third, the first civil right established that a morally sound society "cannot permit human beings to be imprisoned or killed in the absence of due process of law." Reformers fought for the best processes by which to kill, haggling over the age and mental capacity for culpability, over number and quality of lawyers, and over the standards for finding evidence of racial bias. The Democratic battle for racially, processually fair capital punishment culminated with Clinton's Federal Death Penalty Act of 1994. My challenge is to distinguish when and why agendas for processual fairness mitigated or exacerbated, exposed or covered, race-differentiated vulnerability to premature death. That this is a challenge tells us how much liberal law-and-order conceals.

3

Policing the Great Society

Modernizing Law Enforcement and Rehabilitating Criminal Sentencing

"Police recruitment should be modernized to reflect education, personality, and assessment of performance.... The need is urgent for police to improve relations with the poor, minority groups, and juveniles."[1]

—President Lyndon B. Johnson's Commission on Law Enforcement and Administration of Justice, 1967

"When I say 'modernize', incidentally, I do not mean to be soft on crime; I mean exactly the opposite."[2]

—President Richard Nixon describing his proposal to revise the Federal Criminal Code, 1973

"Which side is the federal government on?" John Lewis, chair of the Student Non-violent Coordinating Committee, almost asked in his speech at the March on Washington on August 28, 1963. He was not speaking of the biblical divide between the "dark and desolate valley of segregation" or "the sunlit path of racial justice" that Dr. Martin Luther King Jr. described in his "I Have a Dream" speech. Instead, Lewis spoke of the all-too-real brutal criminal justice system versus the principled struggle for black freedom, aggravated by a meek federal government, unwilling to pick a side. Speaking while every police unit in the District of Columbia was on duty, Lewis charged that pending federal legislation—namely the Kennedy administration's civil rights bill that would later become the Civil Rights Act of 1964—would "not protect young children and old women from police dogs and fire hoses." It would not protect those who "must live in constant fear in a police state." It would "not protect the hundreds of people who have been arrested on trumped-up charges." There was "not one thing" in President Kennedy's civil rights bill "that will protect our people from police brutality." Lewis's draft speech then posed the question that many activists found too confrontational to be included: "I want to know, which side is the federal government on?"[3]

In the five years following the March on Washington, President Lyndon B. Johnson and the Democratic-controlled Congress answered Lewis's question by enacting legislation taking *both* sides—more for *racial* justice and more for *criminal* justice. Along with the Civil Rights Act of 1964, the Voting Rights Act of 1965, and the Fair Housing Act of 1968, Johnson also signed legislation to establish "halfway houses," fund "juvenile delinquency" after-school programs, and provide civil commitment in lieu of prison for drug addicts. As if trying to equalize protection for all who lived in Lewis's police state, Johnson also signed the Criminal Justice Act of 1964, which provided representation for impoverished defendants in federal courts, and the Bail Reform Act of 1966, which established a presumption in favor of release on recognizance.[4]

This chapter investigates policy repercussions from Lyndon B. Johnson's Great Society, "the high tide" of racial liberalism.[5] I direct particular attention to two policies: the Omnibus Crime Control and Safe Streets Act of 1968, which distributed federal money to state and local police, and the Sentencing Reform Act of 1984, which established the U.S. Sentencing Commission. While the Sentencing Reform Act was passed under Republican President Ronald Reagan, its origins lay in liberal strategies blending both civil rights and crime control. Separated by 16 years, these two laws share surprisingly similar stories: both proposals originated in Great Society ambitions for racial fairness, yet both buttressed carceral strength in ways especially detrimental to people of color. Following the tradition of Truman's "security of person," liberal Democrats hoped that a modernized criminal justice system would quell racial violence. Northern Democrats, along with the newly formed U.S. Civil Rights Commission and the NAACP, advocated using federal money to professionalize police and reorganizing the criminal code to minimize disparities.

Insofar as these enactments reformed the administration of justice, they did not choose between explanations such as "root causes" and "individual responsibility," and they did not rest on political catchphrases contrasting "soft" versus "tough." These explanations and catchphrases focused on a clearly decipherable *meaning* to punishment; modernization projects, by contrast, reformed *machinery*, often without consensus on meaning. Indeed, ambiguity facilitated construction of the machine. The epigraphs of this chapter showcase the convenient ambiguity of "modernizing" criminal justice. Johnson's modernization to improve minority relations slipped easily into Nixon's modernization to be tough on crime. In the Safe Streets Act of 1968, Democrats lost Johnson's proposal to distribute money through local categorical grants, and the enacted legislation instead distributed money through state block grants. In the Sentencing Reform Act of 1984, Democrats lost their Johnson-era proposals to regulate criminal sentencing downward, and the rewritten legislation included pro-carceral planks, such as elimination of parole and time off for good behavior. At the mid-1960s nexus of rising crime rates, riots, and emerging norms against overt racism, political parties concurred on "the black crime problem" and the concomitant solution of a race-neutral, fortified criminal justice system.

This chapter unfolds chronologically through two policy case studies, but, as outlined in my first chapter, my larger goal is to understand the dynamics by which racial violence is seen as a problem of administrative deficiency. The players included President Johnson and the crime commissions he established, along with organizations like the American Bar Foundation and the American Legal Institute, whose language and findings were easily decontextualized. To be clear, some used race-liberal approaches strategically, with hopes that better individual process would produce group justice. In other words, some actors may have used race liberal approaches as a path to structural justice. But they spoke about it as a proxy for structural justice, and in so doing helped ossify a framework that viewed well-administered punishment as necessarily just.

Policing the Great Society

Signed by President Lyndon Johnson on June 20, 1968, the Omnibus Crime Control and Safe Streets Act of 1968 was watershed legislation.[6] Title I established the Law Enforcement Assistance Administration (LEAA) to distribute federal money to state planning agencies. From 1968 until 1982, LEAA distributed millions and created the National Institute of Law Enforcement and Criminal Justice (renamed the National Institute of Justice in 1978), the brain to guide modern crime control, lauded by President Johnson as "a modern research and development venture which would put science and the laboratory to work in the detection of criminals and the prevention of crime." But by the mid-1970s, even supporters of the Safe Streets Act of 1968 called it a failure. In most of the sites receiving LEAA money, robbery and violent crime rates actually increased between 1970 and 1975; the goal of the LEAA Impact Cities program was to reduce crime by 20 percent over those five years. In 1975, even the director of the LEAA, Gerald Caplan, admitted, "We have learned little about reducing the incidence of crime and have no reason to believe that significant reductions will be secured in the future." James Q. Wilson, who served on President Johnson's 1966 Task Force on Crime, concluded by 1975 that Title I of the Safe Streets Act was a waste of money.[7]

Liberals past and present see the Safe Streets Act of 1968 just as it was described in a 1969 *New Yorker* article: "a piece of demagoguery devised out of malevolence and enacted in hysteria." Rhetoric employed during the presidential election of 1968 whipped up "hysteria" and evaluated law enforcement in light of rising crime rates, urban uprisings beginning in 1965, and the Supreme Court decisions "handcuffing" the police. The total crime rate jumped 135 percent between 1964 and 1968. In 1968, both violent and property crime rates were at the highest level ever recorded by the FBI. Demographics explained part of the increase: the youngest of the huge baby-boomer cohort hit their teenage years in the mid-1960s, and the population aged 15 to 24 is arrested for roughly 70 percent of all crimes. Another explanation was methodological: sudden improvements in data collection, including new record automation, new 911 emergency calling, and higher reporting rates exaggerated crime's increase as characterized by the *Uniform Crime Reports*.[8] But little of crime's increase came from technological improvements, and the baby-boomer birth cohort made crime rates more expected but no less painful.

Controversies over police power heightened the "hysteria" surrounding the Safe Streets Act of 1968. For Richard Nixon and George Wallace, police officers suffered from a lack of power: rebels hated and legislatures underfunded police, and the Warren Court eviscerated police capacity and empowered criminals. George Wallace positioned crime victims and police officers as helpless against the hypothetical man who "knocks you over the head." In Wallace's scenario, the criminal would get "out of jail" while "the policeman who arrested him will be on trial." Wallace vowed to release police officers from the shackles of legal minutiae sustained by liberal contempt for police power and offered a vision of militarized security. He clamored: "If I were President now, you wouldn't get stabbed or raped in the shadow of the White House, even if we had to call out 30,000 troops and equip them with two-foot-long bayonets and station them every few feet apart." Likewise, Richard Nixon's 1968 stump speeches sympathized with the hypothetical victim whose murderer was "let off," freed by Supreme Court decisions that "have gone too far in weakening the peace forces as against the criminal forces in this country." For others, it was police officers' excessive power and racism that triggered urban uprisings in "ethnoracial ghettos." There were nearly 100 urban uprisings in 1966 and 1967; in 1968, the assassination of Dr. Martin Luther King Jr. ignited protest and insurrection in roughly 175 cities. Police "incidents" sparked many of the urban riots, including the two major 1967 uprisings in Newark and Detroit, the former triggered when police beat an African American taxi driver, the latter triggered after police raided a "speakeasy" patronized mostly by African Americans. Public opinion about police and urban uprisings divided sharply along racial lines, with more than two-thirds of black survey respondents identifying police brutality as the major contributor to riots, while only one in six white survey respondents held this opinion.[9]

Enacted in this context of crime, uprisings, and pre-election talk of a hand-cuffed police force, the Safe Streets Act of 1968 seemed the child of "right-wing rhetoric," a "Frankenstein initiated by Johnson in the wake of the 1966 rioting season." The Safe Streets Act of 1968 does have the appearance of pre-election panic when placed in the landscape of all crime policy enactments from 1963 through 1968, when the Democratic Party had majority control of the House and Senate. The punitive consequences of the Safe Streets Act of 1968 provided additional support for claims that liberals capitulated to conservative values in an election year. The Act swelled the flow of federal funds to state and local police departments that were already using their reserves for domestic militarization. As created and directed by the Safe Streets Act, the Law Enforcement Assistance Administration (LEAA) funded the purchase of helicopters, patrol cars, infra-red cameras, riot gear, and radios by police departments. LEAA also financed Louisiana's purchase of a tank, later used to storm the New Orleans Black Panther headquarters in September 1970. Colorado requested police funds for coun-ties with "college, migrant or minority populations," even after LEAA funneled money to buy 165 riot helmets, 126 gas masks, 118 riot batons, 76 cases of mace, 500 pairs of plastic handcuffs, 13 shotguns, and 33 "riot shields," as well as 94 smoke and gas grenades, projectiles, launching cartridges, and flares.[10]

Viewed at the moment of its enactment, the Safe Streets Act of 1968 appears to be all the critics say. When viewed as policy development, however, it becomes clear that the Safe Streets Act was not the result of election-year panic. Rather, it was part of a long-term liberal agenda, one that reflected a belief that feder-ally subsidized police recruitment and training could become racially fair. This section traces policy development from 1961 through 1967. Picking up threads from the previous chapter, I connect Truman-era demands to modernize police through increased funding to 1960s expansions of criminal justice modern-ization: the 1961 U.S. Commission on Civil Rights, which recommended increased money to professionalize the police; Kennedy's Juvenile Delinquency and Youth Offenses Control Act of 1961, which sponsored programs such as Neighborhood Youth Corps, the Legal Services Corporation, and Head Start; the Law Enforcement Assistance Act of 1965, which created the Office of Law Enforcement Assistance; and President Johnson's 1967 Commission on Law Enforcement and Administration of Justice, which set the groundwork for the Safe Streets Act. By following liberal policy development from 1961 through 1967, the Safe Streets Act of 1968 appears not as election-year racial hysteria, but as a push to the right on a path liberals were already walking.

To Avoid "Destructive Rebellion against the Fabric of Society"

This section evaluates politics and policy to clarify the convergence of race lib-eral and race conservative approaches to criminal justice modernization between

1961 and 1965. For liberal Democrats, dual positions on civil rights and law enforcement sprung from a singular faith in the federal government to correct racial ills through better machinery. Establishing and maintaining civil rights required increased law-and-order to protect racial minorities from white police violence, which would in turn prevent white majorities from being threatened by black insurgent violence. For Republicans and southern Democrats, civil rights seemed to reward black crime and increased risks for white majorities: civil rights validated selective law-breaking and kept the federal government in a position of having to grant more rights to deter black crime. Despite the seeming difference in terms of civil rights causality, both groups equated black violence with lawlessness and crime, and both sought to address this problem with increased procedure in federal crime policy. This section begins in 1961 with the U.S. Civil Rights Commission and President Kennedy's Juvenile Delinquency and Youth Offenses Control Act. It next moves to Goldwater and Johnson's 1964 responses to civil rights legislation alongside the Juvenile Delinquency Act, which sets the stage for my examination of the Law Enforcement Assistance Act of 1965.

Calls for police modernization were longstanding, evolving from Truman Democrats to the U.S. Civil Rights Commission of 1961 to Johnson Democrats. The 1961 U.S. Commission on Civil Rights (USCRC) recommended criminal justice modernization as a pathway to racial justice, where police professionalization was at the heart of their recommendations.[11] In its 307-page survey of criminal justice, the USCRC gave more official recognition to police brutality as an instrument of racial discipline, used to "keep the Negro in his place." Based on Department of Justice data, the USCRC identified 1,328 formal complaints of police brutality between January 1958 and June 1960. Half of all allegations came from African Americans.[12] For the USCRC, police brutality—or, more accurately, *perceived* police brutality—was dangerous because it made black neighborhoods distrustful and therefore impenetrable. Police brutality, wrote the USCRC in 1961, is unfortunate not only "for Negroes but also for the police and the entire community," because criminal investigations rely on information supplied by private persons. "The job of crime control," the USCRC reasoned, "becomes vastly more difficult when a whole segment of the community is wary of any contact with the police."[13]

The USCRC saw police brutality as springing from two problems—one in the flawed behaviors of white police, another in the flawed perceptions of African Americans. Police training promised to salve both issues. Specifically, the USCRC recommended that Congress establish "grants-in-aid" to assist state and local governments to "increase the professional quality of their police forces." Linking its work to the 1931 Wickersham Committee and to Truman's 1946 Presidential Committee on Civil Rights, the 1961 USCRC recommended that federal money go to local police for recruitment, selection tests, training in "scientific crime detection" and "constitutional rights and human relations," and development of college-level education and scholarships in police administration.[14]

Simultaneous with the findings of the USCRC, in 1961 President Kennedy signed the Juvenile Delinquency and Youth Offenses Control Act. This 1961 Act authorized the federal government to fund new local projects for actual and "potential" juvenile delinquents. In monetary terms, the Juvenile Delinquency Act was paltry; it gave only $10 million dollars to new projects. In institutional terms, however, the Juvenile Delinquency Act was weighty. It established the Office of Juvenile Delinquency, which according to sociolegal scholars Malcolm Feeley and Austin Sarat, provided "the most important model for the creation of OLEA [Office of Law Enforcement and Administration] in 1965 and the much larger effort stimulated by the recommendations of the President's Commission on Law Enforcement and the Administration of Criminal Justice in 1966 and 1967." In other words, the 1961 Juvenile Delinquency Act set the stage for the passage of the Law Enforcement Assistance Act of 1965, which created OLEA, and for the President's Commission on Law Enforcement and the Administration of Criminal Justice (the Katzenbach Commission), both of which are discussed in the next section as key precursors to the Safe Streets Act of 1968. The Office of Juvenile Delinquency sponsored proto-typical programs of the Great Society, including Neighborhood Youth Corps, the Legal Services Corporation, and Head Start.[15] Of the Office of Juvenile Delinquency's 16 demonstration-action programs, 14 were located in "the decaying inner core of our large cities," which "provide the least oppor-tunity for behavior acceptable to the larger society," as explained by the Assistant Secretary of Health, Education, and Welfare in 1964.[16] The Juvenile Delinquency and Youth Offenses Control Act's preamble made the connection between social equality and crime: "Delinquency and youth offenses occur disproportionately among school dropouts, unemployed youth faced with limited opportunities and with employment barriers, and youth in deprived family situations."[17]

Programs like those funded through Kennedy's 1961 Office of Juvenile Delinquency were relatively small, but they fueled the political com-plaints of "criminal-coddling" that animated Republican Barry Goldwater's 1964 presidential bid. As he delivered his acceptance speech for the 1964 Republican Party presidential nomination, Goldwater asserted the primacy of law-and-order: "security from domestic violence, no less than from foreign aggression, is the most elementary and fundamental purpose of any govern-ment." This is language Nixon would echo four years later. The "domestic vio-lence" to which Goldwater referred was civil rights activism. After President Lyndon Johnson signed the 1964 Civil Rights Act and while thousands of blacks registered to vote during the 1964 Freedom Summer, Republican presidential candidate Barry Goldwater campaigned using a particular indictment of the black freedom struggle: black civil rights generate crime. The Republican platform of 1964 criticized the Kennedy Administration for "encouraging disorderly and lawless elements" with "extravagant campaign promises."

Throughout his campaign speeches, Goldwater attributed rising crime rates to black civil disobedience, black demands for equality under the law, and black use of the welfare state. In the final pre-election push, Senator Goldwater likened the welfare state to legalized criminality: "If it is entirely proper for government to take from some to give to others, then won't some be led to believe that they can rightfully take from anyone who has more than they?" Quoting the FBI's *Uniform Crime Reports*, Goldwater attributed the "15 percent" rise in crime to those who "have gone to the streets to seek with violence what can only be found in understanding." In seeming reference to his own vote against the Civil Rights Act of 1964, Goldwater presented the well-rehearsed maxim of racial progress embraced by southern Democrats and now many Republicans: "the more the Federal government has attempted to legislate morality, the more it actually has incited hatreds and violence."[18]

As he campaigned through 1964, President Johnson insisted that "there is something mighty wrong when a candidate for the highest office bemoans violence in the streets but votes against the war on poverty," and his landslide victory suggested that many agreed.[19] Setting out to complete Roosevelt's New Deal while rejecting Jim Crow, President Johnson signed legislation to create preschool for poor children through Project Head Start, job training for young people through the Job Corps, and medical care for the aged through Medicare and for the poor through Medicaid.[20] Modernization of law enforcement was not incidental to Johnson's Great Society. Following in the tradition of Kennedy's 1961 Juvenile Delinquency Act, Johnson advocated federal funding for local crime prevention and control programs. But there was a more fundamental way in which his vision of criminality was enmeshed in his Great Society agenda. Johnson understood the Great Society as crime prevention, its resources a balm to the kind of deprivation that compels criminal acts. At the same time, Johnson imbued black people with the kind of violence and criminality structured in a place too personal for policy to touch.

Johnson's famous Howard University speech, delivered in June 1965, clarified the liberal frame that set black criminality as the pathological outcome of racial discrimination. At Howard University, Johnson seemed at first to support a contextualized vision of racist violence and economic subordination: "You do not take a person who, for years, has been hobbled by chains and liberate him, bring him up to the starting line of a race and then say, 'you are free to compete with all the others,' and still justly believe that you have been completely fair."[21] In the same speech, however, Johnson spoke of a sickness beyond the reach of the Great Society. African Americans carried the scars of "ancient brutality, past injustice, and present prejudice," and of these "wounds," perhaps "most important—its influence radiating to every part of life—is the breakdown of the Negro family structure." Johnson's speech referenced a Department of Labor report released in March 1965, titled "The Negro Family: The Case for National Action" but often called the Moynihan report after its author Daniel Patrick Moynihan, Johnson's trusted aide and assistant secretary of labor and policy.

According to the Moynihan report, dominant black mothers and absent black fathers engineered their sons for criminality. The report claimed that the combined impact of poverty and family breakdown yielded the "predicable outcome in a disastrous delinquency and crime rate." This claim was supported by a catalog of arrest and incarceration rates. In 1963, Chicago and Detroit police reported that three-quarters of their arrestees were black, and in 1960 black people constituted 37 percent of state and federal prisons. The report used these statistics to assert that crime was a symptom of "the Negro family's" enduring sickness. When a community "allows large numbers of young men to grow up in broken families, dominated by women, never acquiring any stable relationships to male authority, never acquiring any set of rational expectations about the future—that community asks for and gets chaos." Emphasizing the certainty of biology, the Moynihan report pronounced black criminality to be "inevitable." The report continued: "Crime, violence, unrest, and disorder, are not only to be expected, but they are very near inevitable. And they are richly deserved."[22]

Echoing Truman's *To Secure These Rights*, President Johnson's 1965 Howard University commencement address presented the liberal thermodynamics that converted actual white violence into potential black violence. Johnson sequenced the transfer of violent energy, from joblessness, to hopelessness, to indifference, to rebellion: "Unemployment strikes most swiftly and broadly at the Negro, and this burden erodes hope. Blighted hope breeds despair. Despair brings indifferences to the learning which offers a way out. And despair, coupled with indifferences, is often the source of *destructive rebellion against the fabric of society.*" For all of its egalitarian impulses, Johnson's Howard speech still signaled the looming threat of black crime. This statement reflected race liberal ideological tendencies to universalize while preserving special psychological diagnoses for non-universalizable racial subjects. Law-breaking was law-breaking; simultaneously, black law-breaking was an expression of cultural injury, somehow the structure's fault but the individual's responsibility.

In August 1965, after a Los Angeles police officer stopped a twenty-one-year-old black motorist on suspicion of drunk driving, a crowd witnessed "a scuffle," and rebellion spread. For six days, the Los Angeles community of Watts burned. An estimated 35,000 African Americans participated in the uprising, and it took 16,000 National Guard soldiers as well as Los Angeles police to end it. Of the 34 left dead, 28 were African American—the National Guard killed eight, and the Los Angeles Police Department made more than 3,000 arrests. Images of Watts supplanted images of white police officers beating nonviolent protesters on Bloody Sunday.[23]

Johnson's speech in the immediate aftermath of Watts clarified the logic underlying his earlier Howard speech. "A rioter with a Molotov cocktail in his hands is not fighting for civil rights any more than a Klansman with a sheet on his back and mask on his face," stated President Johnson in his address to the White House Conference on Equal Employment Opportunity on August 21, 1965. It had been only three weeks since Johnson signed the Voting Rights Act of 1965. Standing in front of civil rights supporters, Johnson spoke in the voice of the law: Klansmen and black rioters of Watts are "what the law declares them: law-breakers." "We must not," said Johnson, "in one breath demand laws to protect the rights of all our citizens, and then turn our back, or wink, and in the next breath allow laws to be broken that protect the safety of our citizens." According to President Johnson's trusted adviser Harry McPherson, who claimed credit for drafting Johnson's speech, the Watts rebellion shocked everyone except "the Southerners in Congress." This implied that liberal Democrats could no longer dismiss southern focus on the threat of black violence as "self-serving" efforts to "shift attention away from the terrible problems in the South."[24]

Johnson's conflation of the Watts rebels with the KKK converged with the logic of race conservatives: the law was now clean, so the lawbreakers were truly to blame. Against the black crime problem, conservatives affirmed the neutrality of "law-and-order." By indexing lawless black protesters to lawless white resisters, conservatives positioned law-and-order as the neutral middle. For example, J. Edgar Hoover called for neutral law-and-order, indexing the "pseudoliberals of the extreme left" to the "ultra right" of the Ku Klux Klan, and issuing a lesson to both: "it is reprehensible for any person to select those laws he will obey and those he will ignore. Such defiance is a form of anarchy." In the post–Civil Rights Act world of racial neutrality, equality of law implied renewed commitment to criminal law. In Hoover's equation, "Those who seek equal rights *under* the law should be taught to assume equal responsibility *before* the law. Certainly, civil rights and individual dignity have their vital place in life, but what about the common good and the law-and-order that preserve us all from lapsing back into the jungle?" Similarly, in 1965, Reverend Billy Graham affirmed this neutral center: "If the law says I cannot march or I cannot demonstrate, I ought not to march and I ought not to demonstrate. And if the law tells me that I should send my children to a school where there are both races, I should obey that law also.... Only by maintaining law-and-order are we going to keep our democracy and our nation great."[25] This core logic—racial chaos and black pathology demanded a stronger, yet neutral, criminal justice machinery—was, with different sympathies, also the agenda of the party in power.

To Help "Slum Children Have Respect for the Law"

This section analyzes the Law Enforcement Assistance Act of 1965, which set a key precedent for the passage of the Safe Streets Act by creating a broad and bipartisan consensus on the need for police modernization despite ongoing disagreement as to the reasons. With the Law Enforcement Assistance Act of 1965 (LEAA), Johnson directed Kennedy's local grants-in-aid idea toward local police departments. When President Lyndon B. Johnson signed the LEAA into law in September 1965, he likened police and prisons to teachers and schools: all need federal funding to build a better society. "Material aid to resist crime" was just as "appropriate" as "federal assistance in the fields of housing, employment, mental health, education, transportation and welfare." The Act created a new federal agency, the Office of Law Enforcement Assistance (OLEA, later renamed the Law Enforcement Assistance Administration) and charged it to distribute funds to "adequately trained and well-equipped lawmen." The dollar figure was still quite small—only $10 million dollars for the attorney general to grant to local criminal justice agencies to train personnel and "to collect, evaluate, publish, and disseminate information,"—but sponsors claimed it was essential for police efficacy and legitimacy. As Johnson declared in his signing statement for the Act, "The great society we are striving to build cannot become a reality unless we strike at the roots of crime."[26]

Congress passed the Law Enforcement Assistance Act with almost unanimous support (the House vote was 326-0). The Act gathered backing from strong Republican conservatives such as Senator Roman Hruska (R-Nebraska), from pro–civil rights liberal Republicans such as Senator Jacob Javits, and from southern Democrats such as Senator Sam J. Ervin Jr. of North Carolina. The American Bar Association and the U.S. Civil Rights Commission supported the 1965 Act, and FBI director J. Edgar Hoover applauded its potential to "strengthen the delicate machinery of justice in this country." The Law Enforcement Assistance Act won widespread support, but for divergent and even conflicting reasons. Consensus on police professionalization camouflaged differences on professionalism's *purpose*: some saw police funding as a way to *repress* rioting and lawbreaking; others saw police funding as a way to *suppress* impetuses for rioting by improving "police-community" relations. Some saw funding as *complementary* to civil rights, while conservatives saw it as *compensatory* for court procedural hamstringing. Different groups supported change, believing it would promote different interests.[27] As debates on the floor suggest, some liberal Democrats supported the Act to fund police training for purposes of racial fairness, whereas many members of the conservative coalition supported it to fund police training for racial toughness in regulating urban disruptions.

Democratic Michigan Senator Philip Hart, who had co-sponsored law enforcement assistance bills since 1961, supported federal aid to police as a means to improve "police-community relations." Sometimes called "the conscience of the Senate," Hart had gained a reputation as a civil rights stalwart since he won his Senate seat in 1958, and he vigorously fought for the 1965 Voting Rights Act. He hoped that federal assistance would facilitate connections between local police and federal agencies like the U.S. Civil Rights Commission, the Community Relations Service of the Department of Commerce, and the Department of Health, Education, and Welfare. Similarly, Democratic Senator Birch Bayh of Indiana co-sponsored the 1965 bill by emphasizing the imperative of police legitimacy, saying, "at no time in our history has disrespect for law and those who administer and enforce it been so general and widespread." Senator Bayh supported police professionalization *and* policies for better schools and job training to eradicate "the roots of crime." On the other side, Republican Representative James Martin of Alabama supported the Law Enforcement Assistance Act as a repudiation of "Martin Luther King and Bayard Rustin and other agitators" who call "for the ouster of good police officers." Republican Senator John Tower of Texas supported the bill to fortify law enforcement against civilly disobedient lawbreakers. During a time when people "accept as normal the use of riots, civil disorder, disobedience, and even individual violence," Tower explained, fortifying police would reinforce the "common decency" and "self-control" behind the notion that "Americans need not rob and assault" to achieve "orderly and effective progress."[28]

Commentary on the Law Enforcement Assistance Act of 1965 revealed expectations that "neutral," professionalized police would serve different, even oppositional, racial purposes. Democratic Senator Joseph Tydings of Maryland, who co-sponsored the Act, supported police professionalization as a path to racial fairness as well as national legitimacy. Given the "deep-seated *belief* amongst our Negro citizens that *equal law enforcement* in police practices *does not exist anywhere in our land*," it was to be expected that African Americans would not respect the police. Tydings linked local police abuses to the national legitimacy of criminal law: "when the police in one section of the country" blatantly "defy the very law they are supposed to uphold," then "the problem of enforcing the law is magnified in every section of the country." Senator Tydings believed LEAA was the best solution: increased police salaries, more training, and higher recruitment requirements. Police professionalization would fix police-community relations and thereby teach "slum children [to] have respect for the law."[29]

Professionalization would make police more responsible to "slum children" while making "slum children" more responsible to the police. But the stipulations of LEAA required no distinction between these two purposes. Thus, South Carolina Senator Strom Thurmond could support LEAA while dismissing "*so-called* police brutality" as an "overworked slogan," giving "the green light in this country to insurrection, riots, increased criminal activities, and the breakdown in law-and-order." Black people charging "police brutality" were simply complaining about hurt egos, according to Thurmond. Citing FBI figures of 1,700 complaints between mid-1964 and mid-1965, Thurmond interpreted under-enforcement—only 47 cases were tried, and only five resulted in convictions in federal courts—as evidence that complaints were unfounded. Thurmond entered into record a *U.S. News & World Report* story questioning police brutality as "fact or fiction," and minimized the phenomenon by explaining that "[b]ig-city files bulge with complaints of 'brutality' that boil down to rough language," such as calling a black "man a 'nigger' or a 'boy.' "[30]

The Law Enforcement Assistance Act of 1965 did not specify the content of law enforcement training; it merely stipulated that such assistance be made available, creating OLEA to take on that task and authorizing the attorney general to study all matters relating to law enforcement. In April 1966, the attorney general reported that OLEA had been undertaking research to "address problems of police-community relations and citizen attitudes toward the police."[31] A January 1966 OLEA memo, addressed to applicants for OLEA research grants, explained the "Purpose and Definition of Good Police-Community Relations" in seven bullet points: (1) "To encourage citizens to report crime" or "at least, *not interfere with arrests* and other police work"; (2) "To achieve adequate financial and other support from legislative bodies"; (3) "To improve recruitment"; (4) "To *improve respect* for law and law enforcement which has a direct relationship to the amount of crime"; (5) "To *remove the incidents which can lead to riots*"; (6) "To assist in giving the *public confidence* that the police will enforce the law and provide effective protection without discrimination"; and (7) "To make the police responsive to the public which is essential in a democracy even aside from other pragmatic advantages."[32] Given this definition of "police-community relations," OLEA looks like a public relations agency, engaged in finding ways to improve respect for and public confidence in police. It also implicitly ties this purpose to improved police effectiveness in making arrests and deterring riots.

To "Nourish" Law Enforcement

Along with the creation of OLEA, 1965 also saw another important step in the development of liberal crime policy that led to the Safe Streets Act. In July

1965, President Johnson impaneled the Commission on Law Enforcement and Administration of Justice, called the Katzenbach Commission for its chair Nicholas deB. Katzenbach. In 1967 the Katzenbach Commission reported recommendations that would become, after a brutal amendment process, the Safe Streets Act of 1968. Because of its huge legislative influence, the Katzenbach report deserves special attention, and I will discuss its overall philosophy and its particular recommendations for law enforcement. The Katzenbach Commission affirmed that police discretion was a central problem for the criminal justice system and explicitly connected the Great Society vision of racial peace to federal structure and discipline. The Commission report, entitled *The Challenge of Crime in a Free Society,* hit a now-familiar Democratic punch line: "Warring on poverty, inadequate housing and unemployment, is warring on crime. A civil rights law is a law against crime."[33] The Katzenbach Commission also spoke in the voice of structural law-and-order: "Widespread crime implies a widespread failure by society as a whole." The report therefore advocated a crime reduction plan "to eliminate slums and ghettos, to improve education, to provide jobs."

Criminal justice modernization was a key component to this approach, because criminal justice needed federal support as much as housing programs. The report declared unequivocally: "Every part of the system is undernourished. There is too little manpower and what there is not well enough trained or well enough paid.... To lament the increase in crime and at the same time to *starve* the agencies of law enforcement and justice is to whistle in the wind." The Katzenbach Commission recommended hiring more judges, revising sentencing to make it more uniform, and upgrading prison education and vocational training. As would become relevant to the Safe Streets Act, the Katzenbach Commission recommended federal funding for local law enforcement to recruit and train more police, especially "minority-group officers." In a classic language of modernization, the Katzenbach Commission called state and local law enforcement a "very long-neglected, terribly badly-organized, *backward* thing that nobody has supported." In this vein, Katzenbach supported federal funds as a Great Society subsidy for cities that deserved but could not afford quality police.[34]

The Katzenbach Commission used the language of discretion that had become increasingly popular since the ABF released its data in 1959. ABF Researchers on the Commission, such as Herman Goldstein, gave official voice to the discretion paradigm of the "total criminal justice system" as movement through a line of administrative checkpoints. The Katzenbach report reflected the perspective that discretion permeates the entire criminal justice system: police have discretion most fundamentally on whether to arrest, for "policemen cannot and do not arrest all the offenders they encounter." And prosecutors hold "undisputed sway" over whether to press a case or drop it, how to determine the specific charge against the defendant, and whether and how to "plea bargain" with a defense attorney in the "invisible procedure" of reducing the original charge in return for a plea of guilty.[35]

The Commission report included a "flowchart" of criminal justice procedures, meant to illustrate the process of criminal administration and "the many decision points along its course." The elaborate chart can be summarized as follows for adult felonies: (1) investigation of observed or reported crime; (2) arrest; (3) booking (administrative record of arrest); (4) initial appearance before magistrate, commissioner, or justice of peace (formal notice of charges; advice of rights; bail set); before magistrate with formal notice of charges; (5) preliminary hearing; (6) information (charge filed by prosecutor on basis of information submitted by police); (7) arraignment (appearance for plea); (8) trial; (9) sentencing (subject to appeal; can result in probation, or incarceration followed by parole, etc.). Since police served as the entry point into the system, the Katzenbach Commission recommended increased training to guide police through all permissible activities. It advised shrinking discretionary powers by defining "as precisely as possible when arrest is a proper action and when it is not."[36]

There were several police-specific proposals from the Katzenbach Commission. The Commission recommended a "vastly enlarged program of Federal assistance," particularly in the form of money for criminal justice personnel training, coordinated research and information systems, and grants-in-aid for operational innovations. Training would help police stop taking sides, for example, in all manner of racial conflict, protest, and disruption. The Katzenbach Commission advised more recruitment of "minority" police, since it was axiomatic that more minority police would lead to better police-minority relations. Recruiting police officers from black neighborhoods would improve "police-community relations," bring community knowledge into the police department, and minimize interpersonal conflict on the streets (see Figure 3.1). As symbols, minority officers would correct the image of police officer as enemy to the community. This would assist with the perception that police were oppressors, which according to the commission was at least partially the result of psychological atavism: "the result of accumulated resentment by Negroes of white persons generally, and such prejudice appears to be most prevalent among those who are more poorly educated, have the lowest incomes, and live in high-crime neighborhoods."[37]

Black "prejudice" against white police, in the parlance of the Katzenbach Commission, was accumulated resentment displaced onto the symbol of authority. In a neighborhood of people "suffering from a sense of social injustice and exclusion, many residents will reach the conclusion that the neighborhood is being policed not for the purpose of maintaining law-and-order but for the

Figure 3.1 Join the Oakland Police Department, 1967. *Note*: Recruiting stations, like this
mobile unit in Oakland, "make it known far and wide" in "innercity neighborhoods" that "police
work has many attractions and opportunities." *Source*: President's Commission on Law Enforcement
and Administration of Justice, *The Challenge of Crime in a Free Society* (Washington, DC: GPO,
1967), 109.

purpose of maintaining the status quo." The very presence of a "predominantly
white police force in a Negro community" can be "a dangerous irritant," the
Commission reported. "In order to gain the general confidence and acceptance
of a community," according to the Katzenbach Commission, "personnel within a
police department should be representative of the community as a whole." Thus,
correcting African Americans' misguided "prejudice" was thought to be a matter
of personnel change.[38]

Similar debates over criminal justice modernization were manifest in the 1967
report of another Johnson Commission: the National Advisory Commission on
Civil Disorders. President Johnson formed this commission to evaluate the specific causes of race and urban riots. Known as the Kerner Commission after its
chair Otto Kerner, the Commission identified the underlying causes of urban
riots as "segregation and poverty." These conditions have created in the "racial
ghetto a destructive environment totally unknown to most white Americans." To
address this problem, the Kerner Commission advocated a solution of closing
"the gap between promise and performance." The Kerner Commission used a
structural law-and-order logic often, enough to make Nixon denounce its "undue
emphasis" on "white racists" and lenience on uprising "perpetrators." In terms of
the policing debates of the day, the Kerner Commission was important because
it gave official acknowledgment that police "incidents" triggered roughly half of

the riots. This was incredible rejection of the white public opinion of the day. In 1967 roughly 70 percent of black survey respondents identified police brutality as the major cause of riots, but less than 20 percent of white survey respondents held this opinion.[39] These structural threads in Katzenbach and Kerner were all the more notable given the brewing debates in Congress. Members of the 89th Congress (1965–66) introduced 86 bills prohibiting interstate travel to incite a riot. In 1967, members of Congress introduced 198 riot-related measures, some of which called for research, but most of which called for punishment.[40]

Johnson's "Worst Bill"

The Safe Streets Act of 1968 extended the development traced above, but with a sharpened punitive edge. As originally introduced in 1967, the Safe Streets Act (S. 917, H.R. 5037) proposed funding local law enforcement for training police, getting better equipment, and coordinating between agencies—along with innovation for rehabilitation and prevention. The bill allocated expenditure of $50 million in the first year (with expected expenditure of $300 million in fiscal year 1969) for local law enforcement, giving emphasis to the following six categories: (1) recruitment and training of police, especially police-community relations; (2) modernization of equipment, such as two-way radios; (3) reorganization of personnel structures and coordination between agencies; (4) innovative rehabilitation efforts, such as work-release and community-based corrections; (5) high-speed systems for collecting and transmitting information to police, prosecutors, courts, and corrections agencies; and (6) crime prevention programs in schools and welfare agencies. In each category, the attorney general (then Ramsey Clark) would funnel grants to cities of 50,000 or more.[41] The bill also banned wiretapping and electronic eavesdropping except in cases of national security.

After the Safe Streets Act's introduction in February 1967, President Johnson justified the Act as corrective of a criminal justice system suffering from "decades" of "neglect": local law enforcement remained "undermanned and underpaid," correctional systems "poorly equipped to rehabilitate prisoners," courts "clogged," criminal procedures "archaic," and local juvenile-offender systems "understaffed and largely ineffective." Weak, dated, and disorganized, the criminal justice system needed to be strengthened, updated, and reorganized. For President Johnson, crime reduction was inextricably linked to the promotion of civil rights and anti-poverty programs. With the move toward modernization, Johnson reaffirmed the first civil right, stating that "public order is the first business of government." At the time of its introduction, the bill had broad support from liberal groups such as the American Civil Liberties Union, the U.S. Conference of Mayors, and the U.S. Civil Rights Commission. Adherents to this view sympathized with black criticisms of the police, characterizing the police as a "powerful instrument of the status quo" that has no "legitimacy in the ghetto."[42]

How did the Johnson administration's proposed Safe Streets Act of 1967— forged through the findings of the Katzenbach Commission and a commitment to civil rights—become, in the words of his aide Harry McPherson, "the worst bill you [Johnson] have signed since you took office"? One important explanation is that a conservative coalition of Republicans and southern Democrats modified the bill as it moved through Congress to sharpen its punitive edge. The biggest modification was Title I to fund local law enforcement. The conservative coalition accepted the idea of federal funding for modernization; the controversy was over the *administration* and *prioritization* of funding, not federal funding per se. Partisan and sectional voting revealed that a conservative coalition fought for state block grants aimed at riot control (Table A.2). In the House, William Cahill (R-New Jersey) and Richard Poff (R-Virginia) introduced amendments to replace federal-to-local categorical grants with federal-to-state block grants. Later, in the Senate, Minority Leader Everett Dirksen (R-Illinois) introduced a similar block grant amendment. As in the House, southern Democrats voted with Republicans. The vast majority of Democrats opposed the block grant amendment; of those who supported it, more than 80 percent were from southern states. Funding distribution was a high-stakes controversy. As a simple matter of "pork," liberal Democrats had an interest in distributing money to large cities, which were presumably more liberal, more black, and more Democratic. Ramsey Clark opposed block grants in anticipation that they would undercut cities in the "continuing urban-rural and partisan political controversies."[43]

Beyond changing location from local to state, the change was also from *categorical* grants to *block* grants. Gone were the six categories of police recruitment, modernization, reorganization, information improvement, rehabilitation, and prevention. Instead, on their own, the conservative coalition reorganized distribution through state block grants, reprioritizing funding away from innovative rehabilitation efforts in the tradition of the Juvenile Delinquency Act, and toward selective funding for police preparedness for riot control and organized crime. Again, the majority of Democrats opposed Clark MacGregor's (R-Minnesota) amendment prioritizing riot control over rehabilitation. Of those who supported it, more than 80 percent were from southern states. To justify the focus on riots, southern Democrats emphasized the dangers of selective obedience to the law in terms specific to black collective action. Civil rights leaders "have the arrogance to place themselves above standards of civilized society and to openly defy established principles of law-and-order." Similarly, Representative William Colmer (D-Mississippi) blamed "leaders of SNCC and other similar organizations" for "preaching 'black power' and inciting riots." Representative Charles Bennett (D-Florida) indicted "individuals such as Stokely Carmichael," who "play upon the fears and frustrations of an impressionable minority of Negro youths to vigorously encourage terrorism and violence."[44]

Along with funding battles, the conservative coalition fought over the details of criminal procedure, particularly interrogation (Title II) and wiretapping (Title III). Title II declared that a confession was admissible if a trial judge deemed it so, even if the defendant had not been informed of rights, and even if there was a long delay between arrest and arraignment. In effect, Title II was the congressional response to Supreme Court expansions of criminal procedure in *Mallory* and *Miranda*. A typical complaint against Warren Court expansions to criminal procedure came from Representative John Ashbrook (R-Ohio), who blamed "a series of liberal court decisions hampering law enforcement, rewarding rioters rather than punishing them," and "sociological gobbledygook" for making crime and rioting "a way of life for a small minority of city Negroes." By the time Congress adopted changes to funding and criminal procedure, liberal organizations like the American Civil Liberties Union and the Leadership Conference on Civil Rights opposed the bill as "an invitation to the invasion of privacy." As with block-grant funding, Republicans and southern Democrats voted together in provisions of Title II, and almost all votes kept the more permissive formulations of confessions, eyewitnesses, and wiretapping (Table A.2). Title III expanded wiretapping. The original administration proposal, called the Right to Privacy Act, allowed electronic surveillance only with attorney general and judicial authorization in cases of "national security." The Senate's new Title III, however, allowed any federal assistant attorney general, state district attorney, or local district attorney with judicial approval to wiretap or bug for any crime punishable by imprisonment of more than one year.[45]

Getting "Most of What We Wanted"

It might have been President Johnson's "worst bill," but, in a 1969 interview, Johnson's notoriously liberal attorney general Ramsey Clark concluded that Democrats got "most of what we wanted" from the Safe Streets Act. After noting the losses around wiretapping and funding structure, Ramsey Clark proclaimed victory: "We got the funds we wanted, and we got the opportunity to administer them almost as we wanted," and "we got the authority to support police community relations, and we got the authority to pay" some increases in salaries.[46] Ramsey Clark's gloss of the Safe Streets Act reveals the indeterminacy of liberal law-and-order: liberals won the chance to fund law enforcement—and presumably this would "improve" the local law enforcement by any metric—but they had no way to distribute funds toward any desired outcome. Even before introduction of the first conservative coalition amendment, liberal proposals for police modernization slipped around in a mix of motives—some saw strong law

Table 3.1 **Disparate Penalties for Identical Cases, The Second Circuit Sentencing Study, 1974**

	Most severe sentence	6th most severe sentence	12th most severe sentence	Median sentence	12th least severe sentence	6th least severe sentence	Least severe sentence	# of sentences ranked
Case 1: Extortionate credit transactions; income tax violations.	20 yr. pris.; $65,000	15 yr. pris.; $50,000	15 yr. pris.	10 yr. pris.; $50,000	8 yr. pris.; $20,000	5 yr. pris.; 3 yr. prob. $10,000	3 yr. pris.	45
Case 2: Bank robbery.	18 yr. pris.; $5,000	15 yr. pris.	15 yr. pris.	10 yr. pris.	7.5 yr. pris.	5 yr. pris.	5 yr. pris.	48
Case 3: Sale of heroin.	{10 yr. pris.;}5 yr. prob.	6 yr. pris.; 5 yr. prob.	5 yr. pris.; 5 yr. prob.	5 yr. pris.; 3 yr. prob.	3 yr. pris.; 3 yr. prob.	3 yr. pris.; 3 yr. prob.	1 yr. pris.; 5 yr. prob.	46
Case 4: Theft and possession of stolen goods.	7.5 yr. pris.	5 yr. pris.	4 yr. pris.	3 yr. pris.	3 yr. pris.	2 yr. pris.	4 yr. prob.	45
Case 5: Possession of barbiturates with intent to sell.	5 yr. pris.; 3 yr. prob.	3 yr. pris.; 3 yr. prob.	3 yr. pris.; 3 yr. prob.	2 yr. pris.; 3 yr. prob.	1.5 yr. pris.; 3 yr. prob.	5 yr. prob.; $500.	2 yr. prob.	42
Case 6: Filing false income tax returns.	3 yr. pris.; $5,000.	3 yr. pris.; $5,000.	2 yr. pris.; $5,000.	1 yr. pris.; $5,000.	6 mo pris.; 2.5 yr. prob.; $3,000	6 mo pris.; $5,000	3 mo pris.; $5,000	48
Case 7: Possession of heroin.	2 yr. pris.	2 yr. pris.	1.5 yr. pris.	1 yr. pris.	6 mo pris.; 18 mo prob.	3 mo pris.	1 yr. prob.	39

Note: The Second Circuit Sentencing Study asked judges to render sentences on twenty identical cases, seven of which are excerpted above. Senator Edward Kennedy presented the sentencing ranges as proof of "unjust and arbitrary" judicial discretion. (The *Congressional Record* erroneously omitted a line from "Case 3: Sale of Heroin"; my correction is in curly brackets.)

Source: Senator Edward Kennedy, *Congressional Record*, January 20, 1978, 294, reformatted from Anthony Partridge and William Eldridge, *The Second Circuit Sentencing Study: A Report of the Judges of the Second Circuit* (Washington, DC: Federal Judicial Center, 1974), table 1.

enforcement as an entitlement, others wanted decent officers to inculcate black children with respect for authority, and still others wanted to nourish carceral machinery as an integral part of a healthy Great Society.

Tenuously connected to racial justice, liberal police professionalization obscured three core issues. First, bluster over how to distribute funds eclipsed questions of why to distribute funds. Even though the conservative coalition won state-level distribution, rather than federal to the local level, there was still no purpose in the statute. Malcolm Feeley and Austin Sarat concluded that the Safe Streets Act of 1968 lacked "substantive objectives, specific goals, and a strategy for achieving them"; its goals were "almost purely procedural." The Safe Streets Act of 1968 renamed OLEA the Law Enforcement Assistance Administration (LEAA) and transitioned from federal engagement with local law enforcement to state-level administration. Any potential for federal guidance grew fainter when the connection became to state planning agencies, instead of to local law enforcement. At the level of implementation, state planning agencies had difficulty influencing entrenched local law enforcement. In sheer dollars, state planning agencies regulated less than five percent of the total criminal justice budget in any state, and thus control through finances was limited, especially with larger agencies and larger cities.[47] State plans were, in the words of one study commissioned by Johnson, "pedestrian." Instead of providing strong federal guidance for fair, educated, modernized policing, as originally proposed by the Katzenbach Commission, the Safe Streets Act simply channeled federal funds into "old programs" and higher salaries for "old-line personnel."[48]

The same criticism holds for legal reforms. Just as "neutral" funding turned punitive, "neutral" procedural reforms offered thin protection against the substantive rise of criminalization and the larger apparatus of policing. *Miranda,* for example, ultimately allowed the accused to waive rights to silence and counsel, and allowed police officers to take the waivers. Moreover, one week after *Miranda,* the Supreme Court held that protections applied only prospectively. Police have "adapted" to *Miranda*: once the warning is read and the waiver obtained—as it is in roughly 80 percent of interrogations—*Miranda* does not restrict deceptive or hostile interrogation, or lengthy confinement that may induce a suspect to confess. Stringent protections could have required that all police interrogations be taped, required the presence of an attorney or neutral observer, or banned certain interrogation techniques altogether. Some even summarized *Miranda* as requiring police to say "a few magic words" before obtaining a waiver and commencing the same abusive interrogation techniques challenged more than 40 years ago. In this vein, some critical race scholars conclude that *Miranda,* like *Brown v. Board,* has remained intact because of its limited impact on institutional racism. Reforms from *Mapp* and *Miranda* created negative controls with requirements of formality that were easily accommodated, leading political scientist

Michael Brown to conclude that "professionalization has fostered the illusion of control over police discretion when in fact it has resulted in greater autonomy for the police."[49]

Second, Johnson's profile of "the Negro" as injured-ergo-injuring embedded black pathology into allegedly "colorblind" law-and-order. Black subjects' experience of racial prejudice marked them unable to participate in the universal promise of law-and-order. Perhaps they rightly perceived injustice in the discretionary—and therefore discriminatory—procedures of law enforcement. But black subjects remained caught in a pathological dead-end, unable to perceive the effectiveness of neutral law-and-order, and now in need of crime control themselves. This logic pathologized black resistance to white violence by insisting that only the state's "neutral" law-and-order machinery could fix racial violence.

Third, liberal advocacy to limit race prejudice through police modernization actually legitimated state-based racial violence. Preoccupation with criminal justice "discretion" matched the idea that racism was "prejudice," a deviation from an otherwise race-free process. Fixation on discretionary moments and prejudiced individuals yielded modest calls for reform, such as proposals to incorporate "minority" officers into the existing police force.[50] The reduction of police prejudice—ostensibly achieved by integrating "minority" officers—would increase community respect for police and decrease incidents of black violence (understood as either legitimate resistance or illegitimate crime). Obscured in this approach is the fact that violence against people of color, perpetrated by private actors and state agencies, far exceeded individual acts of assault and murder that constituted the ever-discussed measures of the FBI *Uniform Crime Reports*. In just the 24 months preceding Johnson's June 1965 Howard speech, international and domestic state-sponsored or state-sanctioned racial violence included the murder of military veteran and activist Medgar Evers in June 1963; the killing of four African American girls in the bombing of the 16th Street Baptist Church in September 1963; the lynching of Johnnie Mae Chappell in March 1964; the lynching of Charles Moore and Henry Dee in May 1964; the August 1964 Gulf of Tonkin Resolution and the commencement of bombings on North Vietnam; and police brutality and immediate uprisings in Harlem and Rochester in July 1964 and in Philadelphia in August 1964. Liberal modernization to reduce discretion and prejudice steered attention away from the structural racism permeating state machinery.

"It's Time to Rehabilitate the Sentencing Process"

By the time he signed the Sentencing Reform Act of 1984, President Ronald Reagan had already established his contempt for the "new privileged class"—criminals, those entitled rights-holders who manipulated the "maze of legal technicalities" to get their charges "dropped, postponed, plea-bargained away." Criminals had help. Judges, Reagan said, may be "trained in the law," but they have "no special competence in imposing a sentence that will reflect society's values."[51] If the confluence of rights-exploiting criminals and liberal-elite judges bred lawlessness, then the remedy would discipline criminals and judges alike. This is precisely what the Sentencing Reform Act of 1984 accomplished. The Sentencing Reform Act of 1984 ended indeterminate sentencing, the practice wherein trial judges imparted sentences in broad ranges—say, three-to-five years or five-to-seven years—and parole officials then selected the final release date based on assessments of an incarcerated person's behavior or progress toward rehabilitation. The SRA created the U.S. Sentencing Commission, a seven-person administrative agency, and charged it with creating a sentencing grid, clear and mandatory parameters for criminal sentencing. The resulting U.S. Sentencing Guidelines, released by the U.S. Sentencing Commission in 1987, required federal judges to "plot" convicted criminals on a 6 x 43 table, with a vertical axis for "Offense Level" (1–43) and a horizontal axis for "Criminal History Category" (I–VI). The corresponding cell showed the sentencing range in months of imprisonment, and the judge's job was to impart a sentence from the appropriate cell (see Table A.3).[52] The Guidelines have been mandatory since 1987 and advisory since 2005. President Reagan endorsed the Sentencing Reform Act as a way "to make prison sentencing more certain [and] to end abuses of parole."

Five years after their implementation, the U.S. Sentencing Guidelines had *doubled* the average time served in federal prison and *halved* the percentage of offenders punished with probation rather than prison. Average time served was just under 25 months in 1987; it was 50 months in 1992. The Sentencing Reform Act was "one of the great failures at law reform in U.S. history," according to legal scholars Marc Miller and Ronald Wright, and Michael Tonry called it "the most controversial and disliked sentencing reform initiative in U.S. history." For all its punitive consequences, the Sentencing Reform Act developed from a historical thread of liberal advocates: mid-1960s Great Society aspirations for fairness, early-1970s concern about prisoner "frustrations" with sentencing disparity, and suspicion that judges used their lavish discretionary power in prejudiced ways. Democratic leaders in Maine, California, and New York established determinate sentencing through the mid-1960s, fighting for less incarceration and more rule of law in criminal sentencing.[53]

To understand policy development before the Reagan revolution, I track federal sentencing reform from its Great Society origins, beginning with President Lyndon B. Johnson's 1966 creation of the National Commission of Reform of the Federal Criminal Laws, and following the introduction by Senator Edward

Kennedy (the quintessential liberal Democrat from Massachusetts) of sentencing "grids" who ushered his proposals through to enactment in the Sentencing
Reform Act of 1984.[54] Sentencing reform became a pivotal issue in the 1970s,
connected to broader challenges of the excessive use of incarceration as punishment. By 1984, however, the Sentencing Reform Act would create the harshest
sentencing guidelines the country had ever seen.

To Mend the "Crazy-Quilt Patchwork"

Even as they are engines of carceral expansion, sentencing guidelines have a dis-
tinctly liberal history. The guidelines began as a conversation about rationalizing federal criminal statutes, launched in President Lyndon B. Johnson's Great
Society and inspired by legal scholarship. In March 1966, President Johnson
called for a commission to reclassify and rationalize federal criminal statutes.
As OLEA of 1965 was starting its research projects, he had, by this time, signed
legislation for the Correctional Rehabilitation Study Act of 1965, and he had
already impaneled the Commission on Law Enforcement and Administration of
Justice in 1965 (reported out as the Katzenbach Commission in 1967). So when
President Johnson created the National Commission of Reform of the Federal
Criminal Laws (Brown Commission) in 1966 to study reorganization of the federal criminal code, all the keywords of ordered machinery, consistent practices,
and research were already in place. Johnson wanted the Brown Commission to
address the problem of "obsolete," "inconsistent," and "scattered" laws that, in
Johnson's language, combined to make the "crazy-quilt patchwork" of our criminal code.[55]

The Brown Commission, like the Katzenbach Commission before it, criticized the criminal code as an insult to the idea of the rule of law. The Katzenbach
Commission's 1967 report ridiculed the "anomalies and inconsistencies" in both
federal and state criminal codes. Colorado served as a telling example: state legislators punished *stealing* a dog with up to 10 years imprisonment, but *killing* a dog
carried a maximum of six months imprisonment; first-degree murder received
up to 10 years imprisonment, while lesser-degree murder received up to 15.
Federal and state criminal codes were confusing and internally contradictory by
virtue of their length, their detail, and the sheer number of offenses and penalties. By the mid-1960s the Oregon Penal Code, for example, contained no fewer
than 1,413 offenses and specified no less than 466 penalties.[56] Some disparities
might be attributed to different legislators setting penalties at different times.

The Katzenbach Commission acknowledged the criminal justice system's
disjointed development, which derived from English common law and was
appended with recent reforms like professionalized police, probation, and
parole. American federalist divisions compounded the problem, as every town,

city, county, and state developed its own system, each "somewhat alike" but no two "precisely like," alongside the federal criminal system. The "criminal justice system" was not a system at all. It was merely a "philosophical core," according to the Katzenbach Commission, whose basic principle was that "a person may be punished by the Government if, and only if, it has been proved by an impartial and deliberate process that he has [*sic*] violated a specific law." This philosophy reads like a textbook definition of due process and rule of law, more aspirational than descriptive. The historical reality was quite different: "Around that core layer upon layer of institutions and procedures, some carefully constructed and some improvised, some inspired by principle and some by expediency, have accumulated."[57]

Federal criminal law was an intricate mess. To the extent that there is one, the "U.S. Criminal Code" was compiled in Title 18 of the U.S. Code, "Crimes and Criminal Procedure." Crimes and punishments were scattered, however, through the 51 titles of U.S. Code. Title 21 on Food and Drugs lists narcotics-related crimes; Title 28 on the Judiciary and Judicial Procedures codifies the duties and powers of the DOJ and the U.S. Sentencing Commission; and any statutory provision with a criminal penalty is part of the "U.S. Criminal Code" regardless of which title it is under. As the Brown Commission lamented, the U.S. Code specified 79 culpable states of mind, that is, 79 different mental states that make an act blameworthy. The U.S. Code designated criminal liability if a person acts, for example, "corruptly," "feloniously," "fraudulently," "improperly," "knowingly," "maliciously," "wantonly," "willfully and knowingly," and so on. The Model Penal Code, by contrast, offered only four culpable states of mind; a crime might be committed "purposefully," "knowingly," "recklessly," or "negligently."[58]

Scholars of American Political Development call this phenomenon "layering." That is, new policies and institutions simply "layer" on top of, rather than replace, the old. Lawmakers are most likely to engage in layering when the political-institutional context sets high costs and low rewards for pursuing systemic change. Reorganizing the U.S. Criminal Code was a high-cost proposal; it asked lawmakers to throw open criminal law as a whole, without attending to any particular "pet" crime issue, and, as a result, completing the task would almost certainly take longer than a two-year or even four-year election cycle. In contrast, lawmakers risked little by proposing new criminal statutes, even when such proposals duplicated or contradicted current law. The result was policies and institutions marked by tensions and confusion.[59] Building on this insight from American Political Development, we can say that the Criminal Code may be untenable as "rule of law," but its absurd incoherence is perfectly logical as a product of politics. Criminal law was a palimpsest, and each new criminal statute was inscribed on top of the last, without reconciliation of redundant or even contradictory dicta. Lawmakers constructed and confronted new crime scares, from reefer madness to identity theft to welfare fraud to deliberate spread of HIV. Public fear was fleeting and episodic. Crime waves recede and panics wane, but, as political scientist Marie Gottschalk has demonstrated, the crime policies they inspired remained the law.[60]

It was no coincidence that President Johnson's folksy criticism echoed Herbert Wechsler's characterization of the criminal code as "fragmentary and uneven." Herbert Wechsler, along with Louis Schwartz of the University of Pennsylvania, had co-directed the American Law Institute's (ALI) 10-year effort to create the Model Penal Code of 1962—one of Johnson's inspirations for creating the Brown Commission. The major source of disparity in criminal sentencing, according to Wechsler, was *statutory ambiguity*. Writing in 1955, Wechsler complained that criminal statutes were "disorganized and often accidental in their coverage, a medley of enactment and of common law...a combination of the old and the new that only history explains." Judges deferred to legislative intent, but legislative meaning was indecipherable, a jumbled mess of platitudes and contradictory criminal statutes. The problem of penal law "inhered in the state of our penal *legislation*."[61] Wechsler delivered this criticism directly to the Senate Judiciary Committee in 1974. What the senators referred to as federal criminal law was little more than "a miscellany of modern enactments passed on an ad hoc basis"; this legislative jumble "frequently produc[ed] gross disparities in liability or sentence."[62]

Wechsler's analysis, cited in several congressional reports and floor statements, brought disdain for judicial inconsistency back to Congress' door. Fragmentary, disorganized legislative dicta all but ensured sentencing disparity. The solution: organize the criminal code by offense grade, and set fixed maximum penalties determined by grade. This was, of course, the function of the American Law Institute's (ALI) 1962 *Model Penal Code*. The Model Penal Code classified all crimes into three felony grades and two misdemeanor grades, and each grade carried a maximum penalty, with almost all penalties shorter than those extant in 1962.[63] The ALI's Model Penal Code listed 11 grounds for *withholding* a sentence of incarceration, and it limited trial court discretion with fixed *maximum* sentences—that is, sentencing ceilings, not the sentencing "floors" of mandatory minimums that Congress would become enamored of in the 1980s.[64]

Researchers from the ALI's Model Penal Code staffed President Johnson's Criminal Law Commission (Brown Commission). Chaired by Edmund G. "Pat" Brown, Sr., the former governor of California, the Brown Commission was headed by Professor Louis B. Schwartz, co-author of the ALI's *Model Penal Code*. Congressional documents explicitly traced the origins of sentencing reform to the ALI's Model Penal Code.[65] Many lawmakers praised the Model Penal Code for restoring intellectual respectability to criminal law, and two-thirds of states used at least part of the Model Penal Code as the basis for revision.[66] The Brown Commission, however, was also staffed by other people with "radical" sentencing ideas. Its Deputy Director was Richard Green, former project director of the American Bar Association's (ABA) *Sentencing Alternatives and Procedures*. The ABA's 1968 *Sentencing Alternatives and Procedures* suggested that most sentences should be less than five years, and the ABA set a punishment ceiling of no more than 10 years for all but the most unusual cases.[67] The Brown Commission's Advisory Committee also included Milton Rector, president of the National Council on Crime and Delinquency (NCCD). This nongovernmental organization developed their own Model Sentencing Act in 1972, which recommended the principle of least restrictive sanctions; most nonviolent offenders should receive nothing more than probation, fine, or suspended sentences.[68] The NCCD's Model Sentencing Act also set a high bar for incarceration, and specified that probation, fine, or suspended sentences were most appropriate for the majority of nonviolent offenders. The Model Penal Code promised a kind of order that could create fairness in a system whose "philosophical core" of "impartial and deliberate process" was confused by historical layering. The Brown Commission issued its report in 1970, and immediately thereafter sentencing reform came under scrutiny in relation to a series of prison rebellions.

To Avert Rebellion with "Clear and Comprehensible" Sentencing Protocols

Just as the 1960s rebellions inside cities propelled policing reforms, the 1970s rebellions inside prisons invigorated agendas for sentencing reforms.[69] Since the birth of the prison, inmates have experienced the "numbing monotony, arbitrary rules, the weight of time, claustrophobia, loneliness, the dullness of institutionalism, the loss of liberty, bad food, and the myriad of humiliations, deprivations, and irritations large and small that comprised the pains of imprisonment."[70] Still, changing political and racial consciousness of the 1960s and 1970s inspired more prison rebellions. In 1964, a year of uprisings in New York, Chicago, and five other cities, the director of the Federal Bureau of Prisons warned of an upsurge in "prison riots," citing sentencing disparities as "among the major causes of prison riots." With a hint of empathy, the director explained to the Senate Judiciary Committee that prisoners react rationally to irrational criminal sentencing: when two people convicted of the same crime meet in prison, the person with the longer sentence "cannot be expected to accept his situation with equanimity." Riots were rational. Therefore, the director deduced that sentencing "whimsies" undermine the penological goals of rehabilitating a misguided or addicted person and of instilling respect for the law. Sentencing disparity confirmed that the law did not deserve respect "among the very persons whom the law is supposed to teach that respect."[71]

As prison rebellions persisted into the next decade, more lawmakers accepted sentencing "whimsies" as their major provocation. In January 1970, a guard in California's Soledad prison shot and killed three African American inmates, one of whom had filed suit against the Soledad warden. Despite charges against the guard for retaliation and targeting, the guard's actions were ruled "justifiable homicide." In October 1971, guards in California's San Quentin prison shot and killed prison activist George Jackson in his alleged attempt to escape. People incarcerated in New York's Attica prison protested George Jackson's murder with a day of silence, following which a group of 1,500 politically active African American, Puerto Rican, and white prisoners took control of Attica in what turned into a four-day prison revolt. The September 1971 Attica rebellion ended when New York Governor Nelson Rockefeller ordered 1,000 National Guard and state police troops to retake the prison. By its end, 43 people were killed, 32 of them prisoners.[72]

The Attica Liberation Faction listed 27 demands in its Manifesto of Demands, most of them so fundamental to human life that to call them "demands" betrays the prison's sickness-inducing and exploitative practices. They demanded sanitary food, an end to practices of leaving food unrefrigerated and uncovered for hours before mealtime, and an option to replace pork-saturated food when necessary for religious requirements. They demanded licensed medical practitioners instead of untrained prison staff authorized to dispense medications in error-laden, erratic, and sometimes punitive fashion. They demanded basic freedom of belief and speech: access to books, the ability to receive papers sent to them in the U.S. mail, and an end to intra-prison segregation based on political or religious affiliation. They demanded an end to the practices of beating and solitary confinement for the people who refused to labor. Instead of coercively extracted labor compensated at 40 cents per day, they demanded basic labor protections such as an eight-hour workday compensated at minimum or union-scale wage. With these demands, the Attica Liberation Faction stated its collective grievance: "We, the inmates of Attica prison, have grown to recognize beyond the shadow of a doubt, that because of our posture as prisoners and branded characters as alleged criminals, the administration and prison employees no longer consider or respect us as human beings, but rather as domesticated animals selected to do their bidding in slave labor and furnished as a personal whipping dog for their sadistic, psychopathic hate."

The parole system also shared the death-dealing properties of noxious food, pernicious medical practices, and overall prison administration that treated inmates as "domesticated animals." Of the Attica Liberation Faction's 27 demands, four indicted parole as unconstitutional, secretive, anti-rehabilitative, and rigged against black and brown people. Demand Number One faulted parole hearings as unconstitutional "non-hearings," wherein potential parolees had neither an attorney nor an opportunity to call witnesses. Demand Number Eighteen named the abuses of "indeterminate" sentencing, in which parole boards acted "within secrecy and within vast discretion." As political appointees, parole board members gave heavy weight to prison employees' accusations against potential parolees. The Attica Liberation Faction therefore called for a parole board elected by popular vote to replace the present parole board appointed by the governor. Demand Number Twenty-Two protested parole decisions based on "discrimination in judgment" and political "quota[s] of parole for black and brown people." Demand Number Twenty-Four criticized decisions based exclusively on the potential parolee's criminal record. A record-based decision calculus violated the alleged rehabilitative purpose of indeterminate sentencing. In a functional indeterminate sentencing system, parole board members use a rehabilitation-based decision calculus, not a criminal record-based decision calculus. As they concluded: "Most prisoners are denied parole solely because of their previous records. Life sentences should not confine a man longer than ten years as a seven-year duration is the considered statute for a lifetime out of circulation, and if a man cannot be rehabilitated after a maximum of ten years of constructive programs, etc., then he belongs in a mental hygiene center, not a prison."[73]

In many ways, the 1971 Attica Manifesto was no outlier in the arena of scholarly and activist critiques through the 1970s. Reducing reliance on prisons was part of mainstream discussion, or, at the very least, was not on the radical fringe. President Nixon's 1973 National Advisory Commission on Criminal Justice Standards and Goals recommended closing juvenile penal facilities, as well as a 10-year moratorium on prison construction. Many organizations endorsed sentencing guidelines as a mechanism to reduce incarceration. The American Bar Association, for example, supported tiered, non-carceral punishment, beginning with fines, restitution, and criminal forfeiture, jumping to community supervision and intermittent incarceration, and, finally, only "if all other conditions fail," a term of imprisonment. Like the ABA, the National Council on Crime and Delinquency (NCCD) supported guidelines as a means to compel shorter sentences more consistent with those of other industrialized nations; in 1976 the U.S. incarceration rate of 215 per 100,000 was already twice that of Canada, and the prison boom had just begun. For the NCCD, incarceration was an inherently brutal practice. Anti-carceral advocacy extended to the National Interreligious Task Force on Criminal Justice, a coalition of Jewish, Catholic, and Protestant denominations, which called imprisonment "the harshest, most debilitating sanction available." The National Moratorium on Prison Construction denounced pro-carceral sentencing as "unimaginative" and "hard-line." The

ACLU opposed the pro-incarceration focus on grounds that between 50 and 70 percent of people already in prison did not belong there.[74]

Across the legislative sessions, however, lawmakers transformed demands for organized decarceration into proposals for sentencing uniformity. Denuded as a protest for dignity, "Attica" became a one-word cautionary tale against *arbitrary* sentencing and parole. Consider, for example, the interpretations of the New York State Special Commission on Attica. Also called the McKay Commission for its chair Robert McKay, professor at New York University Law and chair of the New York Civil Liberties Union, the Attica Commission investigated the rebellion by interviewing approximately 1,600 incarcerated persons and 400 correction officers. In its 1972 report, the McKay Commission pronounced unequivocally: "The criminal justice system fails to dispense justice and impose punishment fairly, equally, and swiftly." More specifically, the McKay Commission lobbed its criticisms at Attica's meek or missing protocols. The Commission criticized New York Governor Nelson Rockefeller for sending state police to open fire; the criticism was not, however, of excessive force, but of Governor Rockefeller's failure to visit Attica before ordering the bloodbath. The Commission also faulted New York prison authorities for their ill preparedness and their lack of equipment to quash the rebellion. Attica officers, wrote the McKay Commission, should have had immediate access to lethal weapons.

In this liberal logic of "sympathy" for incarcerated people, prisoners flailed in frustration because procedures were too loose. Mindful of the sentencing process's credibility deficit, the McKay Commission acknowledged that "parole procedures *are* unfair" but added that prisoners overestimated the magnitude of unfairness. Because parole procedures remained opaque, they "*appear* to inmates to be even more inequitable and irrational than they are." The McKay Commission therefore advised that "the grant or denial of parole must be measured by clear and comprehensible standards."[75]

For Robert McKay, within the hundreds of interviews at Attica, "the most persistent complaints were about the unequal treatment in the sentencing process and in the parole process." People in "adjacent cells believed that sentences were unjust because of unexplained disparity in severity of the sentences." According to McKay, parole board decisions were opaque and appeared arbitrary, and the chair of the Attica Commission therefore concluded that "it's time to rehabilitate the sentencing process."[76] Recall that Attica activists did not protest the arbitrary; rather, they protested parole procedures as dehumanizing, racially rigged kangaroo courts wherein parolees sat without attorney, subject to unassailable accusations from prison guards. In political discourse beyond the Attica Manifesto, however, the imperative was to bring order to a carceral system whose chaos, if left unreformed, would breed disrespect and resistance.

Hardening the Guidelines, 1977–1984

Lawmakers answered the call to "rehabilitate the sentencing process," with Democratic Senator Edward Kennedy of Massachusetts leading the way. This section examines five bills, all sponsored or co-sponsored by Senator Kennedy, that sentencing scholars see as milestone proposals: S. 1437 (introduced in 1977); S. 1722 (introduced in 1979); S. 1630 (introduced in 1981); S. 2572 (introduced in 1982); and S. 1762 (introduced in 1983, and enacted as the Sentencing Reform Act of 1984).[77] Focusing on Senator Kennedy's co-sponsored proposals, I attend to crucial subsections on four areas: parole, good time, alternatives to incarceration, and prison capacity. I demonstrate that Kennedy's initial proposals articulated a moderate reluctance to incarcerate, but subsequent bills jettisoned anti-carceral planks.

My attention to Senator Kennedy and to these specific subsections warrants explanation. Tracking Senator Kennedy means I follow the policy "victor" and neglect defeated bills that fell to Kennedy's left (more anti-carceral) and right (more pro-carceral). I therefore cannot determine if Kennedy's bills hardened relative to *all* Senate bills over time; I demonstrate only that Kennedy's bills hardened relative to *his* previous bills. It is possible that Senate sentencing bills hardened so aggressively from 1977 to 1984 that Kennedy's proposals remained left of center throughout. For these reasons and more, my method is limited. At the same time, however, the liberal "lion of the Senate" Ted Kennedy is a hard test case for my claim that Democrats aided, abetted, and legitimated a punitive law-and-order regime. With low ratings from the conservative Americans for Constitutional Action and high ratings from the liberal Americans for Democratic Action, Kennedy's voting record secured his liberal bona fides.[78] Even as the Democratic Leadership Council pushed for a moderate "Third Way" after Reagan's landslide 1984 reelection, Senator Kennedy remained "the avatar of liberalism" and opposed "New Democrat" measures like the Personal Responsibility and Work Responsibility Act of 1996, Clinton's end to welfare as we know it. As the liberals' liberal, Ted Kennedy is the litmus test for the more specific claim that pro–civil rights liberal lawmakers reformed criminal justice with a vision of fairness through uniformity and predictability.

Within five milestone bills, I focus on subsections about parole, "good time," alternatives to incarceration, and prison capacity. Combined, these four provisions drive carceral growth; depending on the configuration of these subsections, sentencing guidelines might dramatically increase or decrease the carceral state. Among other forces, parole, "good time," and alternatives to incarceration set the course for whether and how long one goes to prison. The Sentencing Reform Act abolished parole, curtailed "good time," and discouraged alternatives to incarceration, with enormous consequences. Before implementation of the U.S. Sentencing Guidelines, incarcerated people served between 40 and 70 percent of the sentence imposed by the judge. After enactment of the U.S. Sentencing Guidelines, incarcerated people served between 87 to 100 percent of the sentence.[79] Prison capacity stipulations also mattered. When legislation instructed the sentencing commission to account for prison capacity, there was comparatively less growth in the prison population. When "capacity conscious" guidelines began in Minnesota (1980), Washington (1984), and Oregon (1989), these states kept their respective incarceration rates below the national average. In sum, sentencing guidelines can constrain carceral growth when legislation directs the sentencing commissions to stay within extant population caps.[80]

With each subsequent proposal, Senator Kennedy and his various Republican co-sponsors jettisoned sections that would have *limited* incarceration. Table 3.2 summarizes the hardening to Kennedy's 1977–1984 proposals. The Senate passed S. 1437, but House Democrats rejected it as pro-prison, not pro-fairness. In 1979 the bill from Senators Kennedy, Strom Thurmond, and Orrin Hatch went no further than the Senate Judiciary Committee report, in large part because Kennedy devoted his energy to his 1980 Democratic presidential nomination.[81] In the next Congress, Senators Kennedy, Biden, and Thurmond removed more anti-carceral planks, and, under pressure from the Moral Majority, raised the bill's maximum penalty for rape from 12 years to 25 years. Reagan pocket vetoed the bill on the ground that S. 1722 accrued too much power to the federal government.[82] In 1983 and 1984, Senators Kennedy, Biden, and Thurmond worked together on the bill that finally passed both houses, the Comprehensive Crime Control Act of 1984, which included the Sentencing Reform Act of 1984.

Ending Parole. From 1977 through 1984, Senator Kennedy slowly closed the exit door of parole: his proposals moved from keeping parole, to limiting parole, to abolishing parole. Kennedy's 1977 bill maintained parole.[83] Kennedy's 1979 and 1981 bills, however, proposed a new form of court-imposed "parole" called "supervised release." This enabled the court, not the U.S. Parole Commission, to impose a sentence of incarceration *plus* a sentence of post-incarceration supervision. At the defendant's original criminal sentencing, the court might impose a term of imprisonment, plus up to three years of "supervised release."[84] By 1979 the National Legal Aid and Defenders Association, the organization attending to defendants without financial resources for counsel, complained that Congress had forgotten the goals of "neutrality" and "a balanced approach" apparent in the 1966 Brown Commission. Kennedy's 1979 proposals would increase time served to surpass those of the Soviet Union.[85]

Kennedy's 1982 bill further constrained discretion related to release. The Bureau of Prisons was allowed to grant "pre-release custody" for 10 percent of the sentence, but no more than six months. The thinking was that the U.S. probation system might help the person "adjust" during the months in "pre-release

Table 3.2 **Selected Senate Proposals for Sentencing Guidelines, 1977–1984**

	Status Quo Ante	1977 S. 1437	1979 S. 1722	1981 S. 1630	1982 S. 2572	1983 S. 1762	1984 Sentencing Reform Act
Parole	Maintain	Maintain	Court-imposed "parole"	Court-imposed "parole"	Bureau-imposed "parole"	Abolish	Abolish
"Good Time" Reductions	60–120 days	60–120 days	36 days	36 days	36 days	36 days	54 days
Prison Capacity	No rule	Do not exceed	Do not exceed	Do not exceed	Advise change	Advise change or expansion	Advise change or expansion
Alternatives to Incarceration	No rule	Are appropriate	Are appropriate	Maybe appropriate	Maybe appropriate	Maybe appropriate	Maybe appropriate

Note: This table shows bills as introduced.

Sources: Compiled by author from S. 1437, 95th Cong., 1st sess. (May 2, 1977); S. 1722, 96th Cong., 1st sess. (September 7, 1979); S. 1630, 97th Cong., 1st sess. (September 17, 1981); S. 2572, 97th Cong, 2nd sess. (May 26, 1982); *Sentencing Reform Act of 1984*, Public Law 98-473, U.S. Statutes at Large 98 (1984): 1991–1992, codified as 18 U.S.C. § 3581.

custody." Closing off early release exits would comfort and soothe incarcerated people. To justify parole abolition, the Senate Judiciary Report of 1980
asserted: "prisoner morale will improve with uncertainties as to release dates
removed." The evidence? "The official report on the Attica riots indicates that
uncertainty in release dates was a major cause of the riots. Public respect for the
law will grow when the public knows that the sentence announced in a particular
case represents the real sentence, rather than one subject to constant adjustment
by the Parole Commission." As enacted, the Sentencing Reform Act abolished
the U.S. Parole Commission.[86]

Reducing "Good Time." "Good time" is the accumulated reduction in the
amount of time required to complete a sentence. Prior to the Sentencing Reform
Act, the "good time" system cut sentences by 60 to 120 days per year. Federal
law, as codified in 18 U.S.C. 4161, scaled good time deductions as follows: for
sentences of six months to one year, five days deduction per month; for sentences of one to three years, six days deduction per month; for sentences of three
to five years, seven days deduction per month; for sentences of five to 10 years,
eight days deduction per month; and for sentences of 10 years or more, 10 days
per month.

The Sentencing Reform Act replaced scaled and prospective "good time"
reductions with flat and retrospective "good conduct time" reductions. Instead
of tiered reductions, the new system capped "good conduct time" at 54 days
reduction per year of incarceration.[87] Moreover, the former "good time" system
awarded deductions prospectively, at the start of a prison term; the new system
awarded "good conduct credit" deductions only retrospectively, after the Bureau
of Prisons assessed whether the incarcerated person showed "exemplary com-
pliance."[88] Kennedy's 1977 proposal retained "good time," allowing for 60 to
120 days reduction per year incarcerated. His subsequent proposals, however,
capped "good time" reduction to 36 days per year, regardless of whether the sentence was for one year or 10 years. "Under the bills introduced today," Kennedy
said in 1979, "the *sentence imposed* will be the *sentence served* (subject to time off
for good behavior)." The particular number, 36 days per year, meant a maximum
10 percent reduction per year. Representative Conyers (D-Michigan) opposed
the elimination of "good time," because, in his calculus, "although disparity may
be reduced, the excessive reliance and use of incarceration may increase."[89]

Prison Capacity: From Do Not Exceed to Recommend Expansion. Kennedy
inverted prison capacity clauses: in 1977, his bill directed the Sentencing
Commission to not exceed prison capacity, but by 1984, his bills recommend
expansion of capacity. The 1977 proposal declared flatly that prison capacity
"will *not be exceeded.*"[90] The Kennedy-McClellan bill directed the sentencing
commission to "assure that the available capacities" of federal prisons and other
resources "will not be exceeded." In 1979 and 1981 Kennedy and his Republican

co-sponsors retained the directive that the Sentencing Commission must assure that prison capacity is *not exceeded*. The Senate Judiciary Committee justified the capacity cap with the simple logic that prisons were already overcrowded.[91] In 1982, the Kennedy-Biden-Thurmond proposal deleted the injunction against exceeding prison capacity.[92] The next iteration, the 1983 Kennedy-Thurmond bill, actually rewrote the Commission's directive.

Instead of designing guidelines to cap prison capacity, the Commission should have recommended capacity "change and *expansion*" to accommodate the guidelines' predicted impact—more people imprisoned, longer sentences for all. Kennedy and Thurmond's 1983 bill mandated that the Commission "shall take into account the nature and capacity of the penal, correctional, and other facilities and services available, and shall make recommendations concerning any change or expansion in the nature or capacity of such facilities and services that might become necessary as a result of the guidelines promulgated pursuant to the provisions of this chapter."[93] As finally enacted, the Sentencing Reform Act directed the Commission to recommend "change or expansion" to prison capacity, and, as a vestigial limb from proposals past, it also directed the Commission to "minimize the likelihood that the Federal prison population will exceed the capacity of the Federal prisons, as determined by the Commission."[94] This stipulation, however, did not prohibit overcrowding.

Alternatives to Incarceration: From Appropriate to Reflect Appropriateness. In his early proposals, Kennedy set signposts pointing away from prison. His proposals in 1977 and 1979 set a presumption *against* incarceration for first-time, nonviolent offenders with a statutory principle: it was generally appropriate that guidelines "impose a sentence other than imprisonment" for first-time offenders not convicted of a "violent or other serious crime."[95] The Kennedy-McClellan bill of 1977, S. 1437, prioritized alternatives to incarceration by encouraging both the sentencing commission and the sentencing judge to consider alternatives, such as probation and community service. The Kennedy-McClellan proposal specified that guidelines should impose a sentence other than imprisonment for first-time nonviolent offenders, and there should be a presumption against incarcerating juvenile offenders, as well. The Kennedy-McClellan bill also included specific proposals for liberal decriminalization (and selective liberal criminalization): abolition of the Smith Act, which criminalized advocating overthrow of the government; elimination of penalties for possessing less than 10 grams of marijuana; an increase in maximum fines for corporations; and broadening criminal civil rights laws to include sex discrimination.

Later bills uprooted these do-not-go-directly-to-jail signposts. Instead of asserting that alternatives to incarceration were appropriate, Kennedy's co-sponsored legislation from 1981 onward directed the U.S. Sentencing Commission to "reflect" the "general appropriateness" of incarceration. Note the same language in Kennedy's co-sponsored proposals of S. 2572 (as written in § 994(i)) and S. 1762 (as written in § 994(j)): "The Commission shall insure that the guidelines reflect the general appropriateness of imposing a sentence other than imprisonment in cases in which the defendant is a first offender who has not been convicted of a crime of violence or an otherwise serious offense, *and the general appropriateness of imposing a term of imprisonment on a person convicted of a crime of violence that results in serious bodily injury.*"[96] Revised bills therefore widened paths to prison sentences in two ways: first, by deleting anti-carceral presumptions; second, by asking the Commission to consider the appropriateness of incarceration for serious violent crimes, thereby neutralizing the uniqueness of first-time nonviolent offenders. As finally enacted, the Sentencing Reform Act directed the U.S. Sentencing Commission to "insure that the guidelines reflect the general appropriateness" of incarceration.[97]

By the time President Ronald Reagan signed the bill into law on October 12, 1984, key carceral caps had been removed. In addition to this explicit hardening, the Sentencing Reform Act left statutory ambiguities that allowed the U.S. Sentencing Commission—the administrative body charged with writing the U.S. Sentencing Guidelines—to devise guidelines even more punitive than required by statute. Many scholars fault the U.S. Sentencing Commission for catering to Reagan's DOJ and "the most law-and-order members of the United States Congress."[98] For example, the Commission decided to incorporate mandatory minimums into the fabric of the Guidelines. This incorporation increased all drug-offense sentences, and as Michael Tonry explained, raised the "center of penal gravity of the entire scheme." (A less punitive alternative that the U.S. Sentencing Commission could have pursued: set Guidelines to their own *administrative* center of penal gravity and allow mandatory minimums, with their higher *legislative* center of gravity, to trump Guidelines only in instances of conflict. Many state commissions did this.) Additionally, the Commission required judges to apply Guideline penalties based on all "relevant conduct," that is, conduct for which the defendant was charged and conduct for which the defendant was uncharged or acquitted. (A less punitive alternative that the U.S. Sentencing Commission could have pursued: base the Guideline on conviction offenses, that is, the defendant's conduct during the offense of conviction. This alternative is the norm; the "relevant conduct" standard is unique to the federal Sentencing Guidelines.) Through their own discretion, the U.S. Sentencing Commission chose to define certain immigration offenses, minor property crimes, and low-level embezzling as "serious" offenses, even though these offenses warranted only probation in pre-guidelines.[99] Still, even before the creation of the U.S. Sentencing Commission, Senator Kennedy's sentencing reforms "drifted" rightward, unanchored by normative commitments to mitigating carceral violence.

In the end, lawmakers and the newly formed USSC ignored the research and abandoned animating calls from activists. Lost in this circuitous road to the Sentencing Reform Act were important lessons from researchers and activists. The American Bar Foundation (ABF) studies defined the "total criminal justice system" as an interconnected matrix of police, prosecutors, judges, and legislators. Lawmakers interested in rational, uniformly applied sentencing needed to consider how sentencing grids impact the "total criminal justice system." ABF studies found that fixed sentence schemes are "not uniformly applied *in practice.*" In reality, sentencing grids transferred discretion from judges to prosecutors within this total system.[100] Yet the lessons of the "total criminal justice system" were lost from legislative debates, such that there was little understanding about how limiting judicial discretion would increase discretionary power of prosecutors. Similarly, the American Legal Institute's (ALI) development of the Model Penal Code prioritized clarity and rationality alongside the principle of least restrictive sanctions. Instead of grasping this larger lesson, Democratic lawmakers lifted "discretion" and "disparity" as the keywords for punitive sentencing guidelines. Untethered to the lessons of the ABF or the ALI, sentencing guidelines would bring restrictive visions of civil rights as uniform, colorblind processing through a predictable, bias-free machine.

The Liberal's "Disparity Problem" Had a Disparity Problem

What explains the hardening of sentencing guidelines? It would be difficult to overstate the impact of shifts in partisan power. The 1980 election devastated the national Democratic Party with the voting in of Ronald Reagan to the White House. The last time a candidate defeated an elected, incumbent president was when Roosevelt had beaten Hoover in 1932. Democrats won the Senate majority in 1954 and held control for the following 26 years, but Republicans won the Senate majority in 1980, 1982, and 1984. The last time Republicans controlled the Senate for three consecutive elections was during the presidencies of Calvin Coolidge and Herbert Hoover. Senator Ted Kennedy was a candidate in the 1980 Democratic presidential primary but lost to incumbent Jimmy Carter. The Reagan Republican victories of 1980 signaled ideological shifts to the right and demographic shifts that deflated the power of the Democratic-leaning Northeast relative to the Republican-leaning South and Southwest.[101] Of course, all of these partisan shifts took place within larger contexts of union decline, a widening wealth gap, and deindustrialization.

Even acknowledging the centrality of these partisan shifts and convergences, my point is that the Sentencing Reform Act of 1984 as signed by President Reagan retained its liberal core: fairness (racial and otherwise) administered through grids, without a vision of justice beyond predictability. In the end, the development of the Sentencing Reform Act demonstrates the prioritization of the administrative quality of punishment over the purpose of punishment. As in police professionalization, ambiguity of purpose facilitated support for sentencing rationalization. Without connection to explicit benchmarks of justice, proposals for the U.S. Sentencing Commission were part Rorschach test: supporters saw in sentencing reform their own vision of justice, and competing visions coexisted in the wish for modernization.

Lawmakers agreed on the same solution to the problems of "judicial discretion," even though the problem held different meanings. Conservatives of the Reagan administration, for example, endorsed Guidelines by emphasizing that judges were out of touch with home-spun common sense. If the Warren Court adjudicated battles of police versus criminals, so the political story goes, then judges sided with criminal bullies. In his 1968 Republican presidential campaign, for example, Richard Nixon urged "respect" for "courts and those who serve on them," only then to warn that "some of our courts in their decisions have gone too far in weakening the peace forces as against the criminal forces in this country."[102] In line with this attack on liberal judges, Nixon endorsed limiting judicial discretion with "modernization" of the federal criminal code, the policy precursor to the Sentencing Guidelines. In his 1973 State of the Union Address, the epigraph of this chapter, Nixon advocated "modernizing" the "inadequate, clumsy, and outmoded" federal criminal code. Nixon clarified, however, that "modernization" meant more punishment, and he sought "a new code" to "give us tougher penalties and stronger weapons in the war against dangerous drugs and organized crime."[103]

Liberals objected to judicial discretion on technical grounds: the fragmented, contradictory laws known as the U.S. Criminal Code rendered enforcement necessarily haphazard. At the level of basic mechanics, wide sentencing variation resulted from a slack machine, and, in the spirit of Wechsler, legislators held the tools to tighten criminal statutes. In this sense, Senator Edward Kennedy likened judicial discretion to a coordination problem. The year of its signing, Kennedy stated, "with all due respect...judges themselves have not been willing to face this issue and...remedy this situation."[104] Senator Kennedy characterized his 1984 bill as "revis[ing] Federal sentencing procedures to achieve a rationality, uniformity, and fairness that does [sic] not exist in the current system." He explained: wide judicial disparity in sentencing means a defendant "has no way of knowing or reliably predicting whether he or she will walk out the courtroom on probation or be locked up for a term of years that may consume the rest of his or her life, or something in between." He concluded: "We should narrow the wide discretion we give our judges and parole boards."[105]

The Federal Judicial Center's *Second Circuit Sentencing Study* of 1974 offered proof that sentencing was a "game of chance." When a 1974 experiment presented 50 U.S. district judges with identical criminal cases, the judges proved that sentencing is a "game of chance." In an admirable effort of self-scrutiny, judges submitted to an experiment: 50 judges from the same region (the Second Circuit of New York, Connecticut, and Vermont) were asked to render sentences on 20 hypothetical cases, each with an identical pre-sentence report authored by a fictitious chief probation officer. Judges rendered prison sentences of wildly different length, but, more astounding still, the judges unanimously issued a prison sentence in only four of 20 scenario cases; in the remaining 16 cases, opinion varied so wildly that some judges issued a fine or a probationary term in lieu of prison time. To appreciate the absurd roulette of criminal sentencing, consider hypothetical Case 3, sale of heroin (see Table 3.2). Each judge read the same pre-sentence report of a man, over age 40 and employed as a cab driver at the time of conviction, who pled to sale of heroin, with a prior record of seven convictions, five periods of incarceration, and a "history of cocaine-sniffing." Some Second Circuit judges deemed the middle-aged cab driver deserving of one year in prison; others sentenced him to 10 years in prison. The existence of nonsensical sentencing gulfs grew wider still in the juxtaposition of punishments for heroin selling versus heroin possession. In hypothetical Case 7, the pre-sentence report presented a female, between 26 and 40 years old at time of conviction, who pled to possession of heroin. Her prior record listed over 20 convictions and over 10 jail or prison sentences, principally for prostitution and drug use. Presented with Case 7, seven judges committed the offender to observation under the Narcotic Addict Rehabilitation Act, enacted in 1966 as a short-lived effort to divert drug offenders from criminal prosecution to civil commitments for treatment and probation. Other Second Circuit judges sentenced the heroin-possessing woman to one-year probation, and several judges sentenced her to the maximum penalty of two years imprisonment. The experimental design of the *Second Circuit Study* exposed embarrassing sentencing discrepancies: depending on luck of the draw of judges, a person might serve more time for possessing heroin than for selling it.[106]

Liberal reformers straddled two critiques of discretion: one criticized judicial discretion for its arbitrary outcomes, another for its harsh outcomes. Given that Kennedy occupied both positions, without stated principles about how the two are connected, it is no surprise that Kennedy's proposals slipped into harsher and tougher modes. Spongy language covered the fault lines between the arbitrary and the harsh, and, to make matters worse, notions of unacceptable *racial* disparity also moved between critiques of the arbitrary and the harsh. Lawmakers universally condemned sentencing "disparity" the way anyone might condemn "bias" or inexplicable difference. Many lawmakers bemoaned disparity using the classic (individual-based) definition: disparity exists when people with like case attributes are sentenced differently. But many lawmakers, like Kennedy at the start of his campaign for sentencing reform, bemoaned disparity between groups: disparity exists when some groups (presumably with like worth and "propensity" to crime) are sentenced differently than other groups. Kennedy lamented "harsh and unfair punishment" of "the young and the poor" vis-à-vis corporations and public officials.[107] The liberals' disparity critique stood on weak, uneven ground.

To put it coarsely, the "disparity problem" had a disparity problem. Even the intellectual father of sentencing guidelines, Judge Marvin Frankel, toggled between anti-arbitrary and anti-carceral positions in his treatise, *Criminal Sentencing: Law Without Order.* As President Johnson's 1965 appointee to the U.S. District Court of Southern New York, Marvin Frankel was no tough-on-crime conservative, but his slender monograph lobbed a heavy attack against judicial discretion. Frankel's disdain for discretion oscillated between different, even antithetical, systems of logic. On the one hand, judicial discretion yielded unacceptably *arbitrary* punishment. For Frankel, "wholly unchecked and sweeping" discretion invited judges to indulge their personal whims. For any given judge on any given day, the sentencing "philosophy" at work might be, according to Frankel, "punitive, patriotic, self-righteous, guilt-ridden, and more than customarily dyspeptic." Unfettered discretion was therefore "intolerable" to any society that "professes devotion to the rule of law." On the other hand, judicial discretion yielded unacceptably *harsh* punishment. Frankel designated the United States "the world's cruelest nation—cruelest in terms of incarcerating more people for longer periods than any other country." With this statement, Frankel seemed to block prison expansion on two fronts—fewer entries into prison, quicker exits from prison. Frankel wanted sentencing commissions to teach "the public to accept a *more civilized (generally less harsh)* sentencing regime."[108]

Frankel criticized arbitrary sentencing, that is, a troublingly large standard deviation around *any* mean sentence length. Frankel also criticized harsh sentencing, that is, a troublingly large standard deviation around a troublingly high mean sentence length. In an abstract sense, discretion vitiated rule of law; in an applied sense, discretion vitiated standards of civilization. Frankel proposed ending "justice without law" through creation of an administrative "Commission on Sentencing" that would enact "binding guides" on sentencing courts. For Frankel, legislatures and the administrative agencies they created promised order by using "objective and objectively ascertainable criteria." Frankel's position would receive significant support from Senator Edward Kennedy, who took his recommendations as the foundation of his own sentencing reform efforts. In 1975 Senator Kennedy hosted a dinner party for Judge Frankel, whom he deemed "the father of sentencing reform."[109] Kennedy subsequently launched his campaign for fairness through sentencing guidelines, citing both the Federal

Judicial Center's 1974 *Second Circuit Study* and Marvin Frankel's 1973 *Criminal Sentencing*. Between 1977 and 1984, Senator Kennedy would advocate for the reduction of arbitrariness in sentencing while slowly shedding anti-carceral planks to achieve a winning coalition. Fairness became defined by consistency of sentence, not conditions of punishment.

When Judge Frankel evaluated the very U.S. Sentencing Guidelines that he inspired 20 years later, he distinguished "uniformity" and "harshness" as different, even potentially competing values; any 1993 evaluation of the U.S. Sentencing Guidelines would have to draw this distinction. The retired judge gave his decision: if forced to choose, he would "choose less disparity, even with legislatively decreed harshness, over wide discretion." Senator Kennedy did the same. In 1975 Senator Kennedy wrote a *New York Times* editorial where he staked out his position in relation to sentencing reform. Kennedy viewed better criminal justice machinery as an escape from the impossibly ideological tension between "law-and-order" and "root causes." "It is futile," Kennedy wrote in 1975, "to counter the law-and-order fallacy with the opposite fallacy that crime cannot be controlled unless we demolish city slums and eliminate poverty and discrimination." Great Society aspirations had become a luxury. Senator Kennedy added "We can no longer afford the luxury of confusing social progress with progress in the war on crime. We face the crime menace now.... It is time to fight a more practical, less ideological war on crime. What we need are sound, constructive proposals directed at improving law enforcement and the administration of justice." As an exit from false extremes, Kennedy proposed "a more practical, less ideological" effort aimed at "improving law enforcement and the administration of justice," specifically through the certainty of criminal sentences under sentencing guidelines.[110]

Kennedy's movement away from ideology and toward practicality was echoed in broader disparagements of criminal laws as arbitrary and chaotic (rather than expressing concern over their relative harshness). A 1978 DOJ study counted 134 statutes pertaining to theft and fraud, 89 pertaining to forgery and counterfeiting, 159 pertaining to false statements to government officials, and 84 pertaining to property destruction. Even national newspapers endorsed sentencing commissions by ridiculing the federal criminal code, not necessarily for its "softness" or "toughness," but for its anachronisms and inconsistencies. As debates gained prominence through the late 1970s, the *New York Times* ridiculed antiquated laws such as the federal misdemeanor of detaining a U.S. carrier pigeon, punishable with a fine of up to $1,000, as well as the federal felony of seducing a female passenger on a steamship.[111] As a product of continued layering, the criminal code had overlapping, conflicting, and confusing definitions.

Liberals set two measures for evaluating criminal sentencing—a predictability metric and a severity metric—and they picked two different objects of reform—the criminal justice system and the individual criminal. Calls for reform sometimes identified criminal justice machinery as the target of discipline, such as when the *New York Times* praised sentencing guidelines for forcing "consistency and order to the chaotic and confusing hodgepodge of Federal criminal laws." As a "national scandal" and a "disgrace," criminal sentencing corrupted trust in government and nurtured growing "public cynicism about our institutions."[112] In a 1977 floor speech, Senator Kennedy made it plain that *perceived* fairness mattered more than actual fairness:

> Today Federal correction policy is unjust and arbitrary. Perhaps, *more important, it is perceived to be unjust* by both the prisoner and society. S. 1437 [Kennedy's 1977 proposal for sentencing guidelines] breaks with the correctional myths of the past, and offers a blueprint for reform based upon the idea that prisons cannot cure.
>
> It ends an unfair policy, a policy based on the best of intentions, and it replaces it with a new system grounded in the knowledge that we do not yet know how to mold or predict our human behavior.
>
> I think what we are attempting to do is to get certainty for the defendants and for the public, and this legislation does that in a very important and significant way.[113]

But Senator Kennedy also affirmed that sentencing policy was indeed "unfair." Like Robert McKay's call to "rehabilitate the sentencing process," Kennedy's statement concurred that the system needed rehabilitation. Specifically, the sentencing process needed to be relieved of the delusion that individuals could be reformed or rehabilitated through incarceration. Kennedy flatly asserted, "Prisons cannot cure."

The Sentencing Reform Act of 1984 therefore did not contain a philosophy of punishment; it merely distributed punishment uniformly for all like cases.[114] As finally established in the Act, the Sentencing Commission should devise sentences that avoid "unwarranted sentencing disparities among defendants with similar records who have been found guilty of similar criminal conduct while maintaining sufficient flexibility to permit individualized sentences when warranted." In other words, so long as similarly situated embezzlers were treated similarly, and so long as similarly situated crack possessors were treated similarly, then vast differences between the two groups would not count as "disparity."[115] Disparity between individuals would no longer exist; the system would distribute harshness "fairly" among all individuals caught up in the efficiency of the machine.

For Kennedy, rehabilitation was slack in the machine. For all the changes between bills, Kennedy and his co-sponsors held that "imprisonment is not an appropriate means of promoting correction and rehabilitation."[116] In this sense, liberal reformers affirmed the jeremiad research of the mid-1970s that seemed to herald the impossibility of rehabilitation for prisoners. Robert Martinson's 1974 survey of 231 studies of penal rehabilitation programs was widely cited with the cynical synopsis "nothing works." Political scientist James Q. Wilson concluded in 1975 that the rehabilitative model was yet another failure of social liberalism and lenience, and he therefore proposed fixed-term punishments.[117] But critiques of prisoner rehabilitation were not new, unequivocal, or irrefutable in the 1970s. Sociologist David Garland has demolished the notion that research killed the rehabilitative ideal. Researchers since the 1930s have challenged rehabilitation's viability and value, and therefore research of the 1970s carried no unique transformative power. Moreover, Martinson's research was no flat-footed rejection of rehabilitation. Martinson's "what works" article actually demonstrated that some things do work, and his 1979 research revealed a guarded optimism for prisoner rehabilitation. Additionally, as Garland has argued, challenges to the rehabilitative ideal could have been met with reasonable defenses, such as the claim that rehabilitation programs were under-funded, under-staffed, and undermined by the destructive context of prison.[118]

Notions of order underpin penology, and the object of order for liberal Democrats was the unruly, unpredictable machine. If the nineteenth-century grand penological turn was from punishing the body to disciplining the soul, then late twentieth-century liberal Democrats turned from disciplining individuals to disciplining carceral machinery.

Disciplining the Machine

It was neither paradox nor backlash that crime policies developed so aggressively and in tandem with civil rights policies of the Johnson administration. This chapter focused on the liberal roots of modernization reforms for police professionalization and for sentencing reform. In supporting early versions of these proposals, race liberals and northern Democrats wanted police professionalization to achieve fairness and to win respect for the law from "slum children." Likewise, they advocated sentencing reform to rationalize the disorderly systems that, in liberal perspective, aggravated even the most reasonable of would-be prison rioters.

As policies spearheaded by Truman and Johnson Democrats, both policies were ultimately turned for more punitive ends—policies of police modernization qua racial fairness became policies of police militarization, and policies to modernize the criminal code and reduce racial disparity were ultimately guidelines for longer sentences. Race conservatives modernized toward different ends: these reforms answered the alleged criminological consequences of civil rights, the procedural revolution that "handcuffed" law enforcement, and the legacy of liberal judges. Even with competing logics—modernization to *complement* racial liberalization versus modernization to *correct* racial liberalization— opposing interests converged on rebuilding the carceral state.

There is no master narrative of conservative ascendance. As finally enacted, the Safe Streets Act of 1968 and the Sentencing Reform Act of 1984 entrenched anti-black carceral development, but both bills originated from and retained constitutive elements of liberal law-and-order. For many Democratic lawmakers, unruly policing and unpredictable sentencing provoked the uprisings of Watts and Attica. Liberal law-and-order fought arbitrary administration as the mark and measure of racism, and, in this sense, carceral modernization only enhanced civil rights.

4

The Era of Big Punishment

Mandatory Minimums, Community Policing, and Death Penalty Bidding Wars

"One of my objectives, quite frankly, is to lock Willie Horton up in jail."[1]
—*Democratic Senate Judiciary Chairperson Joseph Biden, 1991*

"The first duty of any government is to try to keep its citizens safe," asserted President William Clinton on August 11, 1993, but the preceding 12 years of Republican administrations meant that "we no longer have freedom from fear for all our citizens." Along with judiciary chairs Senator Joe Biden and Representative Jack Brooks, President Clinton stood in the White House Rose Garden on that summer day promoting his crime bill, centrally a proposal to hire 100,000 new police officers to secure freedom for people "imprisoned in their own apartments behind locked doors." Clinton then retold his campaign stump speech about "the immigrant worker in the New York hotel" who asked Clinton to "make his son free." The president explained, "He meant that his son couldn't walk to school two blocks without his walking with him, his son couldn't play in the park.... He said his son was not free." To deliver us from fear, Clinton promised to break from the partisan "labels of the past," those divisive keywords of "liberal or conservative or tough or compassionate." To fulfill the first duty of government, Clinton's crime bill would "emphasize punishment, police, and protection."[2]

This chapter details the explosion of punitive crime policy from the start of the Reagan administration through the end of the Clinton administration, as the Democratic Party remade "the first civil right" once again. Even in the context of falling crime rates and rising party polarization, lawmakers hardened carceral machinery continuously through the final two decades of the twentieth century, enacting notoriously harsh narcotics penalties in the Anti-Drug Abuse Acts of 1986 and 1988, three-strikes legislation in the Violent Crime Control and Law Enforcement Act of 1994, and more capital crimes with fewer appeals in the Federal

Death Penalty Act of 1994 and the Anti-Terrorism and Effective Death Penalty Act of 1996. The empirical heart of this chapter documents Democratic tough-on-crime policy developments in three areas—drug-related mandatory minimums, community policing, and capital punishment. Democrats attempted to shed their soft-on-crime moniker, especially after Reagan's 1984 reelection, by adopting a new policy approach: détente through punitive assent. Democratic Senator Joe Biden's mission to "lock Willie Horton in jail," as referenced in the epigraph, displayed Democratic efforts to incapacitate Republican attacks by punishing African Americans, in rhetorical and legislative terms.[3] The Democratic punitive turn was a deliberate distancing from racial egalitarianism, and, in perverse terms, the institutional legacies of liberal law-and-order amplified the carceral expansion.

Situating the Democratic punitive turn in the trajectory of postwar liberal law-and-order reveals how past was prelude in cross-cutting terms. On one hand, the damning image of soft-on-crime liberalism pushed centrist Democrats rightward, toward harsher positions and proposals. On the other hand, the actual institutional legacies of Great Society liberalism had fortified carceral machinery. Despite the soft-on-crime branding, Great Society–era liberal law-and-order actually developed a more capacious carceral state.

The Sentencing Reform Act of 1984, the result of Senator Ted Kennedy's eight-year fight for sentencing fairness, created the U.S. Sentencing Commission and charged it with devising Sentencing Guidelines by 1987. Senator Kennedy's proposals began with aspirations for fairness and racial justice, but the institution he helped to create, the U.S. Sentencing Commission, did not retain "aspirations." Instead, the Commission confronted legislative mandates to eliminate parole, cut "good time," and grant no special exemptions for first-time nonviolent offenders. This U.S. Sentencing Commission, then, became the institution that had to reconcile the rash of new mandatory minimums within the new sentencing regime.[4] On April 13, 1987, the U.S. Sentencing Commission submitted to Congress the new Federal Sentencing Guidelines, and it had chosen a particular way to bring coherence to the mandatory minimums that lawmakers had enacted willy-nilly while guidelines were still in the making. Sentencing Guidelines incorporated the 100-to-1 ratio between "crack" and powder cocaine established by Congress the preceding year and, to maintain "proportional" punishments, the U.S. Sentencing Commission inflated other criminal sentences to accommodate the new, high benchmarks of mandatory narcotics minimums.[5]

We see a similar liberal legacy in death penalty escalation. Even though the 1972 Democratic Party platform opposed the death penalty, it did so in mixed logics: liberal complaints of administrative deficiency existed side by side with absolute rejection of the death penalty. By opposing the death penalty on administrative grounds, liberals propelled, however unintentionally, the pursuit of administrative improvements for the death penalty.

Reclaiming What Nixon Stole

Democratic retreat from pro–civil rights carceral modernization is apparent in the transformation of their national party platforms since 1972. The 1972 Democratic platform endorsed felon re-enfranchisement, community-based rehabilitation facilities, and work-release furlough programs, and the 1976 platform promised "jobs, decent housing and educational opportunities [to] provide a real alternative to crime." The 1980 platform attributed crime and drug abuse to "the cumulative effect of joblessness, poor housing conditions and other factors." By 1984, however, the Democratic platform renounced "permissive liberalism" as the answer to crime, and in 1988, Democrats embraced the drug war as a defense for "the security of our nation." By 1992, the Democratic platform echoed Nixon's 1968 pledge "to restore government as the upholder of basic law-and-order for crime-ravaged communities," adding that the "most direct way to restore order in our cities is to put more police on the streets."[6] When President Clinton signed the Violent Crime Control and Law Enforcement Act of 1994, with its 100,000 new police officers and its 60 new capital crimes, he lionized the enactment as "the toughest, largest, smartest Federal attack on crime in the history of our country."[7] Adjectives in that order—tough, large, and then smart—marked Democratic priorities.

Electoral Defense, Racial Offense: Democrats and Mandatory Minimum Escalation

Consequences of Democratic punitive quiescence are evident in the massive proliferation of mandatory minimums from 1980 through 2010. Mandatory minimums trigger legislatively predetermined sentences upon conviction, and they warrant special attention because of their incredible force in driving mass incarceration.[8] On a methodological note, mandatory minimums are comparatively tractable measures of legislative activity. Unlike counts of U.S. Code provisions or statutory sections that carry a criminal penalty, counts of mandatory minimums have the comparative advantage of capturing "units" that meet a common level of punitiveness, that is, requiring incarceration for one year or more.[9] It is reasonable to (very cautiously) compare mandatory minimum enactments over time, and to do so, I traced all legislative enactments to establish, repeal, expand, or contract mandatory minimums from 1790 through year-end 2010 (n = 465). Figure 4.1 shows total congressional changes to mandatory minimums from 1790 to 2010, with total changes counted as the number

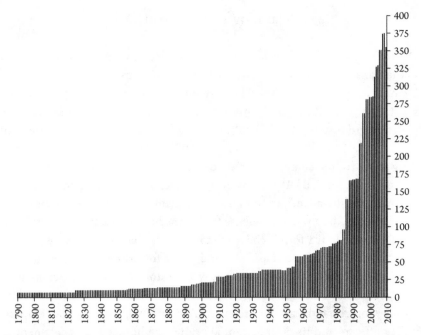

Figure 4.1 Cumulative Net Number of Mandatory Minimum Expansions, 1790–2010.
Note: Each bar represents the cumulative net number of changes to mandatory minimum statutes,
that is, the number of new and expanded mandatory minimums, minus the number of repealed and
reduced mandatory minimums. *Source*: Compiled by author.

of new or expanded mandatory minimums, minus the number of repealed or
contracted mandatory minimums.[10] Congress passed its first mandatory minimum statute in 1790, and the use of mandatory minimums has grown substan-
tially since then.

Between 1790 and 1950, mandatory minimum expansion remained limited,
with a slow steady growth from seven to 38 congressional expansions over more
than 150 years.[11] Moreover, mandatory minimums from 1790 through 1950
generally targeted crimes that were infrequent, minor, and decisively federal
in nature. These early mandatory minimums addressed piracy (life sentence,
passed in 1790), refusing to testify before Congress (one month, passed in
1857), bribing a federal inspector in the Baltimore or New York harbors (six
months, passed in 1888), trespassing on federal land for hunting or shooting
(five days, passed in 1897), forging the U.S. seal (one year, passed in 1906), dis-
obeying a cease-and-desist order (six months, passed in 1922), violation of the
Merchant Marine Act (one year, passed in 1936), and kidnapping during a bank
robbery (10 years, passed in 1948).

Cumulative net expansions quintupled from 1980 to 2000 (from 77 to
284). This staggering increase is all the more noteworthy because two terms
of tough-on-crime Reagan and Bush conservatism, from 1985 to 1992, added

72 cumulative net expansions, only to be outdone by Clinton's two terms that added 116 cumulative net expansions. Mandatory minimums added since 1985 address common crimes with high chances of state apprehension. (See Table A.4 for current federal mandatory minimums statutes.) Minimums passed during this period include a 15-year mandatory minimum for carrying a firearm with two prior convictions (passed in 1986); a one-year mandatory penalty enhancement for drug distribution to a person under age 21 (passed in 1986); a five-year mandatory minimum for possessing five grams of crack cocaine (passed in 1988); and a mandatory life sentence for the second or third violent offense (passed in 1994).

Many Democrats voted for mandatory minimums because they feared electoral reprimand for being soft on crime. Statements from Democrats, particularly House Democrats, revealed their anticipatory fear that a challenger would highlight a vote as soft on crime, and that voters would punish them. In the 1984 legislation, Congress passed the Sentencing Reform Act only when it was attached to a must-pass emergency spending measure. Sponsored by Representative Hamilton Fish (R-New York), the 1984 crime bill was approved by the Senate 91 to one in February 1984. Reagan held a press conference describing his crime bill as "long overdue" and chastising House Democrats for "dragging their feet." On September 25, 1984, Representative Dan Lungren (R-California) motioned to attach a brand new House bill, identical to the Senate bill, to a must-pass appropriations bill and send it to the full House for a vote. If the House delayed or failed to pass it, federal funding would freeze and the entire government would shut down. After months of rewriting and adding new sections to the Senate bill, House Democrats now faced a straight up-or-down vote on the same Senate bill they rejected in February. Under House rules, only five minutes of debate were permitted. After that parliamentary move, failure to pass the legislation would have meant partial government shutdown, a near death-knell for incumbents.

Many House Democrats opposed the legislation, as they had for the previous 11 years, primarily because of civil liberty concerns over preventative detention and the insanity provisions. Recognizing the electoral need to vote for the legislation, despite possible real opposition, House Speaker Thomas O'Neill (D-Massachusetts) told Democratic members to "go ahead" and vote for it if they needed to make a public stand against crime to boost their reelection options.[12] The House voted 243 to 166 to pass the legislation. Similarly, Democrats spoke candidly of how electoral pressures drove them to pass the Anti-Drug Abuse Act of 1986, which increased penalties for most federal drug crimes, authorized $1.7 billion for drug control, and amended the Safe Streets Act of 1968 to include grants to state and local law enforcement for narcotics assistance. As one of the 16 House Democrats to vote against the bill, Representative Mike Lowry (D-Washington) described the process as "legislation by political panic."

Representative Barney Frank (D-Massachusetts), who also voted against the legislation, described it as "the legislative equivalent of crack," as it was "going to give people a short-term high, but it is going to be dangerous in the long run and expensive to boot."[13]

Such statements were unsurprising from Democrats who voted *against* the 1986 legislation, but Democrats who voted *for* it expressed similar sentiments. Although many Democrats expressed reservations about the bill's new mandatory minimums, "how can you get caught voting against them?" asked Representative Nick Rahall II (D-West Virginia) after he joined the 378–16 majority for final passage on October 17, 1986. Rahall worried that excessively stiff penalties would discourage juries from convicting, but he concluded that his election challenger might "distort a no vote on some of these amendments." Representative Patricia Schroeder (D-Colorado) voted for final passage, but lamented that "in football there's a thing called piling on. I think we're seeing political piling on right before the election." Representative David McCurdy (D-Oklahoma) commented that anti-drug legislation was "out of control. But of course I'm for it." Representative Charles Schumer (D-New York), who also voted for final passage, described the "down side" of the 1986 Act as "you come up with policies too quickly" and "the policies are aimed at looking good rather than solving the problem." Representative Claude Pepper (D-Florida), who voted for final passage, characterized the state of Congress this way: "right now, you could put an amendment through to hang, draw and quarter.... That's what happens when you get on an emotional issue like this." The intensity of the anti-drug wave was evident in the 1986 mid-term elections: Republican incumbent Senator Paula Hawkins campaigned as the "General in the Senate's war on drugs," and her Democratic opponent Governor Bob Graham ran television ads showing himself standing next to an airplane found with smuggled drugs, calling for more military interdictions. Democratic incumbent Frank McCloskey of Indiana was forced to replay his admission of trying marijuana once in 1972. In the Democratic primary for Georgia's fifth district, John Lewis of SNCC fame took a drug test and challenged his opponent and fellow civil rights–era activist and icon Julian Bond to do the same.[14]

It was a lesson to the party that in the 1988 presidential campaign, Jesse Jackson criticized Reagan for *weakness* in the drug war and seemed to inspire fear in Republicans that Democrats were "poised to steal from our party what has been a traditional Republican issue—law enforcement." In the aftermath of the 1988 defeat, Charles Schumer (D-New York) in the House and Joseph Biden (D-Delaware) in the Senate strategized on how to put a Democratic "stamp on crime," especially on capital punishment.

Even Democrats who voted for Clinton's 1994 Violent Crime Control and Law Enforcement Act expressed electoral cynicism at their own party's victory.

Senator Sam Nunn (D-Georgia), who also voted for the legislation, stated: "It has become fairly predictable that every two years Congress will be debating a crime bill of some sort—it is a safe guess that, in another two years as the next election looms on the horizon, we will be doing this all over again. In an election-year rush to enact tough anticrime measures, I am concerned the Congress may be creating quick fixes that may sound good, but too often raise unrealistic expectations in the public's mind."[15]

Selecting Who Pays: The "Unacculturated, Unsocialized and Indigestible Lump of Young Men"

On its own, Democratic fear of electoral reprimand cannot explain the rapid escalation of mandatory minimums. The idea that it pays politically to be tough on crime has become a seemingly self-evident catchphrase; this maxim has achieved explanatory currency that is overpowering and, I argue, partially undeserved.[16] Federal lawmakers do not simply react to public fear and vengeance in blunt and uniform fashion; instead, there is a more specific calculus about when it does—and does not—pay to be tough on crime.

In this vein, drug-related mandatory minimums deserve attention for exacting the real-world cost of electoral fear. Between 1984 and 1990, roughly 60,000 people received mandatory minimum sentences; of these, about 90 percent were convicted for drug offenses. By 1999, federal drug offenders received an average sentence of six years, compared to the average sentence of seven years for violent offenders.[17] While most Democrats voted for mandatory minimums from 1984 onward, this Democratic "accommodation" to the punitive 1980s and 1990s was no simple effort to electorally make "crime pay."

The evolution of narcotics mandatory penalties responded to the racial distribution of narcotics arrestees and the construction of drug scares. As shown in Figure 4.2, Congress passed harsh drug-related mandatory minimums in 1951 and 1956, repealed them in 1970 even as public punitiveness hit new highs, and then passed them again in biennial fashion, beginning in 1984. As I discussed in Chapter 3, Congress began using mandatory minimums against entire categories of narcotics with the Boggs Act of 1951, and it fortified those mandatory penalties in the Narcotic Control Act of 1956. Narcotics arrests were 11 percent black and 67 percent white in 1933. By 1950, however, a year before Congress passed the Boggs Act, narcotics arrests were 50 percent black and 46 percent white. A year before Congress fortified narcotics penalties with the 1956 Narcotic Control Act, narcotics arrests were 63 percent black and 36 percent white. Concern about the racial composition of drug addicts infused congressional debates around the 1951 Boggs Acts and the 1956 Narcotic Control Act. Members of Congress were particularly concerned with dealers in

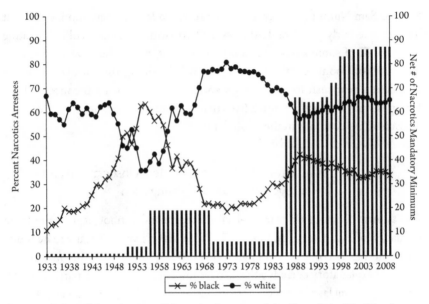

Figure 4.2 Racial Distribution of Narcotics Arrests and the Cumulative Net Number of Expansions to Narcotics Mandatory Minimums, 1933–2000. *Note:* Each bar represents the cumulative net number of changes to narcotics-related mandatory minimum statutes. *Source:* Distribution of arrests according to race, Federal Bureau of Investigation, *Uniform Crime Reports.*

predominantly black Harlem and Southside Chicago who peddled marijuana and heroin to children.[18]

Against the expectations of tough-on-crime opportunism, Congress *repealed* mandatory penalties for all drug violations in the Comprehensive Drug Abuse Prevention and Control Act of 1970. Members of Congress justified repeals with sweeping critiques of mandatory minimums, arguing that they hamper the process of rehabilitation, infringe on proper judicial roles, and exacerbate problems of youth alienation by enforcing a rigid and excessively punitive system. In particular, they rejected the inflexibility of mandatory minimums, suggesting that severe penalties wrongly punished casual violators as if they were hardened criminals.[19] Congressional critiques of mandatory minimums seem disingenuous, however, when we look at the totality of mandatory minimum reform during this period. In the same legislation that repealed drug-related mandatory minimums, Congress passed *new* mandatory penalties for participation in "continuing criminal enterprises." The same 91st Congress created new mandatory penalties in the Organized Crime Control Act of 1970, the D.C. Court Reorganization and Criminal Procedure Act, and the Amendments to the Safe Streets Act of 1968. Together, these new laws created mandatory penalties for carrying a firearm in any felony, for using a firearm in a robbery, for the second armed violent crime, and for using fire or explosives in any felony.

Congressional distrust of mandatory minimums seemed to apply only to drug-related penalties in 1970. Like the years preceding the Boggs Act, the years preceding the 1970 drug penalty repeal also saw a racial reversal in national narcotics arrests. Narcotics arrests in 1954 were 63 percent black and 36 percent white. By 1969, the year before Congress repealed the narcotics penalties of the Boggs Act and its progeny, narcotics arrests were 22 percent black and 77 percent white. In contrast to political rhetoric surrounding the Boggs Act and its progeny, political rhetoric surrounding the 1970 repeals reflected sympathy for drug addicts and sensitivity to how mandatory minimums inflexibly punish upstanding citizens and hardened criminals alike. In words reflecting generalized sympathy for drug addicts, Representative John Jarman (D-Oklahoma) framed drug addiction as "one of the most important health problems existing in the United States today," adding that drug addiction "is a criminal offense only because we have made it one." Members of Congress worried that retaining mandatory penalties for "professional criminals" in "continuing criminal enterprises" could unintentionally injure college students. House Democrats warned that the definition of "professional criminals" could potentially include a group of college students, living together, habitually smoking and exchanging marijuana. Inflexible mandatory penalties, they warned, would make this group wrongly subject to a mandatory 10-year prison sentence.[20]

A decade and a half later, Congress' stance on mandatory drug penalties reversed once again, and Congress passed mandatory drug penalties in 1984, 1986, and 1988. The decade preceding these laws saw a notable change in racial distribution of national narcotics arrests. As shown in Figure 4.2, narcotics arrests were 20 percent black and 78 percent white in 1974. By 1983, the year before Congress began passing narcotics penalties again, narcotics arrests were 30 percent black and 69 percent white, and by 1987 narcotics arrests were 36 percent black and 63 percent white. White arrestees were still in the majority, and this changing racial distribution was not nearly as dramatic as the racial reversals preceding Boggs and the 1970 repeals. Nonetheless, in this round of congressional drug penalty passage, political rhetoric and policy design were forcefully and unmistakably race-laden. Congress gave crack possession and trafficking some of the most punitive mandatory minimums in its history. In the Anti-Drug Abuse Act of 1986, Congress established the infamous 100-to-1 ratio, giving a five-year mandatory minimum for trafficking 500 grams of powder cocaine or five grams of crack cocaine. In the Anti-Drug Abuse Act of 1988, Congress set a five-year mandatory *minimum* for first-time possession of more than five grams of crack; first-time possession for any other illegal substance, however, remained a misdemeanor punishable by a *maximum* of one year in prison.

Consequences of the 1986 and 1988 Anti-Drug Abuse Acts were apparent almost immediately. By 1993, African Americans accounted for 88.3 percent of all federal crack cocaine distribution convictions, Latinos 7.1 percent, whites 4.1 percent, and Asians and Native Americans 0.5 percent. In the same year, racial breakdown for federal powder cocaine distributions were 32.0 percent white, 27.4 percent black, 39.3 percent Latino, and 1.3 percent Asian and Native American. By way of reference, note that the 1991 Household Survey on Drug Use and Health found that, of all those reporting "crack" cocaine use, 52 percent were white, 38 percent were black, and 10 percent were Latino. Of all those reporting powder cocaine use, 75 percent were white, 15 percent were black, and 10 percent were Latino.[21] Mandatory penalties also exacerbate intersectional marginalization. Of the women convicted of drug felonies in state courts, almost half are convicted solely on possession charges. Additionally, sentencing does not account for the possibility of coercion from an abusive male partner who deals, and it is not a "mitigating circumstance" to be the sole guardian caring for a child. Nationally, African American women convicted of drug felonies are sentenced to prison 41 percent of the time, while similarly convicted white women are sentenced to prison 24 percent of the time. Indeed, agents of the Drug Enforcement Agency acknowledge and defend gendered racial profiling. In sworn testimony, DEA agents have attested to the baseline presumption that most drug couriers are black females, and that being Hispanic or black was part of the profile they used to identify drug traffickers.[22]

Enactment of drug-related mandatory minimums varied by racial composition of narcotics arrestees and race-specific constructions of the pharmacological consequences of drug use. In opium scares of the 1880s and 1890s, for example, lawmakers perceived great danger in opium smoking, associated with Chinese Americans, with other forms of opium use considered more benign. Cocaine scares of the 1910s referenced "Negro cocaine madness," as if the pharmacological consequences varied by racial group; marijuana scares of the 1930s linked "reefer madness" to the "Mexican menace," as if the problem of marijuana was a problem of foreign invasion into American life. This kind of race coding of pharmacology and criminalization persisted during the civil rights and post–civil rights era: the harshest narcotics mandatory minimums in American history were enacted in the 1950s, as heroin was constructed as the drug from "Red China," spreading among black communist radicals and jazz musicians. These minimums were then repealed as drug arrests escalated for white people in the 1970s.[23]

With "crack" cocaine as the central punitive target, lawmakers argued that crack reduced its users to their most base selves. As a representation of black degeneration, crack cocaine made the men violent and the women lascivious, with defects transmitted genetically, as the children were born frenzied, uneducable, and menacing. This was Moynihan's dysfunctional black family on drugs. "When we talk about drug abuse," we "are talking about...young males in the inner city," Senator Moynihan (D-New York) announced in 1986, as if spilling a secret. Old Democratic allies agreed. Adam Walinsky, a New York Democrat and former aide to Robert F. Kennedy, published the editorial "Crack as a Scapegoat" in the *New York Times*. Citing Moynihan's 1965 analysis as a model, Walinsky argued that crack was a scapegoat for the real problem of "disintegrating families and neighborhoods." Walinsky noted that in 1966, 75 percent of black children were "still being born into families with fathers present, married to the mothers." But by 1976, "when today's 10-year-olds were born," only about half of black children were born into two-parent families. Single black mothers were "prepar[ing] a disaster: the steady growth in our midst of an unacculturated, unsocialized and indigestible lump of young men" who are likely to see crime as "the definition of self." At root, Walinsky argued, "we must decide that we will not live with a black illegitimacy rate in excess of 60 percent." In the same vein, an editorial by Pulitzer Prize–winning journalist Edwin Yoder Jr. titled "We Know Who Will Lose the Drug War" asserted that "illicit drugs are implicated in the decline in social discipline and control," especially for the "urban underclass" for whom "drugs and crime have become an expression of social defiance and alienation."[24] When confronted with the U.S. Sentencing Commission's 1995 recommendation to reduce crack-related penalties, President Clinton opposed "equalizing" penalties; his obligation to protect devastated communities trumped his heartfelt "concern with the number of young African-Americans who enter the criminal justice system."[25]

Like notions of black degeneration, the conventional wisdom on crack retained its power through racial ideology, not science. From its introduction in the *New England Journal of Medicine* in 1985, the term "crack baby" has troubled researchers. Researchers saw three problems: first, lack of control groups between cocaine and non-cocaine using mothers; second, absence of long-term effects, as differences at birth disappeared by age two; third, and perhaps most important, inability to distinguish differential impacts between powder and crack cocaine. As a pseudo-scientific notion, the idea of the "crack baby" allowed projections from all sides.[26] It was the nightmare of the deprived, self-reproducing "underclass" and the conservative nightmare of costly racial degeneration. After visiting a Harlem hospital in 1986, Senator Moynihan described the horror of one-pound "crack babies" and in 1988 cited the existence of 5,000 children "born with crack in their urine" in New York City hospitals, even though urine tests could not distinguish between powder and crack cocaine. Representative Bruce Vento (D-Minnesota), who also supported crack mandatory minimums, asserted "the past several years have seen an astronomical rise in the incidence of substance abuse among pregnant women, particularly the use of cocaine and crack." In 1986, the year Congress established the 100-to-1 ratio and protected "crack babies," the black infant mortality rate was more than twice the white infant mortality rate, with recent spikes stemming from 1982 Medicaid cuts that limited maternal care.[27]

Punishment was protection—for black children, black communities, and taxpayers alike. Crack babies were "jittery, irritable and hyperactive," explained Senator Paula Hawkins (R-Florida), who added as the policy punch line that, "saving the life of one of these babies can cost as much as $135,000. And tax-payers...will pay for decades for these children." As justification for his 1988 amendment to require a mandatory minimum for crack possession, Republican Senator Jesse Helms of North Carolina cited these harms to children: two-thirds of New York's infant abuse cases involved parents who were drug addicts, and 12 percent of babies born in 1985 were cocaine-exposed. Although Helms marshaled this evidence to criminalize "crack" possession specifically, neither datum was crack-specific. Moynihan and Helms set "crack" mandatory minimums even before *Washington Post* columnist Charles Krauthammer penned the crack baby's birth announcement: "The inner-city crack epidemic is now giving birth to the newest horror, a bio-underclass, a generation of physically damaged cocaine babies whose biological inferiority is stamped at birth."[28]

Lawmakers defended "crack" mandatory minimums as a way of "caring about" African American communities. After the U.S. Sentencing Commission recommended reform in 1995, members of the Congressional Black Caucus, including Maxine Waters, endorsed reduction of the 100-to-1 ratio. In response, Republican Bob Barr of Georgia accused CBC members of "going lenient on people who traffic death in *their communities.*" Members of the CBC were also reminded of their initial endorsement of "crack" mandatory minimums—13 of 20 voting members of the CBC had voted for the Anti-Drug Abuse Act of 1986, and eight of 22 voting members had approved the Anti-Drug Abuse Act of 1988—even though they had now retracted support. Representative McCollum made sure to note that the District of Columbia police chief, chief prosecutor, and chief trial judge, "who are all African-Americans," did not want equalization between powder and "crack" cocaine.[29]

After nearly 25 years of damage, Congress enacted the Fair Sentencing Act of 2010 to eliminate the penalty for simple possession, reducing the ratio from 100-to-1 to 18-to-1. One of the few opponents to the Fair Sentencing Act, Republican Lamar Smith of Texas retold the story of the Anti-Drug Abuse Act of 1986 as a rescue effort: when crack cocaine ravished cities, "these communities cried out for help, and in 1986 Congress responded." For supporters of the Fair Sentencing Act, the crack penalties were good intentions gone awry. California Republican Dan Lungren voted for the Anti-Drug Abuse Acts of 1986 and 1988, and, more than two decades later, he voted for their partial repeal. With some humility, Lungren recalled his 1986 cohort as having acted rashly and uninformed: "We initially came out of committee with a 20-to-1 ratio. By the time we finished on the floor, it was 100-to-1. We didn't really have an evidentiary basis for it, but that's what we did, thinking we were doing the right thing at the time." The lesson, for Lungren, was tragic. "Certainly, one of the sad ironies in this entire episode is that a bill which was characterized by some as a response to the crack epidemic in African American communities has led to racial sentencing disparities which simply cannot be ignored."[30]

Repurposing Big Government

Through three consecutive Republican presidencies, conservatives successfully ensconced crime, drug use, affirmative action, welfare, and immigration in a common language of personal responsibility and just deserts. In this context, Clinton's turn to "punishment, police, and protection" was undoubtedly an electoral strategy. In renouncing the extremes of "tough or compassionate" crime policy, Clinton played the New Democrats' leitmotif of the centrist "third way," its tone of flexibility crafted by the Democratic Leadership Council with hopes of wooing white swing voters and Reagan Democrats. For Clinton Democrats, the strategy was to outbid on a range of issues, some clearly punitive (like long mandatory minimums), some ambiguously punitive (like community policing), and some not punitive (like drug treatment and midnight basketball).

As early as October 1993, staffers warned Clinton about "the prospect of a bidding war in both houses, in which Republicans and even liberal Democrats would compete to prove that they care more about crime than the administration. Senator Biden and others are urging us to *pre-empt this debate by pledging more* resources for cops, drug treatment, and prisons."[31] The strategy of upward bidding was well vetted within the Clinton administration, as evidenced in a memo to him from his advisors Bruce Reed and José Cerda: "Biden strongly believes that the Administration needs to *seize control of the issue by upping the ante.* On Friday, [White House Chief of Staff] Mack McLarty convened a meeting with the Attorney General and White House senior staff to address this matter. There is no disagreement on the merits or the politics of putting more money into the Administration's key anti-crime programs."[32] Crime would become a Democratic asset through the strategy of "upping the ante," with agreement between the White House, the attorney general, and Senator Biden on the merits and politics of more and more. In upping the ante, White House staffers supported mandatory minimums in part because they saw them as inconsequential compared to the larger battle for funding, especially money for community policing and Police Corps, boot camps, drug courts, policing in schools, and deportation of "criminal aliens." In this vein, staffers noted that "adding or not adding 12 new minimums to the federal books is not likely to have much of an impact." Because of this estimation of limited impact, staffers said the administration should "avoid making the more controversial elements of the crime bill a point of public focus."[33]

Upping the ante across issues, and doing so in a single omnibus bill, was central to maintaining a large voting coalition and inhibiting the opposition of liberal House Democrats and the Congressional Black Caucus. White House staff prioritized a large, comprehensive omnibus crime bill, because liberal House Democrats like "Don Edwards, Craig Washington, [and] John Conyers [would] continue to push for the House's approach of passing a series of crime prevention grant programs. This [was] unacceptable from the administration's perspective." The White House staff envisioned a "comprehensive and balanced" crime bill that would include "more cops, boot camps and drug courts; reasonable gun controls; and, where appropriate, increased penalties, including the death penalty."[34] In acknowledging that House Democratic Judiciary Chair Jack Brooks "may have to go further to the left than we would like," staffers anticipated that "the most likely place to attract votes [was] from conservative Democrats and moderate Republicans." With regard to the CBC, Clinton staffers accepted that a majority would not support the bill, and the goal was therefore to "make sure that they [the CBC] [did] not make it one of their priorities to stop the bill." In a telling gesture of racial symbolism, this memo added, under a section headed "CBC," that maybe Clinton should start "reaching out to Norm Early, a Clinton supporter and head of the Black Prosecutors."[35] An omnibus package was thus preferred; it was the parliamentary device that would capture the "blended" stance of Clinton Democrats, the alleged third way of the New Democrats. House Democratic Caucus talking points, as written by Clinton speechwriter Jonathan Prince, repeatedly emphasized, in his words, that "there [was] a lot in it for everyone." Clinton's "third way" was expressed legislatively through omnibus piling, with Clinton's crime philosophy of rejecting "the false choice between tough punishment and smart prevention."[36]

With urgency and self-aware historical weightiness, Clinton's top staffers pressed crime as a realignment issue: "You have a chance to seize one of the two most powerful realignment issues (along with health care) that will come your way, at a time when public concern about crime is the highest it has been since Richard Nixon *stole the issue from the Democrats in 1968*."[37] Advisers pressed the possible historical parallel between Clinton and "Robert Kennedy's day," when "crime was a linchpin that helped hold a Democratic majority together across racial and class lines." Clinton therefore had the opportunity to "unite the country on an issue that . . . divided our party and our nation for three decades," and he was "the first Democratic candidate since RFK to speak credibly about crime."[38] Similarly, Biden's crime strategy memos emphasized Democratic issue ownership throughout. He called for "rapid enactment of the Biden/Clinton" bill "(to reinforce that this is a *Democratic* initiative)," and his strategy goals were to "maintain crime as a Democratic initiative," to "control the agenda" through the 1994 election, and to pass a bill with more police, penalties, and prevention that satisfied "all sectors of the party."[39]

Upping the punitive ante complemented Clinton's imperative to remake big government. Clinton's top domestic policy strategists saw a "natural link between reinventing government and fighting crime." In a stinging example of what some have called carceral neoliberalism, Clinton planned to fund police and prisons with the money "saved" by cutting 252,000 employees from the federal payroll, with a "swap" of funds to occur through creation of the so-called Violent Crime Reduction Trust Fund. The linkage was partly a reflection of government expertise ("steer government away from things it doesn't know how to do, into things government can do best"), and partly a reflection of what counts as a legitimate government job ("reduce the bureaucracy by 100,000 and use the money to help put 100,000 new police on the street").[40]

The cumulative effect of Clinton's "remaking big government" increased the likelihood of being swept into a vast carceral archipelago. New Democrats opened more paths to incarceration, especially for people of color, immigrants, and poor people. For people enmeshed in the web of school policing, immigration control, and drug laws, it became clear the criminal justice system was not "on the other side of a fixed line of law."[41] Community policing, and the extension of policing through immigration and social welfare and schools, repurposed an already meager social safety net to serve as part of the criminal justice net.

As he rallied for community policing, President Clinton's staging and rhetoric reflected the moment of advanced and secondary marginalization, when heightened stratification within and between racial groups only raised the symbolic power of uniformed people of color policing their own.[42] While Truman's 1947 right to safety took aim at the white supremacist violence of lynching and police brutality, Clinton's "first civil right" referenced cities caught in an internecine war, in which African American, Latino, and immigrant people deserved protection from the worst of their own kind. The 1992 national Democratic Party platform referred to geographically discrete inner cities as "crime-ravaged communities" where "crime is not only a symptom but also a major cause of the worsening poverty and demoralization that afflicts inner city communities." Even as New Democrats punished the "Willie Hortons," they also positioned themselves as protectors of respectable, middle-class people of color, a distinction achieved by Clinton's personal rhetorical savvy and, more significant, the internal economic stratification of African Americans. Clinton's Democratic Party politicked on different economic grounds than did Truman Democrats. In 1992, as Clinton campaigned, the poorest quintile of African Americans had *lost* 30 percent of its

1947 income; the richest quintile, however, had gained eight percent over its comparatively high 1947 income.[43]

What became Clinton's flagship Violent Crime Control and Law Enforcement Act of 1994 was decidedly punitive, but the enactment retained certain signatures of liberal law-and-order. In the spirit of fighting (black) crime by engendering trust in carceral machinery, Clinton supported hiring more police officers under the banner of "community-oriented policing," a conveniently ambiguous term easily packaged to suggest that a friendly, racially diverse police force would foster neighborhood goodwill. As he made good on his campaign promise to propose legislation to put 100,000 more cops on the streets, Clinton stood against a backdrop of some two dozen police officers, all in uniform, nearly half of whom appeared to be people of color (Figure 4.3). This was a distorted selection of full-time local police department employees in 1993. Of the roughly 474,000 full-time local police department employees in 1993, only 11.3 percent were black, only 6.2 percent Latino, only 1.5 percent Native American Indian or Asian American. In addition, only 8.8 percent of police department employees were female, by a count that treats each category as distinct. By my count of this photo, there were 25 officers, 11 of which appear to be black or brown.[44]

Two months after Clinton launched his Community Oriented Policing Services (COPS) initiative, his Domestic Policy Council still referred to

Figure 4.3 President Clinton with Police Officers, 1993. *Note*: On August 11, 1993, President Clinton introduced his anti-crime plan using a backdrop of (disproportionately black and brown) law enforcement officers. *Source*: Photograph courtesy of the William J. Clinton Presidential Library.

community policing as a "philosophy—not a program."[45] As a philosophy, "community policing" floated in the ether, along with phrases like "prevention through partnership." Since Title I of the Violent Crime Control and Law Enforcement Act of 1994, which created the COPS program, did not define "community policing," the newly established COPS Office, housed in the DOJ, wrote its own mandate: "Community policing is a philosophy that promotes organizational strategies, which support the systematic use of partnerships and problem-solving techniques, to proactively address the immediate conditions that give rise to public safety issues such as crime, social disorder, and fear of crime."[46] What is striking is not the puffed-up verbiage, reminiscent of a McKinsey & Company mission statement; rather, my interest is in the bundling of such a wide range of issues—"public safety issues such as crime, social disorder, and fear of crime." It is hard to imagine what is excluded from such a definition.

When the National Institute of Justice (NIJ) evaluated COPS grantees, it acknowledged that Title I left "community policing" undefined. To fulfill its charge to evaluate Clinton's "philosophy," the NIJ delivered its own definition of community policing. Community policing, according to the NIJ, had two dominant characteristics: (1) an emphasis on problem solving, and (2) community involvement and partnerships among police, community members, and organizations. With this definition in hand, the NIJ surveyed, interviewed, and visited COPS-grantees of local or county law enforcement to see how their definition matched practice. Based on survey responses, roughly 60 percent of COPS-funded officers spent only some, little, or none of their time performing the core philosophy tasks of community policing—solving problems and building partnerships with communities. Instead, fully one quarter of COPS-funded officers spent "most or all" of their time on "quality of life" policing, that is, the style of aggressive misdemeanor arrests and stop-and-frisks made famous by New York City police commissioner William Bratton. In practice, community policing was the latest catchphrase in a "long tradition of circumlocutions whose purpose is to conceal, mystify, and legitimate police distribution of nonnegotiably coercive force."[47]

Clinton's welfare and immigration reforms expanded "community policing" by another name. With panicked calls to control "illegal immigration," Congress bundled immigration provisions in the Violent Crime Control and Law Enforcement Act of 1994. The legislation allocated $1.2 billion to strengthen border control and enable faster deportation of those denied asylum, and $1.8 billion to help states pay for incarcerating undocumented immigrants convicted of felonies. Funding states to deport "criminal aliens," the 1994 enactment delivered roughly 90 percent of deportation funding to five states: California, Texas, Florida, New Jersey, and New York. White House staffers urged President

Clinton and Vice President Gore to present deportation checks, personally, to each state's governor.[48] The Illegal Immigration Reform and Immigrant Responsibility Act of 1996 (IIRIRA) further enmeshed immigration with criminal justice machinery. It authorized judges to issue deportation orders as part of a probation or plea agreement and required non-citizens to be deported if they committed a crime with a sentence of one or more years (rather than the previous benchmark of five or more years); given the simultaneous mandatory minimum escalation, even the most minor offenses would trigger deportation. IIRIRA also imposed a penalty of up to five years in prison for knowingly helping an undocumented immigrant apply for aid, and it authorized $5 million for a database to track "criminal aliens." In 1984, federal prisons held 1,204 non-citizens for drug offenses, but by the end of the Clinton administration, this figure had increased 15-fold to 18,594, even though undocumented people and legal permanent residents were more likely than U.S. citizens to play a minor, low-level role in the transaction.[49]

The Personal Responsibility and Work Opportunity Reconciliation Act of 1996 (PRWORA) replaced federal income support with a federal block grant program called Temporary Assistance to Needy Families (TANF) that allowed states to create their own welfare programs. Federal provisions tagged some groups for permanent exclusion: people with drug felony convictions, and immigrants (with some exceptions). The 1996 Act banned those with drug felony convictions from using food stamps and temporary assistance.[50] The same legislation banned parole and probation violators from TANF, food stamps, Supplemental Security Income, and housing assistance. The drug felon exclusion, an amendment sponsored by Senator Phil Gramm (R-Texas), passed after two minutes of debate. The only voice of protest came from Senator Edward Kennedy, who underscored criminological inconsistencies, arguing that, "under this amendment, if you are a murderer, a rapist, or a robber, you can get Federal funds; but if you are convicted even for possession of marijuana, you cannot."[51] Given the high rate of drug felony convictions, the Gramm amendment permanently denied eligibility for an enormous population. Of the 347,774 felony drug convictions in state courts in 1996, roughly 40 percent (135,270) were for possession. Since drug felon exclusions were permanent, the cumulative number of persons denied welfare would grow every year. By earmarking drug felons as subject to special punishment, these laws magnified the harm of one of the most racially selective areas of the criminal justice system. Simultaneously, PRWORA repurposed aid for surveillance by requiring agencies that administer welfare block grants, Supplemental Security Income, and housing assistance to provide quarterly reports with the names and addresses of people residing unlawfully in the United States. As a result, the receipt of TANF, food stamps, and Medicaid by lawful permanent residents plummeted after PRWORA.

Though some food stamp cuts were restored in 1998, fear of deportation inhibited parents from applying for food stamps for their eligible children, and many state agencies, confused about eligibility stipulations, mistakenly turned away eligible immigrants.[52]

To Proceduralize Death

In the period of zero executions between 1968 and 1976, it appeared that the United States might follow other democracies and abolish capital punishment. With execution seen as the hallmark of fascism, many countries abolished capital punishment following World War II, and abolition accelerated with rising international consensus that capital punishment violated human rights. Death penalty abolition spread throughout Italy (1944), West Germany (1949), Austria (1950), New Zealand (1961), Great Britain (1969), Portugal (1976), Spain (1978), and France (1981). In the early 1970s, it seemed that liberals were on the precipice of abolishing capital punishment. Executions in non-southern states had dropped through the 1940s, and executions in southern states waned through the 1960s, such that by 1966 there was only one execution in the nation.[53]

This section explores the road not taken—death penalty abolition, a proposal so popular in 1972 that it appeared in the national Democratic Party platform. How is it, then, that the number of crimes punishable by death escalated so dramatically, from only one in 1974, to three in 1988, to 66 by 1994? By tracing proposals in the critical window of expansion, from the 100th to the 103rd Congress, I find that the total number of capital crimes increased via alternate high bids between Democratic and Republican legislators. That is, the trend I discover is a death penalty bidding war in which the two parties vied for the toughest proposal by "upping" the number of death-eligible crimes with a new bill or amendment. In my account of this dramatic escalation, two factors are especially important. First, the road from abolition to escalation was paved with proposals to improve death penalty administration. Liberal abolitionists framed their opposition in conditional administrative terms rather than unconditional anti-violence terms. In so doing, abolitionists left open pathways for implementation of a new, improved, routinized death penalty. Second, in the escalation of capital crime statutes, Democratic Party defensiveness against racial lenience in crime policy propelled their punitive race-to-the-top. In the end, Democratic Party capacity to compete in bidding wars hinged on its willingness to forfeit the Congressional Black Caucus's Racial Justice Act, the legislative answer to *McCleskey* that would have allowed statistically based challenges to the racial fairness of individual death sentences.

From "Unbridled Discretion" to "Clear and Objective Standards"

A trilogy of cases—*Furman v. Georgia* (1972), *Gregg v. Georgia* (1976), and *McCleskey v. Kemp* (1987)—demonstrates how the liberals' racial procedural-ism, with its critique of racism nested within critiques of administrative weak-ness, remained vulnerable to conservative co-optation. The Supreme Court "suspended" the death penalty with *Furman v. Georgia* in 1972, when it deemed unconstitutional the "unbridled discretion" of death penalty administration. The *Furman v. Georgia* case involved a young black man, 25-year-old William Henry Furman, accused of breaking into a house and murdering the white male resi-dent. The five-to-four *Furman* decision hit no single message, with each Justice writing a separate concurrence or dissent, but a common denominator among the majority was that the death penalty was administered in an arbitrary fash-ion. In all murder charges, prosecutors had carte blanche discretion to decide which defendant should face capital punishment. The *Furman* decision hence concluded that, as currently administered, there was "no meaningful basis for distinguishing the few cases" in which capital punishment was imposed from the many cases in which it was not. At the time, Georgia and the 40-plus death sen-tencing jurisdictions instructed one jury to make two judgments: (1) whether the defendant was guilty of the capital crime; and, if so, (2) whether to deliver the verdict of "guilty with mercy" or "guilty without mercy." Jurors received no instructions as to what, if anything, merited mercy.[54]

Overall, *Furman's* challenge to capital punishment was meek: the death pen-alty constituted "cruel and unusual" punishment to the extent that it was admin-istered in arbitrary fashion. Only two justices, William Brennan and Thurgood Marshall, held that the death penalty was intrinsically unconstitutional rather than merely unconstitutionally administered. Justice Marshall also noted in his concurring opinion that, of the 455 persons sentenced to death for rape since 1930, a full 405 were black.[55] In many ways, *Furman's* mixed rejection of capital punishment reflected the scattered liberal advocacy of the day. Through the late 1960s, the NAACP Legal Defense and Educational Fund sought death penalty abolition via administrative perfection. Pursuing litigation to increase proce-dural protections and to liberalize habeas corpus, the NAACP LDF strategized that courts and the public would eventually conclude that error-free capital sen-tencing was impossible. Moreover, they suspected that counties using capital punishment on the cheap could not sustain, in the long run, the costs of meticu-lously proceduralized capital trials. While seeing the death penalty itself as "cruel and unusual punishment," the NAACP LDF pursued a multi-pronged litigation strategy that deemed the death penalty administratively arbitrary *and* intrinsi-cally unconstitutional.[56]

Similarly, various Democrats packaged death penalty opposition in utilitarian, administrative, and racial terms. In 1968, for example, the Senate held hearings on Senator Philip Hart's (D-Michigan) bill to commute all death sentences to life in prison, with Senator Hart's justifications couched in terms of weak deterrent effect and administrative discrimination. At the hearings, Attorney General Ramsey Clark called for abolition because of weak deterrent effect, adding that "racial discrimination occurs in the administration of capital punishment," and it is "the poor, the weak, the ignorant, the hated who are executed." Here, Clark, perceived as among the most radical of Great Society liberal Democrats, indicted capital punishment on criminological, administrative, and racial grounds. Even the 1972 Democratic platform called for "abolishing capital punishment" because it was commonly "recognized as an ineffective deterrent to crime, unequally applied, and cruel and excessive punishment."[57] In sum, many abolitionists critiqued capital punishment for its procedural quality—too much discretion and too little protection for the marginalized.

Herein lay their vulnerability: too many abolitionists rejected capital punishment on (conditional) administrative grounds rather than on (unconditional) principled grounds of the limits of state violence. Ultimately, abolitionist reasoning aligned with the minimalist holding of *Furman*: the death penalty constituted "cruel and unusual" punishment because it was *administered* in arbitrary and discriminatory fashion.[58] If the trouble with capital punishment was "unbridled discretion," then what was the solution? One year after *Furman*, a group of experts appointed to President Nixon's National Commission on Criminal Justice Standards and Goals answered this question in telling extremes. In general, Nixon's Commission prioritized a simplified penalty structure à la the Model Penal Code, and death penalty states needed especially crisp lines of criminal liability. The Commission then concluded its capital punishment discussion with this interpretation of *Furman*:

> Consideration of the scope of aggravated murder and the extent of non-culpability because of mental disease or disorder will be more difficult in a State with the death penalty than in one in which the death penalty has been abolished. However, the character of the debate is markedly different today in light of the Supreme Court's decision that capital punishment in its present form constitutes a denial of equal protection and a form of cruel and unusual punishment. (See *Furman v. Georgia*, 408 U.S. 238 (1972). L. Ed. 2d 346, 92 C Ct. 2726, 40 *Law Week* 4923.) The only option open to a legislature appears to be *to require capital punishment for all persons convicted of the crime to which it attaches, without any exercise of discretion.*[59]

The Nixon Commission offered a simple deduction: if the problem was death via administrative discretion, then the solution was death via requirement. Mandatory capital punishment was the "only option open to a legislature" post-*Furman*. The Nixon Commission therefore advised legislatures to define death-required crimes with precision, to circumscribe the exact scope of aggravated murder, and to set clear standards for exculpatory mental illnesses. Then, if the defendant is found guilty, it should be mandated to execute him or her "without any exercise of discretion." To be clear, the Nixon Commission's statement "to require capital punishment" was not their position of advocacy; it was their interpretation of "the only option."

Following this logic, it becomes clear that condemning capital punishment for its arbitrary nature invited three solutions: execute every convicted murderer, execute no convicted murderer, or enhance administration to maximize rationality. With *Gregg v. Georgia* in 1976, the Supreme Court followed the third solution. *Gregg* outlined procedural mechanisms to structure capital sentencing, through, among other specifications, bifurcated guilt and sentencing phases, and instructions for considering aggravating and mitigating factors in penalty decisions.[60] When the Court upheld the constitutionality of death penalty administration in *Gregg v. Georgia*, it affirmed additional procedures, required separate trials for guilt and for sentencing, and called for the state high court to conduct review on direct appeal.

In *McCleskey v. Kemp* (1987), the Supreme Court faced an Eighth and Fourteenth Amendment challenge to Georgia's administration of the death penalty. The defendant, Warren McCleskey, argued that Georgia administered the death penalty in a racially discriminatory manner, thus violating both the Eighth Amendment and the equal protection clause of the Fourteenth Amendment. The challenge reposed on David Baldus's research of over 2,000 Georgia murder cases in the 1970s. Controlling for 29 nonracial variables, Baldus found that defendants charged with killing white victims were 4.3 times more likely to be condemned to death than those charged with killing black victims. Black defendants were 1.1 times more likely to receive the death penalty than were white defendants.

In a five-to-four decision, the Court rejected statistical disparity as proof of violation of equal protection. Writing for the majority, Justice Powell viewed statistics as insufficient proof of the "purposeful discrimination" necessary for violation of the equal protection clause. Statistics were also insufficient to demonstrate a "constitutionally significant risk of racial bias affecting the... capital-sentencing process" impermissible under the cruel and unusual punishment clause. Scholars rightly explain *McCleskey* as a deadly consequence of interpreting anti-discrimination law as a narrow prohibition of intentional bias. By the *McCleskey* standard, any defendant who alleged an equal protection violation had "the burden of proving 'the existence of purposeful discrimination'" and pinpointing precisely the way in which "the purposeful discrimination 'had a discriminatory effect' on him."[61] In short, the criminal justice system began with the presumption of innocence, that is, the presumption of no racism. Overcoming this presumption required proof of purposeful, intentional, direct discrimination.

By this standard, the *McCleskey* Court searched for discrimination at each criminal justice checkpoint and found no procedural violation and no unacceptable levels of discretion. First, each jury was unique and "selected from a properly constituted venire." Second, while prosecutors could select who was brought on capital charges with wide discretion, clear state laws and federal constitutional requirements adequately circumscribed prosecutorial discretion. Third, the Georgia state legislature had addressed all procedural concerns of *Furman* with new, improved, detailed procedure. Georgia's enhanced death penalty administration provided two separate proceedings, one trial for guilt and another for sentencing proceedings. New statutes enumerated aggravating circumstances to narrow the class of murders subject to capital punishment. Georgia had devised clear standards for the defendant to use mitigating evidence. After considering these administrative improvements, the *McCleskey* Court concluded: "Thus, while some jury discretion still exists, 'the discretion to be exercised is controlled by clear and objective standards so as to produce nondiscriminatory application.'"[62]

In sum, *McCleskey* found the criminal justice system racially innocent by virtue of its overwhelming, inescapable guilt. "In its broadest form," wrote Powell for the majority, "McCleskey's claim of discrimination extend[ed] to every actor in the Georgia capital sentencing process, from the prosecutor who sought the death penalty to the jury that imposed the sentence to the State itself that enacted the capital punishment statute that allows it to remain in effect, despite its allegedly discriminatory application." A charge of discriminatory outcomes implied that all actors were guilty, and Powell concluded flatly, "this claim must fail." Racial disparity was "an inevitable part of our criminal justice system," in Powell's logic. Ergo, if racial disparity constituted discrimination, then the entire system was illegitimate. "If we accepted *McCleskey*'s claim that racial bias has impermissibly tainted the capital sentencing decision," reasoned Powell, then "we could soon be faced with similar claims as to other types of penalty." In response to Powell's acknowledgment of widespread racial disparity throughout the criminal justice system, Justice Brennan wrote in his dissent, "Such a statement seems to suggest a fear of too much justice."[63]

Many abhorred *McCleskey*. A *New York Times* editorial asserted that *McCleskey* "effectively condoned the expression of racism," and Anthony Amsterdam, one of the lawyers who argued for *Furman*, called *McCleskey* "the *Dred Scott* decision of our time." Despite the fact that *McCleskey* met sharp criticism, for members of Congress it provided a constitutional resolution to debates about the relationship among racial disparity, racial discrimination, and fair administration. As legal scholar Rory Little has suggested, the *McCleskey* decision gave formal resolution to racial suspicions and "helped break the legislative logjam" on capital punishment. The mid-1980s confluence of landslide Republican victories, the creation of the "centrist" Democratic Leadership Council, and the *McCleskey* ruling moved Democratic leadership toward a new position on the death penalty.[64]

Death Penalty Bidding Wars, 1988–1994

Before the Federal Death Penalty Act of 1994, housed within Title VI of Clinton's Violent Crime Control and Law Enforcement Act, Congress had enacted only three capital crimes since *Furman*'s 1972 injunction: one related to airplane hijacking in 1974 and two related to drug "kingpins" in 1988. Prior to 1988, Democratic resistance ensured that the number of capital crimes remained low. In establishing the 1974 capital crime, the Senate conservative coalition voted to reinstate the death penalty in its entirety, but House Democrats held the line at death penalty reform for one crime only—murder during a plane hijacking. New procedures applied to that crime exclusively. In 1984, the Senate again voted for full reinstatement, but House Democrats killed the measure. In 1986 a version of the Anti-Drug Abuse Act of 1986 imposed the death penalty for drug-related murders, but this provision was removed after 25 Democrats and moderate Republicans threatened to filibuster.[65]

For centrist New Democrats, however, the addition of 66 new death penalties in the 1994 Federal Death Penalty Act was a point of pride. President Clinton, House Judiciary Chair Jack Brooks, and Senate Judiciary Chair Joseph Biden offered the number as concrete, countable proof that the Democratic Party was not soft on crime. This section traces death penalty bill escalation in the major bills and their amendments from the 100th through 103rd Congress (1987–1994). (For a full listing of federal civilian capital crimes by year of enactment 1974–2010, see Table A.5.)

Federal increases to capital crimes began gingerly, in small numbers, and with actual attention to the content of the crimes punishable by death. In the 100th Congress (1987–1988), lawmakers authorized the death penalty for two major crimes: intentional murder by a drug trafficker and intentional killing of a police officer during a drug-related crime. Title VII was more than two new capital crimes, the first in fourteen years, important though they were. Title VII detailed the procedures for a fair and just death penalty. Procedures specified how attorneys must serve notice of intent to seek the death penalty and outlined death-exempt groups, such as those with "mental disability," as defined in Section 408(l). Section 408(m) listed 10 mitigating factors; one mitigating factor might undercut a death sentence if the defendant established it by a "preponderance of the evidence." Section 408(n) listed 12 possible aggravating factors; one of these might fortify a death sentence if the government established it "beyond a reasonable doubt."[66]

Democrats supported this so-called Drug Kingpin Act, housed in Title VII of the Anti-Drug Abuse Act of 1988, because of the special "crisis" of drug use. The Senate passed the Anti-Drug Abuse Act of 1988, including the capital crimes in Title VII, by an overwhelming majority of 87–3. Only one Democrat, William Proxmire of Wisconsin, voted "no." Democratic Senator Sam Nunn of Georgia explained that the drug war demanded swift if imperfect legislation, and supporting the death penalty reduced any chance of a filibuster. Democratic Senator Moynihan concluded in 1988 that Democrats had already lost the fight against capital punishment. After all, the Senate passed D'Amato's "drug kingpin" capital crimes bill (S. 2455) just four months prior, and by a sizable margin (65–39).[67]

The remainder of this section narrates the death penalty bidding war in some detail. I offer Figures 4.4 and 4.5 as visual summaries of bidding wars, with relevant roll-call votes in Tables A.6 and A.7. In the 101st Congress, legislators moved away from crime-by-crime consideration of capital crime statutes and toward comparisons of the total number of capital crime statutes; that is, rather than debating *which* crimes should be punishable by death, members of Congress began comparing bills in terms of *how many* crimes they made punishable by death. It is clear, however, that there was methodology for counting capital crimes; the unit, "a capital crime," might be counted as the relevant sections, subsections, or sub-subsections of the U.S. Code.[68] It is plausible, for example, to count 18 U.S.C. § 32-34 (death resulting from the destruction of aircrafts, motor vehicles, or their facilities) as *one* capital crime. It was equally tenable to count *two* capital crimes, 18 U.S.C. § 32 (death resulting from destruction of aircraft or aircraft facilities) and 18 U.S.C. § 33 (death resulting from destruction of motor vehicle or motor vehicle facilities), and then cross-reference the penalty, written in 18 U.S.C. § 34. The nonprofit, nonpartisan Death Penalty Information Center counts one capital crime, using the former method; the Congressional Research Service counts two capital crimes, using the latter method.[69] I found only one document listing the Democratic proposal for 64 new death penalties; it was a press release, issued by the House Democratic Judiciary Committee in September 1993. The final column of Table A.5 shows one Democratic count of 64 death-eligible crimes. While the count here is very disaggregated, "inflated" counts fit best, if imperfectly, with counts offered by lawmakers and echoed in news stories. In Table A.5, I completed and updated the count of death-eligible crimes in similar fashion to reflect this inflated tallying method; in an updated count, Congress enacted 92 death-eligible crimes from 1974 to 2010.

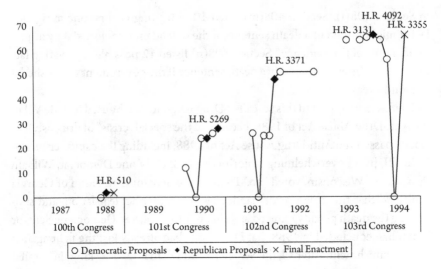

Figure 4.4 Number of Capital Crimes in Selected House Proposals, 1988–1994. *Source:* Compiled by author. See Table A.6 for details and related House votes.

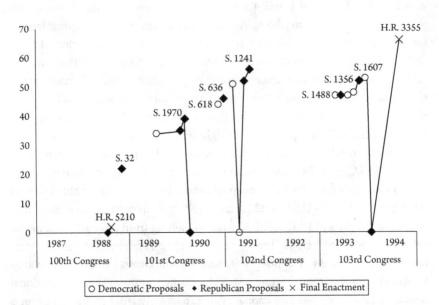

Figure 4.5 Number of Capital Crimes in Selected Senate Proposals, 1988–1994. *Source:* Compiled by author. See Table A.7 for details and related Senate votes.

Members of Congress vied for the highest number of capital crimes during the 101st Congress. In July 1990, House Democratic Judiciary chair Jack Brooks of Texas, introduced a bill (H.R. 5269) with 12 crimes punishable by death. Then, in October 1990, Republican George Gekas of Pennsylvania added an additional 12 capital crimes by amendment, bumping the total number to

24.[70] That same day, Democratic Representative James Traficant of Ohio proposed one capital crime—murdering state or local law enforcement officers assisting a federal investigation—which passed by voice vote. Republican Representative Bill McCollum of Florida then added an additional two capital crimes by amendment, bringing the total to 27 proposed capital crimes. The conservative coalition of Republicans and southern Democrats secured death penalty expansions in the Gekas amendment and the McCollum amendment; northern Democrats opposed both.[71] It would be wrong to impute, however, that a robust majority of northern Democrats of the 101st Congress rejected capital punishment. Consider that, in the same debates over Representative Brooks' bill, one Democrat, Harley Staggers of West Virginia, proposed an amendment to commute all death sentences to life in prison without parole. The Staggers amendment failed, with only half of all voting northern Democrats voting for life sentences in lieu of death sentences. Democrats like Ron Dellums (D-California) attributed the escalation to the Democratic Party's "collective defensiveness" about "being soft on crime."[72]

Senators of the 101st Congress also lobbed competing high bids for capital punishment. In January 1989, Republican Senator Strom Thurmond proposed a bill with 22 new capital crimes (S. 32).[73] In November 1989, Democratic Senator Biden introduced a competing Democratic bill to make 34 crimes punishable by death (S. 1970). At the same time, Senate Democrats were turning against death penalty alternatives. When death penalty opponent Mark Hatfield (R-Oregon) proposed replacing capital punishment with life imprisonment without release, the majority of voting Democrats opposed it. At the end of the 101st Congress, House-Senate conferees abandoned efforts to reach agreement on capital crimes, largely due to disagreement over the Racial Justice Act.

In the 102nd Congress, House Democrats introduced the Violent Crime Control Act of 1991, which devoted 26 separate sections to death-eligible crimes (H.R. 3371). Republican Representative Gekas then won an amendment to replace the Democrats' 26 sections of death-eligible crimes with 36 separate sections defining death-eligible crimes. In the floor debates that followed, not even members of the House Judiciary Committee could identify an exact count. In the October 1991 debates, Hughes proudly endorsed H.R. 3371 for making "48 serious Federal crimes" death eligible, but Schumer credited the same version of the bill with a higher count of "50 or 52" death-eligible crimes. Schumer characterized the bill as "including the death penalty for more than 50 federal offenses," and, with some limitations on defendants' ability to bring appeals, the bill was "hardly a victory for civil libertarians." A Democratic amendment to commute death sentences to life imprisonment without release failed, this time with a slim majority of voting northern Democrats rejecting the amendment (ND: 89-96; SD: 6-70; R: 5-156).[74]

The 102nd Senate took many swings at an omnibus crime bill, with Senate Democrats battling with President Bush in his reelection campaign; each bill failed, but every iteration increased the number of death-eligible crimes. The Democratic Biden bill, introduced on March 12, 1991, established 44 death-eligible crimes.[75] The Republican Bush-Thurmond bill, introduced on March 13, 1991, established 46 death-eligible crimes. In June 1991, the Democratic Biden bill established 51 offenses punishable by death. Biden touted the lethality of the Democratic proposal:

> The Biden crime bill before us calls for the death penalty for 51 offenses. A wag in the newspaper recently wrote something to the effect that Biden has made it a death penalty offense for everything but jaywalking. The President's bill calls for the death penalty on 46 offenses. The difference is negligible. Yet, I am a supporter of the death penalty. I am a supporter of the death penalty without the Racial Justice Act in it. I think it is better with it, but I am a supporter of it without it as well.[76]

Senator Thurmond responded, "The President's death penalty, habeas corpus, and exclusionary rule proposals are tougher on criminals than the pending [Biden] bill." Against Republican challenges, Biden's retort was that he had "written into my bill 51 offenses for which there would be death." Biden pitched his bill as "much tougher than the President's" because it "provides for more penalties for death for more offenses than the [President's] bill." With two additional Republican amendments, the final tally was 53 crimes punishable by death.[77]

The Conference Report for H.R. 3371 won support for audits of punitiveness, with Senator Mikulski (D-Maryland) supporting the bill precisely because "this bill expand[ed] the death penalty to include 53 new offenses, provide[ed] needed crime fighting assistance for policemen and prosecutors, and crack[ed] down on drug and violent crime offenders." Senator Dodd (D-Connecticut) specifically praised the 53 capital crimes. Biden chastised his colleagues who thought the bill was too weak: "If it is so weak, why does the conference bill include every death penalty offense passed by both House and Senate?" Biden answered his own question: "This bill adds 53 death penalty offenses—the single largest expansion of the Federal death penalty in the history of the Congress." Senate Democrats twice failed to get a cloture vote.[78]

The major omnibus crime bill of the 102nd Congress, the so-called Violent Crime Control and Law Enforcement Act of 1991, floundered in a pre-election standoff. With George H. W. Bush running for reelection, some thought that the Republican president was trying to run against Congress, as Democrats had majorities in both the House and Senate. Democrats like Biden marked lethality by number of crimes, and Republicans like Thurmond and Gramm marked lethality by tightening habeas corpus and rules of evidence. Gramm criticized the Democratic bill for "strengthen[ing] criminals' rights," and Biden countered "we do everything but hang people for jaywalking." Gramm then presented a letter from 31 state attorneys general opposing the bill (because the Republican proposal for fewer habeas corpus petitions would reduce legal costs). Biden, for his part, provided letters from police unions supporting the bill (and its $3 billion for local law enforcement).[79] Biden even held a news conference with the Fraternal Order of Police and the National Association of Police Organizations on October 1, the day before the cloture vote, and he publicly offered to strike all habeas corpus provisions to entice Republicans away from filibuster. President Bush opposed the prominent if fairly modest Brady bill to require a five-working-day waiting period and background check for handgun purchases. At the close of the 102nd Congress, with Bill Clinton's campaign well underway, Democrats could not muster enough votes for cloture.[80]

In the 103rd Congress, Democrats enjoyed unified control, and Judiciary Committee leaders Brooks and Biden introduced parallel crime bills, both roughly following the contours of the 1992 conference agreement (H.R. 3371). In the House, Brooks introduced the 434-page Violent Crime Control and Law Enforcement Act of 1993 (H.R. 3131), and its 31 titles included Clinton's campaign promises for more cops, gun control, grants to state prisons, and more drug penalties. Title II of the Brooks-Clinton bill made 64 crimes punishable by death. Schumer introduced a stand-alone version of the same death penalty statutes (H.R. 4032) on March 15, 1994. Chair of the House Judiciary Committee, Jack Brooks, consolidated 13 crime bills approved in committee to create the Omnibus Anti-Crime bill (H.R. 4092) in March 1994.[81]

Democratic amendments to limit capital punishment failed. One amendment, offered by Representative Watt (D-North Carolina) of the CBC, would have eliminated the death penalty for drug "kingpins" in cases in which no death resulted. Watt gave the racial statistics of "kingpin" laws—since the 1988 kingpin statute, 33 of the 37 prosecutions were against black or Latino defendants—and the amendment was defeated, with most Democrats voting against it. Another amendment would have eliminated the death penalty for murder committed during a carjacking, drive-by-shooting, or federal drug and gun crime, offered by Representative Scott (D-Virginia), also in the CBC, on grounds of limiting the federalization of crime, but it was rejected by voice vote. Clinton's Office of Legislative Affairs opposed Scott's amendment as "contrary to the President's support for restoring an enforceable federal death penalty for the most heinous federal crimes." The grandest amendment to eliminate the death penalty and replace it with life imprisonment—introduced by Representative Kopetski (D-Oregon) on behalf of himself as well as Kweisi Mfume (D-Maryland) and

Jose Serrano (D-New York)—was defeated by overwhelming majority, as well as opposition from the White House.[82]

In the Senate, bidding began at a lower number. Biden presented Clinton's bill (S. 1488), with Title II on the death penalty introduced as "the largest ever expansion of the federal death penalty to cover 47 offenses." The competing Republican bill, introduced on August 4 by Dole and Hatch (R-Utah) as the Neighborhood Security Act, also included 47 crimes punishable by death. Even with the same number of capital crimes, Senator Hatch pitched the Dole-Hatch bill as tougher than the Biden bill because it established "an enforceable death penalty for 47 offenses," with emphasis on stricter habeas reforms. As folded into the omnibus bill (S. 1607), the Senate bill thus began with 47 death-eligible crimes. Biden brought the bill to the floor without committee action, and from November 3 to November 19, 1993, senators inflated the number of death provisions. After substituting the text of their own bill (S. 1607) for the House version (H.R. 3355), the Senate increased the $9.6 billion bill to a $22.3 billion bill, including more money for community policing programs, federal prison construction, boot camps, and women's shelters. As enacted, the Violent Crime Control and Law Enforcement Act, signed on September 13, 1994, authorized $30.2 billion over six years for police and prisons, banned 19 assault weapons, and established the Violence Against Women Act.[83]

Democrats bragged about high death penalty counts. Senator Biden boasted that he "added back into the Federal statutes over 50 death penalties—50 circumstances in which, if a person is convicted of a crime at a Federal level, they are eligible for the death penalty." In addition, the bill authorized "over 70 increased penalties—70, seven zero—70 increased penalties in new offenses covering violent crimes, drug trafficking, and gun crimes." Senator Dianne Feinstein (D-California) justified her support by noting that the bill includes "60 death penalties" and new "penalties for more than 70 violent crimes."[84] In party competition, the aggregate number of capital crimes became the focal point of policy comparison. Democratic lawmakers advertised "more than 60" as a concrete, objective number.

By August 1994, Republicans like Senator Hatch accused Democrats of "bowing to the liberal wing of the Democratic Party." Senator Biden defended Democratic toughness on crime policy, citing numerical tallies:

> Let me define the liberal wing of the Democratic Party. The liberal wing of the Democratic Party is now for 60 new death penalties. That is what is in this bill. The liberal wing of the Democratic Party has 70 enhanced penalties, and my friend from California, Senator Feinstein, outlined every one of them. I gave a list to her today. She asked what is in there to every one of them. The liberal wing of the Democratic Party is for

100,000 cops. The liberal wing of the Democratic Party is for 125,000 new State prison cells.

The liberal wing of the Democratic Party is not the old wing I knew. So if that is what he [Republican Senator Orrin Hatch] defines as the liberal wing of the Democratic party, then I suspect I would like to see the conservative wing of the Democratic Party.[85]

Biden restored dignity to "the liberal wing of the Democratic Party" through punitive escalation. This was echoed by Clinton's attorney general, Janet Reno, who stated in her confirmation hearing of March 1993 that she "regularly" asked for the death penalty as Dade County state attorney, and she pledged to help Congress craft new death penalty procedures to cut the protracted appeals that make a "mockery of the justice system." With her support, the DOJ increased the number of prisoners on death row. During the "pre-protocol" period (1988–1994), U.S. Attorneys submitted 52 defendants for initial death penalty review, with the DOJ seeking death for 47 defendants. In the "post-protocol" period (1995–2000), U.S. Attorneys submitted 682 defendants for death penalty review, with the DOJ seeking death for 159.[86]

Democrats neutralized soft-on-crime accusations with punitive outbidding, with the strategy being successful to the extent that the Democrats' approval rating on crime rose from 50 percent in 1994 to 70 percent in 1997. After House passage of the Violent Crime Control and Law Enforcement Act of 1994, Charles Schumer (D-New York) announced, "Democrats have recaptured this issue," impervious to accusations of being "mushy-headed on crime." Republicans spoke openly of concerns that Schumer and Biden might be right, and James Sensenbrenner (R-Wisconsin) wrote in a letter to Republican colleagues that they needed to defeat Clinton's bill and "give the crime issue back to Republicans for the upcoming election."[87] By 1996, Biden noted a blurring of ideological lines, joking that someone asleep for the last 20 years might wake up to think Republicans were representing Abbie Hoffman and Democrats were representing J. Edgar Hoover.[88]

Death via Fair, Racially "Unmodified" Procedures

The Federal Death Penalty Act of 1994 codified new procedures and thereby "enabled" capital crime escalation. Here, I offer the term "enabled" in two senses: new procedures enabled capital punishment to pass constitutional muster, and, more significantly, new procedures enabled a kind of liberal political cover. As a legal technicality, new federal procedure met post-*Gregg* constitutional standards. As enacted, the Federal Death Penalty Act included, like most post-*Gregg* rules, requirements for trial bifurcation into the "guilt phase" for the jury to decide guilt for the death-eligible offense, followed by the "sentencing phase" to establish level of intent and at least one aggravating factor. Some procedures introduced in the Act seemed to be liberal victories. The FDPA required appointment of two lawyers in all federal capital cases, at least one of whom must be "learned in the law" of capital cases. It also prohibited execution of "mentally retarded" persons, or persons who "lack the mental capacity to understand the death penalty and why it was imposed," an exception that Democratic Senator Edward Kennedy had fought for since 1986. Death penalty bidding wars and procedural protections came together within a rhetoric of severity with fairness. As he shepherded Clinton's bill through the Senate, Biden described new penalties with assurances of fair processes and administration—the "intent" standard for sentencing, long lists of mitigating and aggravating factors, exemptions for children and those with "mental retardation," and appellate review. All concluded that "the death penalty provisions are tough and the procedures are fair."[89]

Defeat of the Racial Justice Act reveals the Democratic retreat from even modest procedures for racially fair punishment. In death penalty bidding wars, Democrats like Biden embraced a punitive triumphalism, offering more and more crimes punishable by death, continuously ratcheting up the previous Republican bid. In this process, the center of the Democratic Party cleaved the substantive expansion of capital crimes from procedures that might have aided racial justice. Yet the Congressional Black Caucus created an opportunity to use proceduralism toward racially just ends through their introduction of the Racial Justice Act (RJA). As the Congressional Black Caucus' response to *McCleskey v. Kemp*, the RJA would allow people incarcerated in state and federal prisons to use racial-group statistics to challenge their individual sentences as racially discriminatory.[90] Debates over the RJA revealed Democratic Party struggles to shed itself of its historical association with the civil rights legacy, even in their most procedurally narrow forms.

The Congressional Black Caucus threw its political weight behind the Racial Justice Act provision, telling the House Judiciary Committee that its members would automatically oppose any crime bill with new capital crimes that did not include the RJA. The Chair of the CBC, Representative Kweisi Mfume (D-Maryland), denounced prison in general as "an antiquated approach to crime." CBC member Eleanor Holmes Norton (D-District of Columbia) said that prosecutors "choose blacks for death." Many in the popular media accused the CBC of imprudent Democratic atavism: the New Republic characterized their position as a "reversion to paleoliberalism," *Newsweek* accused Representative Mfume of "showboating," and neo-conservative African American cultural critic Stanley Crouch bluntly jabbed, "let [these monsters] shoot up the CBC and we'll see what happens in the next crime bill."[91]

Since John Conyers (D-Michigan) introduced the Racial Justice Act in 1988, the question of execution hit the replay on procedure versus punishment. Group-based statistics reversed progress, a way to "roll back the clock on our ability to fight crime," as President Bush put it in 1990. As if recycling Nixon's *Miranda*, President Bush described the Act as "tougher on law enforcement than on criminals." Attorney General Richard Thornburgh called RJA "a bizarre racial quota system," more "pro-criminal" than "pro-law enforcement." Deputy Attorney General William Barr labeled the House 1990 RJA a "pro-criminal" attempt to "effectively abolish the death penalty." In the 102nd Congress, Senator Thurmond feared that the RJA would "effectively eliminate the death penalty in every State." The RJA was "a back-door way to *abolish* the death penalty in the name of *restoring* it," in the words of Republican Senator Orrin Hatch.[92] Hatch's statement is intriguing for its twisted accuracy: taking the "back-door" to racial justice was liberal law-and-order writ large.

Through death penalty bidding wars and the relinquished Racial Justice Act, Democrats retreated from the "liberal wing of the Democratic Party." The retreat, however, was not so far: from Johnson Democrats to Conyers Democrats, administrative fixes defined the death penalty debate. Some of the strongest advocates of the RJA, Don Edwards (D-California) and John Conyers (D-Michigan), insisted that the "Racial Justice Act will not abolish the death penalty"; instead, they reassured, it offered broad mechanisms for states to challenge both "the adequacy of the statistical case" and "any inference of racial bias." More pointedly, some liberals supported the RJA as justification for death penalty expansion. For example, New York State Attorney General Robert Abrams endorsed the Racial Justice Act by saying, "If Congress endorses broader use of capital punishment, it must insure a fair and color-blind process." In this same vein, an editorial in the *New York Times* conceded that more capital crimes might become "tolerable [if] accompanied by the Race Justice Act." In this sense, the RJA would have been another procedural patch, expanding substantive punishment while procedurally cleansing it of racial disparity, in the same vein of Democratic efforts to modernize police and sentencing. In the same year of Clinton's victorious addition of 60 new capital crimes, Justice Harry Blackmun rejected all death penalty patchwork, writing in *Callins v. Collins*: "From this day forward, I no longer shall tinker with the machinery of death." This "tinkering," in Justice Blackmun's words, the continual fixation on rules that impart "the mere appearance of fairness," defined the short spectrum of intra-Democratic conflict.[93] By this logic, rigorous procedure justified tough penalties.

Given the intensity with which the CBC advocated for the Racial Justice Act, it is notable that Clinton did not support the measure. His silence was planned. A White House document titled "Draft Q & A / Racial Justice Act" began with the bracketed introduction: "[President gives his statement on the urgency of the crime bill. No mention of RJA.]" As response to the anticipated question of whether Clinton would work with the Black Caucus for a modified RJA, the memo suggested the answer that there was a crisis, and Clinton's imperative was to "pass the bill and get those cops out on the streets." The critical moment of rejecting the Racial Justice Act came in Conference Committee. The House bill (H.R. 3355) included the RJA; the Senate bill did not. As the bill was in conference in the summer of 1994, there was growing consensus among Democratic supporters that, in Representative William Hughes's (D-New Jersey) words, the crime bill was too important to be "held hostage" by the Racial Justice Act.[94] The RJA was finally jettisoned in Conference Committee, and its rejection marked an endpoint to the Democratic Party's half-century grappling with the purpose of procedure. Liberal Democrats, especially through Johnson's "high tide" of racial liberalism, used procedure as a *path* to racial equality, and some saw procedure as a *proxy* for racial equality. Many New Democrats used procedure as a *cover* for perpetuating racial inequality, but Hughes's statement gestured at something more crass: proceduralist racial protections simply obstructed his clearly stated endgame of lethal punishment.

This same position is evident in Clinton's signing of the Anti-Terrorism and Effective Death Penalty Act of 1996. The immediate catalyst for the Act was the bombing of the Murrah Federal Building in Oklahoma City in April 1995, planned and executed by two white Americans in a militia-style attack on the expansive federal government. Within one month after the bombing, 12 state attorneys general wrote to President Clinton supporting habeas restrictions to end the "endless delay and procedural manipulation" that corrupts respect for the law. As enacted, the Anti-Terrorism and Effective Death Penalty Act of 1996 gave state prisoners generally one year after exhausting all appeals in state court, and more than one appeal was very difficult. Death row appeals were stricter still. The Death Penalty Act, the "Special Habeas Corpus Procedures in Capital Cases," set a ceiling of 180 days to file a certiorari, state post-conviction, and a federal habeas petition. It was an unprecedented restriction to habeas corpus. Republicans had pledged to restrict death row appeals since the Reagan administration, and the 1994 "Contract with America" renewed this commitment, an indicator that Clinton's crime bill was too lenient.

Although the Anti-Terrorism and Effective Death Penalty Act of 1996 was ostensibly in response to the Oklahoma City bombing, key provisions of the act were aimed at immigrants. Congress rejected measures that might have had some impact on domestic terrorism, such as marking explosives with chemical identifiers. Instead, it passed a ban on "foreign" groups with terrorist connections and a provision allowing the border patrol to more easily turn away immigrants. In particular, it established a procedure of "summary exclusion," making it easier to turn away those without proper documentation, disregarding the possibility that a refugee fleeing persecution might need to rely on false papers.[95]

Empathic and Lawful Racial Violence

Punitive policies exploded from 1984 through the end of the Clinton administration, demonstrating the Democratic retreat from racial justice that has been so well documented by scholars like Paul Frymer, Claire Kim, Adolph Reed, and Philip Klinkner and Rogers Smith. Democratic distancing from "special interests" was evident in policies on welfare, immigration, gay and lesbian rights, and pay equity, and, as argued in this chapter, in crime policy, where New Democrats performed conspicuous rejection of their racially liberal wing.

Witnessed in the lineage of postwar liberal law-and-order, Democratic punitiveness was not only an expedient electoral strategy; it was also, I argue, the extension of earlier constructions of black pathology and administrative deficiency. Racially liberal Democrats who supported the notion of "old" civil rights conceived of black crime as black sickness, whether as Emanuel Celler's articulation of blacks "warped" by the past or Daniel Moynihan's framework of the "tangle of pathologies." Democratic attacks on crack cocaine as the drug of the dysfunctional, self-replicating "underclass" were the logical extremes of prior visions of black sickness; this was most evident in Moynihan's 1986 explanation that "crack" and "crack babies" were the violent end to his 1965 prognosis. Similarly, to the extent that liberal law-and-order opposed capital punishment on administrative grounds, the Democratic assent in death penalties seems far less unexpected. As a project of pity and administrative order, Clinton and the New Democrats represented "matured" liberal law-and-order.

President Clinton, famous for his "I feel your pain" empathic performances, deemed racial "disparities" worthy of white sympathy. In his speech at the University of Texas at Austin in October 1995, Clinton presented the datum that, of all African American men in their twenties, one in three were on probation, parole, or imprisoned. Clinton asked every white person to imagine how it "would feel if one in three white men were in similar circumstances." He then asked African Americans to "understand and acknowledge the roots of white fear in America."[96] This request for understanding revealed much about the transformation of the first civil right. By the time of Clinton's 1995 speech, state-sanctioned racial violence was so unassailable that even the president could deem it an outcome beyond his control. His call for empathy was the outer limit of racial justice.

The Last Civil Right

Freedom from State-Sanctioned Racial Violence

By the opening of the twenty-first century, blackness signaled a threat so deep that many white people, participating in experiments, experienced a lighting-up in the "fear center" of the brain when they were flashed photos of black faces for less than one second. With the rise of mass incarceration through the 1980s and 1990s, the conflation of blackness, criminality, and carcerality was so extreme that rhetorical shorthand permeated the culture. "Driving while black" and "shopping while black" both played on the phrase "driving while drunk" and denoted the presumption of guilt that black people faced in daily routines. One in three black men lived under probation, parole, or prison on any given day, and viewers of HBO's *The Wire* know that many police officers referenced individuals of this demographic simply as "number one male." For many, the names Rodney King, Amadou Diallo, Abner Louima, Kathryn Johnston, Oscar Grant III, Henry Louis Gates Jr., the Jena Six, and the New Jersey Four were synonymous with anti-black police brutality, "even," as if anyone suspected otherwise, for black women and suit-and-tie attired black men. Clothing signaled race-laden associations with criminality, and in 2007 the cities of Delcambre and Mansfield in Louisiana passed indecency laws, punishable by fines and jail time, for wearing "saggy" pants. As evidenced in the 2012 murder of Trayvon Martin, a black teenager wearing a "hoodie" was prima facie "up to no good," threatening enough to warrant preemptive punishment.[1]

In this context, it is strange to recall the promises of liberal law-and-order. In its 1947 articulation, Truman's right to safety prohibited "arbitrary arrest and punishment" and permitted punishment "only for commission of offenses clearly defined by law and only after trial by due process of law." Yet federal prisons continue to expand by "detaining" people who have not even violated criminal law. Of all the undocumented people in federal prisons (22,230 people in 2010), roughly 40 percent faced immigration charges that were administrative rather than criminal in nature. Immigration and Customs Enforcement occasionally detains and deports U.S. citizens—acts clearly proscribed by law, as ICE has no jurisdiction over U.S. Citizens—and this episodic "lawless violence" compounds the routine legal violence against undocumented people.[2] Truman's right to safety called for freedom from "lawless violence," but the post-9/11 "lawless decade" of illegal detentions and wiretapping depended on expanded federal carceral powers. The PATRIOT Act of 2002 passed with the declaration that "the first civil right of every American is to be free of domestic terrorism," and once again the supremacy of safety justified greater surveillance and more punishment.[3] With its enormous infrastructure, the twenty-first-century carceral state pervades social life.

This concluding chapter situates my argument in *The First Civil Right* in two contexts. In the first half of this conclusion, I situate my findings in the larger context of other civil rights policy areas. This book has treated federal law-and-order as another front in the struggle for racial justice, no less important than fair employment, voting rights, and quality education. Like other civil rights areas, the struggle for racially just law-and-order changed when liberal lawmakers selectively accomodated and opportunistically rearticulated the meaning of racially fair punishment. In the second half of this conclusion, I consider the ways in which liberal law-and-order conceals racial violence in the twenty-first century.

From Carceral Puzzle to Normal Racial Politics

This book began the way many such studies do—by presenting the seeming paradox of one black man in the White House, but one million black men in the Big House. When seen on a timeline of crime rates, fiscal conservatism, neoliberalism, and the conventional wisdom of racial progress, racialized carceral expansion is puzzling indeed. Lawmakers enacted tough-on-crime policies amid the already waning crime rates and anti-government fervor of the 1980s and 1990s. Lawmakers authorized money to build more prisons and hire more police amid the fiscal conservatism from the Reagan Revolution through the ascendance of Clinton New Democrats. Crime policy is frequently presented as an outlier in the conventional wisdom of racial progress.

When liberal law-and-order is recognized as a centerpiece of pro–civil rights agendas, however, the history of carceral expansion is neither puzzling nor exceptional. It is, instead, a tragically commonplace story of civil rights. At midcentury, the black freedom struggle threatened state legitimacy by exposing the criminal justice system as the strong arm of state-sanctioned white violence. If we follow Margaret Levi's admonition to study "the extent to which the state has a monopoly of physical force and the extent to which the use of physical force is legitimate" as variables, not elements of a definition of the state, then it is easier to see that postwar law-and-order was not simply about burglary, robbery, or murder.[4] It was no whipped up moral panic about mugging or juvenile delinquency. Instead, the postwar law-and-order problem was a credible threat to the state's monopoly on legitimate violence, and these threats came from multiple, conflicting racial coalitions. White lawlessness and the complicity of criminal justice were nakedly evident at the height of the "classical" civil rights movement, when the graphic violence of police dogs and fire hoses accelerated liberal development of the civil rights carceral state. White massive resisters and co-signatories of the Southern Manifesto also challenged federal authority and monopoly on legitimate violence. In response to these threats, liberal lawmakers secured legitimacy through administrative reforms that seemed to tame lawless racial violence. My invocation of legitimacy here is no functionalist deduction. As illustrated in this study, lawmakers commonly justified carceral reform as a way to promote trust and perceptions of fairness.

Liberal agendas to deracialize punishment bloomed in a normative haze. Democratic proposals for racial fairness found support from Republicans and southern Democrats who supported carceral modernization, but for different purposes. When Johnson Democrats attempted to correct racism in criminal justice, resulting reforms to "modernize" ultimately strengthened the carceral state, usually with the result of exacerbating racial disparity. As highlighted in this study, civil rights advocates like Emanuel Celler, Philip Hart, the U.S. Civil Rights Commission, and the ACLU supported early Democratic proposals to professionalize police with better training, higher standards, and more money. As finally enacted and administered, however, the Safe Streets Act of 1968 ultimately gave money for police equipment and quasi-militarization, largely because the conservative coalition amended Democratic proposals with alternate priorities and funding administration. Similarly, Johnson-era demands for reduced sentencing disparity (with anti-carceral specifics) were transformed into subsequent bipartisan policies for reduced sentencing disparity (with pro-carceral specifics), culminating with the Sentencing Reform Act of 1984. When Clinton New Democrats enacted legislation for community policing and death penalty expansion, their "rightward" punitive policies reposed on justifications from liberalisms past. The rights-laden liberal system secured the integrity of brutal, even lethal state violence, and the discourse of a community engagement enabled more order-maintenance policing.

Perhaps some liberal lawmakers hoped to cement racial bias out of the machine. Perhaps others hoped to harden machinery to contain racial threat. In the strategic ambiguities of policymaking, it is difficult to distinguish policies for racial fairness from policies for racial discipline. I have argued that, in the logic of liberal law-and-order, this is a distinction without a difference. If legitimate punishment means that the state surveils, confines, and kills with the right techniques and protocols, then liberal law-and-order specified and refined quality administration with the outcome of legitimating the carceral state. In the end, new administrative fixes made violence appear less emotional and more rights-laden.[5]

In the end, the Big House may serve racial conservatism, but it was built on the rock of racial liberalism. Liberal law-and-order promised to deliver freedom from racial violence by way of the civil rights carceral state, with professionalized police and prison guards less likely to provoke Watts and Attica. Despite all their differences, Truman's first essential right of 1947, Johnson's police professionalization, Kennedy's sentencing reform, and even Biden's death penalty proposals landed on a shared metric: criminal justice was racially fair to the extent that it ushered each individual through an ordered, rights-laden machine. Routinized administration of race-neutral laws would mean that racially disparate outcomes would be seen, if seen at all, as individually particularized and thereby not racially motivated. Expunged from institutions and abstracted from the material world, race did its damage in psychic territory. This summons Gunnar Myrdal's heavenly spirit of the American Creed, those virtuous commitments to liberty and democratic egalitarianism that float above the hardware of the U.S. racial state. As original sin, white prejudice left its mark in the form of black criminal propensities, making African Americans the embodiment of "a moral lag in the development of the nation."[6] In this sense, liberal law-and-order was especially powerful in entrenching notions of black criminality. I say especially because liberal law-and-order maintained a politics of pity that, through references to African American family deficits and at-risk youth, softened the hard edges of conservatism and carceral neoliberalism.

Crime policy was akin to other civil rights issues in this sense: when liberal lawmakers selectively accommodated activist demands, they did so in ways that transformed, decontextualized, and even inverted original visions of justice. Like campaigns for fair employment and quality education, campaigns for racially fair law-and-order faced a dilemma best explained by critical race theorist Kimberlé Crenshaw: the very reforms won through rights rhetoric seemed "to undermine the ability to move forward toward a broader vision of racial equality." In other words, while victories for anti-discrimination law yielded many benefits, they simultaneously legitimated a rights regime that could barely confront the abject material conditions of people of color. Thus, Crenshaw concludes: "In the quest for racial justice, winning and losing have been part of the same experience."[7]

The biography of *Brown v. Board of Education* is a case in point. *Brown* reposed on a paltry conception of racial harm, so its victory meant the loss of more ambitious, economic, and international definitions of racism. In particular, the *Brown* ruling reveals how the postwar emphasis on racial classification, stigma, and psychological damage ultimately truncated the broader economic goals of civil rights. *Brown* sanctified the racial common sense equating discrimination with classification; this equation factored out racial harm manifest in material conditions that civil rights legal campaigns of the previous two decades had sought to address. Ordinary rights talk of the late 1930s and early 1940s equated "civil rights" with labor rights, decent wages, union rights, and freedom from peonage and police brutality. The civil rights "victory" of *Brown* actually restricted the meaning of racial justice. Legal historian Risa Goluboff puts it in a clean equation: "once *Brown* was constructed as it was, Jim Crow became synonymous in popular understanding with state-mandated segregation. And the answer to Jim Crow became the 'color-blind' Constitution."[8] Reforms to professionalize police and nationalize due process were no different than *Brown* or the Voting Rights Act of 1965 in the sense that they represented no permanent victory. Instead, every fight over the carceral state, like every fight over anti-discrimination law, "represents an ongoing ideological struggle in which the occasional winners harness the moral, coercive, consensual power of the law."[9]

Liberal Law-and-Order in the Twenty-First Century

The perils of postwar liberal law-and-order are worth recalling in the twenty-first century, when demands for reform are loud but modest in scope and normatively untethered. Parts of the carceral state are too expensive for fiscal conservatives, too intrusive for civil libertarians, and too cruel for human rights advocates. Michelle Alexander's 2010 blockbuster *The New Jim Crow* invigorated opposition to the drug war, and the chorus demanding reform of drug penalties includes everyone from Jimmy Carter to William F. Buckley and Milton Friedman.[10]

At the same time, however, twenty-first-century carceral apparatuses do not suffer any overwhelming credibility problem. If the American public evaluates judges negatively, it is for sentencing too leniently, not too aggressively. Between 1972 and 2012, a national survey asked about how "the courts in this area deal...with criminals," and across all years nearly 85 percent of respondents answered "about right" or "not harshly enough." Recent years have seen a very modest decline in support for courts, yet, in 2012, a majority of respondents (63 percent) deemed courts "not harsh enough" and 21 percent deemed courts "about right."[11] Similarly, a majority of Americans have a great deal of confidence in the police, and most see police officers as fair. In the 20 years of Gallup asking the same question, consistently more than half of respondents said they have "quite a lot" or "a great deal" of confidence in police, while, during the same period, a combined 8 and 16 percent said they had "very little" or "no confidence" in them. A 2005 Gallup poll found that nearly two-thirds of respondents believed that police brutality did not exist in their area.[12] Those evaluations are based more on police adherence to procedural justice rather than instrumental evaluations of police performance in catching rule-breakers, fighting crime, or providing fair outcomes.[13]

Given general assent to the carceral state, it is perhaps no surprise that twenty-first-century reforms lurch about in fits and starts. Between 2009 and 2013, New Mexico, Connecticut, and Maryland voted to abolish the death penalty, but Californians voted to keep the death penalty in a 2012 ballot initiative, showing once more that the death penalty is "rocked but still rolling." California limited but Massachusetts expanded three-strikes legislation in 2012.[14] When twenty-first-century students learn about carceral practices, they tend to propose a number of possible reforms: hire more African American police officers; reinstate judicial discretion; limit police discretion; train police. Like federal lawmakers, they search for ways to improve the administration of justice for fairness and predictability.

The history of liberal law-and-order matters because the same proposals for better administration, proffered with the same good intentions, are likely to reproduce the same monstrous outcomes in the twenty-first century. The problems of a normatively untethered liberal law-and-order regime are clear in the arc of liberal positions on judicial discretion. Mid-century liberals viewed discretion as dangerous individualized justice, tailored to each defendant from each judge's moral cloth in all its idiosyncratic textures. Judicial discretion lurked in law's "twilight zone," dispensing what Judge Marvin Frankel called "law without order." Liberal fear of discretion endured through the mid-1980s, when one could easily characterize the "mainstream liberal thought" as unambiguously opposed to discretionary administrative interpretation and implementation.[15] With the rise of sentencing guidelines and mandatory minimums through the 1980s and 1990s, however, liberals called for more judicial discretion by praising that which they previously reprimanded—justice customized to each individual defendant.[16]

As a project to control the irrationalities of racial bias and administrative discretion, liberal law-and-order ignored empirical lessons and displaced normative questions. Reformers invoked the promises and perils of "discretion" while ignoring the central findings of research. The American Bar Foundation's 1957 survey and the myriad studies it inspired analyzed discretion within the "total criminal justice system." As a system, carceral machinery is not easily corrected by small administrative adjustments: tighten discretion in one place, and the criminal justice system "accommodates," to use the original language of the ABF studies, so that discretion simply becomes more important for a different decision maker.

Accommodation is evident of sentencing guidelines and mandatory minimums, which diminished judicial discretion but effectively increased prosecutorial discretion. When situated with a total system approach, the "amount" of discretion has neither increased nor decreased, concludes Samuel Walker; it has simply moved from one agency to another.[17]

Administrative tinkering does not confront the damning features of the American carceral state, its scale and its racial concentration, which, when taken together reinforce and raise African American vulnerability to premature death. By focusing on the intra-system problems of "discretion," lawmakers displaced questions of justice onto the more manageable, measurable issues of system function. When framed as a problem of discretion—that is, individual decision making permissible by formal rules—then solutions to racial inequality double back to individual administrators and their institutional rules. In this sense, problematizing discretion forces questions of remediation onto sanitary administrative grounds. Should judges be elected or appointed? Should judges administer justice through sentencing guidelines? No guidelines and some mandatory minimums? No mandatory minimums and only mandatory maximums? Will judges or parole boards select the final release date? These questions matter, but they cannot replace clear commitments to racial justice. When they are posed independently of normative goals, process becomes the proxy, not the path, to justice. Without a normatively grounded understanding of racial violence, liberal reforms will do the administrative shuffle.

This book traced a stark half-century turn from confronting white racial violence administered and enabled by carceral apparatuses, to controlling black criminality through a procedurally fortified, race-neutral system. Race liberals institutionalized the "right to safety" while skirting its animating call against state-sanctioned white violence. Fixation on administrative minutiae distracted from the normative core of punishment in a system of persistent racial hierarchy. Unlike administrative tinkering, reforms for decriminalization and decarceration would push debates to their normative core: what warrants punishment, in what form, and why?[18] In place of liberal searches for the ideal procedural path to life incarceration, metrics of racial justice should focus on what Ruth Wilson Gilmore calls "the state-sanctioned or extralegal production and exploitation of group-differentiated vulnerability to premature death."[19] Seeing racism as "group-differentiated vulnerabilities to premature death" gives proper context to acts of violence between individuals. If we situate private violence in relation to group-differentiated reality, we begin to see the tight weave of state and private racial violence. An example often mobilized to repressive ends is the fact that most crimes occur within rather than between racial groups, such that African Americans, Latinos, and Native Americans confront high incarceration rates *and* high victimization rates. This is the complex story of the U.S. racial state, where normal institutional and ideological processes perpetuate the multigenerational transmission of accumulated advantage and accumulated disadvantage.[20] Accumulated advantage imparts a presumption of innocence; inherited wealth enables home ownership in class-segregated areas (i.e., "a safe neighborhood") and medical insurance for diagnosis of conditions and coverage of various prescriptions such as Ritalin (i.e., more effective forms of meth). In contrast, accumulated disadvantage imparts a presumption of guilt.

Seeing racism as the state-sanctioned reproduction of race-differentiated vulnerability to premature death, then, forces us to evaluate the carceral state as adjudicator and perpetrator of racial violence. From this perspective, we might follow Angela Davis's call to reimagine the institutional landscape of punishment without "looking for prisonlike substitutes for the prison, such as house arrest safeguarded by electronic surveillance bracelets." Instead, reformers might envision a continuum of alternatives to imprisonment—demilitarization of schools, revitalization of education at all levels, a health system that provides free physical and mental care to all, and a justice system based on reparation and reconciliation. As a result, "the creation of new institutions that lay claim to the space now occupied by prison can eventually start to crowd out the prison so that it would inhabit increasingly smaller areas of our social and psychic landscape."[21]

To understand how liberal law-and-order continues to hide its own violence, consider two law-enforcement fixes that bookend the twenty-first century to date: the prosecution of hate crimes after 9/11, and the prosecution of the alleged mastermind of 9/11, Khalid Sheikh Muhammed. Immediately following 9/11, the already high levels of "private" violence against Arab, Muslim, and South Asian people increased, with more arson and vandalism of mosques, temples, and gurdwaras, as well as death threats and murders.[22] At the same time, the arsenal of state violence after 9/11 intensified national security-based profiling, deportation, and detention, including new "Special Registration" requirements for Arab and Muslim men. The Department of Homeland Security registered, fingerprinted, and photographed 85,000 immigrants until stopping the program in May 2003, as federal actors increased selective deportation of immigrants and planned strikes on Afghanistan and Iraq. President George W. Bush and his attorney general John Ashcroft denounced private violence as "un-American and unlawful," subject to hate-crime investigations because "such senseless acts violate federal law." Hate crimes were "un-American" in the sense that they violated the American Creed of democracy and equality; they were "unlawful" from the legacy of liberal civil rights efforts.[23]

When President Bush and his attorney general condemned hate crime "incidents" in the midst of organized anti-Arab/Muslim state violence, it summoned, for me, a foundational moment in the history of liberal law-and-order: when President Truman and his attorney general denounced lynching "incidents" in the midst of 1946 systemic enforcement of Jim Crow. Without naming the four murder victims—Mae Murray Dorsey, George Dorsey, Dorothy Malcolm, and Roger Malcolm—Truman commented that lynching exposed a nation "in a pretty bad fix from a law enforcement standpoint." In a sense, Truman's awkward understatement revealed much. For all the unacknowledged racial violence since Reconstruction, suddenly "law enforcement" was in "a pretty bad fix" because lynching was finally recognized as law's logical extension, not law's abnegation. With this, race liberals recast state-sanctioned white violence as a law enforcement problem. This problem was correctable with modernized carceral machinery—rights-laden, rule-bound, and rational—insulated from the whims of personal anger and prejudice.

Consider the other bookend. When President Obama's attorney general set Khalid Sheik Muhammed's trial for federal court in 2009, many rejected the idea that the self-proclaimed mastermind of 9/11 would enjoy all the rights of a U.S. citizen. Pressured by Republicans in Congress, the Obama administration eventually agreed to a military commission trial in Guantanamo Bay, where, as of November 2013, Khalid Sheikh Muhammed remains in pre-trial hearings. Obama's attorney general, defender of constitutional protections, deemed the Guantanamo military hearing a failure because, had the nation heeded his decision in 2009, "the defendants would be on death row as we speak." When President Obama defended civilian over military justice, his logic was similar. In a vigorous defense of the American legal tradition, President Obama announced his "complete confidence" in "our legal traditions" and "tough prosecutors," concluding that all would be satisfied "when he's convicted and when the death penalty is applied to him."[24] In context of his Democratic predecessors, Obama's promise of death through fair legal process was no political lapse, no racial violence. It was a valedictory for liberal law-and-order.

APPENDIX TABLES

Table A.1 **Overview of Major Federal Crime Legislation, 1790–2010**

Crimes Act of 1790* (Ch. 9, 1 Stat. 112, April 30, 1790)	Criminalized piracy, perjury, murder on federal lands, forgery and counterfeiting, bribing of a judge, and suing a foreign minister
Neutrality Act of 1794 (Ch. 50, 1 Stat. 381, June 5, 1794)	Criminalized serving foreign interests against the United States
Sedition Act of 1798 (Ch. 74, 1 Stat. 596, July 14, 1798)	Criminalized libel and conspiracy to oppose any measure of government
Logan Act of 1799 (Ch. 1, 1 Stat. 613, January 30, 1799)	Criminalized correspondence with a foreign government on a matter in dispute with the United States with the intent of influencing that government
Frauds on the Bank of the United States of 1807 (Ch. 20, 2 Stat. 423, February 24, 1807)	Criminalized forgery and frauds against the Bank of the United States
Crimes Act of 1825* (Ch. 65, 4 Stat. 115, March 3, 1825)	Criminalized arson on U.S. property, violent and property crimes on the high seas, extortion by officers of the U.S. government, and buying or receiving stolen goods
Anti-Polygamy Act of 1862 (Ch. 126, 12 Stat. 501, July 1, 1862)	Criminalized polygamy, focusing on the Territory of Utah
Civil Rights Act of 1866 (Ch. 31, 14 Stat. 27, April 9, 1866)	Criminalized deprivation of rights "committed under color of law" and established that all citizens should enjoy full and equal benefit of the laws

(Continued)

Table A.1 **Continued**

Enforcement Act of 1870 (Ch. 113, 16 Stat. 140, May 31, 1870)	Criminalized official interference with voting, criminalized private interference with free exercise of any constitutional right, and federalized certain state crimes
Ku Klux Klan Act of 1871 (Ch. 22, 17 Stat. 13, April 20, 1872)	Criminalized conspiracy to interfere with government functions and provided liability for injuries caused by deprivation of rights
Comstock Law of 1873 (Ch. 258, 17 Stat. 598, March 3, 1873)	Criminalized mailing "obscene, lewd, or lascivious" material, including information about contraception
Civil Rights Act of 1875 (Ch. 114, 18 Stat. 335, March 1, 1975)	Criminalized violation of guaranteed equal access to public accommodation
Edmunds-Tucker Act of 1887 (Ch. 397, 24 Stat. 635, Match 3, 1887)	Lowered burden of proof for criminal prosecution of polygamy
Sherman Antitrust Act of 1890 (Ch. 647, 26 Stat. 209, July 2, 1890)	Criminalized monopoly and conspiracy to monopolize as misdemeanors
Opium Exclusion Act of 1909 (PL 60-221)	Criminalized the manufacturing, buying, or selling of opium without a license
White Slave Traffic Act of 1910 (PL 61-277)	Criminalized the act of transporting women across state lines for sex work or "immoral purposes" (also known as the Mann Act)
Harrison Narcotics Act of 1914 (PL 63-223)	Required those who legally produce and distribute drugs to register with the federal government, record all transactions, and pay sales taxes
Espionage Act of 1917 (PL 65-24)	Criminalized speech "intended to incite, provoke, or encourage" resistance to the United States
Dyer Act of 1919 (PL 89-41)	Criminalized interstate transport of stolen cars
Eighteenth Amendment and Volstead Act of 1919 (PL 66-66)	Criminalized making, importing, or selling liquor
Jones Act of 1929 (PL 70-899)	Stiffened federal penalties for violations of alcohol prohibition
Lindbergh Act of 1932 (PL 72-189)	Criminalized kidnapping across state lines
Volstead Repeal of 1933	Ended alcohol prohibition

(*Continued*)

Table A.1 **Continued**

National Firearms Act of 1934 (PL 48-474)	Taxed and regulated sale of guns
Marijuana Tax Act of 1937 (PL 75-238)	Criminalized the non-medicinal, non-taxed possession and sale of marijuana
Boggs Act of 1951* (PL 82-255)	Created extensive mandatory minimums for drug-related offenses
Narcotics Control Act of 1956 (PL 84-728)*	Raised mandatory minimums established in the Boggs Act of 1951
Civil Rights Act of 1957 (PL 85-315)	Created permanent U.S. Civil Rights Commission and empowered feds to prosecute conspiracies to deny voting rights
Civil Rights Act of 1960 (PL 86-449)	Criminalized obstruction of court orders and fleeing prosecution for property damage
The Interstate Wire Act of 1961 (PL 87-216)	Criminalized interstate travel to conduct or further an illegal gambling
Juvenile Delinquency and Youth Offenses Control Act of 1961 (PL 87-274)	Funded pilot projects for prevention and control of juvenile delinquency
Gambling Devices Act of 1962 (PL 87-840)	Broadened prohibition on interstate travel for organized crime
Criminal Justice Act of 1964 (PL 88-455)	Provided legal counsel for poor federal defendants
Prisoner Rehabilitation Act of 1965 (PL 89-176)	Authorized use of "halfway houses" for prisoners about to be released, permitted emergency leave for prisoners, permitted daytime release for jobs or training
Correctional Rehabilitation Study Act of 1965 (PL 89-178)	Authorized study of personnel and training needs in the field of rehabilitation of prisoners and delinquents
Law Enforcement Assistance Act of 1965 (PL 89-197)	Created the Office of Law Enforcement Assistance to fund and research local police departments and D.C. police
Bail Reform Act of 1966 (PL 89-465)	Established more lenient bail procedures for those accused of non-capital offenses

(Continued)

Table A.1 **Continued**

Narcotic Addict Rehabilitation Act of 1966 (PL 89-793)	Enabled the commitment of convicted addicts to medical institutions instead of prison for long-term treatment and included a provision for aftercare
Juvenile Delinquency Prevention and Control Act of 1968 (PL 90-445)	Authorized block grants to states for juvenile delinquency programs
Gun Control Act of 1968[#] (PL 90-618)	Banned mail-order and most out-of-state purchases of rifles and shotguns, prohibited interstate shipment of handgun ammunition, prohibited convicted felons from purchasing firearms, and required firearm dealers to be licensed by the Federal Bureau of Alcohol, Tobacco and Firearms
Omnibus Crime Control and Safe Streets Act of 1968[#] (PL 90-351)	Authorized federal funds for law enforcement upgrades, barred persons with riot-related convictions from federal employment and widened the scope of the use of warrants; established the Law Enforcement Assistance Administration (LEAA) and the National Institute of Law Enforcement and Criminal Justice.
D.C. Court Reorganization and Criminal Procedure Act of 1970 (PL 91-358)	Authorized pretrial detention, allowed juveniles as young as 15 to be tried as adults, provided for "no-knock" search and arrest warrants, and authorized use of life sentences for third felony convictions
Organized Crime Control Act of 1970[**] (PL 91-452)	Also known as the Racketeering-Influenced and Corrupt Organizations Act (RICO), this Act extended federal jurisdiction over gambling and authorized civil antitrust remedies against businesses infiltrated by racketeers
Drug Abuse and Prevention and Control Act of 1970[**] (PL 91-513)	Repealed most drug-related mandatory minimums, expanded drug abuse education programs, and broadened programs for addict rehabilitation and treatment

(Continued)

Table A.1 **Continued**

Omnibus Crime Control Act of 1970** (PL 91-644)	Increased federal funding for state crime control and required a greater portion of federal funds go to law enforcement
Rehabilitation Act of 1973 (PL 93-112)	Expanded use of furloughs for federal prisoners
Legal Services Act of 1974 (PL 93-355)	Created the Legal Services Corporation to provide legal assistance to poor and established criterion limiting services poor could receive
Juvenile Justice and Delinquency Prevention Act of 1974 (PL 93-415)	Established a federal grant program to aid states in sheltering and counseling teen runaways and funded juvenile halfway houses as an alternative to incarceration
Parole Reorganization Act of 1976 (PL 94-233)	Set standards for parole procedures
Public Safety Officers' Benefits Act of 1976 (PL 94-430)	Amended the Omnibus Crime Control and Safe Streets Act of 1968 to provide benefits to survivors of certain public safety officers who die in the performance of duty
Juvenile Justice Extension of 1977 (PL 95-115)	Renewed the 1974 Juvenile Justice Act and increased the share of federal aid to states
Comprehensive Crime Control Act of 1984** (PL 98-473)	Created the Sentencing Guidelines system, created a cabinet-level "drug czar" position, nearly eliminated federal parole, created preventative detention of defendants, instituted asset forfeiture for drug and organized crime, and instituted a more restrictive insanity defense
Anti-Drug Abuse Act of 1986** (PL 99-570)	Created more mandatory minimums, instituted crack/powder cocaine sentencing disparities, and increased funds for drug enforcement
Anti-Drug Abuse Act of 1988** (PL 100-690)	Authorized the use of the military for civilian drug-related arrests, civil penalties for drug possession, and a mandatory minimum for possession of crack
Drug Enforcement Increases, 1989 (PL 101-226)	Increased funds for drug enforcement

(Continued)

Table A.1 **Continued**

Anti-Crime Act of 1990* (PL 101-647)	Authorized funding for more DEA agents and state law enforcement and created federal boot camps
Brady Handgun Violence Prevention Act of 1993# (PL 103-159)	Banned domestically produced assault vehicles
Abortion Clinic Access Act of 1994# (PL 103-259)	Criminalized intimidating or injuring in order to prevent the attainment of reproductive health services
Violent Crime Control and Law Enforcement Act of 1994*# (PL 103-322)	Included Federal Assaults Weapon Ban#; increased funding for state and local law enforcement; raised penalties for crimes against women; increased mandatory minimums; proceduralized and expanded capital punishment
Anti-Terrorism Act of 1996*# (PL 104-132)	Restricted state and federal prisoner habeas corpus
Child Pornography Prevention Act of 1996* (PL 104-208)	Enhanced criminal penalties for the distribution and transport of child pornography
Immigration Reform and Immigrant Responsibility Act of 1996# (PL 104-208)	Established civil penalties for unlawful U.S. entry and criminal penalties for high-speed flights from checkpoints; appropriated border security funding
The USA PATRIOT Act of 2001# (PL 107-56)	Appropriated money for domestic security against terrorism, diminished due process requirements for suspected terrorism surveillance, and strengthened border control
Corporate Responsibility Act of 2002# (PL 107-204)	Criminalized destroying records in bankruptcy investigations and auditor failures to maintain five-year records; established the Public Company Accounting Oversight Board
Unborn Victims of Violence Act of 2004# (PL 108-212)	Criminalized causing death or injury to a fetus while committing certain federal crimes

(Continued)

Table A.1 **Continued**

Protect Our Children Act of 2008* (PL 110-401)	Enhanced criminal penalties for the manufacture and publication of child pornography
Fair Sentencing Act of 2010* (PL 111-220)	Reduced the disparity between crack and powder cocaine sentencing from 18 to 1, by raising the weight minimum from 5 grams of crack to 28 grams

* Denotes legislation with establishment or repeal of a mandatory minimum penalty.

\# Denotes "important" legislation as determined by David Mayhew's systematic sweeps of congressional enactments from 1947 to 2008.

Source: Compiled by author. David Mayhew, *Divided We Govern: Party Control, Lawmaking, and Investigations 1946–1990* (New Haven: Yale University Press, 1991), 45, table 4.1; David Mayhew, *Divided We Govern: Party Control, Lawmaking, and Investigations 1946–2002,* Second Edition (New Haven: Yale University Press, 2005), table E.2; for updates, see David Mayhew's website at davidmayhew.commons.yale.edu/datasets-divided-we-govern.

Table A.2 **Selected Votes on the Omnibus Crime Control and Safe Streets Act of 1968**

		All Members		Northern Democrats		Southern Democrats		Republicans		Party Vote	Conservative Coalition Vote
		Yes	No	Yes	No	Yes	No	Yes	No		
Funding Amendments											
Cahill (R-NJ) amendment replacing local categorical grants with block grants	8/8/67	256	147	22	131	62	12	172	4	Yes	Yes
Dirksen (R-IL) amendment replacing local categorical grants with block grants	5/23/68	48	29	7	23	9	6	32	0	Yes	Yes
Criminal Procedure											
Tydings (D-MD) amendment to keep Wade	5/21/68	21	63	17	18	0	19	4	26	No	No
Tydings (D-MD) amendment to keep Mallory	5/21/68	26	58	20	14	2	17	4	27	No	Yes
Tydings (D-MD) amendment to keep Miranda	5/21/68	29	55	21	12	1	17	7	26	No	Yes
Tydings (D-MD) amendment to delete entire procedure title	5/21/68	31	51	23	10	1	17	7	24	No	Yes

Wiretapping											
Long (D-MO) amendment against wiretapping	5/23/68	12	68	8	24	1	15	3	29	No	No
Cellar (D-NY) amendment against wiretapping and forced confessions	6/5/68	60	318	50	84	3	69	7	165	No	No
FINAL VOTES ON OMNIBUS BILL											
Final bill in Senate	5/23/68	72	4	27	2	15	0	30	2	No	No
Final bill in House	6/6/68	369	17	126	15	71	1	172	1	No	No

Notes: A party vote occurs when a majority of voting Democrats opposes a majority of voting Republicans. A conservative coalition vote occurs when a majority of voting northern Democrats opposes a majority of voting southern Democrats and a majority of voting Republicans (following Eric Schickler, *Disjointed Pluralism: Institutional Innovation and the Development of the U.S. Congress* (Princeton: Princeton University Press, 2001)). I define the South as the eleven states of the former Confederacy.

Source: Author's tabulations based on data retrieved from Keith T. Poole, Howard Rosenthal, and Boris T. Shor, *Voteview for Windows vers. 3.0.3: Ross Call Displays of the U.S. Congress, 1789–2000* (accessible at voteview.com).

Table A.3 **U.S. Sentencing Guidelines, 1987**

	Offense Level	I (0 or 1)	II (2 or 3)	III (4, 5, 6)	IV (7, 8, 9)	V (10, 11, 12)	VI (13 or more)
		Criminal History Category (Criminal History Points)					
	1	0–6	0–6	0–6	0–6	0–6	0–6
	2	0–6	0–6	0–6	0–6	0–6	1–7
	3	0–6	0–6	0–6	0–6	2–8	3–9
	4	0–6	0–6	0–6	2–8	4–10	6–12
Zone A	**5**	0–6	0–6	1–7	4–10	6–12	9–15
	6	0–6	1–7	2–8	6–12	9–15	12–18
	7	0–6	2–8	4–10	8–14	12–18	15–21
	8	0–6	4–10	6–12	10–16	15–21	18–24
	9	4–10	6–12	8–14	12–18	18–24	21–27
Zone B							
	10	6–12	8–14	10–16	15–21	21–27	24–30
Zone C	**11**	8–14	10–16	12–18	18–24	24–30	27–33
	12	10–16	12–18	15–21	21–27	27–33	30–37
	13	12–18	15–21	18–24	24–30	30–37	33–41
	14	15–21	18–24	21–27	27–33	33–41	37–46
	15	18–24	21–27	24–30	30–37	37–46	41–51
	16	21–27	24–30	27–33	33–41	41–51	46–57
	17	24–30	27–33	30–37	37–46	46–57	51–63
	18	27–33	30–37	33–41	41–51	51–63	57–71
	19	30–37	33–41	37–46	46–57	57–71	63–78
	20	33–41	37–46	41–51	51–63	63–78	70–87
	21	37–46	41–51	46–57	57–71	70–87	77–96
	22	41–51	46–47	51–63	63–78	77–96	84–105
	23	46–57	51–63	57–71	70–87	84–105	92–115
	24	51–63	57–71	63–78	77–96	92–115	100–125
	25	57–71	63–78	70–87	84–105	100–125	110–137
	26	63–78	70–87	78–97	92–115	110–137	120–150
	27	70–87	78–97	87–108	100–125	120–150	130–162
Zone D							
	28	78–97	87–108	97–121	110–137	130–162	140–175
	29	87–108	97–121	108–135	121–151	140–175	151–188

(Continued)

Table A.3 **Continued**

Offense Level	Criminal History Category (Criminal History Points)					
	I (0 or 1)	II (2 or 3)	III (4, 5, 6)	IV (7, 8, 9)	V (10, 11, 12)	VI (13 or more)
30	97–121	108–135	121–151	135–168	151–188	168–210
31	108–135	121–151	135–168	151–188	168–210	188–235
32	121–151	135–168	151–188	168–210	188–235	210–262
33	135–168	151–188	168–210	188–235	210–262	235–293
34	151–188	168–210	188–235	210–262	235–293	262–327
35	168–210	188–235	210–262	235–293	262–327	292–365
36	188–235	210–262	235–293	262–327	292–365	324–405
37	210–262	235–293	262–327	292–365	324–405	360–life
38	235–293	262–327	292–365	324–405	360–life	360–life
39	262–327	292–365	324–405	360–life	360–life	360–life
40	292–365	324–405	360–life	360–life	360–life	360–life
41	324–405	360–life	360–life	360–life	360–lfe	360–life
42	360–life	360–life	360–life	360–life	360–life	360–life
43	life	life	life	life	life	life

Note: The intersection of the Offense Level and Criminal History Category displays the guideline range in months of imprisonment. The U.S. Sentencing Guidelines were mandatory beginning in November 1987 but have been advisory since 2005.

Source: U.S. Sentencing Commission, *Guidelines Manual* (Washington, DC: Government Printing Office, 1987), 5.2.

Table A.4 **Current Federal Mandatory Minimums Statutes, 2010**

	U.S.C.	Description	Mandatory Minimum
1	2 U.S.C. §192	Refusing to testify before Congress	1 month
2	2 U.S.C. §390	Failure to appear, testify, or produce documents when subpoenaed for contested election case before Congress	1 month or fine*
3	7 U.S.C. §13a	Disobeying cease and desist order by registered entity	6 months or fine or both*
4	7 U.S.C. §13b	Disobeying cease and desist order by non-registered entity	6 months or fine or both*
5	7 U.S.C. §15b(k)	Violating provisions of contract regulation of cotton futures	30 days and fine
6	7 U.S.C. §195(3)	Violation of court order by packer or swine contractor concerning packers and stockyards	6 months
7	7 U.S.C. §2024(b)(1)	Second and subsequent offense, unauthorized use, transfer, acquisition, alteration, or possession of food stamps; value of $100 or more	6 months
8	7 U.S.C. §2024(c)	Second and subsequent offense, use of illegally received, transferred, or used food stamps; value of $100 or more	1 year
9	7 U.S.C. §2146, cross references 18 U.S.C. §1111	Murder of a federal animal transportation inspector	Life
10	8 U.S.C. §1324(a)(2)(B)(i)	First or second offense, bringing in or harboring an unlawful alien when there is reason to believe that he or she will commit a felony	3 years
11	8 U.S.C. §1324(a)(2)(B)(i)	Third or subsequent offense, bringing in or harboring an unlawful alien when there is reason to believe that he or she will commit a felony	5 years
12	8 U.S.C. §1324(a)(2)(B)(ii)	Bringing in or harboring an alien when there is reason to believe he or she committed a crime for commercial advantage or private financial gain	3 years

13	8 U.S.C. §1324(a)(2)(B)(ii)	Bringing in or harboring an alien who reasonably might commit a serious crime	5 years
14	8 U.S.C. §1324(a)(1)(B)(iv)	Death resulting from smuggling "aliens" into the United States	Must imprison, may be up to life
15	8 U.S.C. §1326(b)(3)	Entry of alien who has been previously excluded or removed	10 years
16	12 U.S.C. §617	Commodities price fixing	1 year or fine of both*
17	12 U.S.C. §630	Embezzlement, fraud, or false entries by banking officer	2 years
18	15 U.S.C. §8	Trusts made in order to restrain import trade	3 months
19	15 U.S.C. §1245(b)	Possession or use of ballistic knife in commission of federal crime of violence	5 years or fine or both*
20	15 U.S.C. §1825(a)(2)(C)	First-degree murder of an official enforcing horse protection laws	Life
21	15 U.S.C. §1825(a)(2)(C)	Second-degree murder of an official enforcing horse protection laws	Mandatory incarceration, may be up to life
22	16 U.S.C. §414	Trespassing on federal lands for hunting or shooting	5 days or fine or both*
23	18 U.S.C. §32 (penalty listed in 18 U.S.C. §34)	Death resulting from the destruction of aircraft or aircraft facilities	Life
24	18 U.S.C. §33 (penalty listed in 18 U.S.C. §34)	Death resulting from the destruction of motor vehicles or motor vehicle facilities	Life
25	18 U.S.C. §33(b)	Damage to or destruction of a motor vehicle carrying high-level radioactive waste or spent nuclear fuel with intent to endanger safety of person	30 years
26	18 U.S.C. §36(b)(2)(A)	First-degree murder in a drive-by shooting	Must imprison, may be up to life

(*Continued*)

Table A.4 **Continued**

	U.S.C.	Description	Mandatory Minimum
27	18 U.S.C. §36(b)(2)(B)	Murder in a drive-by shooting other than first-degree murder	Must imprison, may be up to life
28	18 U.S.C. §37	Death resulting from violence at an international airport	Must imprison, may be up to life
29	18 U.S.C. §115(b)(2)	Kidnapping a federal official's family member, resulting in death	Life
30	18 U.S.C. §115(b)(3)	First-degree murder of federal official or family member with intent to retaliate	Life
31	18 U.S.C. §175c(c)(1)	Knowingly engineering or acquiring, and threatening to use, variola virus	25 years
32	18 U.S.C. §175c(c)(2)	Conspires to use variola virus	30 years
33	18 U.S.C. §175c(c)(3)	Violation of variola virus laws, resulting in death	Life
34	18 U.S.C. §225	Organizing, managing, or supervising a continuing financial crimes enterprise	10 years
35	18 U.S.C. §225A(a)(1)	Interstate mailing or transporting child pornography, prior conviction	15 years
36	18 U.S.C. §225A(a)(2)	Knowingly receives or distributes child pornography that has been in interstate transport, prior conviction	15 years
37	18 U.S.C. §225A(a)(3)	Knowingly reproduces, advertises, promotes, or distributes child pornography for interstate transportation, prior conviction	15 years
38	18 U.S.C. §225A(a)(4)	Knowingly sells or possesses child pornography that has been in interstate transportation, prior conviction	15 years
39	18 U.S.C. §225A(a)(6)	Knowingly distributes child pornography that has been in interstate transportation to a minor, prior conviction	15 years

40	18 U.S.C. §229A(2)	Death resulting from chemical weapons offenses	Life
41	18 U.S.C. §247(d)(1)	Death resulting from obstruction of religious rights	Must imprison, may be up to life
42	18 U.S.C. §794(a) (18 U.S.C. §3591(a)(1))	Espionage	Must imprison, may be up to life
43	18 U.S.C. §794(b) (18 U.S.C. §3591(a)(1))	Wartime espionage	Must imprison, may be up to life
44	18 U.S.C. §351(a)	Killing congressional, cabinet, and Supreme Court members	Life
45	18 U.S.C. §844(d)	Death resulting from transportation of explosives	Must imprison, may be up to life
46	18 U.S.C. §844(f)(1)	Destruction or attempted destruction of U.S. property	5 years
47	18 U.S.C. §844(f)(2)	Inflicting injury as result of destruction or attempted destruction of U.S. property	7 years
48	18 U.S.C. §844(f)(3)	Death resulting from destruction of government property	20 years
49	18 U.S.C. §844(h)(2)	First offense, use of fire or explosives to commit a felony, penalty enhancement provision	10 years determinate enhancement
50	18 U.S.C. §844(h)(2)	Second offense, use of fire or explosives to commit a felony, penalty enhancement provision	20 years determinate enhancement
51	18 U.S.C. §844(i)	Destruction or attempted destruction of anything used in interstate or foreign commerce	5 years
52	18 U.S.C. §844(i)	Inflicting injury as result of destruction or attempted destruction of anything used in interstate or foreign commerce	7 years

(Continued)

Table A.4 **Continued**

	U.S.C.	Description	Mandatory Minimum
53	18 U.S.C. §844(i)	Death resulting from destruction of property by explosives or fire	Must imprison, may be up to life
54	18 U.S.C. §844(o)	Transfer of explosives for violent or drug crime	10 years
55	18 U.S.C. §844(o)	Second or subsequent offense involving the transfer of explosive materials to be used to commit a crime of violence or a drug trafficking crime	20 year enhancement
56	18 U.S.C. §924(c)(1)	First offense, crime of violence or drug trafficking while using or carrying a firearm	5 years
57	18 U.S.C. §924(c)(1)	First offense, crime of violence or drug trafficking while using or carrying a machine gun or destructive device, or firearm silencer or muffler	30 years
58	18 U.S.C. §924(c)(1)	First offense, using or carrying of short-barreled rifle or shotgun, or semiautomatic assault weapon in crime of violence or drug trafficking	10 years
59	18 U.S.C. §924(c)(1)(A)(i)	First offense, using firearm in crime of violence or drug trafficking; penalty enhancement provision	5 years determinate enhancement
60	18 U.S.C. §924(c)(1)(A)(ii)	First offense, crime of violence or drug trafficking, firearm brandished	7 years
61	18 U.S.C. §924(c)(1)(A)(iii)	First offense, crime of violence or drug trafficking, firearm discharged	10 years
62	18 U.S.C. §924(c)(1)(C)(i)	Second or subsequent offense, violation of §924(c)(1)(A)	25 years
63	18 U.S.C. §924(c)(1)(C)(ii)	Second or subsequent offense, violation of §924 with a machine gun or a destructive device, or is equipped with a firearm silencer or muffler	Life

64	18 U.S.C. §924(c)(5)(A)	Possession or use of armor-piercing ammunition during a crime of violence or drug trafficking; penalty enhancement provision	15 years
65	18 U.S.C. §924(c)(5)(B)(i)	Possession or use of armor-piercing ammunition during a crime of violent or drug trafficking; death results	Must imprison, may be for life
66	18 U.S.C. §924(e)(1)	Possession of a firearm or ammunition by a fugitive or addict who has three convictions for violent felonies or drug offenses	15 years
67	18 U.S.C. §929(a)(1)	Carrying firearm and armor piercing ammunition during crime of violence or drug trafficking; penalty enhancement provision	5 years enhancement
68	18 U.S.C. §930(c)	Homicide or attempted homicide involving a firearm in federal facility	Life
69	18 U.S.C. §1028A(a)(1)	Aggravated identity theft	2 years
70	18 U.S.C. §1028A(a)(2)	Aggravated identity theft related to federal crime of terrorism (18 U.S.C §2332b(g)(5)(B)	5 years
71	18 U.S.C. §1091(b)(1)	Genocide committed in the United States or by U.S. national	Life
72	18 U.S.C. §1111(b)	First-degree murder	Life
73	18 U.S.C. §1111(b)	Second-degree murder	Mandatory incarceration, may be up to life
74	18 U.S.C. §1114(1)	First-degree or attempted murder of a federal official or law enforcement officer	Life
75	18 U.S.C. §§1116(a)	First-degree murder of foreign officials or internationally protected persons	Life
76	18 U.S.C. §1118	Murder by a federal prisoner	Life
77	18 U.S.C. §1119(b)	Murder of a U.S. national in a foreign country	Life
78	18 U.S.C. §1120	Murder by an escaped federal prisoner already sentenced to life	Life

(Continued)

Table A.4 **Continued**

	U.S.C.	Description	Mandatory Minimum
79	18 U.S.C. §1121(a)(1)	Murder of a person aiding federal or state law enforcement officers	Life
80	18 U.S.C. §1121(b)(1)	Murder of a state correctional officer, committed by an incarcerated person	20 years
81	18 U.S.C. §1122	Selling or donating, or the attempt to do so, of HIV-positive tissue or bodily fluids for uses other than medical research	1 year or fine or both
82	18 U.S.C. §1201(a)	Death resulting from a kidnapping	Life
83	18 U.S.C. §1201(g)(1)	Kidnapping a minor (under age of 18, by a non-relative)	20 years
84	18 U.S.C. §1203(a)	Death resulting from hostage taking	Life
85	18 U.S.C. §1389	Assaulting a U.S. serviceperson or their immediate family member	6 months
86	18 U.S.C. §1466A(a)	Possessing, producing, or transporting obscene visual representations of the sexual abuse of children	5 years and 15 years with prior conviction
87	18 U.S.C. §1503(b)(1)	Murder of a juror or court officer	Life
88	18 U.S.C. §1512(a)(1)(A)	Preventing the attendance or testimony of any person in an official proceeding, resulting in death	Life
89	18 U.S.C. §1512(a)(1)(B)	Preventing the production of a record, document, or other object, in an official proceeding, resulting in death	Life
90	18 U.S.C. §1512(a)(1)(C)	Preventing the communication of information to a judge relating to a federal offense, resulting in death	Life
91	18 U.S.C. §1513, cross references 18 U.S.C. §1111	First-degree murder of a witness, victim, or informant in retaliation	Life

92	18 U.S.C. §1591(b)(1)	Sex trafficking of children under the age of 14 by fraud, means of force, threats of force, or coercion	15 years
93	18 U.S.C. §1591(b)(2)	Sex trafficking of children between 14 and 18 years old, by force, fraud, or coercion	10 years
94	18 U.S.C. §1651	Piracy under laws of nations	Life
95	18 U.S.C. §1652	Piracy by U.S. citizen	Life
96	18 U.S.C. §1653	Piracy against U.S. by non-citizen	Life
97	18 U.S.C. §1655	Piracy by a seaman	Life
98	18 U.S.C. §1658(b)	Preventing escape from a sinking vessel or causing a vessel to run aground by use of false light	10 years
99	18 U.S.C. §1661	Robbery by pirates	Life
100	18 U.S.C. §1716	Death results from mailing of injurious articles with intent of kill	Life
101	18 U.S.C. §1751(a)	Murder of president or president's staff	Life
102	18 U.S.C. §1917	Interference with civil service examinations	10 days or fine or both*
103	18 U.S.C. §1956(h)	Conspiracy to commit money laundering offenses	Mandatory minimum for the underlying offense
104	18 U.S.C. §1958(a)	Use of interstate commerce facilities during murder-for-hire	Life
105	18 U.S.C. §1959	Murder in aid of racketeering	Life
106	18 U.S.C. §1959	Kidnapping of a person for compensation of a crime of violence in aid of RICO (Racketeering)	Mandatory incarceration, may be up to life
107	18 U.S.C. §1992	Death resulting from wrecking trains	Must imprison, may be for life

(Continued)

Table A.4 **Continued**

	U.S.C.	Description	Mandatory Minimum
108	18 U.S.C. §2113(e)	Kidnapping during bank robbery or larceny	10 years
109	18 U.S.C. §2113(e)	Death resulting from bank robbery	Life
110	18 U.S.C. §2118(c)(2)	Robbing a DEA registrant of a controlled substance in his or her care, resulting in death	Mandatory incarceration, may be up to life
111	18 U.S.C. §2118(c)(2)	Burglarizing a DEA registrant of a controlled substance on his or her property, resulting in death	Mandatory incarceration, may be up to life
112	18 U.S.C. §2241(c)	First offense, engaging in a sexual act with a child above the age of 12, but under the age of 16	30 years
113	18 U.S.C. §2241(c)	Second or subsequent offense, engaging in a sexual act with a child under 12, or engaging in a sexual act by force with a child between 12 and 16	Life
114	18 U.S.C. §2245	Death resulting from sex abuse crimes as provided in chapter 109A and select additional sections	Must imprison, may be for life
115	18 U.S.C. §2250(c)	Failure to register as a sex offender and committing a crime of violence	5 years
116	18 U.S.C. §2251(a)	Coercing or attempting to coerce a minor to engage in sexually explicit conduct and transporting the depiction	15 years
117	18 U.S.C. §2251(a)	Coercing or attempting to coerce a minor to engage in sexually explicit conduct and transporting the depiction, one prior conviction	25 years
118	18 U.S.C. §2251(a)	Coercing or attempting to coerce a minor to engage in sexually explicit conduct and transporting the depiction, two or more prior convictions	35 years

119	18 U.S.C. §2251(a)	Coercing or attempting to coerce a minor to engage in sexually explicit conduct and transporting the depiction, death results	30 years
120	18 U.S.C. §2251(b)	Engaging or attempting to engage in sexually explicit conduct by a parent with a child and transporting the depiction	15 years
121	18 U.S.C. §2251(b)	Engaging or attempting to engage in sexually explicit conduct by a parent with a child and transporting the depiction, one prior conviction	25 years
122	18 U.S.C. §2251(b)	Engaging or attempting to engage in sexually explicit conduct by a parent with a child and transporting the depiction, two or more prior convictions	35 years
123	18 U.S.C. §2251(b)	Engaging or attempting to engage in sexually explicit conduct by a parent with a child and transporting the depiction, death results	30 years
124	18 U.S.C. §2251(c)	Enticing or coercing a minor to engage in sexually explicit conduct and transporting the depiction	15 years
125	18 U.S.C. §2251(c)	Enticing or coercing a minor to engage in sexually explicit conduct and transporting the depiction, one prior conviction	25 years
126	18 U.S.C. §2251(c)	Enticing or coercing a minor to engage in sexually explicit conduct and transporting the depiction, two or more prior convictions	35 years
127	18 U.S.C. §2251(c)	Enticing or coercing a minor to engage in sexually explicit conduct and transporting the depiction, death results	30 years
128	18 U.S.C. §2251(d)	Knowingly making any advertisement concerning the visual depiction of a minor engaging in sexually explicit conduct	15 years
129	18 U.S.C. §2251(d)	Knowingly making any advertisement concerning the visual depiction of a minor engaging in sexually explicit conduct, one prior conviction	25 years

(Continued)

Table A.4 **Continued**

	U.S.C.	Description	Mandatory Minimum
130	18 U.S.C. §2251(d)	Knowingly making any advertisement concerning the visual depiction of a minor engaging in sexually explicit conduct, two or more prior convictions	35 years
131	18 U.S.C. §2251(d)	Knowingly making any advertisement concerning the visual depiction of a minor engaging in sexually explicit conduct, resulting in death	30 years
132	18 U.S.C. §2251A(a)	Sale or transfer of custody of minor, knowing minor will be sexually exploited	30 years
133	18 U.S.C. §2251A(b)	Purchase or obtain custody of minor, knowing minor will be sexually exploited	30 years
134	18 U.S.C. §2252(a)(1)	First offense, the transport or shipment of child pornography, including conspiracy or attempt	5 years
135	18 U.S.C. §2252(a)(1)	Second or subsequent offense, the transport or shipment of child pornography, including conspiracy or attempt	15 years
136	18 U.S.C. §2252(a)(2)	First offense, receipt of child pornography that has been transported, including conspiracy or attempt	5 years
137	18 U.S.C. §2252(a)(2)	Second or subsequent offense, receipt of child pornography that has been transported, including conspiracy or attempt	15 years
138	18 U.S.C. §2252(a)(3)	First offense, sale, possession, or intent to sell child pornography, including conspiracy or attempt	5 years
139	18 U.S.C. §2252(a)(3)	Second or subsequent offense, sale, possession, or intent to sell child pornography, including conspiracy or attempt	15 years
140	18 U.S.C. §2252(a)(4)	Second or subsequent offense, possession of one or more items of child pornography, including conspiracy or attempt	10 years

141	18 U.S.C. §2252A(a)(1)	Interstate mailing or transporting of child pornography	5 years
142	18 U.S.C. §2252A(a)(2)	Knowingly receives or distributes child pornography that has been in interstate transport	5 years
143	18 U.S.C. §2252A(a)(3)	Knowingly reproduces, advertises, promotes, or distributes child pornography for interstate transportation	5 years
144	18 U.S.C. §2252A(a)(4)	Knowingly sells or possesses child pornography that has been in interstate transportation	5 years
145	18 U.S.C. §2252A(a)(5)	Possession of child pornography, prior conviction	10 years
146	18 U.S.C. §2252A(a)(6)	Knowingly distributes child pornography that has been in interstate transportation to a minor	5 years
147	18 U.S.C. §2252A(b)(1)	Second or subsequent offense, transports, receives, distributes, reproduces child pornography	5 years
148	18 U.S.C. §2252A(b)(2)	Second or subsequent offense, possession of child pornography	2 years
149	18 U.S.C. §2252A(g)	Child exploitation enterprise	20 years
150	18 U.S.C. §2257	Second offense, failure to maintain records, falsifying records, or distributing materials not mentioning the records of sexually explicit performers	2 years
151	18 U.S.C. §2257A(i)(3)	Failure to keep records of depictions of simulated sexual conduct, with a prior conviction under this section	2 years
152	18 U.S.C. §2260(a), cross references 2251(e)	Use of a minor in the production of sexually explicit depictions for importation into the United States	15 years

(Continued)

Table A.4 **Continued**

	U.S.C.	Description	Mandatory Minimum
153	18 U.S.C. §2260(a), cross references 2251(e)	Use of a minor in the production of sexually explicit depictions for importation into the United States, prior conviction	25 years
154	18 U.S.C. §2260(a), cross references 2251(e)	Use of a minor in the production of sexually explicit depictions for importation into the United States, two or more convictions	35 years
155	18 U.S.C. §2260(a), cross references 2251(e)	Use of a minor in the production of sexually explicit depictions for importation into the United States, resulting in death	30 years
156	18 U.S.C. §2260(b), cross references 2252(b)(1)	Use of a visual depiction of a minor engaging in sexually explicit conduct with the intent of importing the depiction	5 years
157	18 U.S.C. §2260(b), cross references 2252(b)(1)	Use of a visual depiction of a minor engaging in sexually explicit conduct with the intent of importing the depiction, second or subsequent offense.	15 years
158	18 U.S.C. §2260A	Penalty enhancement for registered sex offenders who commit specified offenses involving a minor	10 year enhancement
159	18 U.S.C. §2261(b)(6)	Stalking in violation of a restraining order, or other order described in 18 USC §2265	1 year
160	18 U.S.C. §2280	Violence against maritime navigation resulting in death	Must imprison, may be for life
161	18 U.S.C. §2281	Violence against maritime platforms where resulting in death	Must imprison, may be for life
162	18 U.S.C. §2291	Murder in destruction of maritime facilities	Life

163	18 U.S.C. §2332	Murder of a U.S. national overseas	Must imprison, may be for life
164	18 U.S.C. §2332a	Death resulting from use of weapons of mass destruction against U.S. national or within the United States	Must imprison, may be for life
165	18 U.S.C. §2332a(b)	Death resulting from use of weapons of mass destruction by a U.S. national outside of the United States	Must imprison, may be for life
166	18 U.S.C. §2332b	Death resulting from multinational terrorism	Must imprison, may be for life
167	18 U.S.C. §2332f, cross references §2332a(a)	Death resulting from bombing of government facilities, public transportation, or public places or infrastructure	Must imprison, may be for life
168	18 U.S.C. §2332g(c)(1)	Knowingly produces, transfers, or possesses an explosive or incendiary rocket or missile	25 years
169	18 U.S.C. §2332g(c)(2)	Uses, attempts or conspires to use, or possesses and threatens to use, an explosive or incendiary rocket or missile	30 years
170	18 U.S.C. §2332g(c)(3)	Knowingly produces, transfers, or possesses an explosive or incendiary rocket or missile, resulting in death	Life
171	18 U.S.C. §2332h(c)(1)	Knowingly produces, transfers, or possesses any weapon designed to release radiation or radioactivity at a level dangerous to human life	25 years
172	18 U.S.C. §2332h(c)(2)	Uses, attempts or conspires to use, or possesses and threatens to use, any weapon designed to release radiation at a level dangerous to human life	30 years
173	18 U.S.C. §2332h(c)(3)	Knowingly produces, transfers, or possesses any weapon designed to release radiation at a level dangerous to human life, resulting in death	Life

(Continued)

Table A.4 **Continued**

	U.S.C.	Description	Mandatory Minimum
174	18 U.S.C. §2340a	Torture resulting in death	Must imprison, may be for life
175	18 U.S.C. §2381	Treason	5 years
176	18 U.S.C. §2422(b)	Coercion, via mail or any facility of interstate commerce, of a minor for illegal sexual activity	10 years and fine
177	18 U.S.C. §2423(a)	Transporting a minor across state lines for the purpose of prostitution or another sexual activity that can be charged as a criminal offense	10 years and fine
178	18 U.S.C. §2423(e)	Attempt or conspiracy to transport a minor across state lines for the purpose of a sexual activity that can be charged as a criminal offense	10 years and fine
179	18 U.S.C. §3559(c)(1)(A)(i)	Serious violent felony, after two or more serious violent felonies	Life
180	18 U.S.C. §3559(c)(1)(A)(ii)	Serious violent felony, after one or more serious violent felonies and one or more serious drug offenses	Life
181	18 U.S.C. §3559(d)(1)	Crimes against children, where death results and child is less than 14	Life
182	18 U.S.C. §3559(e)(1)	Sentence enhancement; federal sex offense committed against a minor and the offender has a prior sex conviction in which a minor was the victim	Life
183	18 U.S.C. §3559(f)(1)	Sentence enhancement, murder of child less than 18	30 years
184	18 U.S.C. §3559(f)(1)	Sentence enhancement, murder of child less than 18, death results and circumstances meet subsections (A)–(D) of section 3591(a)(2) of this title	Life

185	18 U.S.C. §3559(f)(2)	Sentence enhancement; kidnapping or maiming of a child less than 18	25 years
186	18 U.S.C. §3559(f)(3)	Sentence enhancement; crime of violence resulting in serious bodily injury	10 years
187	18 U.S.C. §3559(f)(3)	Sentence enhancement, if a dangerous weapon is used during and in relation to a crime of violence	10 years
188	19 U.S.C. §283	Failure to report seaboard saloon purchases to customers	3 months
189	21 U.S.C. §212	Practice of pharmacy and sale of poisons in China	1 month or fine*
190	21 U.S.C. §461(c)	Murder of federal poultry inspector	Life
191	21 U.S.C. §461(c)	Second-degree murder of a federal poultry inspector	Must imprison, may be up to life
192	21 U.S.C. §622	Bribery of inspectors and acceptance of bribes	1 year
193	21 U.S.C. §675	Murder of federal meat inspector	Life
194	21 U.S.C. §841(b)(1)(A)	First offense, intent to distribute various substances including heroin, cocaine, marijuana, or methamphetamine, no death or serious bodily injury	10 years
195	21 U.S.C. §841(b)(1)(A)	Second offense, intent to distribute various substances including heroin, cocaine, marijuana, or methamphetamine, no death or serious bodily injury	20 years
196	21 U.S.C. §841(b)(1)(A)	First offense, intent to distribute various substances including heroin, cocaine, marijuana, or methamphetamine, resulting in death or serious bodily injury	20 years
197	21 U.S.C. §841(b)(1)(A)	Second offense, intent to distribute various substances including heroin, cocaine, marijuana, or methamphetamine, resulting in death or serious bodily injury	Life
198	21 U.S.C. §841(b)(1)(A)	Third offense, intent to distribute various substances including heroin, cocaine, marijuana, or methamphetamine	Life

(Continued)

Table A.4 **Continued**

	U.S.C.	Description	Mandatory Minimum
199	21 U.S.C. §841(b)(1)(B)	First offense, intent to distribute smaller amounts of substances including heroin, cocaine, or marijuana, no death or serious bodily injury results	5 years
200	21 U.S.C. §841(b)(1)(B)	Second and all subsequent offense, intent to distribute smaller amounts of substances including heroin, cocaine, or marijuana, no death or serious bodily injury results	10 years
201	21 U.S.C. §841(b)(1)(B)	First offense, intent to distribute smaller amounts of substances including heroin, cocaine, or marijuana, resulting in death or serious bodily injury	20 years
202	21 U.S.C. §841(b)(1)(B)	Second or any subsequent offense, intent to distribute smaller amounts of substances including heroin, cocaine, or marijuana, resulting in death or serious bodily injury	Life
203	21 U.S.C. §841(b)(1)(C)	First offense, intent to distribute various substances including gamma hydroxybutyric acid, death or serious bodily injury results from use	20 years
204	21 U.S.C. §841(b)(1)(C)	One or more prior convictions, intent to distribute various substances including gamma hydroxybutyric acid, death or serious bodily injury results from use	Life
205	21 U.S.C. §844(a)	Second offense, simple possession, all substances other than those containing cocaine base but weight in 3 grams or less	15 days
206	21 U.S.C. §844(a)	Third and all subsequent offenses, simple possession, all substances other than those containing cocaine base but weighing 1 gram or less	90 days
207	21 U.S.C. §846	Attempt and conspiracy under Chapter 13, drug abuse prevention and control subchapter entitled offenses and penalties	Mandatory minimum term specified at offense
208	21 U.S.C. §848(a)	First offense, continuing criminal enterprise	20 years
209	21 U.S.C. §848(a)	Second and all subsequent offenses, continuing criminal enterprise	30 years

210	21 U.S.C. §848(b)	Continuing criminal enterprise, qualifying drug "kingpins"	Life
211	21 U.S.C. §848(e)(1)(A)	Murder committed by a drug "kingpin"	20 years
212	21 U.S.C. §848(e)(1)(B)	Killing law enforcement in drug crime	20 years
213	21 U.S.C. §859(a)(2)	First offense, distribution to persons under age 21	1 year or 841(b), whichever is the greater
214	21 U.S.C. §859(b)(2)	Second offense, distribution to persons under age 21	1 year or 841(b), whichever is the greater
215	21 U.S.C. §859(b), cross reference to 21 U.S.C. 841	Third offense and subsequent offense, distribution to persons under age 21	Life
216	21 U.S.C. §860(a)(2)	First offense, distribution of a controlled substance near a school or similar facility	1 year or 841(b), whichever is the greater
217	21 U.S.C. §860(b)(1)	Second offense, distribution of a controlled substance near a school or similar facility	3 years or 841(b), whichever is greater
218	21 U.S.C. §860(b), cross reference to 21 U.S.C. 841	Third offense, distribution of a controlled substance near a school or similar facility	Life
219	21 U.S.C. §861(a)	Employment or use of persons under 18 years of age in drug operations	Mandatory minimum term at section 841(b)(1)(A)
220	21 U.S.C. §861(b)	First offense, employing, using, or persuading a person under age 18 to engage in a controlled substance offense	1 year or other minimum, whichever is the greater
221	21 U.S.C. §861(c)	Second offense, employing, using, or persuading a person under age 18 to engage in a controlled substance offense	1 year or other minimum, whichever is the greater

(Continued)

Table A.4 **Continued**

	U.S.C.	Description	Mandatory Minimum
222	21 U.S.C. §861(c), cross reference to 21 U.S.C. 841	Third offense, employing, using, or persuading a person under age 18 to engage in a controlled substance offense	Life
223	21 U.S.C. §861(f)	First offense, distribution of controlled substance to pregnant individual	1 year or other minimum, whichever is the greater
224	21 U.S.C. §861(f)	Second offense, distribution of controlled substance to pregnant individual	1 year or other minimum, whichever is the greater
225	21 U.S.C. §861(f)	Third offense, distribution of controlled substance to pregnant individual	Life
226	21 U.S.C. §960(b)(1)	First offense, import or export various substances including heroin, cocaine, or marijuana, no death or serious bodily injury results	10 years
227	21 U.S.C. §960(b)(1)	Second or any subsequent offense, import or export various substances including heroin, cocaine, or marijuana, no death or serious bodily injury results	20 years
228	21 U.S.C. §960(b)(1)	First offense, import or export various substances including heroin, cocaine, or marijuana, resulting in death or serious bodily injury	20 years
229	21 U.S.C. §960(b)(1)	Second or any subsequent offense, import or export various substances including heroin, cocaine, or marijuana, resulting in death or serious bodily injury	Life
230	21 U.S.C. §960(b)(2)	First offense, import or export smaller amounts various substances including heroin, cocaine, or marijuana, no death or serious bodily injury results	5 years
231	21 U.S.C. §960(b)(2)	Second and all subsequent offenses, import or export smaller amounts various substances including heroin, cocaine, or marijuana, no death or serious bodily injury results	10 years

	Statute	Offense	Penalty
232	21 U.S.C. §960(b)(2)	First offense, import or export smaller amounts various substances including heroin, cocaine, or marijuana, death or serious bodily injury results	20 years
233	21 U.S.C. §960(b)(2)	Second or any subsequent offense, import or export smaller amounts various substances including heroin, cocaine, or marijuana, death or serious bodily injury results	Life
234	21 U.S.C. §960(b)(3)	First offense, import or export various substances including gamma hydroxybutyric acid, resulting in death or serious bodily injury	20 years
235	21 U.S.C. §960(b)(3)	Second or any subsequent offense, import or export various substances including gamma hydroxybutyric acid, resulting in death or serious bodily injury	Life
236	21 U.S.C. §960a, cross reference 21 USC §841(b)	Narco-terrorism and knowingly provides anything of pecuniary value to any person or organization that has engaged or engages in terrorist activity	At least twice the minimum under 21 USC § 841(b)(1)
237	21 U.S.C. §963	Attempt and conspiracy under Chapter 13, drug abuse prevention and control subchapter entitled import and export	Mandatory minimum term specified at offense
238	21 U.S.C. §1041(b)	Murder of an egg inspector	Life
239	21 U.S.C. §1041(b)	Second-degree murder of an egg products inspector	Must imprison, may be up to life
240	22 U.S.C. §4221	Forgery of U.S. seal	1 year
241	23 U.S.C. §164(a)(5)(D)(i)	Second offense, driving under the influence	5 days or 30 days community service
242	23 U.S.C. §164(a)(5)(D)(ii)	Third offense, driving under the influence	10 days or 60 days community service

(Continued)

Table A.4 **Continued**

	U.S.C.	Description	Mandatory Minimum
243	33 U.S.C. §410	Navigable water regulation violation	30 days or fine or both*
244	33 U.S.C. §411	Deposit of refuse or obstruction of navigable waterway	30 days or fine or both*
245	33 U.S.C. §441	Depositing refuse in New York or Baltimore harbors	30 days or fine or both
246	33 U.S.C. §447	Bribery of New York or Baltimore harbor inspectors	6 months
247	42 U.S.C. §2272(b)	Violation of prohibitions governing atomic weapons, no death results	25 years and fine
248	42 U.S.C. §2272(b)	Using, attempting to use, or threatening while possessing, an atomic weapon	30 years and fine
249	42 U.S.C. §2272(b)	Violation of prohibitions governing atomic weapons, resulting in death	Life and fine
250	42 U.S.C. §2283, cross reference 18 U.S.C. §1111	Murder of nuclear inspectors	Life
251	46 U.S.C. Appx §1228	Violation of Merchant Marine Act	1 year or fine or both*
252	46 U.S.C. §58109(a)	Individual convicted of violating Merchant Marine Act	1 year or fine or both
253	46 U.S.C. §70506	Intent to manufacture or distribute a controlled substance on a vessel	Mandatory Minimum at 21 USC §§ 960 & 962

254	47 U.S.C. §13	Refusal to operate railroad or telegraph lines	6 months
255	47 U.S.C. §220(e)	Altering or destroying books or accounts of common carrier	1 year or fine or both*
256	49 U.S.C. §46502(a)(2)(A)	Aircraft piracy, no death results	20 years
257	49 U.S.C. §46502(a)(2)(B)	Aircraft piracy, resulting in death	Life
258	49 U.S.C. §46502(b)(1)(A)	Aircraft piracy outside U.S. special aircraft jurisdiction, no death results	20 years
259	49 U.S.C. §46502(b)(1)(B)	Aircraft piracy, outside U.S. special aircraft jurisdiction, resulting in death	Life
260	49 U.S.C. §46506(1)	First-degree murder in special aircraft jurisdiction of the United States	Life
261	49 U.S.C. §46506(1)	Second-degree murder in special aircraft jurisdiction of the United States	Must imprison, may be up to life

Note: This list of civilian crimes with mandatory incarceration penalties excludes crimes with only a mandatory fine. The * indicates a mandatory minimum penalty of incarceration and/or a fine.

Source: Compiled by author.

Table A.5 Capital Crimes, by the 1993 Democratic Count and by Year of Enactment, 1974–2010

"64 death penalties" by Democratic count, September 1993	Year Enacted	Public Law	U.S. Code	Capital Crime	
1	1974	93-366	49 U.S.C. § 46502 (previously 49 U.S.C. §1472)	Aircraft piracy where death results	1
	1988	100-690	21 U.S.C. § 848(e)(1)(A)	Murder committed by drug "kingpin"	2
	1988	100-690	21 U.S.C. § 848(e)(1)(B)	Murder of a law enforcement office during a drug crime	3
	1994	103-322	7 U.S.C. § 2146	Murder of a federal animal transportation inspector	4
	1994	103-322	8 U.S.C. § 1324	Murder related to the smuggling of aliens	5
	1994	103-322	15 U.S.C. 1825	Murder of an official enforcing horse protection laws	6
2	1994	103-322	18 U.S.C. § 32 (18 U.S.C. §34)	Death resulting from destruction of aircrafts	7
3	1994	103-322	18 U.S.C. § 32 (18 U.S.C. §34)	Death resulting from destruction of aircraft facilities	8
4	1994	103-322	18 U.S.C. § 33 (18 U.S.C. §34)	Death resulting from destruction of motor vehicles	9
5	1994	103-322	18 U.S.C. § 33 (18 U.S.C. §34)	Death resulting from destruction of motor vehicle facilities	10
6	1994	103-322	18 U.S.C. § 36	Murder in drive-by shooting	11

7	1994	103-322	18 U.S.C. § 37	Death resulting from violence at an international airport	12
8	1994	103-322	18 U.S.C. § 115	Murder of federal official or family member with intent to retaliate	13
9	1994	103-322	18 U.S.C. § 241	Death resulting from conspiracy against civil rights	14
10	1994	103-322	18 U.S.C. § 242	Death resulting from deprivation of civil rights under color of law	15
11	1994	103-322	18 U.S.C. § 245	Death resulting from deprivation of federally protected activities	16
12	1994	103-322	18 U.S.C. § 247	Death resulting from obstruction of religious rights	17
13	1994	103-322	18 U.S.C. § 351	Murder of a member of Congress	18
14	1994	103-322	18 U.S.C. § 351	Murder of a Cabinet officer	19
15	1994	103-322	18 U.S.C. § 351	Murder of a Supreme Court Justice	20
16	1994	103-322	18 U.S.C. § 351	Murder of a high-level official	21
17	1994	103-322	18 U.S.C. § 794(a) (18 U.S.C. §3591(a)(1))	Espionage	22
18	1994	103-322	18 U.S.C. § 794(b) (18 U.S.C. §3591(a)(1))	Wartime espionage	23
19	1994	103-322	18 U.S.C. § 844(d)	Death resulting from transportation of explosives	24
20	1994	103-322	18 U.S.C. § 844(f)	Death resulting from destruction of government property by explosives	25

Table A.5 **Continued**

"64 death penalties" by Democratic count, September 1993	Year Enacted	Public Law	U.S. Code	Capital Crime	
21	1994	103-322	18 U.S.C. § 844(f)	Death resulting from destruction of government property by fire	26
22	1994	103-322	18 U.S.C. § 844(i)	Death resulting from destruction of property by explosive	27
23	1994	103-322	18 U.S.C. § 844(i)	Death resulting from destruction of property by fire	28
24	1994	103-322	18 U.S.C. § 924	Gun murder during a federal drug crime	29
25	1994	103-322	18 U.S.C. § 924	Gun murder during a federal crime of violence	30
26	1994	103-322	18 U.S.C. § 924	Gun murder during a federal drug trafficking crime	31
27	1994	103-322	18 U.S.C. § 930	Homicide or attempted homicide involving firearm in federal facility	32
28	1994	103-322	18 U.S.C. § 1091	Genocide committed in the United States or by U.S. national	33
29	1994	103-322	18 U.S.C. § 1111	First-degree murder	34
30	1994	103-322	18 U.S.C. § 1114(1)	Murder of a federal official	35
31	1994	103-322	18 U.S.C. § 1114 (1)	Murder of a federal law enforcement officer	36
32	1994	103-322	18 U.S.C. § 1114 (1)	Murder of a federal judge	37
33	1994	103-322	18 U.S.C. § 1116 (a)	Murder of a foreign official	38
34	1994	103-322	18 U.S.C. § 1116 (a)	Murder of a diplomat	39
35	1994	103-322	18 U.S.C. § 1118	Murder by a federal prisoner	40

36	1994	103-322	18 U.S.C. § 1119(b)	Murder of a U.S. national in a foreign country	41
37	1994	103-322	18 U.S.C. § 1120	Murder by an escaped federal prisoner already sentenced to life	42
38	1994	103-322	18 U.S.C. § 1121(a)	Murder of a local official assisting federal law enforcement	43
39	1994	103-322	18 U.S.C. § 1121(a)	Murder of a state official assisting federal law enforcement	44
	1994	103-322	18 U.S.C. § 1121(b)	Murder of a state correctional officer by a person incarcerated under federal law	45
40	1994	103-322	18 U.S.C. § 1201(a)	Death resulting from a kidnapping	46
41	1994	103-322	18 U.S.C. § 1203(a)	Death resulting from hostage taking	47
42	1994	103-322	18 U.S.C. § 1503(b)(1)	Murder of a court officer	48
43	1994	103-322	18 U.S.C. § 1503(b)(1)	Murder of a juror	49
44	1994	103-322	18 U.S.C. § 1512(a)(1)(A)	Preventing the attendance or testimony of any person in an official proceeding, death results	50
	1994	103-322	18 U.S.C. § 1512(a)(1)(B)	Preventing the production of a record or document in an official proceeding, death results	51
	1994	103-322	18 U.S.C. § 1512(a)(1)(C)	Preventing the communication of information to a federal judge, death results	52
45	1994	103-322	18 U.S.C. § 1513	Retaliatory murder of witness	53
46	1994	103-322	18 U.S.C. § 1513	Retaliatory murder of victim	

(Continued)

Table A.5 **Continued**

"64 death penalties" by Democratic count, September 1993	Year Enacted	Public Law	U.S. Code	Capital Crime	
47	1994	103-322	18 U.S.C. § 1513	Retaliatory murder of informant	54
48	1994	103-322	18 U.S.C. § 1716	Death results from mailing of injurious articles with intent of kill	55
49	1994	103-322	18 U.S.C. § 1751(a)	Murder of President	56
50	1994	103-322	18 U.S.C. § 1751(a)	Murder of Vice President	57
51	1994	103-322	18 U.S.C. § 1958(a)	Use of interstate commerce facilities during murder-for-hire	58
52	1994	103-322	18 U.S.C. § 1959	Murder in aid of racketeering	59
53	1994	103-322	18 U.S.C. § 1992	Death resulting from wrecking trains	60
54	1994	103-322	18 U.S.C. § 2113	Death resulting from bank robbery	61
55	1994	103-322	18 U.S.C. § 2119	Death resulting from carjacking	62
56	1994	103-322	18 U.S.C. § 2245	Rape where death results	63
57	1994	103-322	18 U.S.C. § 2245	Death resulting from sexual abuse crimes	64
58	1994	103-322	18 U.S.C. § 2251	Death resulting from sexual exploitation of children	65
59	1994	103-322	18 U.S.C. § 2280	Violence against maritime navigation where death results	66
60	1994	103-322	18 U.S.C. § 2281	Violence against maritime platforms where death results	67

61	1994	18 U.S.C. § 2332	Murder of U.S. national oversees	68
62	1994	18 U.S.C. § 2332a	Death resulting from use of weapons of mass destruction against U.S. national or within U.S.	69
63	1994	18 U.S.C. § 2340A	Torture resulting in death	70
64	1994	18 U.S.C. § 2381, 18 U.S.C. § 2391	Treason	71
	1994	21 U.S.C. § 461(c)	Murder of federal poultry inspector	72
	1994	21 U.S.C. § 675	Murder of federal meat inspector	73
	1994	21 U.S.C. §848(c)(1), 18 U.S.C. §3591(b)(1)	Drug "kingpin" violation involving twice the amount of controlled substances or twice the gross receipts otherwise required (no death necessary)	74
	1994	21 U.S.C. §848(c)(1), 18 U.S.C. §3591(b)(2)	Attempted murder by drug "kingpin" to obstruct justice (no death necessary)	75
	1994	21 U.S.C. § 1041(b)	Murder of an egg inspector	76
	1994	42 U.S.C. § 2283	Murder of nuclear inspectors	77
	1996	18 U.S.C. § 844(f)(3)	Death resulting from destruction of government property	78
	1996	18 U.S.C. §2332a(b)	Death resulting from use of weapons of mass destruction by a U.S. national outside of the United States	79
	1996	18 U.S.C. § 2332b	Death resulting from multinational terrorism	80

(Continued)

Table A.5 **Continued**

"64 death penalties" by Democratic count, September 1993	Year Enacted	Public Law	U.S. Code	Capital Crime	
	1996	104-132	18 U.S.C. § 2332a(c) (previously 18 U.S.C. § 2332c)	Death resulting from use of chemical weapons	81
	1996	104-192	18 U.S.C. § 2441	War crimes	82
	1996	104-208	8 U.S.C. § 1324(a)	Death resulting from smuggling "aliens" into the United States	83
	1998	105-277	18 U.S.C. § 229A(2), 18 U.S.C. § 229	Death resulting from chemical weapons offenses	84
	1998	105-314	18 USC §3559(d)(1)	Death resulting from crimes against child (under age 14)	85
	2000	106-523	18 U.S.C. § 3261	Murder committed by U.S. armed forces or employees thereof	86
	2002	107-197	18 U.S.C. § 2332f	Death resulting from bombing of government facilities, public transportation, or public places	87
	2006	109-177	18 U.S.C. § 2282A	Death resulting from the use of dangerous devices or substances in U.S. waters	88
	2005	109-92	18 U.S.C. § 924(c)(5)(B)	Death resulting from use of armor-piercing ammunition during a crime of violence or drug trafficking	89

2006	109-177	18 U.S.C. § 2291	Murder in destruction of maritime facilities	90
2006	109-248	18 USC §2260(a)	Death resulting from using a minor in the production of sexually explicit depictions for importation into the United States	91
2006	109-248	18 USC §3559(f)(1)	Death resulting from crimes against children (under age 18)	92

Note: Lawmakers compare proposals by the number of death-eligible crimes, but there is no specified or default method for counting the "unit" of one capital crime. In September 1993 the House Democratic Judiciary Committee issued a press release that listed the "64 new death penalties" of Clinton's proposal as sponsored by Texas Democrat Jack Brooks. This appears to be the only itemized list, and it is represented in the first column of this table. For each death-eligible crime, I identified the matching U.S. Code section. Note that the House Democratic Judiciary counts a "single" capital crime by rigorous disaggregation. It divides a single U.S. Code section into multiple crimes, as in, for example, dividing 18 U.S.C. 351, "crimes against high officials," into four capital crimes: "murder of a member of Congress," "murder of a Cabinet officer," "murder of the Supreme Court Justice," and "murder of a high official." I updated and completed this list of death-eligible crimes, erring on the side of high disaggregation to match the "inflated" counts fit proffered by other. By my count, Congress enacted ninety-two death-eligible crimes from 1974 to 2010.

Sources: Compiled by author from the Anti-Drug Abuse Act of 1988, Public Law 100-690, *U.S. Statutes at Large* 102 (1988): 4387–4388; the Violent Crime Control and Law Enforcement Act of 1994, Public Law 103-322, *U.S. Statutes at Large* 108 (1994): 1959–1982; Antiterrorism and Effective Death Penalty Act of 1996, Public Law 104-132, *U.S. Statutes at Large* 110 (1996): 1281–1297; Adam Walsh Child Protection and Safety Act of 2006, Public Law 109-248, *U.S. Statutes at Large* 120 (2006): 587–650; *U.S. Code Annotated*, 2006 Edition, Titles 7, 8, 18, 21, 49; Congressional Research Service, *Present Federal Death Penalty Statutes* (Washington, DC: Office of Congressional Information and Publishing, 1997); U.S. Department of Justice, *The Federal Death Penalty System: A Statistical Survey, 1988–2000* (Washington, DC: U.S. Department of Justice, 2000), Table 6; Congressional Research Service, *Capital Punishment: An Overview of Federal Death Penalty Statutes* (Washington, DC: Office of Congressional Information and Publishing, 2005); Congressional Research Service, *The Death Penalty: Capital Punishment Legislation in the 110th Congress* (Washington, DC: Office of Congressional Information and Publishing, 2008); and, most critically, House Committee on the Judiciary, Press Release "Brooks Introduces Tough Anti-Crime Package," September 23, 1993, Folder: Crime Bill–Strategy Group, Box 75, Reed Crime Papers.

Table A.6 **Selected House Votes on Capital Punishment Proposals, 1988–1994**

Date	House Bills /Amendments	Sponsor	# of CCs in Democrat Proposal (Net CCs)	# of CCs in Republican Proposal (Net CCs)	Outcome	Northern Democrats	Southern Democrats	Republicans
9/8/88	H.R. 5210 Amend. 869	Rangel (D-NY) commutes to life without release	0		Pass 410–1	207–1	34–0	169–0
9/8/88	Amend. 870	Gekas (R-PA) adds for murder during a drug felony		2	Pass 299–111	105–100	33–2	162–9
9/22/88	H.R. 5210	Anti-Drug Abuse Act of 1988, final vote adding 2 capital crimes			Pass 375–30	141–28	66–2	168–0
7/13/90	H.R. 5269	Brooks (D-TX) as introduced	12					
10/3/90	Amend. 820	Staggers (D-WV) to commute to life without release	Life (= 0)		Fail 103–322	92–89	5–70	6–163
10/4/90	Amend. 822	Hughes (D-NJ) to add 12 and to strike racial justice provisions	+12 (=24)		Fail 108–319	101–161	32–42	10–163
10/4/90	Amend. 823	Gekas (R-PA) adds 12 and ends federal provision of legal counsel to indigent death-row prisoners		+12 (=24)	Pass 217–159	50–131	56–19	165–9
10/4/90	Amend. 824	Traficant (D-OH) adds for murder of police, state and local, for assisting federal investigation	+2 (= 26)		Pass VV			

10/4/90	Amend. 825	McCollum (R-FL) adds for drug crimes that result in death and for drug "kingpins"	+2 (= 28)	Pass 295–133	63–116	67–8	165–9
9/23/91	H.R. 3371	Brooks (D-TX) as introduced	26				
10/16/91	Amend. 319	Staggers (D-WV) to commute to life without release	Life (= 0)	Fail 101–322	89–96	6–70	5–156
10/16/91	Amend. 320	Hughes (D-NJ) to create uniform standard for imposing the death penalty for homicide, and it should include "intentionally or knowingly causing the death of an individual"	−1 (= 25)	Fail VV			
10/16/91	Amend. 321	Hughes (D-NJ) to cut drug "kingpin" penalty	−1 (= 25)	Fail 106–317	93–92	8–68	4–157
10/16/91	Amend. 322	Gekas (R-PA) adds for murder of law enforcement officers at all levels, civil rights murders, murder of federal witnesses, murder in drive-by shootings, gun murders during federal violent and drug trafficking crimes	+22 (=48)	Pass 213–206	30–153	33–42	150–10

(Continued)

Table A.6 Continued

Date	House Bills /Amendments	Sponsor	# of CCs in Democrat Proposal (Net CCs)	# of CCs in Republican Proposal (Net CCs)	Outcome	Northern Democrats	Southern Democrats	Republicans
10/17/91	Amend. 326	Brooks (D-TX) adds death penalty for terrorist-related offenses and murder during rape and child molestation	+3 (= 51)		Pass 216–207	195–32	20–14	0–161
11/26/91	H.R. 3371 Conference Report	Brooks (D-TX) Violent Crime Prevention Act of 1991 (On Conference Report)	51		Pass 205–203	143–36	57–14	5–152
9/23/93	H.R. 3131	Brooks (D-TX) as introduced (and listed in Table 5.1)	64					
2/18/94	H.R. 4092	Brooks (D-TX) as introduced	64					
4/14/94	Amend. 499	Brooks (D-TX) adds for murder related to smuggling of "aliens"	+1 (= 65)		Pass 395–25	176–2	71–0	147–23
4/14/94	Amend. 500	Duncan (R-TN) adds for kidnapping resulting in death of a minor		+1 (= 66)	Pass VV			
4/14/94	Amend. 501	Watt (D-NC) to cut death penalty for drug "kingpins" when not responsible for a death	−2 (= 64)		Fail 108–316	85–93	17–59	5–164

4/14/94	Amend. 502	Scott (D-VA) to cut death penalty for murders committed during carjackings (1), drive-by shootings (1), and federal drug and gun crimes(8)	−10 (= 56)	Fail VV			
4/14/94	Amend. 503	Kopetski (D-OR) to commute death to life without release	Life (= 0)	Fail 111–314	89–92	15–57	6–165
8/21/94	Conference Report on H.R. 3355	Final 66		Pass 235–195	143–34	44–30	46–131

Table A.7 **Selected Senate Votes on Capital Punishment Proposals, 1988–1994**

Date	Senate Bills / Amendments	Sponsor	# of CCs in Democrat Proposal (Net CCs)	# of CCs in Republican Proposal (Net CCs)	Outcome	Northern Democrats	Southern Democrats	Republicans
10/13/88	H.R. 5210 S. Amend. 3678	Hatfield (R-OR) to commute death to life without release		0	Fail 25–64	19–23	0–8	6–33
10/14/88	Pass H.R. 5210 in lieu of S. 2852	Anti-Drug Abuse Act of 1988, final vote adding two capital crimes			Passed 87–3	42–1	7–0	38–2
1/25/89	S. 32	Thurmond (R-SC) as introduced		22				
11/21/89	S. 1970	Biden (D-DE) as introduced	34					
6/28/90	Amend. 2097	D'Amato (R-NY) adds for drug "kingpins," no death requirement		+1 (=35)	Pass 66–32	15–26	13–0	38–6
6/28/90	Amend. 2098	Wilson (R-CA) to add civil rights violations resulting in death		+4 (=39)	Fail 43–55	8 to 31	6 to 9	29–15
6/28/90	Amend. 2100	Hatfield (R-OR) to commute death to life without release		Life (=0)	Fail 25–73	20–21	0–13	5 to 39

Date	Number	Description						
3/12/91	S. 618	Biden (D-DE) as introduced	44					
3/13/91	S. 635	Thurmond (R-SC) as introduced	46					
6/6/91	S. 1241	Biden (D-DE) as introduced	51					
6/25/91	Amend. 374	Simon (D-IL) to commute death to life without release	0		Fail 25–73	19–23	1–13	5–57
6/26/91	Amend. 377	Symms (R-ID) adds drug-related homicides in the District of Columbia		+1 (= 52)	Pass 60–39	15–27	9–5	36–7
6/26/91	Amend. 382	D'Amato (R-NY) adds for homicides involving firearms		+4 (= 56)	Pass 65–33	20–22	11–3	34–8
9/23/93	S. 1488	Biden (D-DE) as introduced	47					
8/4/93	S. 1356	Dole (R-KS) as introduced		47				
11/1/93	S. 1607	Biden (D-DE) as introduced	47					

(Continued)

Table A.7 **Continued**

Date	Senate Bills / Amendments	Sponsor	# of CCs in Democrat Proposal (Net CCs)	# of CCs in Republican Proposal (Net CCs)	Outcome	Northern Democrats	Southern Democrats	Republicans
11/8/93	Amend. 1141	Lieberman (D-CT) adds carjacking	+1 (=48)		Pass 65–34	22–22	10–1	33–11
11/9/93	Amend. 1147	D'Amato (R-NY) adds murder with firearm		+4 (=52)	Pass 58–42	17–27	7–5	32–10
11/17/93	Amend. 1199	D'Amato (R-NY) adds drug "kingpins" for engaging in a continuing criminal drug enterprise, no death requirement		+1 (=53)	Pass 74–25	23–20	12–0	39–5
11/17/93	Amend. 1204	Levin (D-MI) to commute to life without release	0		Fail 25–74	20–23	0–12	6–38
8/25/94	Conference Report on H.R. 3355	Final 66			Pass 61–38	43–1	11–1	7–36

AUTHOR'S NOTES AND ACKNOWLEDGMENTS

This book began as a project that asked a straightforward question: what explains the post–civil rights rise of mass incarceration? My initial answer, written as a doctoral dissertation, was reasonable enough: law-and-order was a chisel, deftly wielded by Republicans and southern Democrats, chipping away civil rights with ever-aggressive swings. My story was told through a familiar string of dyads: the war on drugs eroded the benefits of the Civil Rights Act of 1964, felon disenfranchisement undercut the Voting Rights Act of 1965, retribution trumped the rehabilitative ideal, and neoliberalism obliterated Great Society ambitions.

The more I rehearsed the rhythm of this story—the more I beat conservative law-and-order against liberal defenses of civil rights, rehabilitation, and root causes—the more liberal claims sounded a hollow thud. This was when I started to suspect that I was asking the wrong question. To ask how "law-and-order" undercut "civil rights" takes for granted the validity of these categories as distinct, even oppositional, political positions. "Law-and-order" and "civil rights" as such could not be the tools for my investigation; they must be the subjects of my investigation.

The path from conservative backlash to liberal law-and-order was circuitous, confusing, and long, and I have incurred so many debts along the way. My research began in the Department of Political Science at Yale University, where it took shape as a doctoral dissertation supervised by Rogers Smith, Cathy Cohen, and Donald Green. Many acknowledgment sections, in some of my favorite books, attribute to Rogers Smith an unwavering kindness worthy of beatification, and for good reason. He has read many drafts over too many years, each time offering measured criticism and the assurance that he is permanently in my corner. Cathy Cohen's brilliant insights immeasurably improved my work, and, just as crucially, she insisted that research on carceral expansion mattered when I feared it had no place in political science. Donald Green gave astonishingly detailed feedback, and his enthusiastic spirit rallied me to the finish. Additional

Yale faculty members generously volunteered feedback and encouragement, and I am grateful to Daniel Freed, Martin Gilens, Gregory Huber, Debra Minkoff, David Mayhew, and Ian Shapiro. Graduate-student fellow travelers tended to all the quotidian decisions that become the sum of a dissertation. Looking back, I cannot believe my good fortune to have vetted all those questions with such intellectually powerful and deeply caring graduate-student colleagues: Rebecca Bohrman, Elizabeth Cohen, Amy Cabrera Rasmussen, Robin Hayes, Matthew Light, Perlita Muiruri, Dara Strolovitch, and Janelle Wong.

With its strengths in sociolegal studies and race politics, the University of Washington is the ideal place to research the politics of punishment. Stuart A. Scheingold retired before my arrival but enriched my life tremendously—by forging a path through his innovative research, by introducing me to Lee Scheingold, and by giving me scores of books from his prodigious law-and-order library. Law and society scholars gave me a sense of belonging from day one, welcoming me into a vibrant community cultivated by Rachel Cichowski, Rose Ernst, Angelina Godoy, Steve Herbert, Jamie Mayerfeld, Arzoo Osanloo, and Mark Weitzenkamp. George Lovell's kindness, candor, and political sensibilities were a lifeboat for me in more ways than he knows. I am honored and grateful that Katherine Beckett invited me to be her co-author on several projects; her encyclopedic knowledge of carceral practices has simultaneously expanded my perspective and tethered me closer to the realities that elide abstract theorization.

There is no adjective grand enough to convey my respect and appreciation for Michael McCann. He read draft after draft, never once failing to coach, care, and mentor in all the times I turned to him. He pushed me on the hardest questions about power, and his labor created a space—institutionally and epistemologically—for me to burrow in and wrestle with those questions in the way I needed, unhindered by disciplinary norms. Along with Judy Howard, Margaret Levi, Peter May, Steve Majeski, and more advocates than I know, Michael McCann worked to build the race and ethnicity core within political science—their efforts produced a group of faculty and graduate students that invigorated my research. It is fitting that the Stuart A. Scheingold Professorship of Social Justice is held now by Christopher Parker, a colleague who has taught me so much about race, rights, war, and violence. Along with Gary Segura, Matt Barreto, Luis Fraga, and Christopher Parker, Jack Turner kept me energized in an ongoing conversation of African American political thought and critical race theory.

Since arriving at the University of Washington, I have found a community that inspires and challenges me. Habiba Ibrahim and Chandan Reddy were ideal writing partners who brought stability and pleasure to the daily grind. The camaraderie of Miriam Bartha, Alexes Harris, Ralina Joseph, Su Motha, Illeana Rodriguez-Silva, and Sonnet Retman brought me comfort and strength. I am grateful for sage advice and overall kindness from Christine DiStefano, Ellis

Goldberg, Nancy Hartsock, and Mark Smith. Adam Warren and Scot Orriss sheltered me on more than one dark night. Aaron Brethorst's artistic sensibilities and tenderness brought unexpected beauty into my life. Dara Strolovitch is a singularly inspiring scholar. She helped me at every stage, pushing for more precise evidence in each round and pressing me to "ask the other question." Most crucially, she advised me to ignore voices that dismiss research on inequality as "just normative." In matters of scholarship and beyond, Falu Bakrania has always guided me in the right direction. Gillian Harkins is an intensely brilliant interlocutor and an unceasingly generous friend. Manka Varghese's wisdom on matters of racial power and beyond has fortified me when I needed it most.

I have been fortunate to receive considerable institutional support for my research. The Center for the Study of Law and Culture at Columbia Law School, headed by Katherine Franke and Kendall Thomas, supported this project in its fledgling form. From Yale, I received the John F. Enders Research Grant, the Falk Fellowship, and the John Perry Miller Research Grant. I thank Yale's Center for the Study of Race, Inequality, and Politics, guided by Cathy Cohen and Rogers Smith, for funding my research. I am grateful to the Robert Wood Johnson Foundation's Health Policy Research Program at the University of California at Berkeley, where I spent two years with amazing colleagues like Michael Anderson, Anthony Chen, John Ellwood, Cybelle Fox, Ian Haney López, Robert Kagan, Seana Kelly, Jonah Levy, Taeku Lee, Robert Mickey, Aaron Panofsky, Christopher Parker, Jonathan Simon, Constance Wang, Sandra Kalev, and Jordan Matsudaira. Bringing my "must read" list to impossible lengths, Robert Mickey fortified my library and overall well-being. Anthony Chen generously read several drafts, pressed for clarity, and shared his expertise on Truman.

Many colleagues generously engaged the project at workshops and talks, over coffee, and through very long email exchanges. Michael K. Brown shared his immense expertise on policing, and, along with his invaluable papers and books, he has given me the beginnings of my next project. Lisa Miller read the entire manuscript at an early stage, gently advised extending the time horizon before Goldwater crime politics, and thereby changed the project forever. I have also benefitted tremendously from the comments and insights of Lawrie Balfour, Eva Bertram, Sharon Daniel, Andrew Dilts, Alec Ewald, Marie Gottschalk, Milton Heumann, Daniel HoSang, Kimberley Johnson, Desmond King, Philip Klinkner, Regina Kunzel, Raquiba LaBrie, Daniel LaChance, Keith Lawrence and the Aspen Roundtable on Community Change, Ann Lin, Joseph Lowndes, Mona Lynch, James Morone, Julie Novkov, Robert Perkinson, Brian Pinaire, Mark Sawyer, Patricia Strach, Kathleen Sullivan, Robert Tsai, Vesla Weaver, Daniel Wirls, Priscilla Yamin, and David Zlotnick.

For guiding me through primary-source materials, I am grateful to many archivists and librarians, especially Tammy Kelly at the Harry S. Truman Presidential

Library; Allen Fisher at the Lyndon B. Johnson Presidential Library; and Jason Kaplan and Herbert Ragan at the William Jefferson Clinton Presidential Library. I thank April Suwalsky for stellar research assistance. Hannah Walker's criminal justice expertise helped me in the final stages. Erin Adam's fastidious research assistance and whimsical sense of humor eased completion of the manuscript. I have long admired Richard Ross's photography on *The Architecture of Authority*; his images of sanitized, individualized, routinized brutality are so evocative of the perils of liberal law-and-order. Words cannot express my gratefulness that he granted permission to use as cover art his photograph of the interview room at the Los Angeles Secret Service Headquarters.

Steven Teles had faith in the project from the start, and I am forever grateful that he invited me to submit the manuscript to the Studies on Postwar American Political Development series at Oxford University Press. He generously gave constructive criticism, and reality checks and tough love as needed. David McBride is an extraordinary editor, and his feedback inspired major and much-needed revisions in the final stages. Steven and David engaged the project more seriously than I could have imagined, with more patience than I should have asked for. I suspect that Paul Frymer did not know he would be designated my "sherpa" when he joined the board on this Oxford series. His uniquely incisive perspective on institutional racism changed my thinking even before I met him, and I am humbled by his generosity in reading and discussing many drafts over the years. Anonymous reviewers grasped what I was struggling to say, and I appreciate their deeply engaged and cogent commentary. I am also very appreciative of Alexandra Dauler's wisdom and kindness, Elina Sluzhman Carmona's thoughtful, lightning-speed copyediting, and Pete Mavrikis's fastidious, professional grace through the production process.

I am grateful for families of kinship and affinity. Diane Rubinstein, a blessedly unconventional woman, has given me hope for all the possibilities of remaking oneself. She supported me even when the stuff of her life was a great cargo, some of it heavy. I am grateful for what she has given me, but more grateful for who she is. Together with Franck, Louis, Arthur, and Margot, Dina Murakawa Pecceu has anchored my sense of home when I needed it most. Like our ba-chan, Misao Sakai Murakawa, her love is steady and strong. Mark Rubinstein has been unfailingly generous and has offered wise counsel on all secular matters. Dara Strolovitch and Regina Kunzel have given me sustenance and safe haven in Connecticut, Minnesota, Massachusetts, Washington, D.C., and California, and together we will find a new sense of home in New Jersey. I do not know when Yoshio Murakawa started talking to me about prison and the color line, his perspective informed by his childhood incarceration in Topaz and by his three decades of work in probation. But I know that he launched the most important conversation of my life, and I am grateful for his love and sense of justice.

ABBREVIATIONS IN NOTES

Anslinger Papers	Papers of Harry J. Anslinger, Harry S. Truman Presidential Library, Independence, MO
BJS	Bureau of Justice Statistics, Department of Justice
Bontecou Papers	Papers of Eleanor Bontecou, Harry S. Truman Presidential Library, Independence, MO
Clark Papers	Papers of Ramsey Clark, Lyndon B. Johnson Presidential Library, Austin, TX
Claytor Papers	Helen Jackson Claytor Civil Rights Collection, Collection # 308, Grand Rapids Public Library, Grand Rapids, MI
CD	*Chicago Defender*
CQA	*Congressional Quarterly Almanac*
CQWR	*Congressional Quarterly Weekly Report*
CR	*Congressional Record*
CRS	Congressional Research Service
HSTL	Harry S. Truman Presidential Library, Independence, MO
LAT	*Los Angeles Times*
LBJL	Lyndon Baines Johnson Presidential Library, Austin, TX
Nash Papers	Papers of Philleo Nash, Harry S. Truman Presidential Library, Independence, MO
Niles Papers	Papers of David K. Niles, Harry S. Truman Presidential Library, Independence, MO
NYT	*New York Times*
PCCR	Records of the President's Committee on Civil Rights, Harry S. Truman Library, Independence, MO

Prince Papers   Records of Jonathan Prince, Clinton Presidential
                         Records: White House Staff and Office Files,
                         William J. Clinton Presidential Library, Little
                         Rock, AR
Rasco Papers   Carol Rasco Subject Files, Domestic Policy Council
                         Record Series, William J. Clinton Presidential
                         Library, Little Rock, AR
Reed Crime Papers   Bruce Reed Collection, Crime Series, William
                         J. Clinton Presidential Library, Little Rock, AR
Reed Subject Papers   Bruce Reed Collection, Subject File Series, William
                         J. Clinton Presidential Library, Little Rock, AR
Truman Papers   Papers of Harry S. Truman, Official File, Harry
                         S. Truman Library, Independence, MO
USSC   U.S. Sentencing Commission
White Papers   Subject Files of Assistant Attorney General
                         W. Wilson White, 1958–1959, Records of the
                         Department of Justice, Civil Rights Division, NARA
WJCL   William Jefferson Clinton Library, Little Rock, AR
WSJ   Wall Street Journal

NOTES

Chapter 1

1. Richard Nixon, "Address Accepting the Presidential Nomination at the Republican National Convention," August 8, 1968, in *Richard Nixon: Speeches, Writings, Documents,* ed. Rick Perlstein (Princeton: Princeton University Press, 2008), 145–149.
2. The President's Committee on Civil Rights, *To Secure These Rights: The Report of the President's Committee on Civil Rights* (Washington, DC: GPO, 1947), 20.
3. Barack Obama, "Acceptance Speech in Chicago," November 5, 2008. For references to President Obama and the incarcerated million black men, see Ruth Wilson Gilmore, "What Is to Be Done?" *American Quarterly* 63 (2001), 253, 245–265; Angela Davis, interview with Olivia Ward, "Angela Davis on Where Emancipation Went Wrong," The Star.com, March 17, 2013; Benjamin Jealous quoted in Errol Lewis, "In NAACP Speech, President Obama Gives Inspirational Nod to History, but Focus Is on Today," *New York Daily News,* July 16, 2009; Reverend Eugene Rivers quoted in Charles Ogletree, *The Presumption of Guilt: The Arrest of Henry Louis Gates, Jr. and Race, Class, and Crime in America* (New York: Palgrave Macmillan, 2010), 117. For reviews of post-racialism discourse vis-à-vis President Obama, see Louise Seamster and Eduardo Bonilla-Silva, "Introduction: Examining, Debating, and Ranting about the Obama Phenomenon," *Political Power and Social Theory* 22 (2011), 3–15; Habiba Ibrahim, *Troubling the Family: The Promise of Personhood and the Rise of Multiracialism* (Minneapolis: University of Minnesota Press, 2012), 161–176; Karen E. Fields and Barbara J. Fields, *Racecraft: The Soul of Inequality in American Life* (London: Verso, 2012), 1–13; Rogers Smith and Desmond King, "Barack Obama and the Future of American Racial Politics," *Du Bois Review* 6 (Spring 2009), 25–35; Imani Perry, *More Beautiful and More Terrible: The Embrace and Transcendence of Racial Inequality and the United States* (New York: New York University Press, 2011), 2, 13–22, 147–152.
4. Letter from Grace Chung Becker of the DOJ's Civil Rights Division to the Cook County Board President and the Cook County Sheriff, July 11, 2008, especially 26, 47, 73; Memo from the Justice Advisory Council of the County of Cook to the Cook County Board of Commissioners, Examination of Cook County Bond Court, July 12, 2012; *NYT,* July 18, 2008.
5. Many activists and scholars have likened the drug war to Jim Crow, including Ira Glass of the American Civil Liberties Union in 1999, Graham Boyd of the ACLU Drug Policy Litigation Unit in 2002, and Michelle Alexander, *The New Jim Crow* (New York: New Press, 2010). For a trenchant analysis of the "new Jim Crow" analogy, see James Forman Jr., "Racial Critiques of Mass Incarceration: Beyond the New Jim Crow," *New York University Law Review* 87 (April 2012), especially 25–27. The analogy obscures, as Forman explains, black support for punitive policies, class distinctions between African Americans, and repressive crime policies beyond the war on drugs. For Nixon's use of "the first civil right," see Rick Perlstein, *Nixonland: The Rise of a President and the Fracturing of America* (New York: Scribner, 2008),

305–306, 332–340; Michael Flamm, *Law and Order: Street Crime, Civil Unrest, and the Crisis of Liberalism in the 1960s* (New York: Columbia University Press, 2005), 10, 82, 177–178; Dean Kotlowski, *Nixon's Civil Rights: Politics, Principle, and Policy* (Cambridge: Harvard University Press, 2001), 128–129.

6. Anthony S. Chen, *The Fifth Freedom* (Princeton: Princeton University Press, 2009); Risa Goluboff, *The Lost Promise of Civil Rights* (Cambridge: Harvard University Press, 2007); Ira Katznelson, *When Affirmative Action Was White: An Untold History of Racial Inequality in Twentieth-Century America* (New York: W. W. Norton & Company, 2005); Thomas Sugrue, *The Origins of the Urban Crisis: Race and Inequality in Postwar Detroit* (Princeton: Princeton University Press, 1996).

7. Stuart Scheingold merits particular note for his incisive characterization of the crisp divide between volitional and structural criminology. Volitional criminology, anchored in Hobbes and Locke, blames crime on "individual pathologies—be they moral, emotional, or genetic." Structural criminology, anchored in Rousseau and Marx, blames crime on "social disorganization with its roots in hierarchy, deprivation, coercion, and alienation." Using the individual as the unit of analysis, volitional explanations take aim at the offender, generally suggesting punishment and correction of the defective person. Using society as the unit of analysis, structural explanations take aim at the prevailing social order, generally suggesting measures to mitigate economic, social, and political inequality. Stuart Scheingold, *The Politics of Law and Order: Street Crime and Public Policy* (New York: Longman, 1984); Stuart Scheingold, *The Politics of Street Crime: Criminal Process and Cultural Obsession* (Philadelphia: Temple University Press, 1991), 4–7, 23.

8. By "postwar race liberals," I mean those who came to embrace the historically grounded understanding of white prejudice as a problem that corrupts political institutions and damages the psychological, social, political, or economic standing of African Americans. In this understanding, the American race "problem" is a form of individual prejudice, and the "solution" entails making institutions race-neutral and thereby fair barometers of individual merit. In contrast, I use the term "postwar race conservative" to describe those who minimize or deny the existence of white prejudice, and thereby isolate the causes of racial inequality within black people. My definition of postwar racial liberalism draw on a number of sources, especially Daryl Michael Scott, *Contempt & Pity: Social Policy and the Image of the Damaged Black Psyche, 1880–1996* (Chapel Hill: University of North Carolina Press, 1997), xiii; Nikhil Pal Singh, *Black Is a Country: Race and the Unfinished Struggle for Democracy* (Cambridge: Harvard University Press, 2004), 38–42; Daniel Martinez HoSang, *Racial Propositions: Ballot Initiatives and the Making of Postwar California* (Berkeley: University of California Press, 2010), 13–16; Lani Guinier, "From Racial Liberalism to Racial Literacy: Brown v. Board of Education and the Interest-Divergence Dilemma," *Journal of American History* 91 (2006), especially 100–101; Chandan Reddy, *Freedom with Violence: Race, Sexuality, and the US State* (Durham: Duke University Press, 2011), 194; Jodi Melamed, "The Spirit of Neoliberalism: From Racial Liberalism to Neoliberal Multiculturalism," *Social Text* 24 (Winter 2006), 89–91.

   To be clear, I use the term "postwar racial liberalism" to mark a historically embedded common sense. The term therefore denotes something more tractable than the grand philosophical, historical sweep of all that might be called liberalism. For many, the term "liberalism" evokes the political philosophy of morally equal individuals that developed historically in opposition to medieval ideas of political absolutism and social hierarchy. It might also evoke a Lockean liberalism of individual rights that is often evaluated in opposition to republican ideals of participatory citizenship and virtuous sacrifice for the public good. Scholars like Charles Mills, David Theo Goldberg, and Rogers Smith engage in impressive multicentury, often multinational analyses of the ways in which liberalism might incorporate or excuse racial hierarchy. Charles Mills, "Liberalism and the Racial State," in *State of White Supremacy: Racism, Governance, and the United States*, ed. Moon-Kie Jung, João H. Costa Vargas, and Eduardo Bonilla-Silva (Palo Alto: Stanford University Press, 2011), 27; Charles Mills, *The Racial Contract* (Ithaca: Cornell University Press, 1997); David Theo Goldberg, *The Racial State* (Malden: Blackwell, 2002); Rogers Smith, *Civic Ideals: Conflicting Visions of Citizenship in U.S. History* (New Haven: Yale University Press, 1997).

9. Following scholars like Katherine Beckett and Bernard Harcourt, I see the carceral state as "the liminal space where moral opprobrium meets government-sanctioned punishment." The carceral state therefore extends beyond the criminal justice system. State institutions, policies, and personnel become part of the carceral state when and to the extent that they: (1) require exclusion based on a person's criminal justice status (e.g., felon disenfranchisement and exclusion from higher education loans); (2) use prison or jail as reprimand for issues beyond criminal law (e.g., imprisonment for nonpayment of consumer debt or legal financial obligations); (3) integrate criminal justice personnel into regular institutional practices (e.g., police in public schools); and (4) cross-deputize noncriminal justice personnel to enforce criminal law (e.g., border patrol). While this definition is broad, it includes only state institutions, formal laws, and state administrators, and it excludes disciplinary forces that move through "carceral society," wherein observation, measurement, and discipline move through "factories, schools, barracks, [and] hospitals, which all resemble prisons." Bernard Harcourt, "Preface," *The Carceral Notebooks*, vol. 1, October 2005, 1; Katherine Beckett and Naomi Murakawa, "Mapping the Shadow Carceral State: Toward an Institutionally Capacious Approach to Punishment," *Theoretical Criminology* 16 (May 2012), 211–214; Michel Foucault, trans. Alan Sheridan, *Discipline and Punish: The Birth of the Prison* (New York: Random House, 1977), 227. Alexes Harris et al., "Drawing Blood from Stones: Monetary Sanctions, Punishment and Inequality in the Contemporary United States," *American Journal of Sociology* 115 (2010), 1753–1799; Katherine Beckett and Alexis Harris, "On Cash and Conviction: Monetary Sanctions as Misguided Policy," *Criminology & Public Policy* 10 (2011), 505–537; Elizabeth Patterson, "Civil Contempt and the Indigent Child Obliger: The Silent Return of Debtor's Prison," *Cornell Journal of Law and Public Policy* 18 (2008), 95.

10. Risk of criminal victimization is largely independent from levels of fear and punitiveness, and therefore it is difficult to believe that the crime alone simply prompted more punitive attitudes and more punitive measures. Levels of fear remained strikingly constant from 1965 through the 1990s, despite the fact that crime rose markedly in the 1960s and declined significantly in the early 1990s. Similarly, a preponderance of evidence disconfirms the hypothesis that criminal victimization increases support for harsh crime policies. Individual-level data show that people with high risks of criminal victimization are not more punitive, and some studies show the most victimized are the least punitive. Consider, for example, that African Americans experience more criminal victimization than other racial groups, but historically African Americans as a group are not the loudest advocates for punishment expansion; on the contrary, African Americans have opposed drug-related mandatory minimums and capital punishment in higher percentages than their comparatively safe white counterparts. In sum, "the politics of law and order has a life of its own which is quite independent of crime and criminal victimization," as Stuart Scheingold concluded in 1984. For a comprehensive review and refutation of the crime-prompts-punishment thesis, see Katherine Beckett, "Setting the Public Agenda: 'Street Crime' and Drug Use in American Politics," *Social Problems* 41 (1994), 425–447; Katherine Beckett, *Making Crime Pay: Law and Order in Contemporary American Politics* (New York: Oxford University Press, 1997), chapter 2; Stuart Scheingold, *The Politics of Law and Order: Street Crime and Public Policy* (New York: Longman, 1984), xiii; Ruth Wilson Gilmore, *Golden Gulag: Prisons, Surplus, Crisis, and Opposition in Globalizing California* (Berkeley: University of California Press, 2007), 24; Garth Taylor, Kim Scheppele, and Arthur Stinchcombe, "Salience of Crime and Support for Harsher Criminal Sanctions," *Social Problems* 26 (1979), 413–424; Everett Ladd, "Crime and Punishment: An American Odyssey," *The Public Perspective* 8 (1997), 8–38; David Sears et al., "Self-Interest vs. Symbolic Politics in Policy Attitudes and Presidential Voting," *American Political Science Review* 74 (1983), 670–684; Mark Warr, "Fear of Victimization," *The Public Perspective* 5 (1993), 25–28; Mark Warr, "Public Opinion on Crime and Punishment," *Public Opinion Quarterly* 59 (1995), 296–310; Otto Santa Ana, *Brown Tide Rising: Metaphors of Latinos in Contemporary American Discourse* (Austin: University of Texas Press, 2002).

11. Ruth Wilson Gilmore, *Golden Gulag: Prisons, Surplus, Crisis, and Opposition in Globalizing California* (Berkeley: University of California Press, 2007), 245; Loïc Wacquant, *Punishing the Poor: The Neoliberal Government of Social Insecurity* (Durham: Duke University Press, 2009),

10; Lizabeth Cohen, "A Historian's Reflection on the Unsustainable American State," in *The Unsustainable American State,* ed. Lawrence Jacobs and Desmond King (New York: Oxford University Press, 2009), 326–327; Joseph Dillon Davey, *The New Social Contract: America's Journal from Welfare State to Police State* (Westport: Praeger, 1995); Loïc Wacquant, "The Place of the Prison in the New Government of Poverty," in *After the War on Crime: Race, Democracy, and A New Reconstruction,* ed. Mary Louise Frampton, Ian Haney López, and Jonathan Simon (New York: New York University Press, 2008), 23–36.

12. Bruce Western, *Punishment and Inequality in America* (New York: Russell Sage Foundation, 2006), 16; BJS, *Prisoners in 2009* (Washington, DC: DOJ, 2010), appendix table 12.

13. In 2007, more than 1.7 million children had a parent living in a state or federal prison. In that year, one in 15 black children, one in 42 Latino children, and one in 111 white children had a parent living in state or federal prison. The total number of those disenfranchised due to current incarceration or former felony conviction increased from 1.2 million in 1976 to 5.3 million in 2004. Jeff Manza and Christopher Uggen, *Locked Out: Felon Disenfranchisement and American Democracy* (New York: Oxford University Press, 2006), 253; Keesha Middlemass, "Racial Politics and Voter Suppression in Georgia," in *African Americans in Georgia: A Reflection on Politics and Policy in the New South,* ed. Pearl Ford (Macon: Mercer University Press, 2010), 7–24; Alec Ewald, "Civil Death: The Ideological Paradox of Criminal Disenfranchisement Law in the United States," *Wisconsin Law Review* (2002), 1045–1132; BJS, *Prisoners in 2010* (Washington, DC: BJS, 2011); The Sentencing Project, *Incarcerated Parents and Their Children, 2001–2007* (Washington, DC: The Sentencing Project, 2009), 7.

14. While their prediction did not hold, Blumstein and Cohen provided impressive documentation for stability between 1930 and 1970, with incarceration rates an average rate of 110.2 prisoners per 100,000 population and a standard deviation of only 8.9 prisoners per 100,000 population. Counting jails and state and federal prisons, the U.S. incarceration rate (738 per 100,000) is six to eight times greater than that of France (85 per 100,000), Germany (95 per 100,000), England and Wales (148 per 100,000), Canada (107 per 100,000), and Japan (62 per 100,000). Roy Walmsley, *World Prison Population List,* 7th ed. (London: King's College London International Centre for Prison Studies, 2006); Pew Center on the States, *One in 100: Behind Bars in America* (Washington, DC: The Pew Charitable Trusts, 2008). The prison boom was truly a national phenomenon, as every state increased its prison population by at least half between 1972 and 1992. Over those two decades, the average state incarceration rate increased 250 percent, with the lowest increase in West Virginia (a 55 percent increase) and the highest in Delaware (a 690 percent increase). Joseph Dillon Davey, *The Politics of Prison Expansion: Winning Elections by Waging War on Crime* (Westport: Praeger Publishers, 1998), 30.

15. In 1980, parole revocations represented 18 percent of U.S. prison admissions; by 2000, 34 percent of all prison admissions were triggered by parole violations, and nearly 40 percent of such violations are only technical violations of parole stipulations. Vesla Weaver and Amy Lerman, "Political Consequences of the Carceral State," *American Political Science Review 104* (November 2010), 1; BJS, *Correctional Populations in the United States, 2010* (Washington, DC: GPO, 2011), table 1; Mona Lynch, "'Waste Managers'? The New Penology, Crime Fighting, and Parole Agent Identity," *Law & Society Review 32* (1998), 839–869; Mona Lynch, "Rehabilitation as Rhetoric: The Reformable Individual in Contemporary Parole Discourse and Practices," *Punishment and Society 2* (2000), 40–65.

16. Without this massive increase in African American incarceration, the United States would lose its status as the world's number one jailer. The 2010 white incarceration rate of 459 per 100,000 falls below the incarceration rates of several countries, including Cuba, Rwanda, Belize, and Russia. BJS, *Prisoners in 2010* (Washington, DC: GPO), table 14; Roy Walmsley, *World Prison Brief* (London: International Centre for Prison Studies, 2012).

17. Bruce Western, *Punishment and Inequality in America* (New York: Russell Sage Foundation Publications, 2007), 109. The incarcerated population suffers disproportionate illness, as roughly 18 percent of incarcerated persons have hepatitis C, over 7 percent have tuberculosis, and 1.5 percent have HIV/AIDS, all rates higher than those found in the general population. Controlling for underemployment, lack of health insurance, and lower education levels decreases but does not eliminate the deleterious health consequences of incarceration.

National Commission on Correctional Health Care, *The Health Status of Soon-to-Be Released Inmates* (Washington, DC: National Commission on Correctional Health Care, 2002); BJS, *HIV in Prison, 2007–08* (Washington, DC: GPO, 2010); BJS, *Medical Problems of Prisoners, 2004* (Washington, DC: GPO, 2010); Amy Khan et al., "Ongoing Transmission of Hepatitis B Virus Infection Among Inmates at a State Correctional Facility," *American Journal of Public Health* 95 (2005), 1793–1977; Rucker Johnson and Steven Raphael, "The Effects of Male Incarceration Dynamics on Acquired Immune Deficiency Syndrome Infection Rates among African American Women and Men," *Journal of Law and Economics* 52 (2009), 251–293; Jason Schnittker et al., "Incarceration and the Health of the African American Community," *Du Bois Review* 8 (2011), 133–141; Jason Schnittker and Andrea John, "Enduring Stigma: The Long-Term Effects of Incarceration on Health," *Journal of Health and Social Behavior* 16 (2007), 115–130; Benjamin Fleury-Steiner and Carla Crowder, *Dying Inside: The HIV/ AIDS Ward at Limestone Prison* (Ann Arbor: University of Michigan Press, 2008).

18. Marginalized groups, as defined by Dara Strolovitch, lack power along any of a variety of dimensions, including that: they might lack financial resources; they are historical or contemporary targets of de jure or de facto discrimination; they have minimal electoral power and few or no elected representatives; and they might lack cultural capital due to social stigmatization and to inconformity to dominant constructions of morality and patriarchal citizenship. Dara Strolovitch, *Affirmative Advocacy: Race, Class, and Gender in Interest Groups Politics* (Chicago: Chicago University Press, 2007), 24–25. Patricia Hill Collins, *Black Feminist Thought: Knowledge, Consciousness, and the Politics of Empowerment* (Boston: Unwin Hyman, 1990).

19. Of 6,450 transgender and gender nonconforming survey respondents, a full 18 percent of white respondents reported police harassment, but 38 percent of African American, 29 percent of Asian American, 24 percent of Native American, and 23 percent of Latino gender nonconforming people reported higher rates of police harassment. Jamie Grant et al., *Injustice at Every Turn: A Report of the National Transgender Discrimination Survey* (Washington, DC: National Center for Transgender Equality and National Gay and Lesbian Task Force, 2011), 158–173. Regina Kunzel, *Criminal Intimacy: Prison and the Uneven History of Modern American Sexuality* (Chicago: University of Chicago Press, 2008), especially chapter 5; Dean Spade, *Normal Life: Administrative Violence, Critical Trans Politics, and the Limits of the Law* (Brooklyn: Sought End Press, 2011), 89–93; Christopher Man and John Cronan, "Forecasting Sexual Abuse in Prison: The Prison Subculture of Masculinity as a Backdrop for 'Deliberate Indifference,' " *Journal of Criminal Law and Criminology* 92 (Autumn 2001), 127–186. BJS, *Prisoners in 2008* (Washington, DC: GPO, 2010), table 2; The Sentencing Project, *Women in the Criminal Justice System* (Washington, DC: The Sentencing Project, 2007); Western, *Punishment and Inequality in America* (New York: Russell Sage Foundation, 2006).

20. Bryan K. Fair, *Notes of a Racial Caste Baby: Color Blindness and the End of Affirmative Action* (New York: New York University Press, 1997), xxiii. There is a vast literature on the rise of colorblindness in mass opinion and ideology, public policy, and legal doctrine. For the rise of colorblindness and colorblind racism in mass opinion and ideology, see Eduardo Bonilla-Silva, *Racism Without Racists: Color-Blind Racism and the Persistence of Racial Inequality in the United States,* 3rd ed. (Rowman & Little Publishers, 2009); for the rise of political campaigns and initiatives defining color conscious programs as racist, see Lydia Chávez, *The Color Bind: California's Battle to End Affirmative Action* (Berkeley: University of California Press, 1998); Daniel HoSang, *Racial Propositions: Ballot Initiatives and the Making of Postwar California* (Berkeley: University of California Press, 2010); for the rise of reactionary colorblindness in legal doctrine, see Ian F. Haney López, "'A Nation of Minorities': Race, Ethnicity, and Reactionary Colorblindness," *Stanford Law Review* 59 (February 2007): 985–1063.

21. Vesla Weaver offers an especially useful, compact definition of backlash as "the politically and electorally expressed public resentment that arises from perceived racial advance, intervention, or excess." Vesla Weaver, "Frontlash: Race and the Development of Punitive Crime Policy," *Studies in American Political Development* 21 (2007), 237. Katherine Beckett, *Making Crime Pay: Law and Order in Contemporary American Politics* (New York: Oxford University Press, 1997); Katherine Beckett, "Setting the Public Agenda: 'Street Crime' and Drug Use in American Politics," *Social Problems* 41 (1994), 425–447; Michael Flamm, *Law and Order: Street Crime, Civil Unrest, and the Crisis of Liberalism in the 1960s*

(New York: Columbia University Press, 2005); Marie Gottschalk, *The Prison and the Gallows: The Politics of Mass Incarceration in America* (New York: Cambridge University Press, 2006), 2 and chapter 2. Thomas Edsall and Mary Edsall, *Chain Reaction: The Impact of Race, Rights, and Taxes on American Politics* (New York: W. W. Norton & Co., 1992); Michael Flamm, *Law and Order: Street Crime, Civil Unrest, and the Crisis of Liberalism in the 1960s* (New York: Columbia University Press, 2005); Joel Rosch, "Crime as an Issue in American Politics," in *The Politics of Crime and Criminal Justice*, ed. Erika Fairchild and Vincent Webb (Beverly Hills: Sage Publications, 1985), 25; Bruce Western, *Punishment and Inequality in America* (New York: Russell Sage Foundation, 2006); Nancy Marion, *A History of Federal Crime Control Initiatives, 1960–1993* (Westport: Praeger Press, 1994); Gary LaFree, *Losing Legitimacy: Street Crime and the Decline of Social Institutions in America* (Boulder: Westview Press, 1998).

22. Thomas Edsall and Mary Edsall, *Chain Reaction: The Impact of Race, Rights, and Taxes on American Politics* (New York: W. W. Norton, 1992), especially 136–138. Due to its pervasiveness and its concomitant "stretching," I give a skeletal version of the backlash thesis without taking aim at any particular account. Legal scholar James Forman Jr. writes that "beginning in the mid-1960s, Republican politicians—led by presidential candidates Goldwater and Nixon—focused on crime in an effort to tap into white voters' anxiety over increased racial equality and a growing welfare state." Legal scholar Dorothy Roberts highlights backlash strategies from Nixon to Reagan, documenting: "the shift in law enforcement policies at the end of the 1970s that started the astronomical U.S. prison expansion can be seen as a backlash against the reforms achieved by civil rights struggles." Forman, "Racial Critiques of Mass Incarceration"; Dorothy Roberts, "Constructing a Criminal Justice System Free of Racial Bias: An Abolistionist Framework," *Columbia Human Rights Law Review 39* (2007), 272; Jerome Miller, *Search and Destroy: African-American Males in the Criminal Justice System* (Cambridge: Cambridge University Press, 1996); Katherine Beckett, *Making Crime Pay: Law and Order in Contemporary American Politics* (New York: Oxford University Press, 1997); Michael Flamm, *Law and Order: Street Crime, Civil Unrest, and the Crisis of Liberalism in the 1960s* (New York: Columbia University Press, 2005); Joel Rosch, "Crime as an Issue in American Politics," in *The Politics of Crime and Criminal Justice*, ed. Erika Fairchild and Vincent Webb (Beverly Hills: Sage Publications, 1985), 25; Bruce Western, *Punishment and Inequality in America* (New York: Russell Sage Foundation, 2006); Nancy Marion, *A History of Federal Crime Control Initiatives, 1960–1993* (Westport: Praeger Press, 1994); Gary LaFree, *Losing Legitimacy: Street Crime and the Decline of Social Institutions in America* (Boulder: Westview Press, 1998).

23. Catharine MacKinnon, *Toward a Feminist Theory of the State* (Cambridge: Harvard University Press, 1989), 106.

24. Ronald Reagan, "Remarks at the Conservative Political Action Committee Dinner," 1983, quoted in Beckett, *Making Crime Pay*, 49. George H. W. Bush, "Address to Students on Drug Abuse,'" 1989, quoted in Beckett, *Making Crime Pay*, 48; Loic Wacquant, *Punishing the Poor: The Neoliberal Government of Social Insecurity* (Durham: Duke University Press, 2009), 10.

25. Nixon's statement is cited in many academic tomes. It was documented in Joe McGinnis, *Selling the President, 1968* (New York: Simon & Schuster, 1969), 23; Dan Carter, *The Politics of Rage: George Wallace, the Origins of the New Conservatism, and the Transformation of American Politics* (New York: Simon & Schuster, 1995), 352; Philip Klinkner and Rogers Smith, *Unsteady March: The Rise and Decline of Racial Equality in America* (Chicago: University of Chicago Press, 1999), 292; Mendelberg, *The Race Card,* 97; Vesla Weaver, "Frontlash: Race and the Development of Punitive Crime Policy," *Studies in American Political Development 21* (2007), 259; Ian Haney López, "Post-Racial Racism: Racial Stratification and Mass Incarceration in the Age of Obama," *California Law Review 98* (2010), 104; John Hagan, *Who Are the Criminals? The Politics of Crime Policy from the Age of Roosevelt to the Age of Reagan* (Princeton: Princeton University Press, 2010), 150; Alexander, *The New Jim Crow,* 46; Omi and Winant, *Racial Formation in the United States,* 124.

26. Alexander, *The New Jim Crow,* 44–45.

27. Racial criminalization, that is, the "stigmatization of crime as black," partnered with the idea that instances of white crime were a matter of individual failure, not white deficiency. Khalil Gibran Muhammad, *The Condemnation of Blackness: Race, Crime, and the Making of Modern Urban America* (Cambridge: Harvard University Press, 2010), 3; see also Anne Larason Schneider and Helen Ingram, *Policy Design for Democracy* (Lawrence: University of Kansas Press, 1997), 75.

28. Michael Tonry, *Punishing Race: A Continuing American Dilemma* (New York: Oxford University Press, 2011), 110. Political scientist Joseph Lowndes perceptively summarizes (and critiques) the backlash thesis as a surge of white resentment against the perceived excesses of the 1960s, which in turn granted conservatives "the opportunity to assert basic American values of patriotism, family, hard work, independence, and government fiscal responsibility; in doing so, they reclaimed the political field." Lowndes, *From the New Deal to the New Right,* 3.

    Many have criticized that backlash identifies racism as if it exists in a primordial state. White anxiety and resentment were not inevitable reactions, as Joseph Lowndes has explained, but backlash accounts effectively naturalize white racism by eliding the long-term conservative coalition-building that fused racism, anti-government populism, and economic conservatism. Even central metaphors collapse multiply purposed policies and internal complex party politics into single gestures: "backlash" is a mechanical process by which machinery lurches forward and then self-adjusts by lurching back, and "chain reaction" is a chemical or nuclear sequence that is irreversible once activated. Daniel Martinez HoSang, *Racial Propositions: Ballot Initiatives and the Making of Postwar California* (Berkeley: University of California Press, 2010); Joseph Lowndes, *From the New Deal to the New Right: Race and the Southern Origins of Modern Conservatism* (New Haven: Yale University Press, 2009); Daniel Kryder and Robert Mickey, "The Politics of Racial Backlash: Consequences of an American Metaphor" (paper presented at the annual meeting of the Western Political Science Association, Las Vegas, NV, March 8, 2007).

    Just as backlash centralizes emotions of white resentment and anxiety, punishment theories interpret crime policy as expressive of revenge or personal anxiety. In the grammar of vengeance and fear, many see crime policy as partially "the projection of personal insecurities into the policy arena," such that, for example, three-strikes legislation or Megan's Law represented "retaliatory law-making, acting out the punitive urges and controlling anxieties of expressive justice." By examining crime and punishment as "the symbols that our unconscious seeks," Stuart Scheingold concluded that the "politics of law-and-order must be seen at least partially as the projection of personal insecurities into the policy arena." In David Garland's expansive account of late-modernity's *Culture of Control,* harsh three-strikes legislation or Megan's Law are retaliatory expressions that "assuage popular outrage, reassure the public, and restore the credibility of the system." Stuart Scheingold, *The Politics of Law and Order: Street Crime and Public Policy* (New York: Longman, 1984), 68, 71; David Garland, *The Culture of Control: Crime and Social Control in Contemporary Society* (Chicago: University of Chicago Press 2002), 6, 39, 77–78, 158, 173; see also Stuart Scheingold and Austin Sarat, *Cause Lawyering: Political Commitments and Professional Responsibilities* (New York: Oxford University Press, 1998), 864; Jean-Paul Brodeur, "Penal Saturation," in *Post-Critical Criminology,* ed. Thomas O'Reilly-Flemming (Scarsborough: Prentice Hall, 1996).

29. Claire Jean Kim, *Bitter Fruit: The Politics of Black-Korean Conflict in New York City* (New Haven: Yale University Press, 2003), 9. Alan David Freeman, "Legitimizing Racial Discrimination Through Antidiscrimination Law: A Critical Review of Supreme Court Doctrine," *Minnesota Law Review 62* (1978): 1049–1119; Ian Haney López, *White By Law: The Legal Construction of Race* (New York: New York University Press, 1996), 138–140; Kimberlé Crenshaw et al., eds., *Critical Race Theory: The Key Writings That Formed the Movement* (New York: New Press, 1995).

30. Scott, *Contempt & Pity,* xii–xiii.

31. Guinier, "From Racial Liberalism to Racial Literacy," 92-104, 109–112; Scott, *Contempt & Pity,* xiii, 122–124; Daryl Michael Scott, "Postwar Pluralism, *Brown v. Board of Education,* and the Origins of Multicultural Education,"*Journal of American History* 91 (2004), 78–80.

32. John F. Kennedy, "Radio and Television Report to the American People on Civil Rights," June 11, 1963, *Public Papers of the Presidents of the United States: John F. Kennedy, 1963* (Washington, DC: GPO, 1964), 469. Concessions also include Nixon's 1969 "Philadelphia Plan" to require that government construction contractors promise to hire black employees in proportion to their representation in the workforce. Nixon's Secretary of Labor George Shultz advocated affirmative action requirements as "special measures" to address the "explosive" circumstances of black employment, and the plan matched Nixon's "black capitalism" philosophy that "people who own their own homes don't burn their neighborhood." Quoted in Skrentny, *Ironies of Affirmative Action,* 100–102.

33. President's Commission on Law Enforcement and Administration of Justice, *The Challenge of Crime in a Free Society,* viii, x, 15, 293–301.

34. A. Philip Randolph speaking at the White House civil rights conference in June 1966, quoted in Skrentny, *Ironies of Affirmative Action,* 77. Humphrey quoted in CR 1967, 21207; Timothy Thurber, *The Politics of Equality: Hubert H. Humphrey and the African American Freedom Struggle* (New York: Columbia University Press, 1999), 187; Perlstein, *Nixonland,* 349.

35. Hartman, *Scenes of Subjection,* 19–21; Mark Anthony Neal, *Looking for Leroy: Illegible Black Masculinities* (New York: New York University Press, 2013), 4–5.

36. Kimberlé Crenshaw, "Race, Reform, and Retrenchment: Transformation and Legitimation in Antidiscrimination Law," *Harvard Law* Review *101* (May 1988), 1370–1374.

37. Alexander, *The New Jim Crow,* 44–45; Omi and Winant, *Racial Formation in the United States,* 64.

38. The President's Committee on Civil Rights, *To Secure These Rights,* 28–32.

39. President's Commission on Law Enforcement and Administration Justice, *Challenge of Crime in a Free Society,* 7.

40. Eric Schickler, *Disjointed Pluralism: Institutional Innovation and the Development of the U.S. Congress* (Princeton: Princeton University Press, 2001), especially 15–16; Jacob Hacker, "Privatizing Risk without Privatizing the Welfare State: The Hidden Politics of Social Policy Retrenchment in the United States," *American Political Science Review* 98 (May 2004), especially 248; Karen Orren and Stephen Skowronek (2004); Kathleen Thelen, *How Institutions Evolve: The Political Economy of Skills in Germany, Britain, the United States, and Japan* (Cambridge: Cambridge University Press, 2004). Karen Orren and Stephen Skowrenek, *The Search for American Political Development* (New York: Cambridge University Press, 2004).

41. Bartholomew Sparrow, *From the Outside In: World War II and the American State* (Princeton: Princeton University Press, 1996), 16; Gottschalk, *Prison and the Gallows,* 2–4, 42–43; Bob Jessop, "The State and State-Building," in *Oxford Handbook of Political Institutions,* ed. R.A.W. Rhodes, Sarah Binder, and Bert Rockman (New York: Oxford University Press, 2006), 111–130.

42. Daryl Michael Scott, "Postwar Pluralism, *Brown v. Board of Education,* and the Origins of Multicultural Education," *Journal of American History 91* (June 2004), 74; Walter Jackson, *Gunnar Myrdal and America's Conscience: Social Engineering and Racial Liberalism, 1938–1987* (Chapel Hill: University of North Carolina Press, 1994), 279–281; Thomas Pettigrew, *The Sociology of Race Relations: Reflection and Reform* (New York: Free Press, 1980), 132–134.

43. Penny Von Eschen, *Race Against Empire: Black Americans and Anticolonialsim, 1937–1957* (Ithaca: Cornell University Press, 1997), 157; Nikhil Pal Singh, *Black Is a Country: Race and the Unfinished Struggle for Democracy* (Cambridge: Harvard University Press, 2004).

44. Guy Johnson, letter to Robert Carr of the President's Committee on Civil Rights, April 3, 1947, Records of the President's Committee on Civil Rights, Box 13, HSTL; National Lawyers Guild, National Bar Association, National Association for the Advancement of Colored People, "Moderator's Report on Adequacy of Existing Anti-Lynching Legislation Prepared for Legal Conference on Federal Power to Protect Civil Liberties," January 25, 1947, RG 60: Records of the Department of Justice, Civil Rights Division: Subject Files of Assistant Attorney General W. Wilson White, 1958–1959, Box 74, NARA; Gunnar Myrdal, *An American Dilemma: The Negro Problem and Modern Democracy* (New Brunswick: Transaction Publishers, 2000 [1944]), 533; Robert Lieberman, *Shifting the*

Color Line: Race and the American Welfare State (Cambridge: Harvard University Press, 2001); Paul Frymer, *Black and Blue: African Americans, the Labor Movement, and the Decline of the Democratic Party* (Princeton: Princeton University Press, 2008).

45. Gillian Harkins, *Everybody's Family Romance: Reading Incest in Neoliberal America* (Minneapolis: University of Minnesota Press, 2009), 10.

46. Flamm, *Law and Order*, 169.

47. The 1988 presidential campaign featured two television ads criticizing the Massachusetts prison furlough program. "Weekend Passes," made by an independent political group, showed an image of Horton's face; "Revolving Door," made by the Republican Party, described weekend furloughs as a revolving door for murderers and rapists but did not reference Horton directly. Mendelberg, *The Race Card*, 136.

48. When accused of playing the "race card," George H. W. Bush responded, "There is not a racist bone in my body." Bush's campaign manager Lee Atwater denied racial intent even as he called Horton's furlough the campaign's "silver bullet." Even as they disavowed racist intent, the Horton ad was congruous with Reagan-era tough-on-crime appeals mobilized against African Americans, especially punishments for crack cocaine addiction and alleged welfare fraud. W. E. B. DuBois, *The Souls of Black Folk* (1903; reprint, Madison: Cricket House Books, 2013); Theodore Roosevelt, Sixth Annual Message, December 3, 1906; Mendelberg, *The Race Card*, 138–143.

49. Mark Smith, "Intellectuals, Rhetoric, and Context: The Move to Economic Arguments by Conservative Writers," *Studies in American Political Development 20* (Spring 2006), 3.

50. Paul Frymer, *Black and Blue*, 19.

51. Eric Schickler, *Disjointed Pluralism: Institutional Innovation and the Development of the U.S. Congress* (Princeton: Princeton University Press, 2001), especially 13–15; James March, *A Primer on Decision Making: How Decisions Happen* (New York: Free Press, 1994), 171–179; Barbara Sinclair, *Unorthodox Lawmaking: New Legislative Process in the U.S. Congress* (Washington, DC: Congressional Quarterly, 1997); Glen Krutz, "Tactical Maneuvering on Omnibus Bills in Congress," *American Journal of Political Science 45* (January 2001), 210; Barbara Sinclair, "Can Congress Be Trusted with the Constitution? The Effects of Incentives and Procedures," in *Congress and the Constitution*, ed. Neal Devins and Keith Whittington (Durham: Duke University Press, 2005), 297, 305; Brannon Denning and Brooks Smith, "Uneasy Riders: The Case for a Truth-in-Legislation Amendment," *Utah Law Review 957* (1999), 958–959; Garrick Pursley, "Preemption in Congress," *Ohio State Law Journal 71* (2010), 596.

52. *CR*, September 8, 1965, 23111–23112, 23114.

53. Paul Pierson, "The Study of Policy Development," *Journal of Policy Development 17* (2005), 37; Steven Teles, *The Rise of the Conservative Legal Movement: The Battle for Control of the Law* (Princeton: Princeton University Press, 2008), 18–20, 272–279.

54. See Angela Y. Davis, *Are Prisons Obsolete?* (Toronto: Open Media, 2003), chapter 5; Joshua Page, *The Toughest Beat: Politics, Punishment, and the Prison Officers Union in California* (New York: Oxford University Press, 2011); Lisa Miller, *The Perils of Federalism: Race, Poverty, and the Politics of Crime* (New York: Oxford University Press, 2010). Joel Dyer, *The Perpetual Prisoner Machine: How America Profits from Crime* (Boulder: Westview Press, 2000); David Ladipo, "The Rise of America's Prison-Industrial Complex," *New Left Review 7* (2001): 109–123. For perceptive critiques of the explanatory power of the prison industrial complex, see Christian Parenti, *Lockdown America: Police and Prisons in the Age of Crisis* (New York: Verso, 2000); Wacquant, *Punishing the Poor*, 105–107.

55. Scheingold, *The Politics of Street Crime*, 4–7, 23; Anthony King, *Running Scared: Why America's Politicians Campaign Too Much and Govern Too Little* (New York: Free Press, 1997), 140; Gregory Huber and Sanford Gordon, "Accountability and Coercion: Is Justice Blind When It Runs for Office?" *American Journal of Political Science 48* (2004): 247–263: Joseph Dillon Davey, *The Politics of Prison Expansion: Winning Elections by Waging War on Crime* (Westport: Praeger Publishers, 1998).

56. Controlling for socioeconomic status, people subjected to police questioning and arrest (though not convicted or incarcerated) were less likely to vote and to express trust in government. Weaver and Lerman, "Political Consequences of the Carceral State"; Hannah Walker,

"Activating Communities: The Carceral State, Proximal Contact and Race" (working paper, Department of Political Science, University of Washington, Seattle, 2013); Jeff Manza and Christopher Uggen, *Locked Out: Felon Disenfranchisement and American Democracy* (New York: Oxford University Press, 2006); Khalilah L. Brown-Dean, *"One Lens, Multiple Views: Felon Disenfranchisement Laws and American Political Inequality"* (Ph.D. dissertation, Ohio State University, 2003); Alec Ewald, "Civil Death: The Ideological Paradox of Criminal Disenfranchisement Law in the United States," *Wisconsin Law Review* (2002), 1045–1132; Patricia Allard, *Life Sentences: Denying Welfare Benefits to Women Convicted of Drug Offenses* (Washington, DC: The Sentencing Project, 2002).

57. By enhancing carceral power without altering its basic structures, mainstream anti-violence movements extended protections for some women, but such reforms created no protections for men of color subject to unnecessary arrest, and they heightened carceral surveillance of women of color, immigrant women, and women involved in sex work. Beth Richie, *Arrested Justice: Black Women, Violence, and America's Prison Nation* (New York: New York University Press, 2012), 77–97; Dara Strolovitch, *Affirmative Advocacy: Race, Class, and Gender in Interest Group Politics* (Chicago: University of Chicago Press, 2007), 20–21; Gottschalk, *Prison and the Gallows,* chapters 4–9. Peter Bachrach and Morton Baratz, "Two Faces of Power," *American Political Science Review* 56 (December 1962), 947–952. For an excellent account of how the federal venue tends to produce narrower crime policy solutions than do cities and states, see Lisa Miller, "The Representational Biases of Federalism: Scope and Bias in the Political Process, Revisited," *Perspectives on Politics* 5 (June 2007), 305–321.

58. Jacob Hacker: *The Divided Welfare State: The Battle over Public and Private Social Benefits in the United States* (New York: Cambridge University Press, 2002), 284.

59. Saidiya Hartmen, *Scenes of Subjection: Terror, Slavery, and Self-Making in Nineteenth-Century America* (New York: Oxford University Press, 1997), especially 3–8.

60. For this definition of framing, I draw on Mark Smith, "Intellectuals, Rhetoric, and Context: The Move to Economic Arguments by Conservative Writers," *Studies in American Political Development* 20 (2006), 2.

61. Garland rightly emphasizes that criminologists, penologists, and social scientists have challenged the conventional wisdom of punishment, especially prisons, increasingly through the 1960s. Federal lawmakers, unsurprisingly, have not followed suit. David Garland, *Punishment and Modern Society: A Study in Social Theory* (Chicago: University of Chicago Press, 1990), 3–4.

62. Ruth Wilson Gilmore defines racism as "the production and exploitation of group-differentiated vulnerability to premature death," echoing the 1951 definition offered by the Civil Rights Congress in its petition to the United Nations' "We Genocide," which calls racism "the willful creation of conditions making for premature death, poverty, and disease." Gilmore, *Golden Gulag,* 28.

63. Angela Davis, "Race and Criminalization: Black Americans and the Punishment Industry," in *The Angela Y. Davis Reader,* ed. Joy James (New York: Blackwell, 1988), 63; Angela Davis, "Racialized Punishment and Prison Abolition," in *The Angela Y. Davis Reader,* 96–110. George Lipsitz, *The Possessive Investment in Whiteness: How White People Profit from Identity Politics* (Philadelphia: Temple University Press, 1998).

64. William Haltom and Michael McCann, *Distorting the Law: Politics, Media, and the Litigation Crisis* (Chicago: University of Chicago Press), 7–9, 270–272; John Skrentny, "Law and the American State," *Annual Review of Sociology* 32 (2006), 222–224; Reddy, *Freedom with Violence,* 9; Richie, *Arrested Justice,* 125–140.

65. Darnell Hawkins, "Ethnicity, Race, and Crime: A Review of Selected Studies," in *Ethnicity, Race, and Crime: Perspectives Across Time and Place,* ed. Darnell Hawkins (Albany: State University of New York Press, 1995), 12–13, 31; Darnell Hawkins, "On the Horns of a Dilemma: Criminal Wrongs, Civil Rights, and the Administration of Justice in African-American Communities," in *Crime Control and Social Justice: The Delicate Balance,* ed. Darnell Hawkins et al. (Westport, CT: Greenwood Press, 2003), 440; Thomas Pettigrew, *The Sociology of Race Relations: Reflections and Reform* (New York: Free Press, 1980); Khalil Gibran Muhammad, *Condemnation of Blackness: Race, Crime, and the Making of Modern Urban America* (Cambridge: The Presidents and Fellows of Harvard College, 2010), 276–277, 367.

66. Jeffrie Murphy, "Marxism and Retribution," in *Punishment: A Philosophy & Public Affairs Reader*, ed. A. John Simmons et al. (Princeton: Princeton University Press, 1995), 14–15.

67. Todd Clear's phrase "penal harm" summons the inescapable fact that punishment is "a government's organized infliction of harm upon a citizen." Todd Clear, *Harm in American Penology: Offenders, Victims, and Their Communities* (Albany: SUNY Press, 1994), 2–4; Robert Cover, "Violence and the Word," *Yale Law Journal* 95 (1986), 1601, 1619, 1629; Austin Sarat, "Violence Representation, and Responsibility in Capital Trials: The View from the Jury," *Indiana Law Journal* 70 (1995), 1107; Ian Haney López, "The Social Construction of Race: Some Observations on Illusion, Fabrication, and Choice," *Harvard Civil Rights and Civil Liberties Law Review* 29 (1994); Chandan Reddy, *Freedom with Violence: Race, Sexuality, and the US State* (Durham: Duke University Press, 2011), 226–227; Cover, "Violence and the Word," 1601, 1619, 1629. Any given stop-and-frisk might proceed by rights and rules, the gun holstered, but "it is colored from the beginning by the fear of being violently treated."

68. Paul Pierson, "The Study of Policy Development," *Journal of Policy Development* 17 (2005), 36; Paul Pierson, *Politics in Time: History, Institutions, and Social Analysis* (Princeton: Princeton University Press, 2004), 46–47.

69. Stephen Skowronek, *Building a New American State: The Expansion of National Administrative Capacities, 1877–1920* (Cambridge: Cambridge University Press, 1982), viii; Paul Frymer, *Black and Blue* (Princeton: Princeton University Press, 2007), 10; Jacob Hacker and Paul Pierson, "Business Power and Social Policy: Employers and the Formation of the American Welfare State," *Politics & Society* 30 (2002): 285–286; Paul Pierson, "The Study of Policy Development," *Journal of Policy Development* 17 (2005), 36; Paul Pierson, *Politics in Time: History, Institutions, and Social Analysis* (Princeton: Princeton University Press, 2004), 46–47.

70. One account identified four measureable components that might elevate incarceration rates: a higher offense rate, more arrests per offense, more prison commitments per arrest, and longer sentences per prison commitment. From 1980 to1996, the contribution of each stage was lowest for the offense rate (11.5 percent) and arrests per offense (0.5 percent). The greatest contributors to elevated incarceration rates were commitments per arrest (51.4 percent) and time served (36.6 percent). Alfred Blumstein and Allen Beck, "Population Growth in U.S. Prisons, 1980–1996," in *Prisons*, ed. Michael Tonry and Joan Petersilia (Chicago: University of Chicago Press, 1999), 17–61; Michael Tonry, *Sentencing Matters* (New York: Oxford University Press, 1996), 4–6, 30; BJS, *1996 National Survey of State Sentencing Structures* (Washington, DC: DOJ, 1998).

71. Of David Mayhew's list of 370 important laws enacted between 1946 and 2008, there are 17 enactments germane to criminal law and criminal justice administration: (1) Omnibus Crime Control and Safe Streets Act of 1968; (2) Gun Control Act of 1968; (3) Organized Crime Control Act of 1970; (4) Omnibus Crime Control Act of 1970; (5) Narcotics Control Act of 1970; (6) Comprehensive Crime Control Act of 1984; (7) Anti-Drug Abuse Act of 1986; (8) Anti-Drug Abuse Act of 1988; (9) Brady Handgun Violence Prevention Act of 1993; (10) Assault Weapons Ban of 1994; (11) Violent Crime Control and Law Enforcement Act of 1994; (12) Abortion Clinic Access Act of 1994; (13) Anti-Terrorism Act of 1996; (14) Immigration Reform Act of 1996; (15) the USA PATRIOT Act of 2001; (16) Corporate Responsibility Act of 2002; and (17) Unborn Victims of Violence Act of 2004. Certain immigration and terrorism enactments qualify as crime legislation because of their provisions for domestic detention, surveillance, and punishment.

Mayhew identified "important" enactments based on journalists' end-of-year wrap-up stories and policy specialists' retrospective evaluations. Mayhew noted a dearth of expert sources on crime and narcotics, and therefore crime enactments are covered mostly by journalistic reviews. There are 267 important enactments from the 80th to the 101st Congress, listed in *Divided We Govern*; plus 66 enactments from the 102nd to the 107th Congress, listed in its Second Edition; plus 37 enactments from the 108th to the 110th Congress, listed on Mayhew's webpage. David R. Mayhew, *Divided We Govern: Party Control, Lawmaking, and Investigations 1946–1990* (New Haven: Yale University Press, 1991), 45, Table 4.1;

Mayhew, *Divided We Govern*, Table E.2; for updates, see David Mayhew's website at http://pantheon.yale.edu/~dmayhew/data3.html.

72. In the domain of gun control, I do not treat the Gun Control Act of 1968, the Brady Handgun Violence Prevention Act of 1993, and the Assault Weapons Ban of 1994. In the domain of organized and corporate crime, I do not treat the Organized Crime Control Act of 1970 and the Corporate Responsibility Act of 2002. In the domain of hate crimes and violence against women, I do not treat the Abortion Clinic Access Act of 1994, the Violence Against Women Act of 1994 (Title IV of the Violence Crime Control and Law Enforcement Act), and the Unborn Victims of Violence Act of 2004 (framed as protection of women and children). Bernard Harcourt, *The Language of the Gun: Youth, Crime, and Public Policy* (Chicago: University of Chicago Press, 2006), especially chapter 13; Andrea Smith, "Unmasking the State: Racial/Gender Terror and Hate Crimes," *Australia Feminist Law Journal 26* (2007); Angela Davis, "The Color of Violence Against Women," *Color Lines,* October 10, 2000; Marie Gottschalk, *Prison and the Gallows.*

73. Stuart Scheingold, *The Politics of Street Crime: Criminal Process and Cultural Obsession* (Philadelphia: Temple University Press, 1991), 22–28, 182–187; Herbert Jacob, *The Frustrations of Policy: Responses to Crime by American Cities* (Boston: Little, Brown, 1984); Herbert Jacob et al., *Governmental Responses to Crime: Crime on Urban Agendas* (Washington, DC: NIJ, 1982). Lisa Miller's innovative study of interest-group representation across local, state, and national legislatures found that federal governance produces narrower crime solutions than cities and states. Lisa Miller, "The Representational Biases of Federalism: Scope and Bias in the Political Process, Revisited," *Perspectives on Politics 5* (June 2007), 305–321.

74. Various federal laws prohibit people with felony convictions from receiving Temporary Assistance to Needy Families, food stamps, veteran and disability assistance, and financial aid for college. Public housing authorities may evict people with a criminal conviction, a discretionary power extended to them under President George H. W. Bush in 1988, and extended further still when President Clinton authorized local housing officials to deny applicants for housing based on one arrest, a policy Clinton called a "one strike and you're out" standard in his 1996 State of the Union address. Gwen Rubinstein and Debbie Mukamal, "Welfare and Housing—Denial of Benefits to Drug Offenders," in *Invisible Punishment: The Collateral Consequences of Mass Imprisonment,* ed. Marc Mauer and Meda Chesney-Lind (New York: New Press, 2002), 37–49; Jeremy Travis, "Invisible Punishment: An Instrument of Social Exclusion," in *Invisible Punishment: The Collateral Consequences of Mass Imprisonment,* ed. Marc Mauer and Meda Chesney-Lind (New York: New Press, 2002), 15–36; Jonathan Simon, *Governing Through Crime: How the War on Crime Transformed American Democracy and Created a Culture of Fear* (New York: Oxford University Press, 2007), 194–198. Patricia Allard, *Life Sentences: Denying Welfare Benefits to Women Convicted of Drug Offenses* (Washington, DC: The Sentencing Project, 2002).

75. While I challenge strict periodization that begins with Goldwater or Nixon, I do not seek to reperiodize in any terms, much less presidential terms. David Mayhew, "Suggested Guidelines for Periodization," *Polity 37* (October 2005), 531–535.

76. Brian Balough, "The State of the State among Historians," *Social Science History 27* (2003), 455–457.

77. Transcript, Ramsey Clark Oral History Interview V, June 3, 1969, by Harri Baker, Internet Copy, LBJL, 5–6, 10.

78. Charles Epp, *Making Rights Real: Activists, Bureaucrats, and the Creation of the Legalistic State* (Chicago: University of Chicago Press, 2009), 47, 267; David O. Sears, "Black Attitudes toward the Political System in the Aftermath of the Watts Insurrection," *Midwest Journal of Political Science 13* (November 1969), 515–544.

79. Wacquant, *Punishing the Poor,* 307–308; Katherine Beckett, *Making Crime Pay: Law and Order in Contemporary American Politics* (New York: Oxford University Press, 1997); Joseph Dillon Davey, *The Politics of Prison Expansion: Winning Elections by Waging War on Crime* (Westport, CT: Praeger, 1998); Michael Tonry, *Malign Neglect: Race, Crime, and Punishment in America* (New York: Oxford University Press, 1995); Michael Tonry, *Thinking about Crime: Sense and Sensibility in American Penal Culture* (New York: Oxford University

Press, 2004); Steven Donziger, *The Real War on Crime: The Report of the National Criminal Justice Commission* (New York: Harper Perennial, 1996); Marc Mauer, *Race to Incarcerate* (New York: New Press, 1999).

Chapter 2

1. Robert Carr, Memorandum to the President's Committee on Civil Rights, "The Negro in the United States," prepared by Milton Stewart and Herbert Kaufman, June 24, 1947, Box 37, Nash Papers, HSTL.
2. *CR*, March 1, 1960, 4020–4022.
3. Jonathan Daniels, Administrative Assistant to the President, Memorandum to Victor Rotnem, DOJ, August 3, 1943, Civil Rights File, Box 5, Bontecou Papers, HSTL. After the Detroit and Harlem riots of 1943, the DOJ speculated that World War II race riots paralleled the "racial disturbances in the *last* war period," when "mob violence" spread through East St. Louis, Houston, Philadelphia, Chicago, and other cities between 1917 and 1919. See H. Otto Dahlke, "Race and Minority Riots—A Study in the Typology of Violence," *Social Forces 30* (May 1952), 422.
4. The Social Science Institute at Fist University counted 242 battles, quoted in Shapiro, *White Violence and Black Response*, 508; Glenda Gilmore, *Defying Dixie: The Radical Roots of Civil Rights* (New York: W. W. Norton & Company, 2008), 373; Ian Haney López, *Racism on Trial: The Chicano Fight for Justice* (Cambridge: Harvard University Press, 2003), 75–76; Harvard Sitkoff, "Racial Militancy and Interracial Violence in the Second World War," *Journal of American History 58* (December 1971), 661–663.
5. Philleo Nash, Memorandum to Jonathan Daniels, August 31, 1943, emphasis added, Box 28, Nash Papers.
6. Arthur Raper, *The Tragedy of Lynching* (Chapel Hill: University of North Carolina Press, 1933), 20; Christopher Parker, *Fighting for Democracy: Black Veterans and the Struggle Against White Supremacy in the Postwar South* (Princeton: Princeton University Press, 2009), 39–41.
7. Mary Dudziak, *Cold War Civil Rights: Race and the Image of American Democracy* (Princeton: Princeton University Press, 2000); Philip Klinkner with Rogers Smith, *The Unsteady March: The Rise and Decline of Racial Equality in America* (Chicago: University of Chicago Press, 1999); Derrick Bell, "*Brown v. Board of Education* and the Interest-Convergence Dilemma," *Harvard Law Review 93* (January 1980), 523; Howard Winant, *The World Is a Ghetto: Race and Democracy Since World War II* (New York: Basic Books, 2001), 2–6; Sitkoff, "Racial Militancy and Interracial Violence in the Second World War," 661; Lester Jones, "The Editorial Policy of the Negro Newspapers of 1917–1918 as Compared with That of 1941–1942," *Journal of Negro History 29* (January 1944), 24–31; Ralph Davis, "The Negro Newspapers and the War," *Sociology and Social Research 27* (May–June 1943), 373–380; William Berman, *The Politics of Civil Rights in the Truman Administration* (Columbus: Ohio State University Press, 1970), 42; Robert Garson, *The Democratic Party and the Politics of Sectionalism, 1941–1948* (Baton Rouge: Louisiana State University Press, 1974), 21.
8. Charles Tilly, "War Making and State Making as Organized Crime," in *Bringing the State Back In*, ed. Peter Evans, Dietrich Rueschemeyer, and Theda Skocpol (Cambridge: Cambridge University Press, 1985), 171.
9. Philleo Nash, Memorandum to Jonathan Daniels, August 31, 1943, Box 28, Nash Papers; *Newsweek*, July 5, 1943, 35–36; "Dewey Orders State Guard to Stand By; Riots Leave Harlem Stores in Shambles," *PM Daily*, August 3, 1943, 3; Sitkoff, "Racial Militancy," 671–672.
10. National Urban League, "Racial Conflict—A Home Front Danger: Lessons of the Detroit Riot," July 30, 1943, 4, Box 49, Nash Papers; Philleo Nash to Jonathan Daniels, Memorandum on the Handling of the Detroit Riot, September 28, 1943, Box 28, Nash Papers; Sitkoff, "Racial Militancy"; Sugrue, *The Origins of the Urban Crisis*, 29–30.
11. Alfred McClung Lee in cooperation with the American Council on Race Relations, *Race Riots Aren't Necessary* (Chicago: American Council on Race Relations, 1945), 15, Box 47, Nash Papers.

12. Walter Davenport, "Race Riots Coming," *Collier's*, September 18, 1943, 83; Shapiro, *White Violence and Black Response*, 318.

13. Thurgood Marshall as quoted in Samuel Walker, "'A Strange Atmosphere of Consistent Illegality': Myrdal on 'The Police and Other Public Contacts,'" in *An American Dilemma Revisited: Race Relations in a Changing World*, ed. Obie Clayton Jr. (New York: Russell Sage, 1996), 228; National Urban League, "Racial Conflict—A Home Front Danger: Lessons of the Detroit Riot," July 30, 1943, 3, Box 49, Nash Papers; John Skrentny, *The Minority Rights Revolution* (Cambridge: Belknap Press of Harvard University Press, 2004), 27–29; Shapiro, *White Violence and Black Response*, 318–320.

14. Victor W. Rotnem, Memorandum to the Attorney General, August 9, 1943, Box 5, Bontecou Papers; Garson, *The Democratic Party and the Politics of Sectionalism*, 66–68; Sitkoff, "Racial Militancy," 677.

15. Virginius Dabney, "Nearer and Nearer the Precipice," *Atlantic Monthly 171* (January 1943), 94–100, quoted in Berman, *The Politics of Civil Rights in the Truman Administration*, 43; Report of the Governor's Fact-Finding Committee to Governor Harry Kelly on the Detroit Race Riot of June 20–21, as excerpted in *Detroit News*, August 11, 1943.

16. Walter Davenport, "Race Riots Coming," *Collier's*, September 18, 1943, 81.

17. Walter White letter to Harlem and Brooklyn black leaders, June 30, 1943, Box 58, Nash Papers; Peter Kellogg, "Civil Rights Consciousness in the 1940s," *Historian 42* (1979), 26–32.

18. Letter from Randall Tyus, Executive Secretary of the Baltimore NAACP, to Walter White, July 2, 1943, Box 58, Nash Papers; Letter from Theodore Spaulding, President of Philadelphia Branch of the NAACP, to Walter White, July 1, 1943, Box 58, Nash Papers.

19. Kellogg, "Civil Rights Consciousness in the 1940s," 27; Robert Fredrick Burk, *The Eisenhower Administration and Black Civil Rights* (Knoxville: University of Tennessee Press, 1984), 9; Scott, "Postwar Pluralism, *Brown v. Board of Education*, and the Origins of Multicultural Education," 3–7. Alfred McClung Lee in cooperation with the American Council on Race Relations, *Race Riots Aren't Necessary* (Chicago: American Council on Race Relations, 1945), Box 47, Nash Papers, 2–6; Gordon Allport, *ABC's of Scapegoating*, 4th rev. ed. (1948; repr., New York: Anti-Defamation League of B'nai B'rith, 1963), Box 10, Claytor Papers.

20. National Association for the Advancement of Colored People, *Thirty Years of Lynching in the United States, 1889–1918* (New York: Negro Universities Press, 1969 [1919]); A. Raper, *The Tragedy of Lynching* (Chapel Hill: University of North Carolina Press, 1933); Katherine Stovel, "Local Sequential Patterns: The Structure of Lynching in the Deep South, 1882–1930," *Social Forces 79* (March 2001), 843–880; James Clarke, "Without Fear or Shame: Lynching, Capital Punishment and the Subculture of Violence in the American South," *British Journal of Political Science 28* (April 1998), 269–289; Dominic Capeci Jr., "The Lynching of Cleo Wright: Federal Protection of Constitutional Rights during World War II," *Journal of American History 72* (March 1986), 859–887; Tuskegee Institute statistics, quoted in Memo from Robert K. Carr to Members of the President's Committee on Civil Rights, "'Background Notes on the Lynching Problem,' a Memorandum by Robert K. Carr and Nancy Wechsler," July 10, 1947, Box 37, Nash Papers.

21. Evelyn Simien, "Introduction," in *Gender and Lynching: The Politics of Memory*, ed. Evelyn Simien (New York: Palgrave Macmillan, 2011), 2; Jennifer Williams, "'A Woman Was Lynched the Other Day': Memory, Gender, and the Limits of Traumatic Representation," in *Gender and Lynching*, 81–102; Tera Hunter, *To 'Joy My Freedom: Southern Black Women's Lives and Labors after the Civil War* (Cambridge: Harvard University Press, 1997), 33–34; Trudier Harris, *Exorcising Blackness: Historical and Literary Lynching and Burning Rituals* (Bloomington: Indiana University Press, 1984); Kimberley Johnson, *Reforming Jim Crow: Southern Politics and State in the Age Before Brown* (New York: Oxford University Press, 2010), 58–60; Richard Delgado, "The Law of the Noose: A History of Latino Lynching," *Harvard Civil Rights-Civil Liberties Law Review 44* (2009), 299–300; William Carrigan and Clive Webb, "The Lynching of Persons of Mexican Origin or Descent in the United States, 1848 to 1928," *Journal of Social History 37* (2003), 411–412; Robert Zangrando, *The NAACP*

Crusade Against Lynching, 1909–1950 (Philadelphia: Temple University Press, 1980), 165; Michal Belknap, *Federal Law and Southern Order: Racial Violence and Constitutional Conflict in the Post-Brown South* (Athens: University of Georgia Press, 1987), 17–18; "Four Freedoms: Dixie Style," *CD*, May 8, 1943.

22. DOJ Memorandum, September 26, 1946, Box 45, Nash Papers; Carol Anderson, *Eyes Off the Prize* (New York: Cambridge University Press, 2003), 58, 60–61; Berman, *The Politics of Civil Rights in the Truman Administration*, 45; Parker, *Fighting for Democracy*, 47–48; Walter White, Secretary of National Association for Advancement of Colored People, telegram to Matthew Connelly, Secretary to the President, March 16, 1946, Box 549, Truman Papers; Dudziak, *Cold War Civil Rights*, 18–20; Thurgood Marshall to Tom Clark, December 27, 1946, quoted in Anderson, *Eyes Off the Prize*, 62; *NYT*, July 27, 1946, 1, 32; Memorandum from Attorney General Tom C. Clark, n.d., Tennessee, Box 5, Bontecou Papers.

23. Walter White et al. Telegram to Truman, August 6, 1956, quoted in Anderson, *Eyes Off the Prize*, 60; Parker, *Fighting for Democracy*, 48–51.

24. "Talmadge Says His Regime Will Keep Lynchings Down," *Washington Star*, July 29, 1946; Clark's press conference remarks quoted in Dudziak, *Cold War Civil Rights*, 20.

25. President Truman, Executive Order 9808, quoted in The President's Committee on Civil Rights, *To Secure These Rights*, vii–ix. A growing body of scholarship traces partisan shifts on civil rights back from the mid-1960s to the mid-1940s. Accounts that emphasize the mid-1960s tend to analyze the transformation of elite choices and roll-call votes in Congress, whereas accounts that emphasize the 1940s analyze more gradual demographic and intellectual shifts. Eric Schickler, Kathryn Pearson, and Brian Feinstein point out that roll-call votes represent a small fraction of congressional actions, noting that, of the many civil rights bills introduced between 1933 and 1948, there were only 19 House roll-call votes on civil rights. The authors therefore turn to more "upstream" measures like discharge petitions, speeches on the House floor, and bill sponsorship. Eric Schickler, Kathryn Pearson, and Brian Feinstein, "Congressional Parties and Civil Rights Politics from 1933 to 1972," *Journal of Politics* (July 2010), 672–689; Brian Feinstein and Eric Schickler, "Platforms and Partners: The Civil Rights Realignment Reconsidered," *Studies in American Political Development* 22 (2008), 1–31; Anthony Chen, "The Hitlerian Rule of Quotas: Racial Conservatism and the Politics of Fair Employment Legislation in New York State, 1941–1945," *Journal of American History* 92 (March 2006), 1238; David Karol, *Party Position Change in American Politics: Coalition Management* (New York: Cambridge University Press, 2009).

26. One scholar noted that *To Secure These Rights* "went far beyond" what Truman and his advisors expected. Berman, *The Politics of Civil Rights in the Truman Administration*, 70–71.

27. Steven Lawson, "Introduction," in Steven Lawson, ed. to The President's Committee on Civil Rights, *To Secure These Rights: The Report on Harry Truman's Committee on Civil Rights* (Boston: Bedford Press, 2004), 22; Leslie Dunbar, "The Changing Mind of the South: The Exposed Nerve," *Journal of Politics* 26 (February 1964), 14.

28. Robert Garson, *The Democratic Party and the Politics of Sectionalism, 1941–1948* (Baton Rouge: Louisiana State University Press, 1974), 21–22; Kellogg, "Civil Rights Consciousness in the 1940s," 18–41; Myrdal, *An American Dilemma*, chapter 1; John Temple Graves, *The Fighting South* (New York: G.P. Putnam's Sons, 1943), 114.

29. In 1942, the eight states that retained the poll tax were Alabama, Arkansas, Georgia, Mississippi, South Carolina, Tennessee, Texas, and Virginia. Garson, *The Democratic Party and the Politics of Sectionalism*, 21–22, 24; Myrdal, *An American Dilemma*, 416.

30. The President's Committee on Civil Rights, *To Secure These Rights*, 20–78.

31. The President's Committee on Civil Rights, *To Secure These Rights*, 6.

32. The President's Committee on Civil Rights, *To Secure These Rights*, 29–30.

33. Some federal agencies had their own "law enforcement" arms, such as the Postal Inspection Service (established 1840), Customs Inspection (established 1846), the Intelligence Unit of the Bureau of Internal Revenue (established 1868), the Customs Border Patrol (established 1886), and Immigration Border Patrol (established 1925). Arthur Millspaugh, *Crime Control by the National Government* (Washington, DC: The Brookings Institution, 1937), 24–38; Gottschalk, *The Prison and the Gallows*, 42.

34. Speech by Ida B. Wells-Barnett, "This Awful Slaughter," May 8, 1909, in *Great Speeches by African Americans: Frederick Douglas, Sojourner Truth, Dr. Martin Luther King Jr., Barack Obama, and Others*, ed. James Daley (Mineola: Dover Publications, 2006), 100.

35. Robert Carr, Memorandum to President's Committee on Civil Rights, "The Negro in the United States," a Memorandum prepared by Milton D. Stewart and Herbert Kaufman, June 24, 1947, 7, Box 37, Nash Papers; The President's Committee on Civil Rights, *To Secure These Rights*, 155.

36. Remarks by Guy B. Johnson to the President's Committee on Civil Rights, May 14, 1947, Box 13, 220 PCCR Records; The President's Committee on Civil Rights, *To Secure These Rights*, 25–26; Testimony of J. Edgar Hoover to the President's Committee on Civil Rights, March 20, 1947, 41, Box 14, PCCR Records.

37. Myrdal, *An American Dilemma*, 529, quoted in Muhammad, *Condemnation of Blackness*, 276.

38. Myrdal, *An American Dilemma*, 530, 534, italics in original; Samuel Walker, "A Strange Atmosphere of Consistent Illegality: Myrdal on 'The Police and Other Public Contacts'," in *An American Dilemma Revisited: Race Relations in a Changing World*, ed. Obie Clayton Jr. (New York: Russell Sage, 1996).

39. Joseph Cadden, Executive Director of the Civil Rights Congress, in letter to Robert K. Carr, September 17, 1947, Box 11, Records of the President's Committee on Civil Rights, PCCR Records, HSTL.

40. Section 51 allowed punishment of up to 10 years' imprisonment or fine of up to $5,000, and stated that those convicted were "thereafter ineligible to any office or place of honor, profit or trust created by the Constitution or laws of the United States." The PCCR recommended eliminating the disqualification clause, because they feared that it inhibited convictions. Section 52 carried a much lighter penalty—a maximum sentence of one year in prison and a maximum fine of $1,000—and the PCCR recommended raising penalties to those of Section 51. The President's Committee on Civil Rights, *To Secure These Rights*, 116, 156–157; Goluboff, *The Lost Promise of Civil Rights*, 138–147; The President's Committee on Civil Rights, *To Secure These Rights*, 118–119.

41. President Hoover appointed the 11 member National Commission on Law Observance and Enforcement in May 1929, and their primary charge was to investigate alcohol prohibition. Instead of reaching a coherent position on alcohol prohibition—five of the 11 members favored retention, two favored repeal, and four supported revisions—the Commission recommended overall reforms to the criminal justice system. For further analysis, see Henry S. Ruth, "To Dust Shall Ye Return?" *Notre Dame Lawyer 43* (1968), 811–813; Mahoney, *The Politics of the Safe Streets Act*, 22–28.

42. The President's Committee on Civil Rights, *To Secure These Rights*, 25; Johnson, *Reforming Jim Crow*, 62–64.

43. Specifically, the bill proposed adding to Title 18, section 242, the following new section: "Sec. 242A. (1) The right to be immune from exactions of fines, or derivations of property, without due process of law. (2) The right to be immune from punishment for crime or alleged criminal offenses except after a fair trial and upon conviction and sentence pursuant to due process of law. (3) The right to be immune from physical violence applied to exact testimony or to compel confession of crime or alleged offense. (4) The right to be free of illegal restraint of the person. (5) The right to protection of persons and property without discrimination by reason of race, color, religion, or national origin. (6) The right to vote as protected by Federal law."

    For further details, see U.S. Senate, Committee on the Judiciary, *Civil Rights: Hearings on S. 1725 and S. 1734*, 81st Cong., 1st sess., June 17, 1949, 4–5.

44. U.S. Senate, Committee on the Judiciary, *Civil Rights: Hearings on S. 1725 and S. 1734*, 81st Cong., 1st sess., June 17, 1949, 32.

45. Senator James Eastland, *CR*, April 19, 1948, A2337; see also Representative William Norrell, (D-Arkansas), *CR*, March 2, 1948, A1571; Representative William Winstead (D-Mississippi), *CR*, February 3, 1948, 1008; Representative John Rankin (D-Mississippi), *CR*, April 22, 1948, A4739; Representative Stephen Pace (D-Georgia), *CR*, February 9, 1948, 1233.

46. Oshinsky, *Worse than Slavery*, chapter 4.

47. Myrdal, *An American Dilemma*, lxxxi, 75; Jodi Melamed, "The Spirit of Neoliberalism: From Racial Liberalism to Neoliberal Multiculturalism," *Social Text 24* (Winter 2006), 5–7; The President's Committee on Civil Rights, *To Secure These Rights*, 139.

48. The President's Committee on Civil Rights, *To Secure These Rights*, 141, 146.

49. The President's Committee on Civil Rights, *To Secure These Rights*, 145–146.

50. Myrdal, *An American Dilemma*, 764; The President's Committee on Civil Rights, *To Secure These Rights*, 145–146.

51. Scott, *Contempt & Pity*, 94; Myrdal, *An American Dilemma*, 764.

52. This synopsis of *Native Son* relies on Daryl Michael Scott, *Contempt & Pity: Social Policy and the Image of the Damaged Black Psyche 1880–1996* (Chapel Hill: University of North Carolina Press, 1997), 98–103. Scott persuasively identifies Richard Wright's *Native Son* as foundational to subsequent social scientific scholarship on "black rage." Myrdal, *An American Dilemma*, 763; John Dollard, *Caste and Class in a Southern Town* (New Haven: Yale University Press, 1937), 267–276.

53. John Dollard, *Caste and Class in a Southern Town* (1937), 269, quoted in Gunnar Myrdal, *An American Dilemma: The Negro Problem and Modern Democracy* (1944; repr., New Brunswick: Transaction Publishers, 2000), 1395, italics added; Dollard, *Caste and Class in a Southern Town*, 275, quoted in Scott, *Contempt and Pity*, 50–51; Dollard, *Caste and Class in a Southern Town*, 280, quoted in Myrdal, *An American Dilemma*, 1395.

54. Charles S. Johnson, "Backgrounds of the Negro Migrant Population," in *City of Chicago City Planning in Race Relations: Proceedings of the Mayor's Conference on Race Relations* (Chicago: Mayor's Committee on Race Relations, 1944), 14, Box 48, Nash Papers.

55. Kari Frederickson, " 'The Slowest State' and 'Most Backward Community': Racial Violence in South Carolina and Federal Civil-Rights Legislation, 1946–1948," *South Carolina Historical Magazine* 98 (April 1997), 178.

56. James Scott, *Domination and the Arts of Resistance: Hidden Transcripts* (New Haven: Yale University Press, 1990), 145; Evelyn Nakano Glenn, "From Servitude to Service Work: Historical Continuities in the Racial Division of Paid Reproductive Labor," *Signs* 18 (Autumn 1992), 3; Evelyn Nakano Glenn, *Issei, Nisei, War Bride: Three Generations of Japanese American Women in Domestic Service* (Philadelphia: Temple University Press, 1986); Howard Odum, *Race and Rumors of Race: The American South in the Early Forties* (Chapel Hill: University of North Carolina Press, 1943), 57, 97, 100, 113–131; Charles S. Johnson, "The Present Status of Race Relations in the South," *Social Forces* 23 (October 1944), 27–32.

57. Walter Jackson, *Gunnar Myrdal and America's Conscience* (Chapel Hill: University of North Carolina Press, 1990), 16–20; Stephen Steinberg, *Turning Back: The Retreat from Racial Justice in American Thought and Policy* (Boston: Beacon Press, 1995), 23.

58. Guy Johnson, letter to Robert Carr of the President's Committee on Civil Rights, April 3, 1947, Box 13, PCCR Records; Guy Johnson, remarks before the President's Committee on Civil Rights, May 14, 1947, 2, Box 13, PCCR Records.

59. National Lawyers Guild, National Bar Association, National Association for the Advancement of Colored People, "Moderator's Report on Adequacy of Existing Anti-Lynching Legislation Prepared for Legal Conference on Federal Power to Protect Civil Liberties," January 25, 1947, Records of the DOJ, Civil Rights Division: Subject Files of Assistant Attorney General Wilson White, 1958–1959, Box 74, RG 60, NARA; Turner Smith Memo to Assistant Attorney General Theron Caudle, December 12, 1946, Records of the DOJ, Civil Rights Division: Subject Files of Assistant Attorney General W. Wilson White, 1958–1959, Box 74, RG 60, NARA.

60. The National Negro Congress delegation of Dr. Max Yergan, Charles Collins, and Revels Cayton was received by the secretary of the United Nations Human Rights Commission. The NNC printed nearly 100,000 copies of the petition, but it garnered little attention. With waning organizational strength, the NNC merged with the Civil Rights Congress in 1947. *NYT*, June 7, 1946, 9; *NYT*, June 2, 1946, 33; Martin, "Internationalizing the 'The American Dilemma,'" 38; Thomas Borstelmann, "Jim Crow's Coming Out: Race Relations and American Foreign Policy in the Truman Years," *Presidential Studies Quarterly* 29 (September 1999), 549–569; John Skrentny, "The Effect of the Cold War on African-American Civil Rights: America and the World Audience, 1945–1968," *Theory and Society* 27 (April 1988),

237–285; Parker, *Fighting for Democracy,* 47–50; Dudziak, *Cold War Civil Rights;* Klinkner and Smith, *Unsteady March.*

61. The NAACP had hoped that Eleanor Roosevelt would encourage the UN to hold a hearing on the petition, but she told Du Bois that the petition was "embarrassing" to the State Department and "no good could come from such a discussion." Martin, "Internationalizing 'The American Dilemma,'" 38–39; *NYT,* October 12, 1947, 52; Von Eschen, *Race Against Empire,* 157; Singh, *Black Is a Country;* Anderson, *Eyes Off the Prize.*

62. Ninety-four people signed *We Charge Genocide,* including Mary Church Terrell, W. E. B. Du Bois, Howard Fast, Jessica Mitford, Rosalee McGee, and Paul Robeson. *We Charge Genocide* amassed an international audience, but the CRC suffered charges of communist affiliation. Civil Rights Congress, *We Charge Genocide: The Historic Petition to the United Nations and for Relief from a Crime of the United States Government Against the Negro People,* 2nd. ed. William Patterson (New York: International Publishers, 1970); *NYT,* December 18, 1951, 13; Dray, *At the Hands of Persons Unknown,* 408–412; Dudziak, *Cold War Civil Rights,* 58–66; Thomas Sugrue, *Sweet Land of Liberty: The Forgotten Struggle for Civil Rights in the North* (New York: Random House, 2008), 108–110; Anderson, *Eyes Off the Prize.*

63. For transcript of the radio broadcast, see Radio Diaries, "Willie McGee and the Traveling Electric Chair" (assessed at http://www.radiodiaries.org/audiohistory/storypages/t_mcgee.html); Joseph Crespino, *In Search of Another Country: Mississippi and the Conservative Counterrevolution* (Princeton: Princeton University Press, 2007), 53–54.

64. Jeff Woods, *Black Struggle, Red Scare: Segregation and Anti-Communism in the South, 1948–1968* (Baton Rouge: Louisiana State University, 2004), 32; Crespino, *In Search of Another Country,* 53–54; Civil Rights Congress, *We Charge Genocide,* 8–10.

65. Charles Martin, "Internationalizing 'The American Dilemma': The Civil Rights Congress and the 1951 Genocide Petition to the United Nations," *Journal of American Ethnic History,* 16 (Summer 1997), 40, 43, 52.

66. Martin Luther King Jr., Speech at Holt Street Baptist Church, quoted in Shapiro, *White Violence and Black Response,* 435, 519, italics added.

67. *NYT,* January 25, 1957, 7; *NYT,* November 17, 1957, 60.

68. Robert Caro, *Master of the Senate: The Years of Lyndon Johnson* (New York: Knopf, 2002), 954–957; *CR,* July 13, 1956, 12760–61; Numan Bartley, *The Rise of Massive Resistance: Race and Politics in the South during the 1950s* (Baton Rouge: Louisiana State University Press), 148.

69. *CR,* July 16, 1956, 12946. After emancipation, many whites complained that formerly enslaved African Americans deliberately shoved white people off sidewalks. In the 1920s, southern lawmakers warned that disrespectful street behavior would resume if Congress criminalized lynching, adding that blacks shoved whites off the street as a matter of routine in the North. George Rable, "The South and the Politics of Antilynching Legislation, 1920–1940," *Journal of Southern History 51* (1985), 205.

70. *CR,* July 16, 1956, 12939–12943; see also Representative Basil Whitener (D-North Carolina), *CR,* 1957, 8658; *CR,* July 23, 1956, 14154.

71. *CR,* June 10, 1957, 8658; Mendelberg, *The Race Card,* 75.

72. *NYT,* February 26, 1957, 34; *CR,* September 7, 1959, 18384.

73. As proposals to amend Chapters 30 and 39 of Title 18, some proposals allowed for capital punishment or life imprisonment if the illegal use of explosives resulted in death. See, for example, H.R. 1933, introduced by Representative Frank Osmers (R-New Jersey); H.R. 2526, introduced by Representative Isidore Dollinger (D-New York); and H.R. 500 introduced by Representative John Dingell (D-Michigan). *NYT,* April 22, 1960, 14; Belknap, *Federal Law and Southern Order,* 67–69.

74. *CR,* September 7, 1959, 18382, 18385; *CR,* March 1, 1960, 3982.

75. *U.S. News & World Report,* September 14, 1959; *CR,* March 1, 1960, 3983-3984.

76. Prior to the 1951 Boggs Act, Congress had enacted only one drug-related mandatory minimum: a five-year penalty for opium manufacture. Congress enacted the penalty in its 1914 drug scare centered on Chinese Americans as opium pushers. *CQA,* 1951, 193; John Helmer, *Drugs and Minority Oppression* (New York: Seabury Press, 1975), chapter 18.

77. Testimony recirculated the number of 60,000 U.S. narcotics addicts, compared to an estimate of only 500 addicts in England. Other estimates include Harry Anslinger's 1957 count of 35,000 addicts nationwide, of which 61 percent were "Negro," 5 percent Puerto Rican, and 4 percent Mexican American. There are many estimates of the number of "addicts," and vast discrepancies reflect the difficulty of extrapolating on the total number of addicts from poor (and racially selective) measures, as well as variation in definitions of addiction. Scholars like Hans Mattick conclude that "attempts at extrapolation from arrestees to addicts is sheer metaphysics," and Alfred Lindesmith and William Eldridge also wrote important critiques of addiction counts through the 1950s and 1960s. Statement of Senator Daniel, U.S. Congress, Senate, Committee on the Judiciary, Subcommittee on Improvements in the Federal Criminal Code, *Illicit Narcotics Traffic: Causes and Treatment of Drug Addiction,* 84th Cong., 1st sess., November 23, 1955, 4479, 4492; *CR,* May 25, 1956, 9012–9014; Harry Anslinger, "Narcotic Addiction as Seen by the Law Enforcement Officer," *Federal Probation 21* (June 1957), 36; Hans Mattick, "The Epidemiology of Drug Addiction and Reflections on the Problem and Policy in the United States," *Illinois Medical Journal 130* (October 1966), 439; Alfred Lindesmith, *The Addict and the Law* (Bloomington: Indiana University Press, 1965); William Eldridge, *Narcotics and the Law* (Chicago: American Bar Foundation, 1962).
78. Testimony of Harry Anslinger, Senate Judiciary Internal Security Subcommittee, *CQWR,* March 11, 1955, 261; Lois Higgins, "The Status of Narcotic Addiction in the United States," *American Biology Teacher 16* (April 1954), 94–98; Representative Sidney Yates (D-Illinois), Congress, House, Committee on Ways and Means, *Control of Narcotics, Marihuana, and Barbiturates,* 82nd Cong., 1st sess., April 7, 1951, 46.
79. The Illinois Drug Addict Act of 1953, for example, required all addicts to register and carry a registration card; failure to register would trigger a mandatory minimum penalty of six months imprisonment. A complete copy of the Illinois Drug Addict Act is found in Congress, Senate, Committee on the Judiciary, Subcommittee on Improvements in the Federal Criminal Code, *Illicit Narcotic Traffic: Causes and Treatment of Drug Addiction,* 84th Cong., 1st sess., November 21, 1955, 4454; Task Force on Narcotics and Drug Abuse, 1967, 12.
80. Testimony of Russell McCarty, Detective-Inspector, Commanding Narcotics Bureau, Detroit Police Department, U.S. Senate, Committee on the Judiciary, Subcommittee on Improvements in the Federal Criminal Code, *Illicit Narcotics Traffic: Causes and Treatment of Drug Addiction,* 84th Cong., 1st sess., November 23, 1955, 4489; Testimony of Lieutenant Howard Hutchings, Narcotics Squad, Cleveland Police Department, U.S. Senate, Committee on the Judiciary, Subcommittee on Improvements in the Federal Criminal Code, *Illicit Narcotics Traffic: Causes and Treatment of Drug Addiction,* 84th Cong., 1st sess., November 25, 1955, 4694; Testimony of Lieutenant Joseph J. Healy, Narcotics Bureau, Chicago Police Department, U.S. Senate, Committee on the Judiciary, Subcommittee on Improvements in the Federal Criminal Code, *Illicit Narcotic Traffic: Causes and Treatment of Drug Addiction,* 84th Cong., 1st sess., November 21, 1955, 4239, 4246, 4249; Anslinger, "Narcotic Addiction as Seen by the Law Enforcement Officer," 36.
81. U.S. Senate, Committee on the Judiciary, Subcommittee on Improvements in the Federal Criminal Code, *Illicit Narcotics Traffic: Causes and Treatment of Drug Addiction,* 84th Cong., 1st sess., November 25, 1955, 4699; U.S. Senate, Committee on the Judiciary, Subcommittee on Improvements in the Federal Criminal Code, *Illicit Narcotic Traffic: Causes and Treatment of Drug Addiction,* 84th Cong., 1st sess., November 21, 1955, 4250-4251; U.S. Senate, Committee on the Judiciary, Subcommittee on Improvements in the Federal Criminal Code, *Illicit Narcotics Traffic: Causes and Treatment of Drug Addiction,* 84th Cong., 1st sess., November 23, 1955, 4491.
82. Heather Ann Thompson, "Blinded by a 'Barbaric' South: Prison Horrors, Inmate Abuse, and the Ironic History of American Penal Reform," in *The Myth of Southern Exceptionalism,* ed. Matthew Lassiter and Joseph Crespino (New York: Oxford University Press, 2009), 74–75, italics added.
83. Muhammad, *The Condemnation of Blackness,* 4–5; Matthew Lassiter and Joseph Crespino, "Introduction: The End of Southern History," in *The Myth of Southern Exceptionalism,* ed. Matthew Lassiter and Joseph Crespino (New York: Oxford University Press, 2009), 5.

84. In this sense, my work aligns with scholarship that sees discursive realignments as crucial prerequisites to shifts in governing authority. Victoria Hattam and Joseph Lowndes, for example, have demonstrated that colorblind conservatism was "introduced and consolidated discursively" long before Nixon's election and the Reagan Revolution. Victoria Hattam and Joseph Lowndes, "The Ground Beneath Our Feet: Language, Culture, and Political Change," in *Formative Acts: American Politics in the Remaking,* ed. Stephen Skowronek and Matthew Glassman (Princeton: Princeton University Press, 2007), 199–219; Pamela Brandwein, "Law and American Political Development," *Annual Review of Law and Social Science* 7 (2011), 187–216.

Chapter 3

1. President's Commission on Law Enforcement and Administration of Justice, *The Challenge of Crime in a Free Society* (Washington, DC: GPO, 1967), 294–295.
2. Richard Nixon, "Radio Address About the State of the Union Message on Law Enforcement and Drug Abuse Prevention," March 10, 1973, *Public Papers of the Presidents of the United States: Richard Nixon, Concerning the Public Messages, Speeches, and Statements of the President, 1973* (Washington, DC: GPO, 1975), 74, 180.
3. John Lewis and Michael D'Orso, *Walking with the Wind: A Memoir of the Movement* (New York: Simon & Schuster, 1998), 216–228.
4. Between 1964 and 1968, Congress enacted at least four laws true to the party's association with rehabilitation, prevention, and gun control: (1) Prisoner Rehabilitation Act of 1965, which established "halfway houses"; (2) Narcotic Rehabilitation Act of 1966, which created civil commitment as an alternative to incarceration for drug addicts; (3) Juvenile Delinquency Prevention and Control Act of 1968, which funded after-school programs; and (4) Federal Gun Control Act of 1968, which established gun restrictions. Congress also enacted laws to improve criminal procedure for the poor, including the Criminal Justice Act of 1964, which provided representation for impoverished defendants in federal courts, and the Bail Reform Act of 1966, which established a presumption in favor of release on recognizance. Walker, *Taming the System,* 65.
5. Sidney Milkis and Jerome Mileur, eds., *The Great Society and the High Tide of Liberalism* (Amherst: University of Massachusetts Press, 2005).
6. The Omnibus Crime Control and Safe Streets Act of 1968, Public Law 90-351, contained 11 titles. Title I established the Law Enforcement Assistance Administration (LEAA); Title II specified the procedural rights of criminal defendants; and Title III authorized the use of wiretaps by law enforcement officials acting under court order and under certain circumstances. The remaining titles reveal a mix of agendas. Titles IV and VII imposed restrictions on interstate sale of handguns and illegal possession of firearms, but Title V disqualified any person convicted of "inciting a riot or civil disorder" from eligibility for federal employment for five years. Title VI pertained to the Confirmation of the Director of the FBI; Title VII addressed Unlawful Possession of Firearms; Title VIII, Providing for Appeals from Decisions Sustaining Motions to Suppress Evidence; Title IX, Additional Grounds for Issuing Warrant; and Title X, Prohibiting Extortion and Threats in D.C. Even after the LEAA closed in 1982, federal funding to state and local police continued through multiple other agencies, including the Edward Byrne Memorial State and Local Law Enforcement Assistance Formula Grant Program, created in 1988; the Community-Oriented Policing Services Program, created in 1994 with the Violence Crime Control and Law Enforcement Act; as well as the Local Law Enforcement Block Grants Program, launched in 1996. John Worrall, "The Effects of Local Law Enforcement Block Grants on Serious Crime," *Criminology & Public Policy* 7 (September 2008), 327–328; Robert Diegelman, "Federal Financial Assistance for Crime Control: Lessons of LEAA Experience," *Journal of Criminal Law and Criminology* 73 (1982), 996.
7. Johnson's statement quoted in Jonathan Simon, "Governing Through Crime Metaphors," *Brooklyn Law Review* 67 (2002), 1061; Hearings before the Subcommittee on Domestic and International Planning and Analysis, House Committee on Science and Technology, *The Application of Science and Technology to Crime Control,* 94th Congress, 1st sess., (1975),

94, quoted in Barry Mahoney, *The Politics of the Safe Streets Act, 1965–1973: A Case Study in Evolving Federalism and the National Legislative Process* (Ph.D. dissertation, Columbia University, 1976), 267; James Wilson, *Thinking About Crime* (New York: Basic Books, 1975), 208.

8. Richard Harris, *The Fear of Crime* (Santa Barbara: Praeger, 1969), 14, quoted in Jonathan Simon, *Governing Through Crime Metaphors*, 1050. The baby boomer cohort elevated crime rates through the sheer force of their numbers and the age distinctiveness in offending and victimization; conversely, crime's decline three decades later represents the youngest of the baby boomer cohort aging out of the most "criminally active" years. James Allen Fox, "Demographics and U.S. Homicide," in *The Crime Drop in America*, ed. Alfred Blumstein and J. Wallman (New York: Cambridge University Press, 2000); Alfred Blumstein, "Youth Violence, Guns and the Illicit Drug Industry," *Journal of Criminal Law and Criminology 86* (1995), 10–36; Albert Biderman, "Social Indicators and Goals," in *Social Indicators*, ed. Raymond A. Bauer (Cambridge: MIT Press, 1966), 151; Thomas Cronin, Tania Cronin, and Michael Milakovich, *U.S. v. Crime in the Streets* (Bloomington: Indiana University Press, 1981), 8.

9. Wallace quoted in Liva Baker, *Miranda: Crime, Law, and Politics* (New York: Atheneum, 1983), 243–244; Nixon quoted in Fred Graham, *The Self-Inflicted Wound* (New York: Macmillan, 1970), 15; Loïc Wacquant, "Deadly Symbiosis: When Ghetto and Prison Meet and Mesh," *Punishment & Society 3* (2001), 95–133; CQA, 1967, 796.

10. Christian Parenti, *Lockdown America: Police and Prisons in the Age of Crisis* (London: Verso Press, 1999), 8, Gilmore, *Golden Gulag*; Barry Mahoney, *The Politics of the Safe Streets Act, 1965–1973: A Case Study in Evolving Federalism and the National Legislative Process* (Ph.D. dissertation, Columbia University, 1976); Malcolm Feeley and Austin Sarat, *The Policy Dilemma: Federal Crime Policy and the Law Enforcement Assistance Administration, 1968–1978* (Minneapolis: University of Minnesota Press, 1980); Joseph Goulden, "The Cops Hit the Jackpot," *The Nation*, November 23, 1970, 521.

11. Created by the Civil Rights Act of 1957, the U.S. Commission on Civil Rights was a bipartisan agency directed to study and report civil rights problems to the president and Congress. U.S. Civil Rights Commission, *Justice: 1961 United States Commission on Civil Rights Report 5* (Washington, DC: GPO, 1961), ix–xii, 1.

12. Of the 1,328 total allegations of police brutality, there were 12 victims identified as "Indian," 10 "Mexican," one "Mixed," and one "other." Southern states held no monopoly on allegations of police abuse. Southern police officers received many complaints (831 complaints combined from 11 former-confederacy states), but many issued formal complaints about police in New York (54 complaints), Illinois (46 complaints), Pennsylvania (38 complaints), and Michigan (28 complaints). U.S. Civil Rights Commission, *Justice*, 6–8, 12, 26–27, 263–264.

13. The chapter on police brutality concluded with a Detroit county prosecutor confessing his "sadness" that "colored people" are "most apt to know" the perpetrators of "heinous crimes," but they refuse to come forward. "As much as *the good colored people as well as the white people* want criminals apprehended and brought to justice, that if a person knows or has reason to believe it would help us to locate these culprits the chances are, 99 chances out of 100, if he complains he will be treated more as a suspect than as a citizen attempting to reduce crime in the city of Detroit." U.S. Civil Rights Commission, *Justice*, 27–28.

14. Specifically, the 1961 U.S. Civil Rights Commission suggested that grants-in-aid might apply to five areas of police development and maintenance: "(1) recruit selection tests and standards; (2) training programs in scientific crime detection; (3) training programs in constitutional rights and human relations; (4) college-level schools of police administration; and (5) scholarship programs that assist policemen to receive training in schools of police administration." U.S. Civil Rights Commission, *Justice*, 112.

15. Feeley and Sarat, *The Policy Dilemma*, 40; John Moore, "Controlling Delinquency: Executive, Congressional, and Juvenile, 1961–1964," in *Congress and Urban Problems*, ed. Frederick Cleveland (Washington, DC: The Brookings Institute, 1969), 171–172; Gordon Raley, "The JJDP Act: A Second Look," *Juvenile Justice 2* (Fall/Winter 1995), 11–18.

16. Statement of Wilbur Cohen, Assistant Secretary of Health, Education, and Welfare, House Committee on Education and Labor, *Hearings on H.R. 7177, H.R. 7857: Bills to Extend the Juvenile Delinquency and Youth Offenses Control Act of 1961,* 89th Cong., 1st sess. (April 28, 1965), 4, 7.

17. Preamble to the legislation introduced by President Kennedy's Committee on Juvenile Delinquency and Youth Crime in 1961, quoted in LaFree et al., "Race and Crime in Postwar America," 160.

18. Goldwater's message was no subtle subtext. A front page *New York Times* story heralded the title, "Goldwater Links the Welfare State to Rise in Crime." Barry Goldwater, Acceptance Speech for the Republican Presidential Nomination, July 16, 1964; *NYT,* September 11, 1964, 1; *Newsweek,* September 14, 1964, 24; *U.S. News and World Report,* September 14, 1964, 36–41.

19. Lyndon B. Johnson, "Remarks in Dayton, Ohio," October 16, 1964, in *Public Papers of the Presidents of the United States: Lyndon B. Johnson, 1963–64,* vol. II (Washington, DC: GPO, 1965), 1371.

20. Sidney Milkis, "Lyndon Johnson, the Great Society, and the Modern Presidency," in *The Great Society and the High Tide of Liberalism,* ed. Sidney Milkis and Jerome Mileur (Amherst: University of Massachusetts Press, 2005), 1–49.

21. Lyndon B. Johnson, "Commencement Address at Howard University: 'To Fulfill These Rights,'" June 4, 1965, *Public Papers of the Presidents of the United States: Lyndon B. Johnson, 1965,* vol. 2 (Washington, DC: GPO, 1966), 635–640.

22. Daniel Patrick Moynihan, *The Negro Family: The Case for National Action* (Washington, DC: Office of Policy Planning and Research, U.S. Department of Labor, 1965); Ibrahim, *Troubling the Family,* 48–52; Beckett, *Making Crime Pay,* 33–34.

23. Gerald Horne, *Fire This Time: The Watts Uprising and the 1960s* (Charlottesville: University of Virginia Press, 1995); Leigh Raiford, *Imprisoned in a Luminous Glare: Photography and the African American Freedom Struggle* (Chapel Hill: University of North Carolina Press, 2001), 119.

24. Harry McPherson claimed credit for writing the part of the speech denouncing all violence equally. Johnson combined his strong opposition to violence with pro–civil rights assurances, according to McPherson, and Johnson worried even before Watts of "extreme measures" and "violent measures" used to "secure better living conditions for Negroes." Transcript, Harry McPherson Oral History Interview V, Tape 1, April 9, 1969, by T. H. Baker, Internet Copy, 2-3, LBJL.

25. J. Edgar Hoover, Remarks before the Supreme Council, 33° of the Ancient and Accepted Scottish Right of Freemasonry, Southern Jurisdiction, Washington, DC, October 19, 1965, reprinted in *CR,* October 20, 1965, 27622–27623. Billy Graham quoted in Steven Miller, *Billy Graham and the Rise of the Republican South* (Philadelphia: University of Pennsylvania Press, 2009), 89, 113–114. I am grateful to Steven Teles for this reference.

26. Bureau of the Budget, Memo for the President on H.R. 8027, dated September 9, 1965, Folder: P.L. 89–197, H.R. 8027, Box 26, Reports on Enrolled Legislation P.L. 89–192 to P.L. 89–222, LBJL; Senate Judiciary Committee, Report on the Law Enforcement Assistance Act of 1965, H.R. 8027, 89th Cong., 1st Sess., August 31, 1965. Office of the White House Press Secretary, Statement by the President on Signing of H.R. 8027 and SJ Res 102 for Law Enforcement Assistance, September 22, 1965, Folder: P.L. 89–197, H.R. 8027, Box 26, Reports on Enrolled Legislation P.L. 89–192 to P.L. 89–222, LBJL.

27. Senator Hart enumerated the multiple goals of police professionalization: the "primary goal" was improved police performance, but the "additional merit" was federal assistance for "an improved *community relationship* and understanding for the role of the policeman, and a clear appreciation and understanding by the policeman of the many various groups in his community." *CR,* September 8, 1965, 23105, 23113, italics added.

28. *CR,* September 8, 1965, 23114; *CR,* August 25, 1965, 21823; *CR,* September 8, 1965, 23114.

29. *CR,* September 8, 1965, 23111–23112, italics added.

30. *CR,* September 2, 1965, 22736. "'Police Brutality'—Fact or Fiction?," *U.S. News & World Report,* September 6, 1965, entered by Senator Strom Thurmond into the *CR,* September 2, 1965, 22736–22738.

31. Nicholas deB. Katzenbach, "Report to the President and the Congress on Activities Under the Law Enforcement Assistance Act of 1965," April 1, 1966, Folder: Law Enforcement Assistance Act—2, Box 102, Clark Papers.

32. The President's Commission on Law Enforcement and Administration of Justice, "Work Plan: Police-Community Relations," January 14, 1966, Folder: Law Enforcement Assistance Act—1, Box 102, Clark Papers.

33. President's Commission on Law Enforcement and Administration of Justice, *The Challenge of Crime in a Free Society*, viii, x, 15, 293–301.

34. "People in the suburbs just won't pay taxes for central city law enforcement any more than they'll pay for central city education," said Katzenbach. Transcript, Nicholas deB. Katzenbach Oral History Interview I, November 12, 1968, by Paige E. Mulhollan, 34, Internet Copy, LBJL; President's Commission on Law Enforcement and Administration of Justice, *The Challenge of Crime in a Free Society*, viii, x, 15, 293–301.

35. Walker, "Origins of the Contemporary Criminal Justice Paradigm," 47–76, 50; President's Commission on Law Enforcement and Administration of Justice, *The Challenge of Crime in a Free Society*, 10–11.

36. The flowchart separated out felonies, misdemeanors, petty offenses, and juvenile cases, since they follow different paths. President's Commission on Law Enforcement and Administration of Justice, *The Challenge of Crime in a Free Society*, 7–12, 104–106.

37. Transcript, Nicholas deB. Katzenbach Oral History Interview I, November 12, 1968, by Paige E. Mulhollan, Internet Copy, 37, LBJL; Transcript, Harry McPherson Oral History Interview V, Tape 2, April 9, 1969, by T. H. Baker, Internet Copy, 9, LBJL.

38. Liberal reformers have wanted to hire more black or minority police since at least the racial violence of 1943 (outlined in Chapter 3) "gave birth to the modern police-community relations movement" in the words of Samuel Walker. Organizations like the American Council on Race Relations advised police on racial "sensitivity," and California Peace Officers recommended that departments "enroll Negro, Mexican and Filipino men as local police officers or auxiliary deputies" to earn "good will." Given that a 1930 study found not a single black police officer in any city in Mississippi, South Carolina, Louisiana, or Alabama, it is unsurprising that minority recruitment remained controversial. Police departments of the urban North and West hired black officers in proportions less than one-third their city population, sometimes even lower. In 1952–53, African Americans were underrepresented in Detroit (2.4 percent of officers are black, but 16.2 percent of city residents are black); Chicago (3.9 percent of officers, but 13.6 percent of city); New York (3.1 percent of officers, but 9.5 percent of city); Newark (2.0 percent of officers police, but 17.1 percent of city); Washington, D.C. (10.8 percent of officers, but 35.0 percent of city); Philadelphia (3.6 percent of officers, but 18.2 percent of city); St. Louis (5.0 percent of officers, but 17.9 percent of city); and Los Angeles (2.9 percent of officers, but 8.7 percent of city). Elliott Rudwick, "The Negro Policeman Outside of the South" adopted from William M. Kephart, *Racial Factors and Urban Law Enforcement* (Philadelphia: University of Pennsylvania Press, 1957), 135, RG 453: Records of the U.S. Commission on Civil Rights, Federal Programs Division, Records Relating to Equal Protection and the Administration of Justice, 1961–1965, Box 9; President's Commission on Law Enforcement and Administration of Justice, *Task Force Report: The Police*, 167.

39. For Nixon, talk of race was racist talk. He acknowledged the existence of "prejudice," but added that "this talk" tends to "divide people. U.S. Riot Commission, *Report of the National Advisory Commission on Civil Disorders* (New York: Bantam Books, 1968); *NYT*, March 6, 1968, 1; *CQA*, 1967, 796.

40. Of the 1967 bills, some proposed investigating riot triggers (33), but most were punitive rather than investigatory. Of these71 prohibited interstate travel to incite a riot; another 23 increased penalties for interfering with, assaulting, or killing a firefighter or member of the armed services during a riot. Ten cut off federal benefits for riot participants, and another five proposed funding local police specifically for riot control. Author's count of bills, resolutions, and amendments tagged as riot-related under the subject headings "crime" and "crime and criminals" in the end-of-session *Congressional Record Index*. Any bill listed under more than one heading is counted once. The 89th Congress (1965–67) introduced 19,874 bills,

and the 90th Congress (1967–68) introduced 22,060 bills. Norm Ornstein, Thomas Mann, and Michael Malbin, *Vital Statistics on Congress* (Washington, DC: American Enterprise Institute Press, 1999), table 6-1.

41. The list of categorical grants comes from a statement by Attorney General Ramsey Clark; see Clark's statement before the Senate Subcommittee on Criminal Laws and Procedures on the Safe Streets Act, S. 917, March 7, 1967, Box 108, Clark Papers; House Committee on the Judiciary, *Hearings on H.R. 5037,* 90th Cong., 1st sess., 30; Howard Peskoe, "The 1968 Safe Streets Act: Congressional Response to the Growing Crime Problem," *Columbia Human Rights Law Review* 5 (1973), 69–116.

42. Lyndon B. Johnson's Message on Crime, February 7, 1968, reprinted in *CQA,* 1968, 43-A, 44-A; *CQA,* 1967, 848–854; *NYT,* August 9, 1967, 1; Representative William Ryan (D-New York), *CR,* 1967, 21102; Cronin, Cronin, and Milakovich, *U.S. v. Crime in the Streets,* 45–50.

43. Harry McPherson, *A Political Education: A Washington Memoir* (Austin: University of Texas Press, 1995), 280; Cronin, Cronin, and Milakovich, *U.S. v. Crime in the Streets,* 50–53; "Major Differences Between Subcommittee Bill and New Draft of Safe Streets and Crime Control Act, S. 917," n.d., Folder: Legislation 1968—Safe Streets, Box 107, Clark Papers.

44. Sec. 307 (a) of the Safe Streets Act specified that the Administration and State Planning Agency shall give special emphasis to programs and projects "dealing with the prevention, detention, and control of organized crime and of riots and other violent civil disorders." Folder: Legislation 1968— Safe Streets, Box 107, Clark Papers; Representative Roy Taylor, (D-North Carolina), *CR,* July 19, 1967, 19352.

45. *CQA,* 1967, 19961; *CQA,* 1968, 226–229; *CD,* June 29, 1968, 10; *CD,* June 18, 1968, 13; Flamm, *Law and Order,* 132–141.

46. Transcript, Ramsey Clark Oral History Interview V, June 3, 1969, by Harri Baker, Internet Copy, 6, LBJL.

47. Feeley and Sarat, *The Policy Dilemma,* 135–146.

48. National Commission on the Causes and Prevention of Violence, *Law-and-Order Reconsidered: Report to the Task Force on Law and Law Enforcement to the National Commission on the Causes and Prevention of Violence* (Washington, DC: GPO, 1969), 273–274.

49. Roughly 78 to 96 percent of suspects waive their *Miranda* rights. Richard Leo, "*Miranda* and the Problem of False Confessions," in *The Miranda Debate: Law, Justice, and Policing,* ed. Richard Leo and George Thomas III (Boston: Northeastern University Press, 1998), 275; George Thomas III, "Then End of the Road for *Miranda v. Arizona?* On the History and Future of Rules for Police Interrogation," *American Criminal Law Review* 37 (2000), 1–39; Richard Leo, "Questioning the Relevance of *Miranda* in the Twenty-First Century," *Michigan Law Review* 99 (March 2001), 1015; Stuntz, "The Uneasy Relationship Between Criminal Procedure and Criminal Law," 3–4, 49–52; Louis Michael Seidman, "*Brown* and *Miranda,*" *California Law Review* 80 (May 1992), 673–753; Blume, Johnson, and Feldmann, "Education and Interrogation," 321–345; Michael Brown, *Working the Street: Police Discretion and the Dilemmas of Reform* (New York: Russell Sage, 1981), chapter 10.

50. David Harris, *Profiles in Injustice: Why Racial Profiling Cannot Work* (New York: New Press, 2002), 100–103. Cities like Atlanta, for example, grappled with the alleged dearth of qualified applicants by giving young "ghetto" men intermediary jobs as "Community Service Officers," for which they don the uniform, walk the neighborhood, but do not carry firearms. National Commission on the Causes and Prevention of Violence, *Law and Order Reconsidered,* 304–305.

51. Ronald Reagan, "Remarks Announcing Federal Initiatives Against Drug Trafficking and Organized Crime," October 14, 1982, in *Public Papers of the Presidents of the United States Ronald Reagan, July 3 to December 31, 1982,* vol. 2 (Washington, DC: GPO, 1982), 1314; *NYT,* October 15, 1982, A20; Kate Stith and José Cabranes, *Fear of Judging: Sentencing Guidelines in the Federal Courts* (Chicago: University of Chicago Press, 1998), 44. For excellent accounts of judicial retrenchment, see David Zlotnick, "The War Within the War on Crime: The Congressional Assault on Judicial Sentencing," *Southern Methodist University Law Review* 57 (2004), 211–267; Sarah Staszak, "Institutions, Rulemaking, and the Politics of Judicial Retrenchment, *Studies in American Political Development* 24 (October 2010), 168–189.

52. Sentencing Reform Act of 1984 was Title II of the Comprehensive Crime Control Act of 1984, which was attached to the fiscal 1985 continuing appropriations act, Public Law 98–473 (1984). *The Sentencing Reform Act*, Public Law 98–473, *U.S. Statutes at Large* 98 (1984): 1987–2040; USSC, *Supplementary Report on the Initial Sentencing Guidelines and Policy Statements* (Washington, DC: USSC, 1987); Stephen Breyer, "The Federal Sentencing Guidelines and the Key Compromises Upon Which They Rest," *Hofstra Law Review* 17 (Fall 1988), 1–50; Charles Ogletree, "The Death of Discretion? Reflections on the Federal Sentencing Guidelines," *Harvard Law Review* 101 (1988), 1938–1960.

53. USSC, *Fifteen Years of Guidelines Sentencing* (Washington, DC: USSC, 2004), v–vi; Marc Miller and Ronald Wright, "Your Cheatin' Heart(land): The Long Search for Administrative Sentencing Justice," *Buffalo Criminal Law Review* 2 (1999), 726; Michael Tonry, *Sentencing Matters* (New York: Oxford University Press, 1996), 72; Pamala Griset, *Determinate Sentencing: The Promise and the Reality of Retributive Justice* (Albany: State University of New York, 1991), 35.

54. There is rich scholarship on the Sentencing Reform Act of 1984, and I draw particularly from Kate Stith and Steve Koh, "The Politics of Sentencing Reform: The Legislative History of the Federal Sentencing Guidelines," *Wake Forest Law Review* 28 (1993), 223–290; Tonry, *Sentencing Matters*; Stith and Cabranes, *Fear of Judging*; Ronald Gainer, "Federal Criminal Code Reform: Past and Future," *Buffalo Criminal Law Review* 2 (April 1998), 45–159; Frank Bowman III, "The Failure of the Federal Sentencing Guidelines," *Columbia Law Review* 105 (2005), 1315–1350; Daniel Freed, "Federal Sentencing in the Wake of Guidelines: Unacceptable Limits on the Discretion of Sentencers," *Yale Law Journal* 101 (1992), 1681.

55. Public Law 89–801; *CR*, March 9, 1966, 5368–5370.

56. President's Commission on Law Enforcement and Administration of Justice, *The Challenge of Crime in a Free Society*, 142.

57. President's Commission on Law Enforcement and Administration of Justice, *The Challenge of Crime in a Free Society*, 7.

58. National Commission on Reform of Federal Criminal Laws, *Working Papers* (Washington, DC: GPO, 1970), 118–120; American Enterprise Institute, *Reform of Federal Criminal Laws* (Washington, DC: American Enterprise Institute for Public Policy Research, 1978), 14.

59. Schickler, *Disjointed Pluralism*, 15–16; Kathleen Thelen, *How Institutions Evolve: The Political Economy of Skills in Germany, Britain, the United States, and Japan* (Cambridge: Cambridge University Press, 2004); Jacob Hacker, "Privatizing Risk Without Privatizing the Welfare State: The Hidden Politics of Social Policy Retrenchment in the United States," *American Political Science Review* 98 (May 2004), 248.

60. Gottschalk, *Prison and the Gallows*, 42–43; Kathleen Frydl, "Kidnapping and State Development in the United States," *Studies in American Political Development* 20 (April 2006), 18–44; Gainer, "Federal Criminal Code Reform," 57.

61. While the Model Penal Code addressed disparity through legislative controls, it should be noted that there were other mechanisms for reform on the table, including education and training on sentencing norms, administrative review, and civilian oversight. Herbert Wechsler, "A Thoughtful Code of Substantive Law," *Journal of Criminal Law, Criminology & Police Science* 45 (1955), 524–526; Robert Dawson, *Sentencing: The Decision as to Type, Length, and Conditions of Sentence* (Boston: Little Brown, 1969), 380–405.

62. Senate Committee on the Judiciary, *Criminal Justice Codification, Revision, and Reform Act of 1974*, 93rd Cong., 2nd sess., 1974, Report No. 93-0000, 9.

63. Herbert Wechsler, "Sentencing, Correction, and the Model Penal Code," *University of Pennsylvania Law Review* 109 (161), 476–477; President's Commission on Law Enforcement and Administration of Justice, *The Challenge of Crime in a Free Society*, 142. The Commission praised the Model Penal Code, calling it an "imaginative and constructive approach to simplifying and standardizing" sentencing.

64. Model Penal Code § 7.01 (Proposed Official Draft, 1962): "The Court shall deal with a person who has been convicted of a crime without imposing sentence of imprisonment unless, having regard to the nature and circumstances of the crime and the history, character and condition of the defendant, it is of the opinion that his imprisonment is necessary

for the protection of the public because: (a) there is undue risk that during the period of a suspended sentence or probation the defendant will commit another crime; or (b) the defendant is in need of correctional treatment that can be provided most effectively by his commitment to an institution; or (c) a lesser sentence will depreciate the seriousness of the defendant's crime."

65. Senate Judiciary Committee, *Criminal Justice Codification, Revision, and Reform Act of 1974*, 93rd Cong., 2nd sess., 1974, Report No. 93-0000, 9. Johnson's Sentencing Commission followed the Model Penal Code, see, for example, David Robinson Jr., "The Decline and Potential Collapse of Federal Guideline Sentencing," *Washington University Law Quarterly* 74 (1996), 891; Gainer, "Federal Criminal Code Reform," 96–97.

66. The Katzenbach Commission wrote of the Model Penal Code in laudatory terms, calling it an "imaginative and constructive approach to simplifying and standardizing" sentencing. President's Commission on Law Enforcement and Administration of Justice, *The Challenge of Crime in a Free Society*, 142; Herbert L. Packer, "The Model Penal Code and Beyond," *Columbia Law Review 63* (1963), 594; Gainer, "Federal Criminal Code Reform," 92.

67. American Bar Association, *Project on Minimum Standards for Criminal Sentences, Sentencing Alternatives and Procedures* (New York: American Bar Association, 1968).

68. Statement of Milton Rector, President of the National Council on Crime and Delinquency, House Subcommittee on Criminal Justice, House Judiciary Committee, Hearings on Legislation to Revise and Recodify Federal Criminal Laws, H.R. 6869, 95th Cong., 2nd Sess., 1978, 1752.

69. Franklin Zimring, "Sentencing Reform in the States: Some Sobering Lessons from the 1970s," *Northern Illinois University Law Review 2* (1981), 2–4.

70. Regina Kunzel, *Criminal Intimacy: Prison and the Uneven History of Modern American Sexuality* (Chicago: University of Chicago Press, 2010), 160.

71. Testimony of James V. Bennett, Director of the Federal Bureau of Prisons, Senate Judiciary Committee, Of Prisons and Justice, 88th Cong., 2nd Sess., 1964, as quoted in Dawson, *Sentencing*, 216.

72. Kunzel, *Criminal Intimacy*, 159–169; Joy James, "Introduction" in *Imprisoned Intellectuals: America's Political Prisoners Write on Life, Liberation, and Rebellion*, ed. Joy James (Lanham, MD: Rowman and Littlefield, 2003), 26

73. The Attica Liberation Faction, Manifesto of Demands and Anti-Depression Platform, 1971, reprinted in *Race & Class* 53 (2001), 28–35.

74. Liz Samuels, "Improvising on Reality: The Roots of Prison Abolition," in *The Hidden 1970s: Histories of Racialism*, ed. Dan Berger (New Brunswick: Rutgers University Press, 2010); Heather Schoenfeld, "Mass Incarceration and the Paradox of Prison Conditions Litigation," *Law & Society Review 44* (September/December 2010), 757; Gottschalk, *Prison and the Gallows*, 10; Statement William Greenhalgh, Chair of Committee on Criminal Code Revision, Criminal Justice Section of ABA, House Subcommittee on Criminal Justice, House Judiciary Committee, Hearings on Legislation to Revise and Recodify Federal Criminal Laws, H.R. 6869, 95th Cong., 2nd Sess., 1978, 1777–1778; Statement of Milton Rector, President of the National Council on Crime and Delinquency, House Subcommittee on Criminal Justice, House Judiciary Committee, Hearings on Legislation to Revise and Recodify Federal Criminal Laws, H.R. 6869, 95th Cong., 2nd Sess., 1978, 1736–1738.

75. New York State Special Commission on Attica, *Attica: The Official Report of the New York State Special Commission on Attica* (New York: Bantam Books, 1972), xviiii, xix.

76. Robert McKay, "It's Time to Rehabilitate the Sentencing Process," entered into the *Congressional Record* by Senator Charles Percy, a moderate Rockefeller Republican from Illinois. *CR*, March 10, 1977, 7211; Robert McKay, "It's Time to Rehabilitate the Sentencing Process," *Judicature 60* (December 1976), 223–228.

77. Stith and Koh present the SRA's legislative history through these five Senate bills, plus Senator Kennedy's S. 2966 (introduced 1975); USSC, *Fifteen Years of Guidelines Sentencing*, 4–5. Democratic bills to "rationalize" the criminal code began as proposals for recodification, not sentencing guidelines. In the 92nd and 93rd Congresses, Senator Kennedy proposed code recodification, but the bills, dubbed S. 1 in both Congresses, collapsed under the controversy of Republican-sponsored punitive amendments to curtail the insanity defense and

expand capital punishment. Kennedy ultimately rejected S. 1 as an "unwise and unnecessary encroachment upon civil liberties and lawful political dissent." Senators Kennedy and McClellan introduced S. 1437 as a mix of Senator McClellan's failed S. 1 for criminal code recodification and Senator Kennedy's sentencing commission. Senator Kennedy told Senator McClellan that liberals would embrace a version of S.1, so long as it had sentencing reform without repressive additions, and McClellan, nearing the end of his service and a long-time supporter of S.1, agreed to co-sponsor the bill. Senate Committee on the Judiciary, Criminal Justice Codification, Revision, and Reform Act of 1974, 93rd Cong., 2nd sess., 1974, Report No. 93-0000, 900–901; *NYT*, August 2, 1979, A1, D18; Edward Kennedy, "Reforming the Federal Criminal Code: A Congressional Response," *North Carolina Central Law Journal* 8 (1976), 8–9; *NYT*, March 14, 1977, A30; *NYT*, May 2, 1977, 69; *NYT*, November 14, 1977, A33.

78. Gilda Daniels, "Senator Edward Kennedy: A Lion on Voting Rights," *Legislation and Public Policy 14* (2011), 415–444; E. J. Dionne Jr., *WP*, January 14, 2005, A19.

79. Of course, there are other important sections, like those directing the Sentencing Commission to minimize a person's background characteristics and to maximize the number of severity levels. Stith and Koh, "The Politics of Sentencing Reform," 223; USSC, *Fifteen Years of Sentencing Guidelines: An Assessment of How Well the Federal Criminal Justice System if Achieving The Goals of Sentencing Reform* (Washington, DC: USSC, 2004), iv, D-5.

80. That the national averages ballooned makes this a small victory, smaller still as Minnesota and Washington legislators stiffened penalties and increased the actual capacity of which commissions should be conscious. Thomas Marvell, "Sentencing Guidelines and Prison Population Growth," *Journal of Criminal Law and Criminology 85* (1995), 704; Tonry, *Sentencing Matters,* 58–59.

81. S. 1722, 96th Cong., 1st sess. (September 7, 1979).

82. *NYT*, November 19, 1981, A22.

83. S. 1437 §§ 3831–3835 as introduced allowed early release through parole, but the amended bill did not. For full documentation, see Senate Judiciary Committee, Reform on the Federal Criminal Laws, 10009, 10013.

84. S. 1722, § 2303; S. 1630 § 2303. Both bills authorized tiered supervised release, graded as follows: not more than three years for Class A or B felonies; not more than two years for Class C or D felonies; and, not more than one year for Class E felonies, or for two or more misdemeanors. Stith and Koh, "The Politics of Sentencing Reform," 234–236.

85. In an incendiary comparison, the representative of National Legal Aid testified: "I would like to suggest that the terms of imprisonment that were established here by the Senate [S. 1722 and S. 1723] make me embarrassed when we compare those sentences to other civilized nations in the world. The Soviet Union has a general 'top' of 10 years, some rare offenses, 15 years, and death in only a few enumerated cases. One of the problems with our bill is that we start with life imprisonment, then 20 years, and then working down. We are the 'Greatest' when it comes to imprisonment of any nation in the world." Statement of John Cleary, Legal Aid and Defenders Association, Senate Judiciary Committee, Reform of the Federal Criminal Laws: Hearings on S. 1722 and S. 1723, 96th Cong., 1st Sess., 10100.

86. U.S. Senate Judiciary Committee, Criminal Code Reform Act of 1981 to Accompany S. 1630, S. Report No. 307, 97th Cong., 1st sess., December 22, 1981, 972; Senate Judiciary Committee, Comprehensive Crime Control Act of 1983: Report of the Committee on the Judiciary United States Senate on S. 1762, 98th Cong., 1st Sess., Senate Rep. No. 98-225 (Washington, DC: GPO, 1983), 53.

87. See PL 98–473, codified at 18 U.S.C. § 3624(b).

88. Between 2009 and 2011, roughly 87 percent of federal prisoners received all of the "good conduct time" credit. U.S. Government Accountability Office, *Report of Congressional Requesters: Bureau of Prisons: Eligibility and Capacity Impact Use of Flexibilities to Reduce Inmates' Time in Prison* (Washington, DC: GPO, 2012), 21.

89. S. 1437 § 3834(b); S. 1722 § 3824(b); S. 1630 §3824(b); S. 2572 § 3624; S. 1762 § 3624. See U.S. Senate Judiciary Committee, Reform on the Federal Criminal Laws, 10012. *CR,* September 7, 1979, 23539; *CR*, May 16, 1982, 12008; *CR*, February 25, 1980, 3676.

90. S. 1437 § 124 (1977), italics added.

91. S. 1722 § 994(g) (1979) directs the Commission to "assure that the available capacity of the facilities and services is not exceeded." S. 1630 § 994(g) (1981) directs the Commission to "tak[e] into account the nature and capacity of the penal, correctional, and other facilities and services available in order not only to assure that the most appropriate facilities and services are utilized to fulfill the applicable purposes but also to assure that the available capacities of such facilities and services will not be exceeded." U.S. Senate Judiciary Committee, Criminal Code Reform Act of 1979, Report No. 553, 96th Cong., 2nd sess. (January 17, 1980), 1244, italics added.

92. S. 2572 § 994(g) (1982) states that the Commission "shall take into account the nature and capacity of the penal, correctional, and other facilities and services available, and shall make appropriate recommendations to the Congress concerning such facilities." Italics added.

93. S. 1762 § 994(g)(1983), italics added.

94. Stith and Koh, "The Politics of Sentencing Reform," 267–268. As SRA was codified at 28 U.S.C. § 994(g): The Commission "shall take into account the nature and capacity of the penal, correctional, and other facilities and services available, and shall make recommendations concerning any change or expansion in the nature or capacity of such facilities and services that might become necessary as a result of the guidelines promulgated pursuant to the provisions of this chapter. The sentencing guidelines prescribed under this chapter shall be formulated to minimize the likelihood that the Federal prison population will exceed the capacity of the Federal prisons, as determined by the Commission."

95. S. 1437 § 241; S. 1722 § 994(a).

96. S. 2572 § 994(i); S. 1762 § 994(j).

97. 28 U.S.C. § 994(j) directs the USSC to "insure that the guidelines reflect the general appropriateness" of alternative to incarceration for first-time, nonviolent offenders. Prepared Testimony of Judge Patti. B. Saris, Chair, USSC, Before the Subcommittee on Crime, Terrorism, and Homeland Security, House Committee on the Judiciary, USSC, Washington, DC (October 12, 2011), 59, http://www.ussc.gov/Legislative_and_Public_Affairs/Congressional_Testimony_and_Reports/Testimony/20111012_Saris_Testimony.pdf; S. 1762, 98th Cong. (1983). USSC, *Fifteen Years of Guidelines Sentencing: An Assessment of How Well the Federal Criminal Justice System Is Achieving the Goals of Sentencing Reform* (Washington, DC: USSC, 2004); Stith and Cabranes, *Fear of Judging*, 38.

98. George Lovell, *Legislative Deferrals: Statutory Ambiguity, Judicial Power, and American Democracy* (Cambridge: Cambridge University Press, 2003), 10–14; Michael Tonry, "The Success of Judge Frankel's Sentencing Commission," *University of Colorado Law Review* 64 (1993), 712–714; Marc Miller and Ronald Wright, "Your Cheatin' Heart(land): The Long Search for Administrative Sentencing Justice," *Buffalo Criminal Law Review* 2 (1999), 723–813.

99. Michael Tonry persuasively demonstrates that the USSC surpassed the statutory requirements of the Sentencing Reform Act. My interpretation of the SRA differs from Tonry's only with regard to the clause of incarcerating nonviolent first-time offenders (994(j)). Tonry interprets the clause as "a statutory presumption that non-violent first offenders should receive nonincarcerative sentences." Based on the clause's history, however, I believe that lawmakers considered but ultimately rejected this presumption. Early versions of the clause gave presumption of non-incarcerative sentences, but the enacted legislation only requires the Commission to "reflect" on "the general appropriateness" of incarcerating nonviolent first-time offenders. See Tonry, *Sentencing Matters*, 91–92; Stith and Cabranes, *Fear of Judging*, 70; Bernard Harcourt, "From the Ne'er-Do-Well to the Criminal History Category: The Refinement of the Actuarial Model in Criminal Law," *Law and Contemporary Problems* 66 (2003), 101.

100. Michael Tonry, "Foreword" in *Discretion in Criminal Justice: The Tension Between Individualization and Uniformity*, ed. Lloyd Ohlin and Frank Remington (Albany: State University of New York Press, 1993), xvi; Dawson, *Sentencing*, 217.

101. Douglas Hibbs, Jr., "President Reagan's Mandate from the 1980 Elections: A Shift to the Right?" *American Politics Quarterly* 10 (October 1982), 387; Morris Fiorina, "The Reagan Years: Turning to the Right or Groping Toward the Middle?" in *The Resurgence of*

Conservatism in Anglo-American Democracies, ed. Barry Cooper, Allan Kornberg, and William Mishler (Durham: Duke University Press, 1988), 438–439.

102. Richard Nixon, Nomination Acceptance Address, August 8, 1968.

103. Richard Nixon, "Radio Address About the State of the Union Message on Law Enforcement and Drug Abuse Prevention," *Public Papers of the Presidents* 74 (March 10, 1973), 180.

104. *CR*, January 31, 1984, 975; Stith and Cabranes, *Fear of Judging*, 44.

105. *CR*, February 2, 1984, 1644.

106. *CR*, February 2, 1984, 1644; Anthony Partridge and William Eldridge, *The Second Circuit Sentencing Study: A Report to the Judges of the Second Circuit* (Washington, DC: Federal Judicial Center, 1974), 1–3, 9, A-10, A-18. Sentencing maximums of the 1974 U.S. Code acknowledged difference between selling and possessing. For sale of heroin, the U.S. Code allowed the judge to sentence imprisonment of up to fifteen years and/or $25,000 fine. For heroin possession, the U.S. Code allowed the judge to sentence imprisonment of up to two years and/or $25,000 fine (as specified in 21 U.S.C. §841(a) §844).

107. Alfred Blumstein, Jacqueline Cohen, Susan Martin, and Michael Tonry, *Research on Sentencing: The Search for Reform*, vol. 1 (Washington, DC: National Academy Press, 1983), 72; Cassia Spohn, "Thirty Years of Sentencing Reform: The Quest for a Racially Neutral Sentencing Process," in *Policies, Processes, and Decisions of the Criminal Justice System*, vol. 3 (Washington, DC: NIJ, 2000), 432–433; *CR*, May 2, 1977, 13067.

108. Marvin Frankel, *Criminal Sentencing: Law Without Order* (New York: Hill and Wang, 1973), 5, 11, 23; Stith and Cabranes, *Fear of Judging*, 35–36; Tonry, *Sentencing Matters*, 9–10, 12–13, 24–26. For a trenchant evaluation of Frankel, see Lynn Adelman and Jon Deitrich, "Marvin Frankel's Mistakes and the Need to Rethink Federal Sentencing," *Berkeley Journal of Criminal Law 13* (2008), 239–260.

109. Frankel, *Criminal Sentencing*, 122–123; Stith and Cabranes, *Fear of Judging*, 35–36; Tonry, *Sentencing Matters*, 9–10, 12–13, 24–26.

110. Marvin Frankel and Leonard Orland, "A Conversation About Sentencing Commissions and Guidelines," *University of Colorado Law Review 64* (1993), 655–662; *NYT*, December 6, 1975, 29; *NYT*, November 14, 1977, 33.

111. Gainer, "Federal Criminal Code Reform," 62; Subcommittee on Criminal Justice of the House Judiciary Committee, *Impact of S. 1437 Upon Present Federal Criminal Laws*, 95th Cong., 2nd Sess., 1978. The *New York Times* repeatedly endorsed the Kennedy-McClellan 1977 proposal. *NYT*, March 10, 1977, 34; *NYT*, March 14, 1977, 29; *NYT*, May 9, 1977, 30.

112. *NYT*, January 16, 1979, A14; *NYT*, November 19, 1981, A22; *CR*, May 2, 1977, 13067.

113. *CR*, January 20, 1978, 295, italics added.

114. As codified, the Sentencing Reform Act directs judges to consider the purposes of punishment as listed in 18 U.S.C. § 3553 (a):

"(a) Factors to Be Considered in Imposing a Sentence. The court shall impose a sentence sufficient, but not greater than necessary, to comply with the purposes set forth in paragraph (2) of the subsection. The court, in determining the particular sentence to be imposed, shall consider—

(1) the nature and circumstances of the offense and the history and characteristics of the defendant;

(2) the need for the sentence imposed—

(A) to reflect the seriousness of the offense, to promote respect for the law, and to provide just punishment for the offense;

(B) to afford adequate deterrence to criminal conduct;

(C) to protect the public from further crimes of the defendant; and

(D) to provide the defendant with needed educational or vocational training, medical care, or other correction treatment in the most effective matter."

For excellent discussion of the evaluation of purposes, see Marc Miller, "Purposes at Sentencing," *Southern California Law Review 66* (1992), 413–481.

115. 28 U.S.C. s 991(b)(1)(B)(1988), italics added.

"The purposes of the United States Sentencing Commission are to—

(1) establish sentencing policies and practices for the Federal criminal justice system that—

   (A) assure the meeting of the purposes of sentencing as set forth in section 3553 (a) (2) of title 18, United States Code;

   (B) provide certainty and fairness in meeting the purposes of sentencing, avoiding unwarranted sentencing disparities among defendants with similar records who have been found guilty of similar criminal conduct while maintaining sufficient flexibility to permit individualized sentences when warranted by mitigating or aggravating factors not taken into account in the establishment of general sentencing practices; and

   (C) reflect, to the extent practicable, advancement in knowledge of human behavior as it relates to the criminal justice process; and

(2) develop means of measuring the degree to which the sentencing, penal, and correctional practices are effective in meeting the purposes of sentencing as set forth in section 3553 (a)(2) of title 18, United States Code." 29 U.S.C. 991(b); Bernard Harcourt, "From the Ne'er-Do-Well to the Criminal History Category: The Refinement of the Actuarial Model in Criminal Law," *Law and Contemporary Problems 66* (2003), 101.

116. S. 1660 § 2302(a).
117. Stith and Cabranes, *Fear of Judging*, 11–14; Ogletree, "The Death of Discretion?"; Robert Martinson, "What Works?—Questions and Answers About Prison Reform," *The Public Interest* 35 (1974), 22, 24–5, 48; Wilson, *Thinking About Crime*, 170–171.
118. Robert Martinson, "New Findings, New Views: A Note of Caution Regarding Sentencing Reform," *Hofstra Law Review* 7 (Winter 1979), 243–258; Garland, *Culture of Control*, 63, 65.

Chapter 4

1. *CQA*, 1991, 487.
2. C-SPAN Video Library, "Crime Legislation Introduction Ceremony," August 11, 1993, http://www.c-spanvideo.org/program/IntroductionC (accessed July 23, 2013); Office of the Press Secretary, "Remarks by the President in Anti-Crime Initiative Announcement," August 11, 1993, Folder: Crime Bill—Strategy Group, Box 75, Reed Crime Papers; *WSJ*, August 12, 1993, A16; *LAT*, August 12, 1993, A1; William Clinton, "The President's Radio Address," August 13, 1994, *Public Papers of the Presidents of the United States: William J. Clinton 1994*, vol. 2 (Washington, DC: GPO, 1995), 1466.
3. Beckett, *Making Crime Pay*; Davey, *The Politics of Prison Expansion*; Michael Tonry, *Malign Neglect: Race, Crime, and Punishment in America* (New York: Oxford University Press, 1995); Michael Tonry, *Thinking about Crime: Sense and Sensibility in American Penal Culture* (New York: Oxford University Press, 2004); Steven Donziger, *The Real War on Crime: The Report of the National Criminal Justice Commission* (New York: Harper Perennial, 1996); Mauer, *Race to Incarcerate*; Weaver, "Frontlash."
4. Pierson, *Politics in Time*, 112–115, 137.
5. Charles Ogletree, "The Death of Discretion? Reflections on the Federal Sentencing Guidelines," *Harvard Law Review 101* (1988), 1938–1960; Tonry, *Sentencing Matters*, 91–92; Stith and Cabranes, *Fear of Judging*, 70; Harcourt, "From the Ne'er-Do-Well to the Criminal History Category, 101.
6. Paul Frymer, *Uneasy Alliances: Race and Party Competition in America* (Princeton: Princeton University Press, 1999), 89–91. Klinkner and Smith, *The Unsteady March*, chapter 9; Adolph Reed, Jr. *Without Justice for All: The New Liberalism and Our Retreat from Racial Equality* (Boulder: Westview Press, 2001).
7. As an early display of his racial toughness, Clinton interrupted his 1992 presidential campaign to observe the execution of Ricky Ray Rector, a brain-damaged black man convicted of murder. It was one of four execution orders Clinton signed during his tenure as governor of Arkansas. Ronald Kramer and Raymond Michalowski, "The Iron Fist and the Velvet Tongue: Crime Control Policies in the Clinton Administration," *Social Justice 22* (Summer 1995), 87–101; Frymer, *Uneasy Alliances*, especially chapter 5; *NYT*, July 29, 1994, A1.

8. Mandatory minimums have been the target of widespread scholarly and judicial criticism, and opponents argue that mandatory penalties inflate public expense by increasing trial rates and case processing time, that they displace discretion from judges to prosecutors, that their inflexibility undermines sentence proportionality, and that they heighten racial disparity in sentencing. Tonry, *Sentencing Matters*, 159–161; USSC, *Special Report to the Congress: Mandatory Minimum Penalties in the Federal Criminal Justice System* (Washington, DC: USSC, 1991); Leadership Conference on Civil Rights, *Justice on Trial: Racial Disparities in the American Criminal Justice System* (Washington, DC: Leadership Conference on Civil Rights, 2000); Paula Kautt, *Separating and Estimating the Effects of the Federal Sentencing Guidelines and the Federal Mandatory Minimums: Isolating the Sources of Racial Disparity* (Dissertation, Criminal Justice, University of Nebraska, Omaha, 2000); Doris Marie Provine, "Too Many Black Men: The Sentencing Judge's Dilemma," *Law and Social Inquiry 23* (1998), 823–856. Particularly notable are the appraisals of how mandatory minimums undermine sentence proportionality, mostly through mixture inflations and sentencing cliffs. Mixture inflations occur because mandatory minimums stipulate that total drug weight is constituted by the weight of any "*mixture* or substance containing a detectable amount" of the illegal drug (21 U.S.C. § 841). Mixture stipulations have created some strange problems, such as courts having to decide how to count total drug weight when narcotics bond to suitcases, paper, or drug laboratory equipment. Sentencing cliffs arise because the intrinsic rigidity of mandatory minimums amplifies minor difference between, for example, possessing 4.9 versus 5.1 grams of crack cocaine. While magnifying minor drug weight differences, mandatory minimums minimize major differences in prior offense status, making robbery count as a "strike" with the same force as rape and murder. Barbara Vincent and Paul Hofer, *The Consequences of Mandatory Minimum Prison Terms: A Summary of Recent Findings* (Washington, DC: Federal Judicial Center, 1994), 25.

9. By counting U.S.C. provisions that carried a criminal penalty, a 1989 study identified 3,000 federal crimes, and, following this methodology, a 1998 study found 3,300 federal crimes. The American Bar Association identified 1,020 statutory sections, codified between 1864 and 1996, with criminal provisions. From this ABA count, roughly one quarter of all criminal provisions were enacted between 1980 and 1996. Researchers wisely urge us to remain cautious about the precision of such counts. While Title 18 of the U.S.C. is often called the Federal Criminal Code, criminal penalties litter the other 49 titles, and the sections and subsections of the U.S.C. might be counted in different ways.

    Ronald Gainer, "Report to the Attorney General on Federal Criminal Code Reform," *Criminal Law Forum 1* (1989); Ronald Gainer, "Federal Criminal Code Reform: Past and Future," *Buffalo Criminal Law Review 2* (1998); Task Force on the Federalization of Criminal Law, *The Federalization of Criminal Law* (Washington, DC: American Bar Foundation Criminal Justice Section, 1998), 7–12, appendix C.

10. To identify the universe of congressional acts that establish, expand, repeal, or contract mandatory minimum terms of imprisonment from 1790 to 2010, I began with old lists of mandatory minimums and cross-referenced relevant sections in the U.S.C. Annotated to mark amendments or repeals. I consulted USSC, *Special Report to the Congress: Mandatory Minimum Penalties in the Federal Criminal Justice System* (Washington, DC: USSC, 1991), appendix A; USSC, *Guidelines Manual* (Washington, DC: USSC, 2000), appendix B; USSC, *Report to Congress: Mandatory Minimum Penalties in the Federal Criminal Justice System* (Washington, DC: USSC, 2011), appendix A.

    In total, I identified 465 congressional "actions" on statutory mandatory minimums from 1790–2010 (1st–111th Congresses). There were 410 "tightening actions," that is, provisions to establish a mandatory minimum, to increase the mandatory punishment, or to broaden the definition of a crime to which a mandatory penalty already applies. There were 55 "loosening actions," that is, provisions to repeal a mandatory minimum, to decrease the mandatory punishment, or to contract the definition of a crime to which a mandatory penalty already applies.

11. In rough terms, a similar trajectory holds at the state level. Colonial legislatures established fixed penalties for many criminal offenses, but, by the early nineteenth century, most states granted trial courts greater sentencing discretion. The New York legislature of 1926 enacted

an early three-strikes statute that required a life sentence upon the third felony conviction, and some states followed suit. Aside from a handful of recidivism and drug-related statutes, most state-level mandatory minimums did not appear until the 1970s. Gary Lowenthal, "Mandatory Sentencing Laws: Undermining the Effectiveness of Determinate Sentencing Reform," *California Law Review 81* (1993), 68.

12. Dan Baum, *Smoke and Mirrors* (Boston: Little, Brown and Company, 1996), 203, 197; *CQWR*, September 29, 1984, 2357.

13. *Anti-Drug Abuse Act of 1986*, Public Law 99-570, *U.S. Statutes at Large* 100 (1986): 3207. In a small provision that significantly enmeshed crime, drugs, and immigration, the 1986 Act amended the Immigration and Nationality Act to authorize exclusion or deportation of any "alien" for drug law violations, and it required law enforcement officials to notify the Immigration and Naturalization Service of any drug arrests of suspected "illegal aliens." Brian Duffy, "War on Drugs: More than a 'Short-term High?' *U.S. News & World Report*," September 29, 1986, 28.

14. *LAT*, September 10, 1986, 1; *CQA*, 1986, 92–106; Craig Reinarman and Harry Levine, "Crack in Context: Politics and Media in the Making of a Drug Scare," *Contemporary Drug Problems 16* (1989), 564; *NYT*, November 17, 1986, A1; Duffy, "War on Drugs," 28; *CQWR*, October 18, 1986, 2599–2600.

15. *CQWR*, May 14, 1988, 1281; Harry Chernoff, Christopher Kelly, and John Kroger, "The Politics of Crime," *Harvard Journal on Legislation 33* (1996), 527–579. Both Chernoff and Kroger served as legislative assistants to Charles Schumer. *CR*, August 24, 1994, S12457.

16. Tonry, *Sentencing Matters*, 160; Lord Windlesham, *Politics, Punishment, and Populism* (New York: Oxford University Press, 1998), 12. Mandatory minimum escalation runs counter to trends in both crime rates and public opinion. Public fear and vengeance have been high and stable since the early 1970s, but rather than steady or uniform "pandering" during this period, Congress escalated mandatory minimums in lurching fashion, with steepest escalation after 1984. Against the expectations of the tough on crime "democracy at work" thesis, Congress did not simply pass more and more mandatory minimums uniformly during this period. Beckett, *Making Crime Pay*, 14–27; Mark Warr, "Fear of Victimization" *The Public Perspective 5* (1993), 25–28.

17. Federal Bureau of Prisons, *State of the Bureau 2000* (Washington, DC: GPO), 52–54; USSC, *Annual Report 1992* (Washington, DC: USSC, 1992), 44–45. Average sentence length for possession and non-trafficking drug offenses was only four months shy of the average sentence length for murder. Lawrence Greenfeld, *Compendium of Federal Justice Statistics, 2001* (Washington, DC: GPO, 2003). The three responsible mandatory minimum statutes were 21 U.S.C. § 841 (38,214 offenders) for possessing, manufacturing, or distributing illegal drugs; 21 U.S.C. § 844 (10,218 offenders) for simple possession offenses; and 21 U.S.C. § 960 (6,135 offenders) for unlawful importation or exportation of drugs. USSC, *Special Report to the Congress: Mandatory Minimum Penalties in the Federal Criminal Justice System* (Washington, DC: USSC, 1991), 10.

18. Prior to the 1951 Boggs Act, there was only one federal drug-related mandatory minimum. In 1914, Congress enacted a five-year mandatory minimum for opium manufacture. Like other drug-related mandatory minimums, the opium penalty emerged in racially loaded terms, this time centering on Chinese Americans. Police in northern cities targeted jazz clubs for heightened surveillance, and "practically all the outstanding players of bop were arrested during this period." Ortiz Walton, *Music: Black, White, and Blue* (New York: William Morrow, 1972), 98; John Helmer, *Drugs and Minority Oppression* (New York: Seabury Press, 1975), chapter 18; *CQA*, 1951, 347; *CR*, May 25, 1956, 9018–9022.

19. House Committee on Interstate and Foreign Commerce, Report on the Comprehensive Drug Abuse and Prevention Control Act of 1970, H.R. 18583, H. Rep. No. 1444, 91st Congress, 2nd sess., September 10, 1970; House of Representatives 1970, quoted in USSC, *Special Report to the Congress: Mandatory Minimum Penalties in the Federal Criminal Justice System* (Washington, DC: USSC, 1991), 6–7.

20. *CQA*, 1970, 536; *CQWR*, September 18, 1970, 2259.

21. USSC, *Cocaine and Federal Sentencing Policy*, v, xi.

22. BJS, *Prisoners in 2002* (Washington, DC: GPO, 2003), tables 13 and 14; *Sourcebook of Criminal Justice Statistics, 2001* (Albany: University at Albany, Hindelang Criminal Justice Resource Center, 2001), 494; Amnesty International, *"Not Part of my Sentence:" Violations of the Human Rights of Women in Custody* (New York: Amnesty International, 1999); BJS, *Women Offenders* (Washington, DC: GPO, 1999); BJS, *State Court Sentencing of Convicted Felons, 1994* (Washington, DC: GPO, 1998); National Council of La Raza, *The Mainstreaming of Hate: A Report of Latinos and Harassment, Hate Violence, and Law Enforcement Abuse in the 90s* (Washington, DC: National Council of La Raza, 1999). Gender and racial disparities arise not simply from police, prosecutors, and judges, but are inscribed into the structure of sentencing guidelines. Women often play minor roles in drug dealing and therefore lack information to plea bargain down their sentences. Myrna Raeder, "Gender and Sentencing: Single Mom, Battered Women, and Other Sex-Based Anomalies in the Gender-Free World of the Federal Sentencing Guidelines," *Pepperdine Law Review 20* (1993).

23. James Morone, "Enemies of the People: The Moral Dimensions to Public Health," *Journal of Health Politics 22* (1997), 993–1020; Doris Marie Provine, *Unequal Under the Law: Race in the War on Drugs* (Chicago: University of Chicago Press, 2007); David Musto, *The American Disease: Origins of Narcotics Control* (New York: Oxford University Press, 1987), especially 220–223, 282–283; Naomi Murakawa, "Toothless: The Methamphetamine 'Epidemic,' 'Meth Mouth,' and the Racial Construction of Drug Scares," *Du Bois Review 8* (Spring 2011), 219–229.

24. *CR*, September 26, 1986, S13762–S13763, italics added. Some lawmakers speculated that Caribbean countries exported crack. Senator Moynihan said that "crack came from the Bahamas in 1983 [and] hit Harlem in 1985," and Senator Helms (R-North Carolina) blamed a "Jamaican 'posse' for muscling in and inundating Kansas City with crack." *CR*, October 19 1988, S16803; *CR*, October 21, 1988, S17320.

25. The Office of Legislative Affairs at the DOJ also discouraged the reduction, claiming that maintenance of the 100-to-1 disparity was "consistent with the program of the President." Statement by the President, Office of the Press Secretary, October 30, 1995, Folder: Crack, Box 71, Reed Crime Papers; Kent Markus, acting assistant attorney general, in letter to House Speaker Newt Gingrich, n.d. (fax timestamp June 2, 1995), Folder: Cocaine, Box 70, Reed Crime Papers.

26. Given this dearth of evidence, a group of 30 neonatologists and pediatricians wrote a 2004 open letter requesting that news media drop the terms "crack baby" and "crack addicted baby." They explained that in almost 20 years of research, "none of us has identified a recognizable condition, syndrome or disorder that should be termed 'crack baby.'" David Lewis et al., Open Letter to Media, "Physicians, Scientists to Media: Stop Using the Term 'Crack Baby' 2004," February 25, 2004; see John Morgan, and Lynn Zimmer, "The Social Pharmacology of Smokeable Cocaine: Not All It's Cracked Up to Be," in *Crack in America: Demon Drugs and Social Justice*, ed. Craig Reinarman and Harry Levine (Berkeley: University of California Press, 1997), 131–170; D. Neuspiel and R. Hamel, "Cocaine and Infant Behavior," *Journal of Developmental Behavior and Pediatrics 12* (1991), 55–64; Ira Chasnoff Griffith, D. R. Freier, and J. C. Murray, "Cocaine/Polydrug Use in Pregnancy: Two-Year Follow Up," *Pediatrics 89* (1992), 284–289; L. Mayes, C. Granger, R. Bornstein, and M. Zuckerman, "The Problem of Prenatal Cocaine Exposure: A Rush to Judgment," *Journal of American Medical Association 267* (1992), 406–408; Lynn Paltrow and Katherine Jack, "Pregnant Women, Junk Science, and Zealous Defense," *Champion 34* (2010), 30–37; Dorothy Roberts, *Killing the Black Body: Race, Reproduction, and the Meaning of Liberty* (New York: Pantheon Books, 1997); Doris Marie Provine, *Unequal Under the Law: Race in the War on Drugs* (Chicago: University of Chicago Press, 2007).

27. *CR*, September 26, 1986, S13771; *CR*, October 21, 1988, H11229–H11230; Center for Disease Control and Prevention, *National Linked File of Live Births and Infant Deaths* (Washington, DC: National Center for Health Statistics, 2002).

28. *CR*, September 27, 1986, S13968–S13970; Charles Krauthammer's 1989 *WP* column, cited in Harriet Washington, *Medical Apartheid: The Dark History of Medical Experimentation on Black Americans from Colonial Times to Present* (New York: Doubleday, 2006), 213.

29. *CR*, October 18, 1995, H10266; *CR*, October 18, 1995, H10277, italics added; *CR*, October 18, 1995, H10258.

30. *CR*, July 28, 2010, H6197–H6206.
31. Memo from Bruce Reed and Jose Cerda III to the President, "Crime Bill Funding," October 25, 1993, Box 85, Memos to POTUS Folder, Reed Crime Papers.
32. Attorney General Janet Reno accepted Clinton's proposals for cops, boot camps, and drug courts. She protested, however, the idea that new programs might diminish budgetary allocations for the FBI and the DEA. Memo from Bruce Reed and Jose Cerda III to the President, "Crime Bill Funding," October 25, 1993, Memos to POTUS Folder, Box 85, Reed Crime Papers.
33. Memo from Bruce Reed and Jose Cerda III to Carol Rasco, "Crime Bill Conference," December 1, 1993, Box 75, Reed Crime Papers, digital archive.
34. Memo from Bruce Reed and Jose Cerda III to Carol Rasco, "Crime Bill Conference," December 1, 1993, Box 75, Reed Crime Papers.
35. "Crime Strategy Outline," n.d., Box 75, Reed Crime Papers.
36. President William Clinton Radio Address, Philadelphia, Pennsylvania, July 16, 1994 [Taped July 15, 1994], Folder: 1994 Crime Bill—General, Box 3, Prince Papers. Memo from Jonathan Prince for Leon Panetta on "House Democratic Caucus Talking Points on Crime," August 9, 1994, Folder: 1994 Crime Bill—Strategy Memos, Box 3, Prince Papers.
37. Memo from Bruce Reed and Jose Cerda III to the President, "Possible Biden-Dole Deal on Crime," October 27, 1993, Folder: Memos to POTUS, Box 85, Reed Crime Papers, italics added.
38. Memo from Bruce Reed and Jose Cerda III to the President, "Possible Biden-Dole Deal on Crime," October 27, 1993, Folder: 1994 Crime Bill—Memos to POTUS, Box 85, Reed Crime Papers.
39. Nancy Marion, "Symbolic Policies in Clinton's Crime Control Agenda," *Buffalo Criminal Law Review 1* (April 1997), 67–108; David Holian, "He's Stealing My Issues! Clinton's Crime Rhetoric and the Dynamics of Issue Ownership," *Political Behavior 26* (June 1994), 375–394; Chernoff, Kelly, and Kroger, "The Politics of Crime," 527–579; Ronald Kramer and Raymond Michalowski, "The Iron Fist and the Velvet Tongue: Crime Control Policies in the Clinton Administration," *Social Justice 22* (Summer 1995), 87–101; "Schedule for Crime Strategy," Faxed from Senator Biden to David Gergen, n.d. [fax date January 28, 1994], Folder: Crime Bill—Senate [1], Box 74, Reed Crime Papers, underlining in original.
40. Memo from Bruce Reed and Jose Cerda III to Carol Rasco, "Crime Bill Conference," December 1, 1993, Box 75, Reed Crime Papers, digital archive; Memo from Bruce Reed and Jose Cerda III to President Clinton, "Crime Bill Funding," October 25, 1993, Memos to POTUS Folder, Box 85, Reed Crime Papers; Parenti, *Lockdown America*; Wacquant, *Punishing the Poor.*
41. Gilmore, *Golden Gulag*, 221. I am grateful to Hannah Walker for directing me to this analysis, and for her insights on race, space, and power more broadly.
42. Cohen, *Boundaries of Blackness*, 63–76; Strolovitch, *Affirmative Advocacy.*
43. Jennifer Hochschild, *Facing Up to the American Dream: Race, Class and the Soul of the Nation* (Princeton: Princeton University Press, 1995), 48–49.
44. Matthew Hickman and Brian Reaves, *Local Police Departments, 1993: Law Enforcement Management and Administrative Statistics* (Washington, DC: GPO, 1996); Samuel Walker and K. Turner, *A Decade of Modest Progress: Employment of Black and Hispanic Police Officers, 1983–1992* (Omaha: University of Nebraska at Omaha, 1992).
45. White House Domestic Policy Council called community policing a "philosophy—not a program." "The Clinton Crime Plan," Draft distributed at Crime Meeting October 12, 1993, Folder: Clinton Crime Plan, Box 70, Reed Crime Papers.
46. Community Oriented Policing Services, *Community Policing Defined* (Washington, DC: GPO, 2012).
47. NIJ, *National Evaluation of the COPS Program: Title I of the 1994 Crime Act* (Washington, DC: GPO, 2000), 183, 113–114; Carl Klockars, "The Rhetoric of Community Policing," in *Community Policing: Rhetoric or Reality*, ed. Jack Greene and Stephen Mastrofski (New York: Praeger, 1991), 239–258; for a devastating critique of quality-of-life policing, see Bernard Harcourt, *Illusion of Order: The False Promise of Broken Windows Policing* (Cambridge: Harvard University Press, 2001).

48. Memo from Rahm Emanuel, Bruce Reed, Ron Klain, and Jonathan Price to Leon Panetta, "Crime Planning," September 15, 1994, Folder: 1994 Crime Bill—Strategy Memos, Box 3, Prince Papers.

49. BJS, *Noncitizens in the Federal Criminal Justice System, 1984–94* (Washington, DC: GPO, 1996); BJS, *Compendium of Federal Justice Statistics, 1999* (Washington, DC: GPO, 2001); BJS, *Immigration Offenders in the Federal Criminal Justice System, 2000* (Washington, DC: GPO, 2002).

50. *Personal Responsibility and Work Opportunity Reconciliation Act of 1996*, Public Law 104–193, *U.S. Statutes at Large* 110 (1996), 2105, with drug felony exclusions codified in 21 U.S.C. S 862a. Federal legislation allows states to opt out of the ban or modify its scope. As of 2004, only nine states entirely opted out of both TANF and Food Stamp exclusions (Maine, New Hampshire, New Mexico, New York, Ohio, Oklahoma, Oregon, Rhode Island, and Vermont). U.S. Government Accountability Office, Drug Offenders: Various Factors May Limit the Impacts of Federal Laws That Provide for Denial of Selected Benefits (Washington, DC: US Government Accountability Office, 2005), appendix II.

51. *Personal Responsibility and Work Opportunity Reconciliation Act of 1996*, Public Law 104–193, *U.S. Statutes at Large* 110 (1996): 2105, with food stamp exclusions codified at 7 U.S.C. § 2015, SSI exclusions codified at 42 U.S.C. § 1382, and public housing exclusions codified at 42 U.S.C. § 1437. Kaaryn Gustafson, "The Criminalization of Poverty," *Journal of Criminal Law and Criminology* 99 (2009), 643–716; *CR*, July 23, 1996, S8498; Rukaiyah Adams, David Onek, and Alissa Riker, *Double Jeopardy: An Assessment of the Felony Drug Provision of the Welfare Reform Act* (San Francisco: The Justice Policy Institute, 1998).

52. I am indebted to Rebecca Bohrman for her insights on immigration policy. Tonry, *Malign Neglect*; Miller, *Search and Destroy*; Personal Responsibility Act, H.R. 4, sec. 100, cited in Dorothy Roberts, *Killing the Black Body: Race, Reproduction, and the Meaning of Liberty* (New York: Pantheon Books 1997), 215; Marc Berk, Claudia Schur, Leo Chavez, and Martin Frankel, "Health Care Use Among Undocumented Latino Immigrants," *Health Affairs* 19 (2000), 51–64; Michael Fix and Ron Haskins, *Welfare Benefits for Non-Citizens* (Washington, DC: Brookings Institution, 2002); *NYT*, January 21, 1999; Department of Agriculture, *The Decline in Food Stamp Participation* (Washington, DC: GPO, 2001); General Accounting Office, *Immigration Reform: Employer Sanctions and the Question of Discrimination* (Washington, DC: GPO, 1990).

53. Franklin Zimring, *The Contradictions of American Capital Punishment* (New York: Oxford University Press, 2003), chapter 2; Lee Epstein and Joseph Kobylka, *The Supreme Court & Legal Change: Abortion and the Death Penalty* (Chapel Hill: University of North Carolina Press, 1992), table 3.1; Franklin Zimring and Gordon Hawkins, *Capital Punishment and the American Agenda* (New York: Cambridge, 1986), 26, 30–32.

54. James Lieberman, "Slow Dancing with Death: The Supreme Court and Capital Punishment, 1963–2006," *Columbia Law Review* 107 (January 2004), 7–8.

55. *Furman v. Georgia*, 408 U.S. 238 (1972). Hugo Adam Bedau, "Racism, Wrongful Convictions, and the Death Penalty," *Tennessee Law Review* 76 (2009), 615; Craig Haney, *Death By Design: Capital Punishment as a Social Psychological System* (New York: Oxford University Press, 2005), 8–11.

56. In *Boykin v. Alabama* (1969), for example, the NAACP LDF argued that capital punishment constituted cruel and unusual punishment in every instance. The NAACP LDF challenged capital punishment also on procedural grounds, because "the politics of abolition" required creation of a "death-row logjam." Liebman, "The Overproduction of Death," 2033–2038; Michael Meltsner, *Cruel and Unusual: The Supreme Court and Capital Punishment* (New York: Random House, 1973), 66.

57. *CQA*, 1968, 693.

58. *Furman v. Georgia*, 408 U.S. 364 (1972). Like so many Supreme Court criminal procedure cases, the specific case involved a young black male defendant, 25-year-old William Henry Furman, accused of breaking into the home of a white family and killing the father. Hugo Adam Bedau, "Racism, Wrongful Convictions, and the Death Penalty," *Tennessee Law Review* 76 (2009), 615.

59. National Advisory Commission on Criminal Justice Standards and Goals, *Report on the Criminal Justice System* (Washington, DC: GPO, 1973), 181, italics added.

60. Epstein and Kobylka, *The Supreme Court & Legal Change*, chapters 3 and 4; Haney, *Death By Design*, 11–13; Lieberman, "Slow Dancing with Death."

61. *McCleskey v. Kemp*, 481 U.S. 279 (1987), 293, 339. Justice Powell authored the opinion for the Court, joined by Chief Justice Rehnquist and Justices White, O'Connor, and Scalia. Justices Brennan, Marshall, Blackmun, and Stevens dissented. Charles Ogletree, "The Death of Discretion? Reflections on the Federal Sentencing Guidelines," *Harvard Law Review* 101 (1988), 1938–1960; Lieberman, "Slow Dancing with Death"; Naomi Murakawa and Katherine Beckett, "The Penology of Racial Innocence: The Erasure of Race in the Study and Practice of Punishment," *Law and Society Review* 44(2010), 695–730. James, *Resisting State Violence*, 36–37.

62. Justice Powell, *McCleskey v. Kemp* 481 U.S. at 295–304; Powel quoted *Gregg v. Georgia* 428 U.S. at 197–198.

63. Justice Powell, *McCleskey v. Kemp* 481 U.S. at 292–305; *McCleskey v. Kemp* 481 U.S. at 315. *McCleskey v. Kemp* 481 U.S. at 339.

64. Anthony Lewis, "Bowing to Racism," *NYT*, April 28, 1987, A31; "New Look at Death Sentences and Race," *NYT*, April 29, 2008; Little, "The Federal Death Penalty," 379, 381.

65. Senators Carl Levin (D-Michigan) and Charles McC. Mathias Jr. (R-Maryland) led the fili-buster threat. Rory Little, "The Federal Death Penalty: History and Some Thoughts about the DOJ's Role," *Fordham Urban Law Journal* 26 (1999), 377–379; *CQA*, 1984, 227; *CQWR*, October 18, 1986, 2594; *CQWR*, October 25, 1986, 2699.

66. *Anti-Drug Abuse Act of 1988*, Public Law 100-690, 102 (1988): 4181, section 408 (g)–(r), 4388–4395.

67. Senator Mark Hatfield (R-Oregon) rejected the retributive "eye-for-an-eye" mentality of capital punishment. Senator Daniel Evans (R-Washington) opposed the legislation on grounds that it was simply "an election slam dunk" that "won't even slow down the drug problem." *CQWR*, October 15, 1988, 1598, 2979; *CQA*, 1988, 1658. *CQWR*, June 11, 1988, 1598; *CQWR*, June 18, 1988, 1658; *NYT*, October 4, 1988, A29; *CQWR*, October 8, 1988, 2799; Dara Strolovitch, "Of Mancessions and Hecoveries: Race, Gender, and the Political Construction of Economic Crises and Recoveries," *Perspectives on Politics* 11 (March 2013), 167–176.

68. Charles Boettcher, Comment, "Testing the Federal Death Penalty Act of 1994, 18 U.S.C. §§ 3591–98 (914): *United States v. Jones*, 132 F.3d 232 (5th Cir. 1998)," *Texas Tech Law Review* 29 (1998), 1058–1059.

69. CRS, *Present Federal Death Penalty Statutes* (Washington, DC: Office of Congressional Information and Publishing, 1997); CRS, *Capital Punishment: An Overview of Federal Death Penalty Statutes* (Washington, DC: Office of Congressional Information and Publishing, 2005); CRS, *The Death Penalty: Capital Punishment Legislation in the 110th Congress* (Washington, DC: Office of Congressional Information and Publishing, 2008).

70. Gekas's amendment won over a Democratic amendment that also added 12 capital crimes (Amendments 822 and 823 to H.R. 5269). Democratic Representative William Hughes sponsored the amendment. Instead of explaining why each capital crime justified death, Hughes spoke in the aggregate: his amendment added "12 more substantive offenses to the list of the some 12 death penalty crimes already in H.R. 5269." The difference was the defini-tion of murder. Hughes defined murder as "intentional killing," but Gekas used the more capacious language of "reckless disregard." *CR*, October 4, 1990, 27511–27519.

71. Gekas amendment (ND: 5–131; SD: 56–19; R: 165–9) and the McCollum amendment (ND: 63–116; SD: 67–8; R: 165–9); Little, "The Federal Death Penalty," especially 349–350, 373; text of H.R. 5269, *CR*, July 13, 1990.

72. Democrat Harley Staggers of West Virginia proposed the amendment to change death sentences to life sentences, but most in his party opposed him (ND: 92–89; SD: 5–70; R: 6–163); Dellums, *CR*, October 5, 1990, 27695.

73. The Judiciary Committee adopted Senator Kennedy's racial justice amendment and sent it back to the floor without recommendation. This version of the RJA, adapted from Kennedy's bill 1989 bill (S. 1696), required prosecutors to demonstrate with "clear and convincing" evidence that racial disparities reflected nonracial factors. The amendment was adopted 7–6, supported by the lone Republican Arlen Spector, (R-Pennsylvania), and the committee then split 7–7 on approving the amended bill. They ultimately agreed by voice vote to send

the report to the floor without recommendation. *CQA*, 1989, 260–262; *CQWR*, May 19, 1990, 1557.

74. Author's count of Sections 2402–2427, Title XXIV, H.R. 3371 as introduced in House, September 23, 1991. Neither Brooks nor Schumer announced the number of death-eligible crimes in the bill. Section 103–138, Title XXIII, H.R. 3371, Gekas Amendment to H.R. 3371, *CR*, October 16, 1991, 26614–26621; Brooks, *CR*, October 16, 1991, 26552; Schumer, *CR*, October 16, 1991, 26622; *WP*, August 5, 1992, A1; *NYT*, February 1, 1992, 21.

75. *CQA*, 1992, 311.

76. *CR*, June 20, 1991, S8243, italics added, and S8248–51. Biden repeatedly compared his Democratic bill and the Republican Thurmond bill in terms of its higher death-eligible count, as he had "no reservations" about defending his as "the tougher crime bill." *CQWR*, June 22, 1991.

77. The *Washington Post* set "the standard count" for Biden's capital crimes at 53. Note, however, that *Congressional Quarterly Weekly Report*, a publication dedicated to following congressional details, cautiously set its count at "about 50" new capital crimes. *WP*, November 29, 1991, A29; *CR*, June 20, 1991, S8259, S8302; *CQWR*, August 3, 1991, 2171; *CQWR*, September 28, 1991, 2788; for Biden's count, see *CR*, March 4, 1992, S2818–2819.

78. *CR*, March 19, 1992, S3934; *CQA*, 1991, 311–313; *CQA*, 1992, 311–313, 8–S, 34-S. In the failed cloture votes of March and October 1992, the only Democrats to vote against cloture represented Alabama (Senators Heflin and Shelby) and Louisiana (Senators Breaux and Johnston). By some news sources, the September 1992 bill contained 55 death-eligible crimes. *St. Louis Post-Dispatch*, September 28, 1992, A1.

79. By fall of 1992, the National Association of Police Officers, the International Union of Police Associations, and the Combined Law Enforcement Associations of Texas had already endorsed Clinton. *WP*, August 5, 1992, A1; *Houston Chronicle*, September 27, 1992, A22; *WP*, November 2, 1992, A23; *Chicago Sun-Times*, October 3, 1992, 17.

80. ND: 37–0; SD: 15–4; R: 3–39. Senate Democrats fell short of the 60 votes needed for cloture, 55–43, with 52 Democrats and three Republicans for it and four Democrats and 39 Republicans opposed. *CQA*, 1992, 311–313; *Chicago Sun-Times*, October 3, 1992, 17.

81. *CQA*, 1993, 294; H.R. 4032, "To Provide the Penalty of Death for Certain Offenses," introduced by Schumer on March 15, 1994; "Brooks Introduces Tough Anti-Crime Package," New Release from House Committee on the Judiciary, September 23, 1993, Box 75, Crime Bill—Strategy Group Folder, Reed Crime Papers; *CQWR*, March 26, 1994, 743. A comparison of H.R. 3131, Title II, sec. 202–219 with H.R. 4032, sec. 2–15, reveals that the list included the same death-eligible crimes but in different order.

82. In response to Watt's remarks on racial disparity, Dan Burton (R-Indiana) delivered classic criminological colorblindness: the crime problem was "an American issue" unmodified, unmarked as "a white issue, a black issue, a red issue, a pink issue." *CR*, April 14, 1994, 7439–7441; *CR*, April 14, 1994, 7440; *CR*, April 14, 1994, 7441–7442; Office of Legislative Affairs, Draft Statement of Administrative Policy on H.R. 4092, April 7, 1994, Folder: 1994 Crime Bill—Amendments, Box 71, Reed Crime Papers. For debate over the Kopetski, Mfume, Serrano amendment, see *CR*, April 14, 1994, 7442; *NYT*, April 15, 1994, A23. Clinton's Office of Legislative Affairs opposed the Kopetski amendment.

83. Hatch, *CR*, November 3, 1993, S14941, S14944; *CR*, September 23, 1993, S12442. Biden introduced S. 1488 with the claim that it authorized the death penalty for 47 offenses. *CR*, November 3, 1993, S14918–S14919. *Congressional Quarterly Almanac* confirmed that S. 1488 began with 47 federal capital offenses and H.R. 3131, introduced by Jack Brooks (D-Texas), contained 64 death-eligible offenses. *CQA*, 1993, 294; *CQA*, 1993, 295. Memo from Bruce Reed and Jose Cerda III to Carol Rasco, "Crime Bill Conference," December 1, 1993, Folder: Strategy Group, Box 75, Reed Crime Papers.

84. *CR*, August 22, 1994, S12258; *CR*, August 24, 1994, S12414.

85. *CR*, August 24, 1994, S12427.

86. As a standard judicial troupe that law trumps opinion, Reno stated that she was "personally" opposed to capital punishment even as she described herself as a death-penalty-seeking, tough-on-crime attorney. *WP*, March 10, 1993, A9. Four capital crimes accounted for 540 of the 926 capital charges from 1995–2000: murder with firearm during federal violent crime or drug crime (18 U.S.C. 924), violent crimes in aid of racketeering (18 U.S.C. 1959(a)), murder by a drug "kingpin" (21 U.S.C. 848(e)(1)(A)), and murder during a carjacking

(18 U.S.C. 2119)). Single defendants can be charged with multiple capital offenses, so the number of defendants submitted for review (682) was less than the number of capital charges (926). U.S. DOJ, *The Federal Death Penalty System: A Statistical Survey (1988–2000)* (Washington, DC: GPO, 2000), 8, T-28, T-29.

87. Claire Kim, "Managing the Racial Breach: Clinton, Black-White Polarization, and the Race Initiative," *Political Science Quarterly 117* (2002), 66; Sensenbrenner, quoted in *USA Today*, April 22, 1994, A4.

88. *CQWR*, December 7, 1996, 3342–3343.

89. Aggravating factors vary by nature of offense, with different factors listed for espionage and treason (18 U.S.C. § 3592(b)), homicide (18 U.S.C. § 3592(c)), and drug offenses (18 U.S.C. § 3592(d)). See lawyer qualifications codified at 18 U.S.C. § 3005 (1994); Little, "The Federal Death Penalty," 404; Biden introducing S. 1607, *CR*, November 3, 1993, S14918–S14919.

90. This approach to discrimination had also been used for evaluating racial disparity in jury selection. In *Batson v. Kentucky* (1986), the Supreme Court held that racial patterns of striking prospective jurors constitutes prima facie discrimination, and therefore the burden shifts to the prosecution to explain peremptory challenges in nonracial terms. Erwin Chemerinsky, "Eliminating Discrimination in Administering the Death Penalty: The Need for the Racial Justice Act," *Santa Clara Law Review 35* (1994), 519–534. Laurence Tribe, letter to Senator Edward Kennedy, reprinted in *CR*, May 24, 1990, S6891–6892.

91. *CQA*, 1994, 280; Hanna Rosin, "Action Jackson," *New Republic*, March 21, 1994, 17; Bob Cohn, "Buying Off the Black Caucus," *Newsweek*, August 1, 1994, 24.

92. *NYT*, January 24, 1990, A20; *NYT*, September 26, 1990, A24; *NYT*, October 8, 1990, A16. Like Senator Hatch's statement (italics added), Senator Phil Gramm (R-Texas) dubbed the RJA the "Death Penalty Abolition Act of 1991," and Bill McCollum (R-Florida) agreed that it "would abolish the death penalty in America." *CR*, June 20, 1991, S8249, 8251–8252, S8282; *NYT*, April 22, 1994, A26; *NYT*, October 18, 1990, A24; *NYT*, November 1, 1990, A28.

93. Don Edwards and John Conyers Jr., "The Racial Justice Act—A Simple Matter of Justice," *University of Dayton Law Review 20* (1995): 699–713; *NYT*, October 6, 1990, 1; *NYT*, July 22, 1994, A26; Justice Harry Blackmun, *Callins v. Collins* 510 U.S. 1141 (1994). Even Justice Lewis Powell, author for the *McCleskey* majority, ultimately endorsed abolition. When biographer John Jeffries asked the retired Justice Powell if he would change his vote in any case, Powell replied: "Yes, *McCleskey v. Kemp*." Justice Powell added that he has come to believe that "capital punishment should be abolished." John Jeffries, *Justice Lewis F. Powell, Jr.: A Biography* (New York: Fordham University Press, 2001), 451. Charles Ogletree and Austin Sarat, "Toward and Beyond the Abolition of Capital Punishment," in *The Road to Abolition? The Future of Capital Punishment in the United States*, ed. Charles Ogletree and Austin Sarat (New York: New York University Press, 2009), 1–18.

94. In the end, many CBC legislators supported the RJA-free bill because it banned certain assault weapons and authorized $8 billion for prevention programs in urban areas. "Draft Q & A: Racial Justice Act," n.d., Box 78, Reed Papers, digital library, WJCL; *NYT*, July 14, 1994, D23; Chemerinsky, "Eliminating Discrimination in Administering the Death Penalty"; Edwards and Conyers, "The Racial Justice Act," 699–713; *NYT*, May 13, 1994, A30; *NYT*, June 27, 1994, A14; *NYT*, July 14, 1994, D23; *NYT*, July 15, 1994, A26; *NYT*, July 21, 1994, A20; *LAT*, August 21, 1994, M3.

95. *NYT*, October 1, 2001; Contract with America; *CQWR*, December 14, 1996, 3381.

96. Remarks by President Clinton in his Address to the Liz Sutherland Carpenter Distinguished Lectureship in the Humanities and Science, University of Texas at Austin, October 15, 1995, transcript by White House office of the Press Secretary, Folder: Race-San Diego Speech, Box 125, Reed Subject Papers.

Chapter 5

1. Amadou Diallo was a 23-year-old black man from Guinea who was shot at 41 times by four New York City police officers in 1999. Officers thought Mr. Diallo was pulling out a gun when really he was reaching for his wallet to offer identification. Abner Louima is a man from Haiti who was arrested and raped with a plunger handle by New York City police officers

in 1997. Kathryn Johnston was a 92-year-old African American woman who was shot by three Atlanta police officers in 2006. Plainclothes officers forcibly entered Ms. Johnston's home without warning or warrant, and, when the elderly woman fired one shot, the officers opened fire on her. Oscar Grant III was a 22-year-old African American man who was shot and killed by a transit police officer. The four African American women known as the "New Jersey Four," Terrain Dandridge, Renata Hill, Vernice Brown, and Patreese Johnson, were arrested and charged with "gang assault." Their "gang activity" began after a man shouted anti-gay slurs at the women and followed them down a Greenwich Village street, spitting on one woman and tossing a lighted cigarette at another. Elizabeth Phelps et al., "Performance on Indirect Measures of Race Evaluation Predicts Amygdala Activation," *Journal of Cognitive Neuroscience 12* (2000), 729–738; Dara Strolovitch, *Affirmative Advocacy: Race, Class, and Gender in Interest Group Politics* (Chicago: University of Chicago Press, 2007), 70–71; Imani Perry, *More Beautiful and More Terrible: The Embrace and Transcendence of Racial Inequality in the United States* (New York: New York University Press, 2011), 51, 73; Beth Richie, *Arrested Justice: Black Women, Violence, and America's Prison Nation* (New York: New York University Press, 2012), 12–14; *NYT*, August 30, 2007.

2. BJS, *Immigration Offenders in the Federal Justice System, 2010* (Washington, DC: GPO, 2012), 35; Jacqueline Stevens, "U.S. Government Unlawfully Detaining and Deporting U.S. Citizens as Aliens," *Virginia Journal of Social Policy & the Law 18* (Spring 2011), 606–720.

3. James Sensenbrenner, on supporting the US PATRIOT Act, 2002. National Republican Party, *A Pledge to America: A New Governing Agenda Built on the Priorities of Our Nation, the Principles We Stand For, & America's Founding Values*, 37–40.

4. Margaret Levi, "The State of the Study of the State," in *Political Science: The State of the Discipline*, ed. Ira Katznelson and Helen Milner (New York: Norton, 2002), 40.

5. Westley, "The Escalation of Violence Through Legitimation," 120–126.

6. Michael Rudolph West, *The Education of Booker T. Washington: American Democracy and the Idea of Race Relations* (New York: Columbia University Press, 2006), 34–37.

7. Kimberlé Williams Crenshaw, "Race, Reform, and Retrenchment: Transformation and Legitimation in Antidiscrimination Law," *Harvard Law Review 101* (May 1988), 1335, 1376–1379, 1384–1385.

8. Goluboff, *The Lost Promise of Civil Rights*; George Lovell, *This Is Not Civil Rights: Discovering Rights Talk in 1939 America* (Chicago: University of Chicago Press, 2012).

9. Crenshaw, "Race, Reform, and Retrenchment," 1387; Michael McCann, *Rights at Work: Pay Equity Reform and the Politics of Legal Mobilization* (Chicago: University of Chicago Press, 1994).

10. For a recent account of evangelical and libertarian campaigns against mass incarceration, see David Dugan and Steven Teles, "The Conservative War on Prisons," *Washington Monthly* (November/December 2012); for analyses of evangelical prison programs, see Tanya Ezren, "Testimonial Politics: The Christian Right's Faith-Based Approach to Marriage and Imprisonment," *American Quarterly 59* (September 2007), 991–1015; Alexander, *The New Jim Crow*; Eva Bertram et al., *Drug War Politics: The Price of Denial* (Berkeley: University of California Press, 1996), 181.

11. GSS question wording: "In general, do you think the courts in this area deal too harshly or not harshly enough with criminals?" Some survey participants volunteered the "about right" response. National Opinion Research Center, *General Social Surveys* (Storrs: The Roper Center for Public Opinion Research, University of Connecticut, 1972–2012).

12. Harris question wording: "Do you think that police brutality against blacks and Hispanics in your community happens often, occasionally or never?" Only 11 percent of respondents in a 2002 Harris Poll believed that "police brutality against blacks and Hispanics in your community happens often," and 35 percent categorically rejected the existence of race-specific police brutality in their community, answering that it "never" happens. iPoll Databank (Roper Center for Public Opinion Research, University of Connecticut), http:// www.ropercenter.uconn.edu/ipoll.html, Harris Poll (Roper Organization, February 13–16, 2002, USHARRIS.032002.R3, accessed September 26, 2011). Gallup 2013 question wording: "Now I am going to read you a list of institutions in American Society. Please tell me how much confidence you, yourself, have in each on – a great deal, quite a lot, some, or very little?

The Police..." http://www.gallup.com/poll/1603/Crime.aspx#2, Gallup Poll (Gallup, Inc 1993-2013). Gallup 2005 question wording: "In some places in the nation there have been charges of police brutality. Do you think there is any police brutality in your area, or not?" iPoll Databank (Roper Center for Public Opinion Research, University of Connecticut), http://www.ropercenter.uconn.edu/ipoll.html, Gallup Poll (Roper Organization, October 13–16, 2005, USGALLUP.05OTOB13.R17, accessed September 26, 2011). Liqun Cao et al., "Race, Community Context and Confidence in the Police," *American Journal of Police 15* (1996), 3–22; Wilson Huang and Michael Vaughn, "Support and Confidence: Public Attitudes Toward the Police," in *Americans View Crime and Justice: A National Opinion Survey*, ed. Timothy Flanagan and Dennis Longmire (Thousand Oaks: Sage Publications, 1996).

13. Whites support criminal justice institutions at higher levels than any other racial group. Roughly 87 percent of whites feel that the police were fair, compared to 67 percent of African Americans, for example. Wilson Huang and Michael Vaughn, "Support and Confidence: Public Attitudes Toward the Police," in *Americans View Crime and Justice: A National Opinion Survey*, ed. Timothy Flanagan and Dennis Longmire (Thousand Oaks: Sage Publications, 1996). It is also notable that evaluations of legitimacy do not pivot on instrumental efficacy in reducing crime. In public support for policing, evaluations are based more on police adherence to procedural justice rather than on instrumental evaluations of police performance. Jason Sunshine and Tom Tyler, "The Role of Procedural Justice and Legitimacy in Shaping Public Support for Policing," *Law & Society Review 37* (2003), 513–547; Tom Tyler and Yuen Huo, *Trust in the Law: Encouraging Public Cooperation With the Police and Courts* (New York: Russell-Sage, 2002); Tom Tyler and Yuen Huo, *Trust in the Law: Encouraging Public Cooperation With the Police and Courts* (New York: Russell-Sage, 2002).

14. Michael McCann and David Johnson, "Rocked but Still Rolling: The Enduring Institution of Capital Punishment in Historical and Comparative Perspective," in *The Road to Abolition? The Future of Capital Punishment in United States*, ed. Charles Ogletree and Austin Sarat (New York: New York University Press, 2009).

15. Carl Pinkele, "Discretion Fits Democracy: An Advocate's Argument," in *Discretion, Justice, and Democracy: A Public Policy Perspective,* ed. Carl Pinkele and William Louthan (Ames: Iowa State University Press, 1985), 4.

16. Marc Mauer, Executive Director of The Sentencing Project, Testimony before the USSC, *The Sentencing Project: Research and Advocacy Forum*, February 16, 2012, http://www.ussc. gov/Legislative_and_Public_Affairs/Public_Hearings_and_Meetings/20120215-16/ Testimony_16_Mauer.pdf; Paul Hofer et al., *Fifteen Years of Guidelines Sentencing: An Assessment of How Well the Federal Criminal Justice System is Achieving the Goals of Sentencing Reform* (Washington, DC: USSC, 2004), 135.

17. Samuel Walker, *Popular Justice: A History of American Criminal Justice* (New York: Oxford University Press, 1980), 6; Cassia Spohn and Pauline Brennan, "The Joint Effects of Offender Race/Ethnicity and Gender on Substantial Assistance Departures in Federal Courts," *Race and Justice 1* (2011), 49–78; Angela J. Davis, *Arbitrary Justice: The Power of the American Prosecutor* (New York: Oxford University Press, 2007).

18. Scholars like Sanford Kadish and William Stuntz have endorsed decriminalization of "nuisance statutes" (e.g., loitering and disorderly conduct); "illness statutes" (e.g., public drunkenness and drug addiction); and "moral statutes" (e.g., gambling and recreational drug use). As modest proposals for decriminalization, these reforms would have enormous impact. Of the eight million arrests in 2011, there were approximately 954,000 drug-abuse arrests; 766,000 driving under the influence arrests; 370,000 drunkenness arrests; 327,000 liquor law arrests; 367,000 disorderly conduct arrests; 179,000 vandalism offenses; 52,000 curfew and loitering arrests; 34,000 prostitution arrests; and 18,000 vagrancy arrests. Another obvious category for decriminalization would be "carceral status" penalties, that is, acts criminalized only if committed by people with previous carceral entanglement. Consider technical violations of parole. Of the 650,000 people sent to state prisons in 2005, more than half entered due to parole violation, and roughly one-third of these violations were on technical grounds such as failure to pay fees or restitution costs, missing treatment programs, or being arrested for misdemeanors or felony but not being convicted. National Commission on the Causes and Prevention of Violence, *Law and Order Reconsidered* (Washington, DC: GPO, 1969),

551–570; Sanford Kadish, "The Crisis of Overcriminalization," *American Criminal Law Quarterly* 7 (1968), 17–34; James Austin et al., *Unlocking America: Why and How to Reduce America's Prison Population* (Washington, DC: JFA Institute, 2007). Stuntz, "The Uneasy Relationship Between Criminal Procedure and Criminal Justice," 66–67. Sourcebook of Criminal Justice Statistics Online, "Table 4.6.2011: Arrests," (March 27, 2013), www.albany .edu/sourcebook/pdf/t462011.pdf.

19. Gilmore, *Golden Gulag,* 28; Spade, *Normal Life,* 46.

20. African Americans are seven times more likely than whites to be homicide victims. Lisa Miller, "The Invisible Black Victim," *Law & Society Review* (Fall 2010); Omi and Winant, *The Racial State*; Joe Feagin, *Racist America: Roots, Current Realities, and Future Reparations* (New York: Routledge, 2000).

21. Angela Davis, *Are Prisons Obsolete?* (New York: Seven Stories Press, 2003), 107–108.

22. Muneer Ahmad, "A Rage Shared by Law: Post–September 11 Racial Violence as Crimes of Passion," *California Law Review* 92 (October 2004), 1266; Asian American Legal Defense and Education Fund, *World Trade Center and Pentagon Attacks: The Anti-Asian American Backlash* (2002); *LAT,* October 17, 2001.

23. In a similar vein, President Clinton urged Congress to toughen hate crime laws after the 1999 murders of Matthew Shepard and James Byrd because, inter alia, suppressing vigi-lante violence was "important for our leadership at home and around the world." Hyde Post et al., "Murder at Moore's Ford," *Atlanta Journal-Constitution,* May 31, 1946, A1, quoted in Anderson, *Eyes Off the Prize,* 61; Desmond King, *Separate and Unequal: Black Americans and the U.S. Federal Government* (New York: Oxford University Press, 1995); Ahmad, "A Rage Shared by Law," 1287; Terry Maroney, "The Struggle Against Hate Crime: Movement at a Crossroads," *New York University Law Review* 73 (1998), especially 585; Richie, *Arrested Justice.*

24. *LAT,* November 19, 2009; *WSJ,* November 4, 2013.

INDEX

Abernathy, Thomas, 59
abolitionists (of the death penalty), 131–6,
    141–2, 145, 152–3, 248n93
Abrams, Robert, 145
Abzug, Bella, 56
administrative deracialization, 1–4, 11–19, 44–8,
    69–99, 105–12, 143–6, 150, 232n27
Afghanistan, 155
African Americans
    anti-black animus and, 5, 8–14, 31, 36–7,
        40–53, 67–8, 127, 148
    civil rights expansions and, 1, 4–5, 7, 17, 34–6,
        40–4, 47, 57–66, 78, 149
    class divisions within, 125–31
    drug war and, 1–2, 119–25, 229n77, 229n79,
        241nn9–10, 242n18
    incarceration rates and, 1, 4–7, 18–19, 45,
        62–3, 119–25
    pathology discourses and, 3, 8–19, 35–7, 37,
        48–57, 66–7, 76, 90, 147, 151
    police recruiting and, 82–5, 151, 153, 233n38
    riots and, 9, 12, 27–37, 54, 77–90, 95–9, 102,
        232n24, 233n40
    See also carceral state; liberal law-and-order;
        specific organizations and people
Agnew, Spiro, 10
Alexander, Michelle, 152
Allport, Gordon, 36–7
Amendments to the Safe Street Act of 1968, 120
American Bar Association, 71, 79, 95
American Bar Foundation, 105, 153
American Civil Liberties Union (ACLU), 48, 54,
    85–7, 98, 150
American Council on Race Relations, 33, 36, 37
An American Dilemma (Myrdal), 15, 40–6, 50–4
American Jewish Congress, 48
American Law Institute, 94
American Legal Institute, 71, 105
Americans for Constitutional Action, 99

Americans for Democratic Action, 99
Amsterdam, Anthony, 135
animus (as racism explanation), 5, 8–11, 13–14,
    31, 36–7, 40–53, 127
Anslinger, Harry, 64–5
Anti-Defamation League of B'nai B'rith, 18, 36,
    48
Anti-Drug Abuse Act of 1986 and 1988, 64,
    113–14, 117–18, 121, 124, 136–7
anti-functionalism, 19–29
Anti-Terrorism and Effective Death Penalty Act
    of 1996, 114, 146–8
An Appeal to the World (Du Bois), 55
Ashbrook, John, 87
Ashcroft, John, 155
Attica Liberation Faction, 96–9
Attica prison, 96–9, 102, 151
Atwater, Lee, 219n49

backlash thesis, 5–8, 14, 57–68, 215n21, 216n22,
    217n28
Baldus, David, 134
Baltimore, 34
Barr, Bob, 124
Barr, William, 145
Batson v. Kentucky, 248n90
Bayh, Birch, 80
Beckett, Katherine, 213n9
Bennett, Charles, 86
Biden, Joe, 100, 103, 113–15, 118, 125–31,
    140–4, 151, 247n76
Bingham, John, 54
Birth of a Nation (Griffith), 14
Blackmun, Harry, 145
Bloody Sunday, 78
Boggs, Hale, 61–2
Boggs Act of 1951, 30, 61, 64–6, 119, 121,
    242n18
Bond, Julian, 118

Brennan, William, 132, 135
Brooks, Jack, 113–15, 126, 136, 138–9
Broughton, J. Melville, 35
Brown, Edumund G., 94
Brown, Michael, 90
Brown, Vernice, 248n1
Brown Commission. *See* National Commission
  of Reform of the Federal Criminal
  Laws
Brownell, Herbert, Jr., 58
Brown v, Board of Education, 9, 30, 89, 151–2
Buckley, William F., 152
Burton, Dan, 247n82
Bush, George H. W., 8, 14, 24, 116, 140, 145,
  219n49, 222n76
Bush, George W., 155
Byrd, James, 251n23

Cahill, William, 86
California Correctional Peace Officers
  Association, 16
Callins v. Collins, 145
capital crime statutes, 24–5, 136–43, 190–204
  See also death penalty
capital punishment. *See* death penalty
Caplan, Gerald, 71
carceral state
  administrative deracialization and, 1–4,
    11–19, 29–30, 44–8, 69–90, 92–9, 105–12,
    143–6, 150, 232n27
  definitions of, 213n9
  drug crimes and, 1–2, 115–31, 136–7, 141,
    229n77, 229n79, 241nn9–10, 242n18
  immigration and, 125–31
  incarceration's alternatives and, 23, 99–100,
    102–5, 250n18
  legitimacy of, 13, 21, 25–6
  liberalism and, 12–19, 85–7, 92–105
  pity and racial criminalization in, 3, 8–19,
    35–7, 48–57, 66–7, 76, 90, 147–51
  sentencing legislation and, 2, 12, 90–111,
    168–89
  as social safety net, 4, 16–17, 119–31
  See also liberal law-and-order; police and
    policing; sentencing procedures; violence
Carmichael, Stokely, 86–7
Carnegie Corporation, 54
Carr, Robert, 27
Carter, Jimmy, 105, 152
Caste and Class in the Southern Town (Dollard),
  51–2
Cayton, Revels, 227n60
Celler, Emanuel, 60, 150
Cerda, José, 125
Chain Reaction (Edsall and Edsall), 7
The Challenge of Crime in a Free Society
  (Katzenbach Commission), 82–5
Chappell, Johnnie Mae, 90

Chicago, 65
Chicago Defender, 38
civil rights
  criminogenic charges and, 57–68, 71, 75–7
  drug legislation and, 117–19
  racial neutrality and, 1–4, 9–19, 22, 27–8,
    32–44, 48–57, 78–85, 89–90, 127–8, 148
  safety as, 1–2, 12, 23, 29, 39–53, 69–75,
    84–90, 113–15, 126–7, 144–9, 154
  See also liberal law-and-order; police and
    policing; sentencing procedures; violence
Civil Rights Act of 1957, 30, 58–9
Civil Rights Act of 1960, 30, 57, 60–1
Civil Rights Act of 1964, 2, 57, 69, 75–6
Civil Rights Bill of 1949, 47
Civil Rights Congress, 18, 23, 29, 39, 55–7
Clark, Kenneth and Mamie, 9
Clark, Ramsey, 24, 85, 87, 133
Clark, Tom, 38–9
Cleveland, 22, 65
Clinton, Bill, 4, 25, 68, 99, 113–19, 125–31,
  136–48, 222n76, 240n7, 251n23
cocaine, 64, 114–15, 121, 123–5, 241n8, 243n26
Cold War, 29, 31, 49, 55–7, 64
Collier's magazine, 33, 33, 34
Collins, Charles, 227n60
Colmer, William, 58, 86
colorblindness, 4–11
Commission on Civil Rights (Eisenhower), 58
Commission on Law Enforcement and the
  Administration of Justice, 9–14, 69, 71, 75,
  81–6, 89, 92
Committee on Civil Rights (of Truman), 2, 27,
  29, 38–48, 50–4, 74, 226n40
Community Oriented Policing Services (COPS),
  25, 128–31
community policing, 17, 20, 113–15, 125, 127–
  31, 150, 233n38
Comprehensive Crime Control Act of 1984, 100
  See also Sentencing Reform Act of 1984
Comprehensive Drug Abuse Prevention and
  Control Act of 1970, 120
concealed aggression, 49–53
Congressional Black Caucus, 24–5, 124, 126,
  131–2, 141, 143–8
Congress of Racial Equality (CORE), 31–2
conservatism
  backlash thesis and, 5–7, 57–68, 75–6,
    215n21, 216n22, 217n28
  black criminality and, 9–10
  carceral expansion and, 5, 72–5, 84, 90–2,
    104–11, 115–31, 219n49
  death penalty and, 136–43
  definitions of, 53
  policing issues and, 79–81, 85–90
  racial constructions of, 13–15, 28–9
  sentence reform and, 90–2, 105–12
Conyers, John, 102, 126, 145

Cook County Jail, 1–2
Coolidge, Calvin, 105
Correctional Rehabilitation Study Act of 1965, 92
Cover, Robert, 19
crack cocaine, 114–15, 121, 123–5, 241n8, 243n26
Crenshaw, Kimberlé, 23, 151
crime rates, 3–4, 31, 71–2, 75–7, 113–14, 154–5, 213n10, 214n14, 242n16
Criminal Sentencing (Frankel), 108–9
Crouch, Stanley, 144

Daily Worker, 56
D'Amato, Alfonse, 137
Dandridge, Terrain, 248n1
Daniel, Price, 64–6
Davis, Angela, 155
Davis, James, 59
D.C. Court Reorganization and Criminal Procedure Act, 120
death penalty
    administrative objections to, 13, 18, 56, 113–15, 132–6, 143–7, 247n82, 248n90
    capital crime statutes and, 24–5, 136–43, 190–204
    mental capacity and, 134, 136–7, 144, 240n7
    outbidding dynamic and, 24–5, 115–31, 136–47, 150, 198–204, 246n70
    See also carceral state; liberal law-and-order; violence
Death Penalty Information Center, 137
Dee, Henry, 90
Dellums, Ron, 139
Democratic Party
    black pathologies and, 3, 8–9, 12–15
    electoral politics and, 113–15, 136–47
    justice system's modernization and, 27–8
    liberal law-and-order discourses and, 39, 100–11
    "New Democrats" and, 17, 24, 99, 113–15, 125–49
    sectional friction in, 12, 21–3, 27–46, 57–67, 73–4, 86
Detroit, 33–6, 65, 72
Detroit Free Press, 34
Diallo, Amadou, 148, 248n1
Dirksen, Everett, 86
discretion
    judicial-, 20–5, 61–6, 99–111, 115–31, 168–89, 241n8, 241nn9–10
    liberal mistrust of, 12–19, 27–9, 57–61, 82–5, 90, 98–112, 131–47, 149–56
    racial disparities and, 92–5, 111–12
    See also carceral state; police and policing; racism; sentencing procedures
Dodd, Christopher, 140
Dole, Bob, 142

Dollard, John, 51–2
"doll experiment" (Clark and Clark), 9
Dorsey, George, 38
Drug Kingpin Act, 137, 141
drugs
    punitive penalties and, 4, 8, 107, 114–15, 119–25, 241n8
    racial overtones of, 29–30, 61–6, 119–25, 129–31, 211n5, 229n77
Du Bois, W. E. B., 7, 55, 228n61
Dukakis, Michael, 14

Early, Norm, 126
Eastland, James, 27, 30, 60–1
Edsall, Thomas and Mary, 7
education, 8, 16–17, 127, 151
Edwards, Don, 126, 145
Eighth Amendment, 134
Eisenhower, Dwight, 58
Eleanor Clubs, 52–3
The Emerging Republican Majority (Phillips), 7–8
Evans, Daniel, 246n67
Evers, Medgar, 90
Executive Order 8802, 41
Executive Order 9808, 39–40

Fair Employment Practices Committee, 36, 41
Fair Sentencing Act, 124
fascism, 30–4, 36, 55, 131
Federal Bureau of Prisons, 44, 95
Federal Death Penalty Act of 1994, 24, 68, 136–48
Federal Gun Control Act of 1968, 230n4
Federal Judicial Center, 106–9
Feeley, Malcolm, 75, 89
Feinstein, Brian, 225n25
felon disenfranchisement, 4, 17, 214n13, 222n76
first civil right
    Clinton's construction of, 113–15, 127, 144–7
    Johnson's construction of, 70, 72–4, 85–90, 154
    Nixon's construction of, 1–2, 29, 69–75, 84, 126
    Truman's construction of, 1–2, 23, 27, 39–48, 50–3, 70, 127, 148–9
Fish, Hamilton, 117
food stamps, 130–1
Forman, James, Jr., 211n5, 216n22
Forrester, Elijah, 58
"Four Essential Rights" (PCCR), 42
"The Four Freedoms: Dixie Style" (cartoon), 37–9
Fourteenth Amendment, 46, 54–5, 59, 134
Frank, Barney, 118
Frankel, Marvin, 108–9, 153
Fraternal Order of Police, 141
Friedman, Milton, 152

Frymer, Paul, 15, 147
Fulbright, William, 61
functionalism (theoretical), 19–20
Furman, William Henry, 132, 245n58
Furman v. Georgia, 132–5, 245n58

Garland, David, 17, 111
Gates, Henry Louis, Jr., 148
Gekas, George, 138–9
gender, 7, 52–3, 122, 215n19, 243n22
Gilmore, Ruth Wilson, 154, 220n64
Goldstein, Herman, 82
Goldwater, Barry, 7, 28, 67, 74–6
Goluboff, Risa, 152
good time, 23, 71, 99, 102, 114–15
Gottschalk, Marie, 94
Governor's Committee on the Causes of the
    Detroit Race Riot, 35
Graham, Billy, 78
Graham, Bob, 118
Gramm, Phil, 130, 141
Granger, Lester, 31
Grant, Oscar, III, 148, 248n1
Graves, John Temple, II, 40, 56–7
Great Society legislation. *See* civil rights;
    Johnson, Lyndon B.; police and policing;
    specific acts and agencies
Green, Richard, 95
Gregg v. Georgia, 132, 134, 143
Griffith, D. W., 14
Guinier, Lani, 11
Gulf of Tonkin Resolution, 90
habeas corpus reforms, 132, 140–2, 146–8

Harcourt, Bernard, 213n9
Harkins, Gillian, 12
Harlem, 34, 90
Hart, Phillip, 80, 133, 150, 232n27
Hastie, William, 34–5
Hatch, Orrin, 100, 142, 145
hate crimes, 155, 251n23
Hatfield, Mark, 246n67
Hattam, Victoria, 230n84
Hawkins, Darnell, 19
Hawkins, Paula, 118
Head Start, 73, 75–6
Helms, Jesse, 124
heroin, 64–5
Higgins, Lois, 64
Hill, Renata, 248n1
Holy Street Baptist Church, 57, 90
Hoover, Herbert, 47, 61, 105, 226n41
Hoover, J. Edgar, 45, 78–9
Horton, Willie, 7, 14, 113–15, 219n48
HoSang, Daniel, 11
Household Survey on Drug Use and Health, 122
Howard University, 76–7, 90
Hruska, Roman, 79

Hughes, William, 139, 146, 246n70
Humphrey, Hubert, 10
Hunter, Tera, 224n21

Illegal Immigration Reform and Immigrant
    Responsibility Act of 1996, 130
Illinois Drug Addict Act of 1953, 229n79
immigration, 4, 125–31
Immigration and Nationality Act, 242n13
incarceration. *See* carceral state; crime rates;
    liberal law-and-order
indeterminate sentencing, 20
    See also sentencing procedures
intersectionality, 7, 52–3, 122, 215n19, 243n22
Iraq, 155

Jackson, George, 96
Jackson, Jesse, 118
Jackson, Walter, 54
Japanese Americans, 32, 44, 53
Jarman, John, 121
Javits, Jacob, 60, 79
Jeffries, Edward, 33
Jeffries, John, 248n93
Jena Six, 148
Jim Crow policies, 2, 4, 12, 31, 53, 57, 67, 152,
    155–6, 211n5
Job Corps, 76
Johnson, Charles, 52
Johnson, Guy, 54
Johnson, Lyndon B.
    Commission on Law Enforcement and
        Administration of Justice and, 9, 11,
        67–8
    police professionalism and, 81–5, 87–90, 151
    racial violence and, 13, 24, 69, 73–4, 111–12
    root causes and, 76–9
    sentencing modernization and, 91–5, 108
Johnson, Patreese, 148, 248n1
Johnston, Kathryn, 148, 248n1
Johnston, Olin, 61
Juvenile Delinquency and Youth Offenses
    Control Act of 1961, 23, 73–6, 86, 230n4

Kadish, Sanford, 250n18
Katzenbach, Nicholas deB., 82
Katzenbach Commission. *See* Commission on
    Law Enforcement and the Administration
    of Justice
Kennedy, Edward, 23, 25, 68, 91–2, 99–111,
    114–15, 130, 144, 151, 236n77
Kennedy, John F., 9, 28, 69, 75–6
Kennedy, Robert F., 126
Kerner, Otto, 84
Kerner Commission, 84–5
Kim, Claire, 8, 147
King, Martin Luther, Jr., 26, 57, 69, 72, 80
King, Rodney, 148

Klinkner, Philip, 147
Koh, Steve, 235n54, 236n77
Krauthammer, Charles, 124
Ku Klux Klan, 36, 78
Kunzel, Regina, 207–8

Law Enforcement Assistance Act (and
    Administration), 23, 47, 71–4, 79–81
layering, 11, 22, 92–5, 109
Leadership Conference on Civil Rights, 87
least restrictive sanctions (principle), 95
Legal Services Corporation, 73, 75
Levi, Margaret, 149
Lewis, John, 69, 118
liberal law-and-order
    administrative deracialization and, 1–4,
        11–19, 21, 28–32, 40–8, 69–71, 90–111,
        128–47, 154
    illegal white violence and, 5–9, 12–19, 44–8,
        74–6, 151–2
    police militarization and, 72–3, 79–90,
        111–12, 150
    race conservatives and, 58–67, 78–9, 148–53
    racial criminalization and pity and, 8, 13–15,
        24, 53–7, 66–70, 76–9, 81–5, 111–12,
        119–25
    racial discipline and, 148–53
    racialized criminalization and pity and, 8, 15,
        24, 48–68, 81–5, 111–12
    racial violence as exceptional to, 38–9
    racism's construction and, 38–9, 43–57
    sentencing guidelines and, 95–105, 236n77
    state-sponsored violence and, 28–9, 32, 43–4,
        53–7, 73, 119–31, 149–53
    structural racism and, 11, 23, 43–4, 49, 53–7,
        66, 119–25, 148–53
    See also carceral state; death penalty; police
        and policing; sentencing procedures
Little, Rory, 136
Los Angeles, 27–8
Louima, Abner, 148
Lovell, George, 206
Lowndes, Joseph, 230n84
Lowry, Mike, 117
Lungren, Dan, 117, 124–5
lynching, 2, 10, 14–15, 18, 22, 29–33, 36–40,
    53–7, 90, 127, 155–6

MacGregor, Clark, 86
Mallory v. U.S., 87
mandatory minimums, 20–5, 61–6, 99–105,
    115–31, 153, 168–89, 241n8, 241nn9–10
    See also sentencing procedures
Mapp v. Ohio, 89
March on Washington Movement, 31
Marshall, Thurgood, 34, 38, 48, 132
Martin, James, 80
Martin, Trayvon, 148

Martinson, Robert, 111
Mattick, Hans, 229n77
Mayhew, David, 20–1, 222n73
McCann, Michael, 206
McCleskey v. Kemp, 131–2, 134–6, 144, 248n93
McCloskey, Frank, 118
McCollum, Bill, 139
McCurdy, David, 118
McGee, Willie, 56
McKay Commission, 98–9, 110
McLarty, Mack, 125
McPherson, Harry, 78, 86
Medicaid, 130
Melamed, Jodi, 11
mental illness, 134–7, 144, 240n7
Mexican Americans, 27–31, 38, 43, 53, 64–5,
    122, 231n12
Mfume, Keisi, 141–2, 144
Mikulski, Barbara, 140
Miller, Lisa, 222n75
Miller, Mark, 91
Miranda v. Arizona, 20, 25–26, 87, 89, 145
Mitchell, Clarence, 58
Model Penal Code of 1962, 93–5, 105, 133
Mohammad, Khalid Sheikh, 155–6
Montgomery Bus Boycotts, 57–8
Moore, Charles, 90
Moynihan, Daniel Patrick, 77–8, 122–4, 137
Moynihan Report, 77–8, 122–3
Muck, William, 58
Muhammad, Khalil Gibran, 66
Myrdal, Gunnar, 15, 22, 40–6, 49–54, 151

Narcotic Addict Rehabilitation Act of 1966,
    107, 230n4
Narcotic Control Act of 1956, 64, 119
Nash, Philleo, 28
National Advisory Commission on Civil
    Disorders, 84–5
National Advisory Commission on Criminal
    Justice Standards and Goals, 97
National Association for the Advancement of
    Colored People (NAACP), 12, 31, 34–6,
    38–9, 48, 54–8, 60, 70, 132, 228n61
National Association of Colored Women, 38
National Association of Police Organizations, 141
National Bar Association, 54
National Citizens' Council on Civil Rights, 48
National Commission of Reform of the Federal
    Criminal Laws, 92–5, 100
National Council on Crime and Delinquency
    (NCCD), 95, 97
National Institute of Justice, 71, 129
National Interreligious Task Force on Criminal
    Justice, 97
National Lawyers Guild, 54
National Legal Aid and Defenders Association,
    100

National Negro Congress, 12, 18, 29, 39, 54–5, 227n60

Native Son (Wright), 15, 51

"The Negro Family" (Moynihan), 77–8, 122–3

Neighborhood Security Act, 142

Neighborhood Youth Corps, 73, 75

neoliberalism. *See* New Democrats

Newark, 72

New Deal, 40–1, 76

New Democrats, 17, 24, 99, 125–49

New England Journal of Medicine, 123

New Jersey Four, 148, 248n1

The New Jim Crow (Alexander), 152

New Yorker, 71–2

New York State Special Commission on Attica, 98–9, 110

New York Times, 110, 123, 145

Nixon, Richard
　safety discourses and, 1–2, 10, 29, 69, 72–3, 75, 126
　sentencing guidelines and, 64, 97, 106, 133–4
　Southern Strategy of, 7–8, 28, 84

Norton, Eleanor Holmes, 144

Nunn, Sam, 119, 137

Obama, Barack, 1

Odum, Howard, 52–3

Office for Law Enforcement Assistance (OLEA), 75, 79, 81, 89, 92

Office of War Information, 27

Old Age Insurance, 40

Omnibus Crime Control and Safe Streets Act of 1968, 23, 71, 85–90, 164–5, 230n6
　See also Safe Streets Act (1968)

O'Neill, Thomas, 117

Organized Crime Control Act of 1970, 120

outbidding (political dynamic), 24–5, 115–31, 136–47, 198–204, 246n70

Parker, Christopher, 206–7

parole, 23, 98–101, 114–15, 130, 250n18

paternalism. *See* African Americans; pity (politics of)

PATRIOT Act of 2002, 149

PCCR. *See* Committee on Civil Rights (of Truman)

Pearson, Kathryn, 225n25

Pepper, Claude, 118

Perry, Imani, 211n3, 248n1

Personal Responsibility and Work Responsibility Act of 1996, 99, 130

"Petition to the United Nations on Behalf of 13 Million Oppressed Negro Citizens of the United States of America" (NNC), 55–6

Phillips, Kevin, 7–8

Pittsburgh Courier, 53

pity (politics of), 3, 8–19, 35–7, 48–57, 66–7, 76, 90, 147, 151

Pity and Contempt (Scott), 8

Plessy v. Ferguson, 9

Poff, Richard, 86

police and policing
　brutality and, 1, 12, 18, 33–4, 38, 45–8, 56, 72, 74, 90, 127, 152–3, 231n12
　community policing and, 17, 20, 79–85, 113–15, 125, 127–31, 150, 233n38
　liberal law-and-order funding for, 71–3, 85–90
　professionalization discourses and, 16, 22–9, 44–8, 79–87, 111–12, 151–2, 232n27
　racialized violence and, 30, 32–3, 33, 38, 65, 86, 113–15
　post-racial triumphalism and, 1–2, 4, 22
　postwar racial liberalism, 212n8
　　See also African Americans; Democratic Party; liberal law-and-order; racial liberalism

Powell, Adam Clayton, 38

Powell, Lewis, 134–5, 248n93

President's Committee on Civil Rights. *See* Committee on Civil Rights (of Truman)

Prince, Jonathan, 126

Prisoner Rehabilitation Act of 1965, 230n4

prisons, 95–9
　See also carceral state; rioting; *specific prisons*

probation, 17, 66, 83, 91, 100–1, 104, 130, 147–8

procedural uniformity
　conservative uses of, 90–2, 99–111, 131–47
　death penalty and, 131–47, 247n82
　police professionalization and, 24, 71, 79–85, 152
　punitive punishments and, 143–6
　race neutrality of, 1–4, 11–19, 22, 67–8, 71, 78–9, 82–5, 89–90, 127–36, 143–6, 148, 151
　racialized effects of, 25–6, 69–71, 148–53
　sentencing reforms and, 99–111

Progressive Party, 40

Proxmire, William, 137

Puerto Ricans, 8, 61, 65, 96, 229n77

race
　backlash thesis and, 5–9, 57–68, 74–6, 215n21, 216n22, 217n28
　criminalization and, 3–4, 9, 29–30, 36, 51–3, 73–4, 86–7, 111–12, 119–25
　gender's intersections with, 7, 52–3, 122, 215n19, 243n22
　incarceration rates and, 1, 3–11, 5–6, 62–3, 154–5, 214n14
　racial discipline, 148–53

Racial Justice Act (RJA), 25, 131–2, 140, 143–8, 246n73

racial liberalism
　black pathology discourses and, 2–3, 7–19, 25–37, 40–4, 48–66, 90, 154
　definitions of, 212n8

disciplining dynamic and, 148–53
drug war and, 29–30, 61–6, 114–15, 119–25, 136–7
racism
  definitions of, 19, 44, 151–2, 220n64
  international embarrassment and, 29, 31, 36, 55–7, 80, 237n85
  private irrationality and, 2, 5, 8–19, 36–53, 67–8, 90, 127, 148
  structural-, 11, 23, 43–4, 49, 53–7, 66, 119–25, 148–53
  See also carceral state; civil rights; liberal law-and-order; police and policing; sentencing procedures
Rahall, Nick, II, 118
Randolph, A. Philip, 31, 35
rape, 14–15, 32, 56, 61, 67, 100, 132
Reagan, Ronald, 24, 90–2, 104–11, 113–14, 116–17, 149
Rector, Milton, 95
Rector, Ricky Ray, 240n7
Reddy, Chandan, 11
Reed, Adolph, 147
Reed, Bruce, 125
Reno, Janet, 143, 247n86
Republican Party, 86
  safety rights and, 1–3
Richmond Times Dispatch, 35
Right to Privacy Act, 87
rioting, 12, 27–37, 48–57, 77–81, 86–7, 90, 95–9, 102, 232n24, 233n40
Roberts, Dorothy, 216n22
Rockefeller, Nelson, 96, 98–9
Roosevelt, Eleanor, 52–3, 228n61
Roosevelt, Franklin D., 27–8, 34–5, 37–41, 76, 105
Roosevelt, Theodore, 15, 40
root causes discourses, 8, 12, 24, 48–57, 70, 76–9, 81–5, 111–12
Rotnem, Victor, 34
Rustin, Bayard, 80

Safe Streets Act (1968), 47, 67, 71–3, 81, 85–90, 111–12, 117, 120, 150, 164–5, 230n6
safety
  from black criminality, 2–3, 58–61, 69–75, 84, 126
  from oneself, 119–25
  from racial animus, 1–3, 5, 8–14, 31, 36–7, 40–53, 67–8, 127, 148
  from terrorism, 114, 146–9
San Quentin prison, 96
Sarat, Austin, 75, 89
scapegoatism, 36–7, 50, 123
Schattsschneider, E.., 16
Scheingold, Stuart, 212n7, 213n10
Schickler, Eric, 225n25
Schroeder, Patricia, 118
Schumer, Charles, 118, 143

Schwartz, Louis, 94
Scott, Daryl Michael, 8, 51
Scott, James, 53
Scott, Robert, 141
Screws v. United States, 46–7
Second Circuit Sentencing Study (Federal Judicial Center), 106–9
Sensenbrenner, James, 143
Sentencing Alternatives and Procedures (ABA), 95
sentencing disparities, *88*, 92–9, 105–11, 132–6, 248n90
sentencing procedures
  death penalty and, 143–6
  drug penalties and, 20, 61–2, 64–6, 107, 114–15, 119–25, 136–7, 229n77, 229n79, 241nn9–10, 242n18
  incarceration's reductions and, 95–9
  mandatory minimums and, 115–31, 168–89, 241n8, 241nn9–10
  outbidding dynamic and, 24–5, 115–31, 136–47, 198–204, 246n70
  racial disparities in, *88*, 92–5, 99–111, 132–6, 248n90
  standardization of, 12, 16, 20, 23, 95–9, 151, 153
Sentencing Reform Act of 1984, 23, 68, 70–1, 90–2, 99–111, 114–15, 235n54, 236n77, 238n94
Serrano, Jose, 142
Shepard, Matthew, 251n23
Singh, Nikhil, 11
Sitkoff, Harvard, 31, 33
Smith, Lamar, 124
Smith, Rogers, 147
Smith, Turner, 55
Smith Act, 103
Soledad prison, 96
Southern Manifesto, 58, 150
Southern Regional Congress, 54
Southern Regional Council, 40, 45
"Southern Strategy" (Nixon), 7–8, 14
Sparks, Chauncey, 35
Staggers, Harley, 139
state-sponsored violence, 36–40, 53–7, 90, 127, 155–6
Stith, Kate, 235n54, 236n77
Strolovitch, Dara, 215n18
structural racism and, 11, 23, 43–4, 49, 53–7, 66, 148–53
Student Non-violent Coordinating Committee (SNCC), 69, 86, 118
Stuntz, William, 250n18
Supreme Court (U.S.). *See specific decisions*

Temporary Assistance to Needy Families (TANF), 130, 222n76
Thomas, Bigger (character), 14, 51–3

Thompson, Heather Ann, 66
Three Strikes and You're Out initiative, 4, 16, 113–14, 153
Thurmond, Strom, 60, 81, 100, 103, 139–41, 145, 247n76
Till, Emmett, 57
Tilly, Charles, 32
Tonry, Michael, 91, 104, 238n99
To Secure These Rights (PCCR report), 40–8, 50–4, 77
Tower, John, 16, 80
Traficant, James, 139
transgender and gender-nonconforming people, 7, 215n19
Truman, Harry S.
    civil rights efforts of, 2, 27–9, 39, 49–53, 74, 148–9
    drug addiction and, 64–6
    racialized violence and, 1, 38–44, 66–7, 155–6
Tydings, Joseph, 16, 80

Uniform Crime Reports, 47, 72, 76, 90
United Nations, 55, 227n60
Universal Declaration of Human Rights (UN), 55
Urban League, 31, 34
U.S. Civil Rights Commission, 70, 73–5, 79–80, 85–6, 150
U.S. Conference of Mayors, 85–6
U.S. Criminal Code, 92–5, 105–6
U.S. criminal codes and, 92–5, 106, 157–63
U.S. News & World Report, 61, 81
U.S. Parole Commission, 100–1
U.S. Sentencing Commission, 23, 25, 91–2, 100–6, 114–15, 123, 238n99
U.S. Sentencing Guidelines, 91–2, 100, 109, 166–7
U.S. v. Harris, 55

Vento, Bruce, 123
Vietnam War, 90
violence
    lynching and, 12, 23, 36–40, 53–7, 90, 127, 155–6
    policing and, 30–3, 44–8, 60, 74, 79–81, 90, 231n12
    race and, 1, 3–4, 8–11, 23, 69–70, 72, 76–9
    rioting and, 27–37, 77–81, 86–90, 92–9, 102, 232n24, 233n40
    state-sponsored, 28–9, 32, 43–4, 53–7, 90, 95–9, 136–53
    See also carceral state; death penalty; liberal law-and-order
Violence Against Women Act, 142
Violent Crime Control Act of 1991, 139–40

Violent Crime Control and Law Enforcement Act of 1994, 24, 113–15, 118–19, 127–31, 136–43
Violent Crime Reduction Trust Fund, 127
Voting Rights Act of 1965, 2, 78, 80, 152

Walinsky, Adam, 123
Walker, Hannah, 244n41
Walker, Samuel, 154
Wallace, George, 72
"Warning of Grave Dangers" (Muck, Colmer, and Willis), 58
Warren Court, 2, 21, 67, 72, 87, 106
    See also specific decisions and justices
Washington, Craig, 126
Washington Post, 124
Waters, Maxine, 124
Watt, Mel, 141, 247n82
Watts riots, 77–8, 151, 232n24
Weaver, Vesla, 215n21
We Charge Genocide (CRC), 55, 228n62
Wechsler, Herbert, 94, 106
"We Know Who Will Lose the Drug War" (Yoder), 123
Wells, Ida B., 12, 44
Western, Bruce, 6–7
White, Walter, 31, 36, 38, 56–7
White Citizens' Councils, 59
White House Conference on Equal Employment Opportunity, 78
Whitener, Basil, 59
whiteness
    mob violence and, 2–3, 18, 29–30, 36–40, 53–7, 90, 127, 155–6
    racial animus and, 2, 5–15, 31, 36–7, 40–53, 67–8, 127, 148
    sentimentalism and, 2–3, 8–19, 35–7, 48–57, 66–7, 76, 90, 147, 151
    state-sponsored violence and, 28–9, 32, 43–4, 53–7, 90, 95–9, 136–53
Wickersham Commission, 47, 74
Wilkins, Roy, 60
Willie Horton advertisement, 7, 14, 219n48
Willis, Edwin, 58
Wilson, James Q., 71, 111
Wilson, Woodrow, 40
Winant, Howard, 31
Wirth, Louis, 36
Woodard, Isaac, Jr., 38
World War II, 29–34, 40–1, 55
Wright, Richard, 15, 51
Wright, Ronald, 91

Yergan, Max, 227n60
Yoder, Edwin, Jr., 123

zoot suit riots, 27–9